高等学校翻译专业本科教材

总主编

同声传译基础

A Coursebook of Simultaneous Interpreting Between English and Chinese

主编：仲伟合

编者：仲伟合 钱芳 余怿 李承

外语教学与研究出版社
FOREIGN LANGUAGE TEACHING AND RESEARCH PRESS
北京 BEIJING

图书在版编目（CIP）数据

同声传译基础 / 仲伟合主编；仲伟合等编．— 北京：外语教学与研究出版社，2010.10
（2022.6重印）
高等学校翻译专业本科教材 / 仲伟合，何刚强主编
ISBN 978—7—5135—0233—7

Ⅰ. ①同… Ⅱ. ①仲… Ⅲ. ①英语－口译－高等学校－教材 Ⅳ. ①H315.9

中国版本图书馆CIP数据核字(2010)第197485号

出 版 人　王　芳
项目负责　屈海燕
责任编辑　屈海燕
装帧设计　覃一彪
版式设计　付玉梅
出版发行　外语教学与研究出版社
社　　址　北京市西三环北路19号（100089）
网　　址　http://www.fltrp.com
印　　刷　中农印务有限公司
开　　本　787×1092　1/16
印　　张　18.5
版　　次　2010年10月第1版　2022年6月第15次印刷
书　　号　ISBN 978—7—5135—0233—7
定　　价　38.90元（附MP3光盘一张）

购书咨询：(010)88819926　电子邮箱：club@fltrp.com
外研书店：https://waiyants.tmall.com
凡印刷、装订质量问题，请联系我社印制部
联系电话：(010)61207896　电子邮箱：zhijian@fltrp.com
凡侵权、盗版书籍线索，请联系我社法律事务部
举报电话：(010)88817519　电子邮箱：banquan@fltrp.com
物料号：202330001

目录

- 编写说明　　III

- 教学建议　　VI

- 第 1 单元　同声传译概论
An Introduction to Simultaneous Interpreting　　*1*

- 第 2 单元　同声传译听辨
Listening and Analysis in Simultaneous Interpreting　　*8*

- 第 3 单元　同声传译的多任务处理
Multi-tasking in Simultaneous Interpreting　　*20*

- 第 4 单元　同声传译设备
Simultaneous Interpreting Equipment　　*32*

- 第 5 单元　同声传译基本原则
Principles of Simultaneous Interpreting　　*43*

▶ 第 6 单元　同声传译常用技巧
Techniques in Simultaneous Interpreting　　　*62*

▶ 第 7 单元　同声传译视译
Sight Interpreting　　　*90*

▶ 第 8 单元　带稿同声传译
Simultaneous Interpreting with Texts　　　*109*

▶ 第 9 单元　无稿同声传译
Simultaneous Interpreting Without Texts　　　*128*

▶ 第 10 单元　同声传译专向技能训练
Skill Training for Simultaneous Interpreting　　　*152*

▶ 第 11 单元　同声传译综合训练
Comprehensive Training for Simultaneous Interpreting　　　*171*

▶ 附录 1　参考译文　　　*191*

▶ 附录 2　参考文献　　　*283*

编写说明

《同声传译基础》是由外语教学与研究出版社组织编写的高等学校翻译专业本科教材中的一种,使用对象是翻译本科专业及英语专业高年级学生,以及具备一定口译实践工作经验并希望自学同声传译课程的口译爱好者与翻译工作者。

随着近年来我国对职业译员需求的增加,许多高校纷纷在本科和硕士研究生阶段开设了同声传译课程。2006 年,教育部首次批准广东外语外贸大学等国内三所院校试办翻译本科专业,其专业设置方案中就有同声传译课程。同声传译既是翻译本科专业学位课程设置中的核心课程,也是目前社会上许多有志于从事更高层次口译工作的青年迫切希望学习的一项技能。但是,大多数院校同声传译课程开设的时间相对较短,多数授课教师不具备相应的同声传译工作经验,市面上专门介绍同声传译技能的教材更是寥寥无几。正是在这样的背景下,我们结合广东外语外贸大学高级翻译学院同声传译课程多年的教学实践,尝试编写了这本同声传译入门教材——《同声传译基础》,希望为国内众多在本科阶段开设同声传译课程的院校提供一本方便、实用的教材。

《同声传译基础》的编写体例遵循了以下几个原则:

1. 以同声传译技能为主线安排教程编写框架,同时突出口译练习的专题,做到技能性原则与实践性原则并举。教程共 11 个单元,涵盖了"同声传译概论、同声传译听辨、同声传译的多任务处理、同声传译设备、同声传译基本原则、同声传译常用技巧、同声传译视译、带稿同声传译、无稿同声传译、同声传译专项技能训练、同声传译综合技能训练"等内容；同时，教程还包括了"旅游、创新、会展、教育、经贸、金融、文化、科技、体育、环境"等多个专题的全真会议材料和录音以供同传实际操练，以强化学员对同传技能的掌握。

2. 结构紧凑合理，内容全面丰富，易于课堂操作及课后自学。教程第1单元介绍同声传译的发展简史和相关基本理论，从第2单元开始由浅入深介绍了同传基本技能、原则和技巧，每一单元都由"同传技能"、"案例讲解"、"术语拓展"和"同传实战"四部分组成，其中"同传技能"简要介绍了同声传译的某些重要技能或某些方面的知识和理论，"案例讲解"选择"同传实战"的重点语段结合"同传技能"进行详细精讲，并配有参考译文，"术语拓展"帮助学员拓展相关主题词汇，"同传实战"为四篇会议发言，用于课堂或课外同声传译练习。考虑到学员自我检测练习效果的需要，我们在书后提供了全部同声传译练习的参考译文。

3. 以全真会议录音作为训练材料，强调同声传译训练的真实性原则。本教程所选材料一半以上来自国际会议发言的原声录音，且未经任何加工处理，语料十分难得。为了进一步确保口译现场训练的仿真性，原声录音中发言人的口误、习惯性口头语等口语特点均得以保留，以使学员有身临其境之感，进一步提高训练效果。

参与《同声传译基础》编写工作的是广东外语外贸大学几位多年从事口译教学、研究并具备丰富同声传译实践经验的教师。他们分别是：

仲伟合：广东外语外贸大学校长、博士、教授、翻译学博士生导师。曾先后留学英国、美国。目前兼任国务院学位委员会"全国翻译硕士专业学位教育指导委员会"副主任委员、教育部高校外语专业教学指导委员会委员、全国翻译专业资格（水平）考试英语专家委员会委员、中国翻译工作者协会副会长等职务。国家级精品课程"英语口译（课程系列）"主持人、广东省高等教育教学名师、国家"新世纪百千万人才工程"国家级人选、教育部"新世纪优秀人才支持计划"人选、全国优秀教师及广东省青年"五四"奖章获得者。曾为多位国家、省市领导人及外国国家元首、政商要人等担任口译工作。已主编出版国家级规划专业口译教材三部，其他著作、词典等多部，在《中国翻译》等学术期刊发表论文50余篇，承担多项省部级科研项目。

钱芳：广东外语外贸大学高级翻译学院口译系讲师，中国翻译协会会员，中华人民共和国人事部认证会议口译译员。广东外语外贸大学硕士，方向为国际会议传译。曾任广西壮族自治区人事厅同声传译培训班、广东高校外事干部培训班、南洋理工大学–广东外语外贸大学课程班口译讲师。曾多次为国家、省、市领导人及外国政商要人担任口译工作，口译实战经验丰富。

余怿：广东外语外贸大学高级翻译学院口译系教师，广东外语外贸大学英语（高级翻译）学士，英国利兹大学（University of Leeds）口笔译研究优等硕士。持有中华人民共和国人事部口译二级证书。具有丰富的口笔译实战经验，曾在联合国（维也纳）口译处实习，并先后为国内外多个政府部门及知名企业担任口译译员。

李承：广东外语外贸大学英文学院讲师、四年级口译课程主讲教师，翻译方向硕士。截至2008年底，为近两百场国际会议提供同声传译或交替传译服务。曾任广西壮族自治区人事厅高级翻译培训班和广州外事翻译学会高级英语译员培训班讲师，并担任过澳门理工学院语言暨翻译高等学校同声传译课程客座讲师。

编写本教程对我们来说也仅是一个尝试，因此，书中错漏在所难免，祈望使用者不吝指正。本书使用了很多会议的全真声音、文字资料，我们对相关的会议组织单位及个人表示衷心的感谢！本书在编写和后期制作过程中得到了外语教学与研究出版社屈海燕等编辑的大力支持，在此一并表示感谢！

仲伟合

2010年7月

教学建议

一、同声传译课程教学理念

《同声传译基础》教材使用对象为翻译本科专业及英语专业高年级学生。本教程以技能与专题相结合为特色，全书编写以同声传译技能为主线，每个单元相对围绕一个专题（如经贸、会展、金融、体育等）提供练习材料，并提供该专题相关词汇。

作为本科阶段的同声传译教材，本课程的教学目标为：

1. 帮助学生理解同声传译发展历史、相关概念以及基本工作原理；
2. 帮助学生掌握同声传译基本技能，培养学生基本的听说同步能力，并学习如何处理同声传译中的信息难点；
3. 帮助学生学习热点专题知识、了解相关词汇，学会如何做好译前准备工作。

二、教材内容结构与教学安排

本教程各单元的内容结构与教学安排如下：

第一部分：同传技能。该部分是对每单元涉及的同声传译理论或技能知识进行的介绍或讲解。学生可以在课前对该部分内容进行预习，或者由教师在课堂上结合案例分析进行讲解。

第二部分：案例分析。该部分结合第一部分的理论或技能知识，选用篇章练习部分的口译段落/句子来作详细分析，讲解段落/句子的处理方式、步骤及其原因，并附参考译文。教师可结合第一部分进行讲解，并用该部分的段落/句子给学生作视译练习，以使学生初步了解同传工作模式。

第三部分：术语拓展。该部分结合单元练习主题提供英汉汉英对照词汇及专业术语，包括且不限于单元口译练习材料中出现的词汇或术语。学生可课后自学此部分，用于扩展词汇储备。

第四部分：篇章练习。该部分选择实际会议材料，英译汉及汉译英各两篇，每篇练习材料均附参考译文。该部分为课堂教学主体部分，教师可在学生提前预习的基础上让学生进行当堂练习，并视学生口译水平决定练习形式（带稿同传或无稿同传）和练习长度（截取篇章练习或全部篇章练习）。

上述四个部分中，理论介绍与技能讲解部分为学生了解该单元所涉技能提供基本信息，术语拓展部分为学生提供专题扩展词汇，案例分析与篇章练习部分旨在帮助学生掌握基本的英汉汉英双语同传技能，提高学生处理难点信息的能力。

本教材设计为一学期同声传译课程使用，全书共 11 个单元，建议除第 1 单元以外按每单元两周的进度实施教学。

本课程的期末考试主要考查学生对同声传译技能的掌握程度以及对难点信息的处理情况。课程中后期可安排一至两次模拟会议练习，也可将期末考试以模拟会议的形式进行。

三、单元教学操作（以第 5 单元为例）

本单元内容：

1. 口译技巧：同声传译的基本原则
2. 练习主题：教育

教学时数：

4 个课时（160 分钟）

教学内容：

1. 同声传译五大基本原则介绍
2. 基本原则案例分析
3. 专题词汇术语拓展
4. 专题同声传译练习

教学步骤：

1. 学生课前预习
2. 课堂教学

（1）抽查学生预习情况（术语掌握情况、主题知识了解情况）　15 min

（2）口译技能介绍　25 min

　　教师结合案例分析部分介绍同声传译五大基本原则，其目的在于使学生充分理解基本原则的概念及其操作。教师可结合学生实际水平适当补充案例，加深学生的理解。

（3）口译热身练习　20 min

　　此部分教师可要求学生进行影子跟读练习，以同步听说的形式用源语将听到的篇章重述出来。此部分的练习目标在于使学生迅速进入同步听说的工作状态，为下一步的同步听译做好准备。教师在学生练习同时应全程监听，对于不良的学习习惯应及时指出并加以纠正。对于程度较好的学生，练习时间可以适当缩短。

（4）篇章分析　20 min

　　基础同传阶段的主要教学目的是帮助学生获得同步听说的能力，并掌握基本的同声传译技能。因此，在进入篇章同传练习之前，教师可让学生分析即将处理的篇章，通过对文章的快速阅读迅速把握内容大意、篇章结构、中心思想等，并在重难点部分作出标记。

（5）篇章练习　50 min

　　学生进入同传厢，边听录音边做同传。教师可以邀请其他学生一起进行监听，以备共同点评。学生可分成不同小组，轮流进厢练习。

（6）教师与同学点评　20 min

　　教师与学生共同点评进厢练习学生的优缺点。注意：教师和同学点评不应仅仅限于指出错译、漏译等失误之处，而是要帮助其分析客观原因。

（7）练习总结　10 min

　　学生自我总结同声传译训练心得。

3. 课后复习与巩固

（1）主题知识查漏补缺；

（2）同传技能巩固练习。

第1单元 同声传译概论
An Introduction to Simultaneous Interpreting

单元学习目标
1. 了解同声传译的概念、应用、工作原理等。
2. 了解同传译员应具备的素质并以此确立学习目标。
3. 进行长交传练习，巩固口译技巧。

第一部分 同声传译的概念、特征

口译就其工作方式而言，一般可以分为两类：连续传译（consecutive interpreting，或称交替传译）和同声传译（simultaneous interpreting）。连续传译是指发言人说完一段话后，由口译员在现场立即翻译成目的语给听众的口译形式，发言与口译交替着进行。而同声传译则是指发言人在发言的同时，译员把发言的内容翻译给听众，发言与翻译几乎同时进行，不需要停顿。

在大多数情况下，同声传译是通过专门的同传设备进行的。译员坐在特制的同传厢（booth）中，通过耳机接收发言人的讲话内容，并使用麦克风把翻译的内容传播给听众。这样就能做到发言、翻译互不干扰。而同时，每位听众都会拿到一个无线接收设备，可以选择所需要的语言，通过耳机聆听翻译后的发言内容。

从交传和同传的概念上来比较，我们可以看出同传的几个特征：

1. 听与说几乎同步进行，这是同传与其他口译形式相比最明显的特征。当然，这种"同步"并不是绝对的同步，毕竟译员需要先听取源语信息后才能快速地反应，因此在源语信息和译入语信息传递之间存在一定的时间差。但由于发言和翻译可以持续进行，不需要间断，相对于交传，可以节省出几乎一半的时间。所以，这也是同传较之交传最大的优势所在。

2. 同传的翻译速度受到发言速度的直接影响。由于要保证口译与发言的同步进行，发言人的语速就成了制约译员语速的直接因素。发言人的语速还常常影响同传的质量。发言人语速过快，信息密集，将导致译员没有足够的时间接收并处理信息，往往会造成翻译信息的大量遗漏。而语速过慢则不利于译员短时间内接收和处理完整的信息，有可能导致译入语停顿过长，不流畅。

3. 译入语要求保持连贯且明白易懂。与交传相比，同传译入语的质量要求相对低一些。这是因为，在交传中，译员是先听后说，在听完一整段发言后可以对源语信息进行必要的调整，对没有把握的地方，还可以向发言人求证，因此译出来的信息相对更完整、准确，译文也更通顺流畅。而在同传中，译员是边听边说，没有时间对大段信息进行加工重组；同时，译员独自在厢中工作，遇到不确定的信息也不可能与发言人确认，因此，译入语无论在信息的完整度、准确度，还是译文的流畅程度上，都不可能与交传的要求相当。同传的译入语最基本的要求就是要保持连贯，不能有太多的停顿或前言不搭后语的情况，同时做到清楚明白即可。

值得注意的是，由于同声传译工作方式比较特殊，有别于人们日常的先听后说的习惯，因此，不少人把同传"神化"成了翻译的"九段"，并认为同传要比交替传译高级。事实上，它们并没有高低之分，两者对译员的素质都提出了很高的要求，只是工作方式有所不同，对译入语的质量有不同的衡量标准而已。同传的优点很明显，可以节省会议时间；同时，听众可以不间断地聆听译成目的语的发言，思路连贯。而在另一些场合，则交传的工作方式更为合适：在一些谈判或讨论的场合，发言人需要不断地接受新信息，并思考下一段的发言，因此，交传译员翻译时，刚好为他们的思考准备留出了一段宝贵的时间。

第二部分　同声传译的历史

口译到底有多长的历史，无从查考。据说是自从人类有了语言交往后，便有了口译。和口译比起来，同声传译的历史要短得多。同传首次正式公开的亮相是在1919年的"巴黎和会"上，会议部分尝试采用了翻译与发言同步进行的方式。不过，由于当时的设备比较简单，没有专门的同传厢和收发装置，发言人与译员都同时用各自的麦克风说话，对发言和翻译都产生了很大的干扰。在后来的"纽伦堡审判"(1945-1946)上，需要同时使用英、法、德、俄四种语言，如果要用传统的连续传译的方式，那会议流程将会变得相当复杂拖沓。因此，"大审判"大规模地采用了同传。会议还采用了一套由美国人发明的装置——临时的独立翻译室，译员在其中使用耳机听源语发言，同时用麦克风将译语传播出去，这样发言、翻译互不干扰——此装置不断发展，演变成了今日使用的同传厢。"纽伦堡审判"使人们意识到了同声传译的便利快捷，由于翻译无需占用会议时间，会程几乎缩短了一半。有意思的是,纳粹战犯戈林责备同声传译缩短了他的生命。因为,如果要采用连续传译的形式,大审判还得再多审上几年。

鉴于"纽伦堡大审判"中采用同声传译且十分成功,联合国也开始在其机构内试验。1947年开始正式使用同声传译;而到了1950年,讨论重大问题的安理会也开始使用同声传译,至此,同传在联合国的各个专门机构开始了大规模的应用。随着全球化趋势的不断深入发展,国际交流日益频繁,社会对同传的需求也不断增长。现如今,在联合国、欧盟等国际组织中,每天都有十几种语言通过同传的方式传递;而同传也被广泛地应用于各种商业会议、政府或民间团体的交流活动中。有人曾统计,现在世界上95%的国际会议都采用同声传译。

在口译发展史中,1953年是一个值得纪念的时刻。这一年,最早的一批同传译员在瑞士日内瓦成立了"国际会议口译工作者协会(L'Association Internationale des Interprètes de Conférence, AIIC)。这个协会针对会员的专业水平、资格、语言能力、职业道德和准则等都作出了详细的规定,并同时针对译员待遇、工作时间、工作条件等方面提出了一系列要求,旨在保障译员的合法权益。AIIC的建立标志着口译职业化的开始。

我国首次使用同声传译是在1952年北京召开的亚洲地区和平会议上,但在恢复联合国合法地位前,使用非常有限。直到1979年,联合国与北京外国语学院(北京外国语大学)合作开办了联合国译员培训项目,开始了我国同声传译员的专业化训练,并先后为联合国培养了近两百名译员。改革开放后,由于沿海地区对外交流的需求日益增大,一些沿海地区外语院校相继开设专业的口译及同声传译课程。而今,全国各地很多高校增设了口译专业及同传课程,以适应市场对高质量口译员,特别是同声传译员的需求。

第三部分　同声传译的程序

同声传译的程序可以简单地用下面这个图来表示:

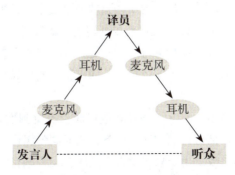

如图所示，同声传译的工作流程基本如下：发言人的源语讲话通过麦克风传入译员的耳机中，译员在通过耳机接收信息的同时迅速处理信息，并以目的语通过麦克风传达给听众，而听众则需要通过同传接收耳机听取翻译的内容。虽然图上将同传分成了好几个步骤，但其实这些步骤几乎都在同时完成，同传译员的工作强度和压力可想而知。

从图上我们不难看出同传的质量受到以下几个方面的制约：

1. 发言人：源语信息的发出者，是翻译质量的"第一道关卡"。发言的内容，信息密度，专业程度，语速和流利程度，逻辑性和口音都会影响译员对源语信息的理解，进而对最终的译入语质量造成影响。

2. 设备：同传设备肩负着向译员传递源语信息，向听众传递译入语信息的双向"重任"，因此设备的好坏，调试是否到位，译员操作是否熟练是翻译质量能否得到保障的重要条件。质量合格且调试妥当的设备应当运行稳定，反应灵敏准确；麦克风和耳机都应该清晰无杂音。同时译员工作的同传厢也要设计合理，有较为舒适的空间、工作台、座椅等，还要通风良好，有足够的光线或安装有台灯。

3. 译员：译员是翻译活动的完成者。如果说发言人、设备是影响翻译质量的"外因"，那么译员的素质则是"内因"。译员在工作中好像一台"多任务处理器"——听、想、记、译同步完成，同时还要应对各种突发状况，承受现场的压力等。因此，合格的译员一方面要有良好的专业素养、深厚的语言功底、熟练的翻译技巧、认真负责的工作态度；另一方，还要有过硬的心理素质，能承受强大的工作压力，沉着地处理突发状况。

第四部分　同声传译的应用

目前，同声传译已成为各种国际会议中普遍采用的口译方式，在联合国、欧盟等国际组织中同传也担负着绝大多数会议的翻译任务。随着各国信息文化传播和交流的日益深入，我们常常还能在电视新闻转播、邀请外宾参加的访谈节目中听到同传译员为观众译出的外语发言。例如，中央电视台在进行伊拉克战争报道和2016年奥运会申办转播时就采用了同传。同传几乎适用于包括正式演讲、双/多方谈判、问答交流等所有的会议形式和场合。而在实际的应用中，为了适应不同场合的不同需要，同传又可以分为以下几种方式：

1. 常规同传（无稿同传）：译员在翻译时没有拿到发言稿或幻灯片等，只是耳听现场发言，结合自己的译前准备，完成同传工作。这对译员的个人能力提出了极大的挑战。由于只了解大会主题、发言题目、发言人姓名头衔等有限的资料，译员要做大量的译前准备，熟悉会议、发言人的背景，了解相关主题，准备和熟悉大量专业词汇术语等。还常常要参考类似的会议资料或是以往接触过的有关会议的资料。准备工作量非常大。工作时，现场压力也相当大。由于没有任何发言资料，大多数时候也不熟悉发言人的说话方式，只能凭借自己的翻译技能，边听、边理解、处理、边翻译。

2. 视译：译员事先拿到了发言稿或者幻灯片演示文件，翻译时一边听发言，一边对照讲稿完成翻译。发言稿或演示文件又分为两种情况。一种是译员事先拿到发言稿原文，即源语材料，在译前准备时要熟悉材料，了解相关专业知识，查出特定的词汇、术语等，并在必要的地方作出调整标记，方便翻译。另一种情况是译员事先拿到的是发言稿的翻译稿。这种情况一般出现在一些特别重大的场合，如国家元首在联合国大会上的发言。由于会议场合非常严肃，发言的措辞非常标准、谨慎。发言稿及其译稿都是经过专业团队不断研究推敲而得出的，不宜再作改动。工作时，译员须谨慎地跟着发言人的速度，把译稿连贯地读出，不可超越发言人抢读，也不可因粗心而漏读、跳读。

3. 耳语同传：译员不是坐在同传厢中，而是坐在与会代表的身边，一边听发言，一边对身边的代表轻声地翻译。这种翻译方式原来只适合于个别语言不通的与会代表，但随着技术的进步，现在出现了一些耳语同传专用的小型信号收发装置，原来只能服务一两个人的耳语同传，如今也能为会场中的一些小型团队服务了。但总的来说，由于译员没有独立的工作空间，现场的噪音和人员干扰比较大，缺少设备或是设备没有同传厢中的完备精密，耳语同传的质量要求相对厢子里的同传稍低。有时译员常被要求"翻个大意"，让身边的代表明白"现场在发生什么事儿"就可以了。

4. 接力同传：在使用三种或三种以上语言的国际会议中广泛应用。以一场使用三种语言的会议为例，发言人用源语（A语）发言后，同传厢①内译员以B语进行同传，而他同传的内容将传播到B语听众和同传厢②中，厢②里的译员根据B语的翻译再将信息译成C语并传送给C语听众。由于进行接力的C语译员无法直接听取源语A语的信息（听不懂A语，或A语非其本场工作语言），只能依赖于B语译员的翻译，因此，B语译员任何的理解错误或翻译差错都将影响到C语的最终翻译。可见，接力同传不仅对每种语言的翻译提出严格的要求，也需要不同语种的译员相互配合。现在，由于具备了完善的技术支持，在联合国、欧盟等组织中，常可见到同时使用十几种语言的会议，一位代表的发言，有可能在译员那里"转了好几道手"才最终到达目标听众的耳机里。

第五部分　同声传译员的素质

同声传译是一项非常复杂的工作，对译员的个人素质要求很高，总结起来，有以下几个方面：

1. 扎实的语言功底和口头表达能力。同传总是和"外语"打交道，因此，大家通常理解同传译员的外语水平一定要非常高，听力敏锐、口语流利、词汇丰富。其实口译，尤其是同传，对母语水平也有很高的要求，包括对母语文字的理解力、表达力，对语域和语体的把握，以及对母语成语典故、诗歌词赋的了解掌握等。国内很多口译学员专注于提高自己的外语水平，却忽略了中文，结果虽然外语听说都很流利，却在转换成中文的时候很困难，说出的中文不像中文，遣词造句也不甚得体。这样的人，外语水平再高，也成不了一名合格的译员。

2. 熟练的口译技巧。长期以来，人们对"口译"这个职业存在着误解，以为能说外语的人，或者外语专业的毕业生就能做口译。实际上，大量的事实证明口译是一项专业技能，必须经过专门的培训（当然也出现过极少数极具天赋的人，未经培训也成为了职业翻译）。而同声传译的工作方式有别于人们正常的听说方式，更需要经过专门的培训。通过培训，译员在记忆力、注意力、表达能力和心理素质等方面都能得到很大的提高，方能胜任同传这项特殊的工作。

3. 丰富的百科知识。多项研究表明口译员的背景知识储备与口译质量成正比。也就是说，口译员对口译任务所涉题材了解得越多，翻译起来越轻松，而口译的质量也越高。由于国际会议所涉主题多样，会上大多交流的是某一领域的最新发展，这就要求口译员要有丰富的百科知识，留心收集国内外重大新闻，并培养对知识的广泛兴趣，随时注意学习和储备。

4. 过硬的心理素质。同声传译是一项压力巨大的工作。同传译员往往是在精神极度紧张的状况下完成任务，还必须要对自己的翻译质量负责。这就要求译员必须具备过硬的心理素质和超人的抗压能力，保证高质量完成任务并能从容应对会议现场的各种突发状况。例如，在一次某省政府的记者招待会上，现场的麦克风突然发生故障，同传厢中的译员无法通过耳机接听到发言。而此次招待会十分重大且是电视直播的，口译不能中断。译员急中生智，果断地打开厢子的门窗，摘下耳机，直接听取发言并继续口译，直到所有设备恢复正常。试想，如果译员心理素质不过硬，在遇到设备故障时可能就已经乱了阵脚，不知所措，更不用说能在极其紧张的状态下想办法保证翻译顺利进行了。

5. 合作精神和职业操守。正常情况下，一个同声传译任务是由2到3人的小组共同完成的。由于压力极大，每位译员翻译20分钟左右，注意力就开始下降，需要休息一下，由另一位译员轮换顶替。而轮休的译员除了及时放松调整外，还要协助同伴记笔记、找资料、协助检查当值译员的输出频道是否正确，或是在发生设备故障的情况下，立即求助，甚至还包括帮同伴递水等小事。这些小事杂事虽然微不足道，但却是口译得以顺利进行的重要保障。如果小组的译员各自为政，不能及时发现同伴的需求，那么整个过程可能频繁出现差错和状况。从 AIIC 成立之时起，就为译员立下了一系列的职业道德准则，如对客户给予的资料和会议内容严格保密，口译过程中保持中立，保证口译质量，信守合约，不接受不能胜任的口译任务，不因后来的任务报酬高、条件好而推掉先前已经接受的任务等。译员遵守职业道德不仅是保障客户的利益，也是保护自己的事业，一个违反职业道德的译员最终只能被市场淘汰。

第2单元 同声传译听辨
Listening and Analysis in Simultaneous Interpreting

单元学习目标
1. 掌握同传听辨技巧。
2. 熟悉旅游这一口译主题的常用汉英术语和表达方式。
3. 能够对较复杂的中英文演讲进行源语及目的语复述。

第一部分 同传技能

1. 吉尔（Daniel Gile）的同声传译脑力分配模式

我们可以把整个同传过程分成好几步，有些步骤是经常性出现的，而有些步骤则是时而有所表现。著名的释意派创始人之一勒代雷（Marianne Lederer）女士曾指出，同传的经常性步骤有以下四个：1）听；2）理解；3）把语言转化成概念，即将一连串的话语形成的语段与先前的知识综合起来，形成记忆；4）根据记忆来表达。由此我们可以看出在译员张口"说"（表达）之前，至少还要做三件事：听取发言、理解信息、处理信息并记忆。而听与理解则是其他过程的前奏和基础，我们把这两个步骤称为同声传译的听辨。

实际上，从以上提到的同传的四个经常性步骤中，我们可以看出，同声传译其实并不是一项单一的任务，译员在做"同传"这件事情的时候实际上同时完成了好几项任务。而每个人的精力都是有限的，如何能保证这所有的任务都能同时顺利完成呢？著名的口译研究学者吉尔提出注意力分配模式（effort model）：

$$SI = L + M + P + C$$

即：同声传译（simultaneous interpreting）= 听力与分析（listening and analysis）+ 短时记忆（short-term memory）+ 言语产出（speech production）+ 协调（coordination）。

从这个模式中我们可以看出，同传活动需要大量的脑力支持，而脑力往往是有限的；工作时，有限的脑力会被全部占用，执行不同的任务，而当用在某一项任务上的脑力增大时，必然会导致另外几项上的脑力减少；换言之，如果我们能通过训练，将脑力合理有效地分配，就能使得整个同传过程协调顺利地进行。值得注意的是，这个模式所展示的是一个动态的过程。在同传过程中，每项任务所分配到的脑力不是一成不变的，相反，根据每一时间段任务的不同特点，译员所采取的应对策略会不断地发生改变，甚至每隔几秒钟就会发生一次改变。比如说，某一段的发言需要译员调动大量的脑力去听和分析，而在翻译另一段的发言时译员则需要花更多的脑力思考如何措词表达（即言语产出）。

一般说来，我们要干好某件事情，至少我们应该具有这件事情所要求的能力，如果我们的能力大于要求，那么干好这件事的几率就会大大提高。同传也不例外。从总量上看，我们的脑力应该等于或大于一项同传任务所要求的脑力；而我们在"听"、"记"、"产出"、"协调"上的能力也应该分别等于或高于四项任务的要求。因此，我们的训练目标是逐项提高各项任务的处理能力，最终获得足够应付同传任务的脑力。而作为整个同传过程第一步的"听力与分析"自然成为了我们攻克难关的第一步。

2. 同传听辨与英语学习中的听力训练

从小学的第一堂英语课开始，听力训练就一直贯穿于我们整个英语学习的过程。经过多年的英语学习，特别是大学专业的英语学习，我们已经具备了相当的英语听力，而口译课正是建立在学习者具备敏锐的英语听力的基础上。口译是英语学习中的一项高级技能，如果尚未具备良好的听力就盲目开始学口译，就如同揠苗助长，适得其反。虽然英语学习与同传的基础都是听，但两者在目的、方法、训练技巧上大有区别，不可混为一谈。

1) 听的目的

普通的英语听力课是为了训练学生捕捉某一类型的信息而设计，比如听辨数字、口音等。通过专项训练，学生对各种信息的敏感度提高了，从而提高了对整个听力材料的理解力和信息捕捉能力。另外，英语听力课还是英语口语学习的基础，听是信息的"输入（input）"环节，而说则是"产出（output）"环节，只有先积累了一定的词汇、表达、知识，才有可能说出正确的英语。

同声传译听辨训练的目的是帮助学生顺利地完成"译"这项任务。正如之前"注意力分配模式"中分析的那样，如果"听力分析"这项任务耗费的脑力较少，则有较多的脑力可以分配到同传过程的其他任务中去。而且，"听与分析"是同传的第一环节，其完成的好坏将直接影响到同传的质量。"听"只是同传听辨任务的一半，另外一半则是要"分析"，这是与普通听力训练最大的区别。同传听辨训练中，我们不仅要准确地抓到信息，还要主动出击，对信息加以梳理归纳，使它更富有逻辑性，便于用目的语准确地表达。

2）听的技巧

在普通的听力课中，我们训练的一般程序都是先听（或先看）问题，再带着问题去听材料，找答案，只要找到答案就算是圆满完成任务，目的性很强。甚至很多指导书会教我们"只要听到这一题的答案就不要再继续听了，应该马上看看下一题的问题"。在这样的训练中，我们很少有机会关注听力材料的原文，分析它的结构和特征；也不太注重去捕捉每一个细节。

而在同传中，这样的方法显然是行不通的。因为没有人会事先告知译员要听什么，人们只会说"我要听发言里的所有内容"，所以，译员不可能听一段漏一段，所有的内容都是同样重要的。这也就决定了我们在同传听辨的训练中必须采取有别于普通听力课的方法。训练学生从全局来把握发言，尽可能地抓住每一个细节；从始至终都必须主动地理解、分析、处理听到的信息，而不是被动地等待答案的到来。

3）训练方法

普通听力课的训练主要采用被动地听＋记录的方法。课堂上，教师会告知学生要聚精会神，一旦找到答案要及时记录，多采用问答的形式来检测学生的听力水平。

相比之下，同传听辨训练的方法更多样，要求也更高。常用的训练方法有听并全文复述、归纳总结、预测、分析等。通过各种方法调动大脑的主动性，将听力、记忆力和理解分析能力紧密结合起来。

3. 听辨要素

1）英文功底

并不是所有英语专业的学生最终都要学同传，只有那些英文功底扎实、口头表达能力好的学生才是同传课的合适人选。听力基础是同传听辨的根本，必须首先具备敏锐的听力，能轻松准确地捕捉发言材料的各种信息。其次，必须具备较丰富的词汇量和扎实的语法功底，能理解各种不同领域的材料，游刃有余地应对不同文体、语域。最后，还应该具有较广的知识面，因为训练材料涉及各个领域，没有一定的知识储备是很难把握的。

2）口译记忆

记忆贯穿于口译的整个过程。听辨训练中，我们听到的所有信息都将会暂时储存在短时记忆中。而我们对材料的理解和全面分析则要依靠听到的信息辅以我们的长时记忆（即知识储备）。"听"与"记"在同传中看似是先后两个程序，实际上两者是密不可分的。不可能"听"而不"记"，也不可能"记"而不"听"。

3）思考分析

思考分析是同传听辨中的主动因素，也是有别于普通听力的最显著特点。"听辨"一词中,"听"与"辨",即分析,各占50%,说明两者具有同样的重要性。分析其实是一个主动处理信息的过程。通过不断地思考分析,我们能及时梳理发言的逻辑,有利于我们更准确地理解上文和预测下文。

第二部分　训练提示

听辨训练可以从最简单的听—复述开始,方法与交替传译的记忆训练类似。熟练之后可以开始进行归纳总结的练习,即听一段文字,对其进行源语或目的语的归纳;刚开始时,要求能归纳出主题、大意即可,循序渐进地将要求提高,逐步达到听一段文字后能整理归纳出一段结构清晰、逻辑性强的文字,不仅能说出大意,还能加上适当的细节以支持主要观点。经过一番整理后,复述语段应比源语段更清晰明了。

在听辨能力得到一定的提高后,可以进一步增加难度。可以选听一些逻辑稍差、结构散乱的语段,重新整合复述;或选取一些不完整段落(如只有例证,没有观点;只分析原因,没有结果),听后根据文字的逻辑,合理补充语段丢失的部分。

在复述归纳的过程中,不要求使用原文的词汇和表达,甚至鼓励在保持意思不变的情况下改变原文的词句。复述应比原文更有逻辑性、结构更清晰、表达更简洁;如果原文的某些地方逻辑混乱,或用词不当,应在听辨的过程中发现并在复述归纳时改正过来。总之,复述的语言质量应高于原文的质量。

第三部分　术语拓展

汉译英

巴厘岛	Bali Island
背包旅行(者)	backpacking (er)
布吉岛	Phuket Island
出境游	out-bound tourism
佛教名山	famous Buddhist mountains
跟团旅行	package tour
广西壮族自治区旅游局	Tourism Administration of Guangxi Zhuang Autonomous Region

国际航线	international routes
海滨旅游	beach tourism
红色旅游	tourism featuring revolutionary heritage
湖光山色	landscape of lakes and hills
廉价航班	Low Cost Airlines (LCA)
旅游集散中心	tourist distribution centre
旅游套票	set ticket
民俗风情	folk custom
名山大川	famous mountains and great rivers
名胜古迹	scenic spots and historical sites
农家乐	rural fun
人文景观	places of historic figures and cultural heritage
入境游	in-bound tourism
生态旅游	eco-tourism
手工艺品	artefacts (or artifacts)
文化遗产	cultural heritage
五岳	the five great mountians (in China)
休闲旅游	leisure tourism
一票通	all-in-one ticket
遗产旅游	heritage tourism
异地联网售票	inter-city ticket selling and ordering
园林建筑	garden architecture
中国广西 – 东盟国际旅游合作论坛	China (Guangxi)—ASEAN International Tourism Cooperation Forum
中国国家旅游局	China National Tourism Administration
自驾游	self-drive tour
自然景观	natural scenery

英译汉

ancient architectural complex	古建筑群
anti-poverty project	扶贫项目
boarding pass	登机牌
check in	入住 / 办理登机手续
check out	退房

check-in counter	值班柜台
cruise terminal	邮轮码头
departure lounge	候机室
flight number	航班号
Forbestraveler.com	福布斯旅游网
groundbreaking ceremony	动土仪式，奠基仪式
guest house	旅社，客栈
handbag tag	行李牌
holiday resort	度假胜地
Hong Kong Wine and Dine Festival	香港美酒佳肴巡礼
itinerary	行程
Lonely Planet	全球最大的旅游指南和数字媒体出版商
motel	汽车旅馆
national park	国家公园
nature reserve	自然保护区
Pan-Pearl River Delta Tourism Business Promotion Conference of Guangdong 2008 International Tourism and Culture Festival	2008广东国际旅游文化节暨泛珠三角旅游推介大会
room service	客房服务
route	航线，路线
security inspection	安检
star-rated hotel	星级酒店
terminal building	航站楼
the occupancy rate of the hotel	酒店入住率
theme park	主题公园
tourism destination	旅游目的地
vacation tour	假日旅游
World Tourism Organization	世界旅游组织
youth hostel	青年旅社

第四部分　同传实战

 Listen to the following four speeches and interpret them into the target language segment by segment.

Text 1

最后一点，我谈一下这个中国的旅游宣传的定位问题。多年来讲，中国作为一个旅游目的地，一般的概念都是一种文化历史的概念，长城也好，故宫也好，但是始终没有一个口号，始终没有一个真正能够反映这个旅游产品的一个 tag line，一个真正的这个招揽物。

那么我们世界旅游组织在这方面没有真正在中国宏观上作过尝试，但是也作过一两个尝试。比如中国黑龙江的哈尔滨，它并不是一个特别吸引人的旅游城市，不是一个顶级资源的城市，在这种情况下如何来设计旅游口号的问题。我们最后想来想去，就叫做"中国酷都"，Cool Capital。c-o-o-l，酷都。如今年轻人来不来就是这个酷，那个酷。那么我们为什么找这个呢，想了它这样几个资源，它为什么叫酷都呢？首先第一夏天的概念，噢，不是夏天，第一是冬天的概念，是冰雪之都，所以是"酷"，冷酷的概念；第二呢，是清凉世界，到了那儿，哈尔滨，太阳岛，要从这个角度；第三呢就是从时尚之都，毕竟是当年的东方莫斯科，所以三者结合找到一个词儿，实际上也是玩儿文字游戏，但是一旦找到了就坚持下去，好像目前哈尔滨一直还在用着我们提出的这个口号。

再有一个就是海南省作为整体口号如何提的问题，海南实际上也蛮难提的，如果是从海滨旅游开发，对于国内人士来讲都是小菜一盘，所有人都知道，但是没有外国人真正知道，海南作为一个，一个可以去度假、海滨旅游的概念，它的知名度是远远不如印尼的巴厘岛和泰国的布吉岛，在这种情况下如何来突出它，我们最后想来想去就提出把它叫做 Tropical China——热带的中国，为什么呢？人一说中国，首先想到的就是历史的中国，文化的中国，谁也不会想到热带的中国，所以就提出了这样的口号，看看有没有可能吸引住大家吧。

中国目前的旅游业发展我认为是在一个战略转移的过程当中。这个转移，最主要的呢应该是说从观光型向休闲型发展，从数字型向质量型发展，也应该是从这个大众旅游型向特殊旅游发展；这样一个过渡当中，我认为最主要的，就是一定要强调可持续发展。只有在可持续发展的大前提下，我们才能够保证旅游业发展的生命力，所以我也给大家一句忠告，那就是希望不要太多的加法，应该是减法多一点，少而精，谢谢大家。

(2005年12月16日，世界旅游组织亚太区主任徐京在"国际旅游与酒店业发展论坛"上的讲话节选，根据录音材料整理）

Text 2

Jay (Rasulo), Distinguished Guests, Ladies and Gentlemen,

Good morning.

It is my great pleasure to join you all for the groundbreaking ceremony of the Hong Kong Disneyland expansion project. Today marks a significant milestone for both Hong Kong Disneyland and the tourism industry in Hong Kong.

Hong Kong Disneyland is an important component of our tourism infrastructure. Since its opening in September 2005, the park has welcomed over 19 million visitors and contributed more than $10 billion of value added to our economy. The park has also created over 10,000 jobs over the year.

The expansion project will add three new themed areas to Hong Kong Disneyland featuring more than 30 new attractions and experiences. Some of the attractions will be unique to Hong Kong Disneyland. A larger park with more attractions will continue to draw the crowds and provide even more fun and excitement for our visitors.

Last year, we received in Hong Kong almost 30 million visitors from around the world. Despite the global financial crisis, we expect tourist numbers to be about the same this year.

We will continue to enhance our portfolio of attractions to further strengthen Hong Kong's appeal as a preferred travel destination.

Over the past few years, Hong Kong has invested over $30 billion in attractions. In the coming few years, we are investing another $17 billion in tourism infrastructure. Preparatory site work has started on a world-class cruise terminal, and we will seek to enhance the attractiveness of popular tourist spots, such as Tsim Sha Tsui, Ngong Ping and Lei Yue Mun.

Hong Kong is a dynamic and vibrant city. Throughout the year, we have many signature events that appeal to both locals and visitors. The Hong Kong Wine and Dine Festival earlier this year has been rated one of the top 10 international food and wine festivals by Forbestraveler.com. Our Chinese New Year celebrations have also been named as the "Best Value Entertainment around the World" by Lonely Planet.

The $100 million Mega Events Fund launched this year will continue to attract international arts, culture and sports events to our city.

Together with the magic of an expanded Hong Kong Disneyland, I am confident that Hong Kong will continue to be a premier destination for our friends of all ages from all corners of the world.

Thank you very much and have a great day.

(Full text of speech by John Tseng, Financial Secretary of Hong Kong SAR, at Groundbreaking Ceremony for the expansion of Hong Kong Disneyland)

Text 3

尊敬的各位代表，女士们、先生们：

由广西壮族自治区旅游局、广西社科院、《中国旅游》报社联合主办的、为期两天的"中国广西－东盟国际旅游合作论坛"马上就要闭幕了。两天来，来自东盟国家、我国国内的、区内的著名专家、学者和旅游部门的负责人，围绕"中国广西与东盟国际旅游合作"这一主题，在友谊、合作、发展的这一框架内，就中国广西与东盟进行旅游合作与交流的相关问题，展开了深入的研讨。其中，还提出了很多有参考价值的意见和建议。这对进一步推动中国广西与东盟的旅游合作将会起着积极的推动作用。通过这两天的论坛的讨论，与会代表以高度的负责精神和高昂的热情，提出了非常好的意见和建议。我想本次论坛在以下三个方面取得了丰硕的成果。

第一，广泛地增进了我们的友谊。虽然会议只有短短的两天时间，各位代表在非常紧张的情况下，就共同关注的主题话题，就是"广西与东盟旅游合作"这个主题，通过聆听演讲报告、互相交流学习，结识了很多朋友，甚至打破了我们在文化、语言等各种方面的障碍。通过短短的两天，结下了很深的友谊。我们也为东盟和我们国内的一些专家克服了很多困难来积极参加本次研讨会，深受感动。比如泰国的代表，维舍吴东陈女士，她是坚持带病参加的会议。那么，昨天发病送到医院治疗，今天正在康复当中。这时我们才知道，她四天前刚做的手术，同样坚持参加会议、发表论文；而且昨天自助餐的时候，还和我们旅游局、社科院就一些合作的课题进行商谈。所以我们对她表示最深切的祝福。很多专家，包括国外的专家和国内的专家，为参加本次论坛，辗转很多国际航线；为这次论坛的演讲做了精心的准备。我想，他们是为友谊而来，为合作而来。这些，我们都应该永远地进行珍惜。

第二，通过本次论坛，进一步加深了相互之间的了解。在两天论坛时间中，许多专家学者，包括旅游部门的实际工作者，都介绍了各自国家和地区发展旅游业的一些基本情况和做法，也介绍了他们旅游发展的先进的经验，同时也宣传了本国、本地区的旅游资源、旅游产品，以及跟广西旅游合作的现状，通报了他们进一步谋求合作，共谋发展的许多具体的想法。同时也客观地分析了目前中国广西与东盟旅游合作过程中的一些问题，比如：旅游安全及舒适度的问题、语言的障碍问题、客源目标市场的定位问题、双边旅游宣传促销的一些脱节的问题、交通不畅的问题、市场不规范的问题、通关不便利的问题、缺乏双边合作机制，等等问题，非常客观地分析了我们合作中存在的一些的突出问题。既表达合作的强烈愿望，又肯定我们现在合作的成绩，同时又冷静地分析在加快合作中必须解决的问题。我想这些都促进了我们双方在合作中的了解，为我们今后深入地探讨解决这些问题，找到了一些努力的方向，创造了相关的条件。

　　第三，通过两天的研讨，我们最重要的成果是共同探讨了旅游合作的问题。在两天的会议中，大家认真分析了相互合作的基础，提出了许多加强旅游合作的途径和办法，展望了中国广西和东盟加强国际区域旅游合作的美好的前景。我想本次论坛，为我们今后广西与东盟开展国际旅游合作迈出了重要的一步。与会人员认为，中国广西与东盟的旅游资源各具特色，互补性强，同时有着长期合作的基础。随着中国－东盟自由贸易区的建立，合作的前景会更加广阔。

　　（2004年11月，广西旅游局局长肖建刚在"中国广西－东盟国际旅游合作论坛"上的讲话节选，根据录音材料整理）

Text 4

　　Ladies and Gentlemen, Dear Friends,

　　Today, the Pan-Pearl River Delta Tourism Business Promotion Conference of Guangdong 2008 International Tourism and Culture Festival ceremoniously opens in the beautiful city of Guangzhou. I am very glad and honored to attend this grand and significant event. On behalf of the World Tourism Organization, I'd like to extend my warmest congratulations on the convening of the Conference & Festival!

　　Since the mid-20th century, modern tourism industry has been springing up rapidly all over the world, which has become one of the most remarkable achievements of the present age. With continuous expansion of its industrial scale and remarkable upgrade of its economic position, the tourist activities have become an increasingly important channel for the people worldwide to carry through cultural exchanges, strengthen friendship and to expand communication, which have exerted extensive influence on both the human life and the social development. Upon the entry of the 21st century, tremendous changes have taken place in the global tourism structure. The Asia-Pacific region has upsprung to the second place in the world in terms of the tourism industry, and the tripartite situation of Europe, Asia-Pacific region and America has been authentically shaped. As a foregoer in East Asia as well as in the Asia-Pacific region, China has made significant achievements in the tourism industry in recent years. It has now become an eyecatching tourism destination in the world with the richest tourist resources and boasts the largest domestic tourism market in the world. At present, China has 150 million international tourists and 1.5 billion domestic tourists per year, with a high annual growth rate of 5%. According to the forecast by WTO, China will exceed the traditional tourist destination countries such as France, Spain and America, and will rank the first among other countries by the year of 2020.

The bright prospect has brought about the golden chance for tourism investment. China has presently become a universal hot spot for tourism investment. According to a preliminary estimation, the annual average capital newly invested in China's tourism industry has reached more than RMB 100 billion in recent years, and investment has become one of the supporting pillars of the tourism industrial development.

Located in the southern part of China's mainland, the Pan-Pearl River Delta is an amazing land full of hope and infinite business opportunities. It is like a magnet that draws tourists not only from neighboring Hong Kong and Macao, but also in and out of Asia. One of the prominent characteristics of Guangdong International Tourism and Culture Festival is that tourism industry in the Pan-Pearl River Delta is promoted to the world as an integrated image. The successful holding of this conference will definitely serve as a platform for strengthening regional cooperation, establishing a wide network for investment and financing as well as jointly exploiting the domestic and foreign tourism business markets. The tourism industry of the Pan-Pearl River Delta will grow much larger and stronger in the future.

In recent years, the World Tourism Organization has cooperated well with many provinces in the Pan-Pearl River Delta. For example, we have participated in the compilation of the overall plans of tourism development in Yunnan, Sichuan, Guizhou and Hainan, etc. Together with the World Bank, we have also got involved in anti-poverty projects by developing tourism industry in Guizhou and other provinces. Also, we have enjoyed a very good cooperative relationship with Guangdong. The Ministerial Conference of the Aisan-Pacific Tourism Policies sponsored by World Tourism Organization in 2006 was held in Macao and while making investigation in Zhuhai, the attendees were warmly welcomed by the relevant department of Guangdong. We hope to further develop the cooperative relationships with Guangdong, Hong Kong SAR and Macao SAR and even the other regions in the Pan-Pearl River Delta. Because this area is the heart of Asian tourism business and the cornerstone of its prosperity.

In the years to come, on the basis of the existing friendship with these provinces and regions, we will continue to pay close attention and provide great support to the development of China's tourism industry, actively assist and participate in the international tourism market exploitation & investment promotion work in PPRD areas, and do our best to further promote the prosperity of the tourism industry of PPRD areas and of China as a whole.

I wish the PPRD Tourism Business Promotion Conference of Guangdong 2008 International Tourism and Culture Festival a very success!

(Full text of speech by Xu Jing, Regional Representative of Asia and Pacific of the World Tourism Organisation, at Pan-Pearl River Delta Tourism Business Promotion Conference of Guangdong 2008 International Tourism and Culture Festival, December 14, 2008)

第 3 单元　同声传译的多任务处理
Multi-tasking in Simultaneous Interpreting

> **单元学习目标**
> 1. 掌握同传多任务处理的基本方法及技巧。
> 2. 熟悉创新这一口译主题的常用汉英术语和表达方式。
> 3. 能够完成"影子"跟读、数数跟读、目的语跟读等同传干扰练习。

第一部分　同传技能

我们知道，同声传译是一个"一心多用"的过程。译员在极短的时间里应对听、理解、翻译、说等多重任务，与我们日常先听后说的交流方式最大的区别在于译员的"边听边说"——嘴里翻译着上一句，耳朵却已经在听下一句了。如果没有经过特别训练，一般人很难做到这种非正常的听说。在同传训练的起步阶段，"影子训练（shadowing）"能有效帮助我们逐步适应边听边说的方式，逐步提高多任务处理能力。

"影子训练"是用与所听材料同样的语言（源语），几乎同步或稍有延迟地跟读。"影子训练"阶段实际上还不能算是真正的同传训练阶段，因为这个时候，我们仍然没有引入翻译练习。"影子训练"一般按如下步骤进行。

1. 源语跟读与源语复述

"影子训练"的第一阶段，一般只要求紧紧跟随源语发言，用同样的语言同步复述出发言内容即可。训练时只要开始听懂一个意思，就可以马上开口复述。刚开始练习会出现听说不协调、张口说话就"听不到"声音等现象。这些都是正常的，不要着急或慌张，只要将听到的内容完整复述即可。在复述过程中，必须坚持的一点是：只有在听懂意思的情况下才开口说，务必保持发音清晰，音量适中，语句完整连贯。切忌没听懂意思就跟着机械地模仿发音，复述出一堆毫无意义的音节。

在逐渐适应影子跟读练习后，可增加难度。跟读一小段发言后，即用源语概括这段话的大意，以强化短时记忆。这时你会发现，自己回忆起发言的内容来，比以前单纯的听后复述或概括费劲多了。这是因为你的大脑比以前多处理了一项任务，耗费了更多的精力。

进行了一段时间的源语同步复述之后，可以进行下一阶段的"影子训练"——延迟复述，即在源语发言开始后，有意延迟半句到一句进行跟读。在整个跟读练习中也应有意识地延迟，保持一个合理的听说时差（EVS, ear voice span），不要跟得太紧。在脑力允许的情况下尽可能延迟，但也要避免落后太远，以免影响语篇的理解和复述的完整与流畅。

2. 注意力分配干扰练习

进行了一段时间的源语跟读和复述练习之后，可以再将难度进一步提高，开始注意力分配干扰练习，即在跟读基础上刻意地安排一些与听说无关的练习，向脑力提出进一步的挑战。

常用的训练方法是数数，也就是在跟读的同时，用笔在纸上数数。刚开始时，先从1、2、3数起，并将数字段限制得短一些。如从1数到20，再回头重数，直至跟读练习结束。然后回头看看纸上的数字是否有漏数、倒数。数数不宜太慢，一般至少一秒钟数一个数。

当数数练习逐渐变得简单之后，可继续增大难度，练习倒数，从100数到1；或者跳数，如2、4、6、8……一直数到200；或者从3开始每隔3位数一次，如3、6、9、12……。在跟读数数完成后，还可以进一步地要求用源语复述或概括出发言内容。

当纸上数数干扰练习变得熟练之后，还可以进行听说干扰练习，即在听发言的同时，嘴里大声、清晰地数数。从简单的顺数开始，直到倒数、跳数。有条件的话，应录下数数的声音，以便检查是否数错，声音是否清晰。在听完发言后，立即要求复述或概括刚才所听到的内容。

3. 目的语复述与跟读

跟读及注意力干扰训练往往需要持续一两个月。大家会发现经历了一个多月的练习后，注意力比刚开始时更容易集中，大脑也越来越"协调"了。在处理听、读、记、数各项任务时不再像以前那样窘迫了。大脑好像被分成了好几块，能互不干扰地处理不同任务，边听边说也变得越来越自信。这时，可以开始加入目的语的练习。先用源语跟读发言，然后用目的语复述或概括。在听第二遍发言的同时，用较概括的目的语简单叙述自己听到的内容。要特别注意的是目的语的跟读不是机械地翻译零星的单词，而是叙述出一个完整的意思。要保证所说的句子都是完整的，都能表达一定的意义；而一个语段跟读下来，能让自己或旁人听出这段话的大意。

第二部分　训练提示

"影子跟读"练习常常受到质疑。有人认为这种方法是让学生"鹦鹉学舌"——机械地重复听到的声音，而非积极动脑思考话语的意义；培养的是学生全神贯注地听，而非自然放松地听和分配注意力。在这里要特别指出的是：以上这些质疑也许误解了本章所述的训练方法，而质疑中所提出的错误的方式——机械地重复听到的声音——也正是本章所反对的。

"影子跟读"完全是建立在对意义的理解之上，是在听懂了一个意义单位之后才能开口跟读。跟读的过程中必须保证所复述的内容都是理解以后的内容。没有理解的部分不能开口，不能简单地模仿发音，而应等到能全部把握意思后再恢复跟读。经过一段时间的训练后，鼓励在源语跟读过程中刻意找一些近义词替代发言中的源语，或进行词性转换、句子切分，在不改变语段意义的前提下尽量转换表达方法。

在做数数干扰练习时，要尽量保证数数的速度均匀，书写整齐。在数数与听读相互干扰时，优先保证听读。如果发现数数对跟读练习干扰较大，以致跟读内容基本无意义，或无法理解语段大部分内容时，说明现在还不是进行干扰训练的好时机。应该回头再练习一段时间的无干扰跟读，不宜操之过急。

在目的语跟读练习的早期，出现刚说了两句就说不下去的现象是正常的，不要灰心，可以停下来多听一遍发言，甚至先用源语跟读一遍，进一步理解语段内容并将注意力调整到最佳状态。切忌听到一个单词就翻译一个单词，使得所说的内容完全不能连贯成意义；也不要着急赶着去表述所听到的每一个内容，一个句子没说完就忙着给另一句起头了，宁愿漏掉几句，也要保证所说的每一句话都是完整的。

第三部分　术语拓展

汉译英

插画家	illustrator
产业集群创新平台	innovation launch pads for industrial clustering
盗版行为	piracy
电子数据交换	electronic data interchange
发明	invention
分散式加工活动	distributed processing activity
风险管理	risk management

工业产权	industrial property
国际产业转移	international industrial relocation
国际视角	international perspective
国家高新区	National High-tech District
基地效应	driving force of setting up bases
技术方案	technical solution
技术秘密	technical know-how
节能减排	energy conservation and emission reduction
科技工业园	high-tech industrial park
科技含量	technological benefit
科学发展观	scientific outlook of development
两高一资	high energy consumption, high pollution and resource-intensive
清洁发展机制	clean development mechanism
融汇效应	fusion effect
三来一补（来料加工、来样加工、来件装配和补偿贸易）	The "Three-plus-one" trading-mix (custom manufacturing with materials, designs or samples supplied and compensation trade)
三资企业（中外合资经营企业、中外合作经营企业、外商独资企业）	three types of foreign-invested enterprises in China, including Sino-foreign joint ventures, enterprises with Sino-foreign cooperation, and wholly foreign-owned enterprises
商务流动	business mobility
商业秘密	trade secret
实用新型	utility model
世界制造业工厂	world factory
适宜性技术	appropriate technology
体制创新	institutional innovation
外观设计	design
无形财产	intangible property
行销	marketing
循环经济	circular economy
循环效应	circular effect
要素驱动型发展	factor-driven development
知识产权	intellectual property right (IPR)

知识经济	knowledge economy
著作权	copyright
专有技术	know-how

英译汉

algae-to-energy	藻类转化能源
all-rounded service	全方位服务
authentication	身份认证
biomass/bio energy	生物质能源
biopharmaceutical industry	生物医药产业
chromosome	染色体
clone	克隆
comprehensive information service	全面的信息服务
computer integrated manufacturing system (CIMS)	计算机集成制造系统
deep water cooling system	深水冷却系统
digital access	数字准入
digital gap	数字鸿沟
digital revolution	数字革命
DNA double helix structure	DNA 双螺旋结构
DuPont Apollo	杜邦太阳能公司
DuPont China Holding Limited	杜邦中国有限公司
economy of agglomeration	经济积聚
electronics and information manufacturer	电子信息生产企业
fossil fuel	化石燃料
frontier	前沿
genetic chip/biochip	基因芯片
genetic engineering/cell engineering	基因工程 / 细胞工程
geothermal resource	地热资源
global positioning system (GPS)	全球定位系统
high-def (high definition)	高清晰度
high-performance computer	高性能计算机

human genome sequence	人类基因组序列
information and communication technology (ICT)	信息与通信技术
informatisation and digitisation	信息化，数字化
interdisciplinary	跨学科的
Internet infrastructure	网络基础设施
liquidity	流动性
market volatility	市场波动
nanotechnology	纳米科技
ocean thermal energy	海洋热能
photovoltaic	光伏电能的
renewable energy resource	可再生能源资源
seawater air conditioning	海水空调系统
self-dependent research and development	自主研发
Shenzhen-Hong Kong Innovation Circle	深圳－香港创新圈
speech-recognition	语音识别
state-of-the-art	尖端的（科技）
technology solution	技术解决方案
thin film transistor (TFT)	薄膜晶体管
the Human Genome Project	人类基因组计划
think tank	智囊团，智库
trackball	轨迹球
wave energy	风浪能
wind farm	风能发电场
wind power	风能

第四部分　同传实战

 Listen to the following four speeches and count backwards aloud at the same time. Reproduce the speeches in source language after each segment.

Text 1

　　所以，现在每个人都会问我，这些是怎么样开始的？很简单的说，就是五年前，那时候非常地年轻，而且非常地无法无天，觉得自己有创业的能力，然后有很多想法。正好又有金主，就是我妈，然后找到一些不错的酒肉朋友，这样一起做点事情，那时候就觉得信心满满，觉得应该就是马上要成功的。开始以后才发现，那才刚开始而已，都是老师没有教过的内容。开始创业以后，你发现设计其实是个服务业，就是说客户，其实，客户不是请你来做你想要做的东西，而是请你来做他们想要的东西。后来也发现就是说，你当初在设计学校的时候，老师跟你说作品很棒的时候，就 stand for itself, 他自己就帮你做行销。创业之后就发现事实上完全不是这样的，你需要很会卖你的作品。很多人进了艺术学校，也是通常把数学丢到一边去，等你可以开公司以后，你就会发现数学其实还蛮重要的，你需要懂会计，你需要算员工的薪水，你需要能够算出来你每一个小时要……要多少钱。你真正才发现管理学才是艺术，就是说你现在做的东西都是服务。所以创业就等于开始学做生意，这是很多设计师一开始的时候，应该是没有……没有想过这一点的。所以如果现在回到四年半以前的话，我可能会拿左边那个蓝色的 peer。

所以很多朋友现在都问我说，你是为什么会决定想要创业，就是说你们觉得我可以吗？很多朋友都会这样子问。创业之前有几件事情一定要先问一下你自己，就是说你创业是为了要赚钱吗？还是说你觉得设计公司都很漂亮，然后你可以穿得美美的，然后尽情地做你喜欢做的设计。然后觉得可以接触到非常有趣的人吗？那现实就是幻灭的开始，或者说你也可以转一个方法来说：幻灭是现实的开始。这个照片是我们公司的同事在加班加到第几天的时候，自己在地板上面做的动作。哈，所以我们的情况跟一般的产业其实是差不了多少的。其实你开了设计公司以后，除了本身有的能力以外，这些都是你会遇到的一些问题。我想这些应该是我们在艺术学校里面都没有被教到的一堂课。

我自己本身是一个设计师，做到后来的时候，我自己就想说，有什么你能够用设计或者用自己本身的能力来改变这样的情况。因为我们是网路设计，所以我能够想到的第一个就是做一个网路的 platform。那一边是设计师一边是市场，就是 buyer 这边是市场。很多设计师他们有 artwork，他们做很多平面设计，或者说摄影师或者说插画家。我们要怎么样帮助这些跟我们一样做设计产业的人，在不懂得这些商业化运作的情况下，给他们提供 web-platform，帮他们接触到市场端。所以我们想到做的就是一个 virtual community，就是说一个线上设计的创作社团。那当然我们就会给大家一些免费的 e-commerce 的 tools。然后上面我们会建立一个，creator 的一个 network，那它里面也会有些 market place，所以设计师和艺术家可以在里面分享他们的创作品。

我们花了一整年的时间，研发了一套网路的系统，这个是一个线上刻制的一个工具，我们自己本身这家公司，web-platform 这家公司，会帮设计师，不管他是艺术家或其他什么设计者，我们帮他把他的作品产品化。我们也会跟台湾的一些manufacturer，制造商，跟他们达成某一、某些类型的backing的一些support，将设计作品变成一个产品。

（2008年12月1日，台湾企业家Nancy Chan在"英中创意企业家网络启动"上的讲话节选，根据录音整理）

Text 2

Good morning Mr. Liu, Mr. Wang, Mr. Tseng, Distinguished Guests, Ladies and Gentlemen,

I would like to take this opportunity to thank the government of Shenzhen and of Hong Kong for their continuous support. The creation of the Shenzhen-Hong Kong Innovation Circle makes possible the ideal environment for us to launch our photovoltaic business. And so I thank the governments. I thank our partners and I thank our customers for making today possible. This is the moment when the world needs to define our energy future. The abundant natural resources that we rely on and that we've enjoyed are scarce resources. And always depending on fossil fuels is a global concern. And whether we look at this on a standpoint of energy security, or whether we look at it in terms of environment, we recognize that we need to conserve energy, and we also need to develop renewable source of energy. And it is this common concern that brings us together today.

The R&D and manufacturing expertise of DuPont Apollo is part of the solution to the problem. DuPont Apollo is unique and it represents within China the first integrated solar system provider solution. DuPont Apollo is equipped with advanced technology and the state-of-the-art manufacturing facilities that will contribute to the solar energy future. Our team is an energetic one. And they put together both the technology and the manufacturing facility that will allow us to succeed. Two decades ago, DuPont was the first company to establish within China a wholly-owned foreign enterprise. We see this in the cooperation of DuPont China Holding Limited in Shenzhen. Today's opening marks another major milestone for DuPont in China. We've combined our research capability with the state-of-the-art manufacturing facility here in Shenzhen to support our growth in photovoltaic market.

And once again I thank the government of Shenzhen and of Hong Kong for bringing us together to the Innovation Circle. The capability found in the Shenzhen-Hong Kong Innovation Circle is in reality the reason why we are all here today. With the support of the governments, and with DuPont's R&D that combines with local universities, we have the faith of the commercial development and success. We hope that more and more other enterprises can follow this example, and take the unique advantage we find here in the Pearl River Delta region in order to develop and commercialize technology. And while there are many other entrances into the photovoltaic market, DuPont with our 25 years' experience will continue to bring new products and new solution to photovoltaic to increase the efficiency and performance and lifetime of photovoltaic modules. We thank you once again for your interests in this project and we would like to thank DuPont Photovoltaic team here in DuPont Apollo. Congratulations to your success. And again my thanks to the governments, to our partners and our customers for contributing to this success. Thank you very much!

(Full text of speech by Dr. Thomas Connelly, Executive Vice President and Chief Innovation Officer of DuPont, at the Grand Opening Ceremony of DuPont Apollo Thin Film Photovoltaic Manufacturing Facility in Shenzhen on November 17, 2009)

Text 3

总结过去 30 年的发展,"创新"无疑成为广东经济发展的第一推动力,广东已经成为中国改革开放的先行者、国际化进程中的探索者,体制创新、组织创新、技术创新的实验者。广东已经成为中华民族伟大复兴的排头兵,广东模式为发展中国家和地区提供了一个可供借鉴的发展道路。广东未来的发展也必须不断创新发展模式,从而保持其在世界经济格局中、在中国现代化进程中的特殊重要地位。我们寄望,广东的创新。

首先,支撑广东开放型经济发展的体制创新取得重大突破。

改革开放 30 多年来,广东以创新精神推动着改革开放的伟大实践,率先创办经济特区,率先发展"三来一补",率先引进海外的先进技术设备和管理经验及创办"三资"企业,率先进行外贸体制改革、投资促进体制改革,率先进行价格改革,率先进行金融体制改革,率先实行土地有偿转让,率先实行产权制度改革等等,在建立和完善社会主义市场经济体制方面走在全国前列,实现了从计划经济体制向社会主义市场经济体制的历史性转变,初步建立了有利于开放型经济发展的体制和制度环境。

其次,经济发展模式创新,开放型经济成为广东经济发展的重要推动力量。

"中国模式"已经成为世界经济发展史上的奇迹,而广东过去 30 年的经济发展成为"中国模式"的典范,即以出口和外资为经济发展的主要推动力。通过开放型经济发展,广东积累了资本,要素的配置效率与技术效率取得了长足的进展,国际竞争力显著增强,通过经济发展模式的创新,开放型经济已经成为广东经济增长的重要推动力量,解决了广东和国内其余部分省份的大量剩余劳动力,显著带动了内源经济发展,初步奠定了"世界制造业工厂"的地位。

第三,基于"干中学"的技术创新能力不断提升。

广东开放型经济发展过程中的技术进步是一种基于"干中学"的赶超型技术进步,其主要特征是随着自身技术存量的不断积累,获得外部技术转移的能力越来越强,并通过技术改造成为"适宜性技术"。过去30多年,通过完善技术创新的体制机制和政策环境,初步构建了开放型区域创新体系,技术进步已经成为支撑广东经济发展的重要力量,这为未来广东开放型经济向更高水平发展、向全球价值链高端攀升奠定了良好的基础。

第四,创新要素利用机制,要素集聚能力和要素培育能力显著增强。

国际分工与合作的实质是不同国家和地区间生产要素的分工与合作。过去30多年广东利用难得的发展创新要素利用机制,不断集聚和培育与开放型经济发展相适应的生产要素。一方面,集聚了低成本且具有一定技能的劳动力、中高层管理者、技术人员、境外资本和国内资本;另一方面,通过逐步完善投资环境,建设了较为完善的基础设施,从多方面为集聚与培育中高级生产要素奠定了良好的基础。

第五,积极推进产业组织创新,产业国际化程度逐年加深。

改革开放30多年来,广东省通过积极推进产业组织创新,加速与国际产业分工体系的融合,有效地吸收了国际产业转移,承接国际市场知识密集型的高附加值服务外包和转包正逐年增加,与港澳台的经济一体化程度正逐年加深,正逐步融入亚太经济圈,产品的国际市场占有率大幅度提高,初步形成了若干具有国际竞争力的产业集群和一批大型企业和企业集团。同时产业结构调整取得重大进展,产业高级化和适度重型化趋势明显,服务业吸收外资的比例正逐步提高,九大产业的主导作用显著增强,产业布局和结构日趋合理,为构建现代产业体系奠定了坚实的基础。

(2009年11月13日,广东外语外贸大学校长隋广军在"广东开放论坛暨广东国际战略研究院揭牌仪式"上的讲话节选)

Text 4

But before we get to that, I want to go back to 1991, when Apple announced and shipped its first PowerBooks. This was the first modern laptop computer. Apple actually invented the modern laptop computer with its PowerBooks. It was the first laptop that has the TFT screen—the first modern LCD screens. It was the first laptop that push the keyboard up creating palm rests, and had intergraded pointing devices—in this case, the trackball. Well, of course almost 20 years later, we've got incredible laptops now. Just a few years ago in 2007, Apple reinvented the phone with the iPhone. And a few years later, we got the great iPhone 3GS, the best phone in the world. And so all of us use laptops and smartphones now. Everybody uses a laptop and a smartphone. And the question is, in recent, lately, is there room for a third category of device in the middle—something that's between the laptop and the smartphone? And of course, we pondered this question for years as well. The bar is pretty high in order to really create a new category of devices. Those devices are gonna have to be far better at doing some key tasks. They have to be far better at doing some really important things—better than a laptop, better than a smartphone. What kind of tasks? Well, things like browsing the web. That's pretty tough work. Something is better at browsing the web than a laptop? OK, doing email. Enjoying and sharing photographs. Video, watching videos. Enjoying your music collection. Playing games. Reading eBooks. If there is gonna be a third category of device, they have to be better at this kind of tasks than laptops or smartphones, otherwise, it has no reason for being.

Now, some people have thought that's a netbook. The problem is netbooks aren't better at anything. They are slow, they have low quality displays and they run clunky old PC software. So they are not better than a laptop at anything, they are just cheaper. They are just cheap laptops. And we don't think they are the third category device. But we think we got something that is. And we'd like to show it to you today for the first time. And we call it the iPad. So, let me show it to you now. This is what it looks like. I happen to have one. Right here. That's what it looks like, very thin. So, to give you an overview. It's very thin. And you can change the background screen, the home screen to personalize it anyway you want. People put on their own photos on it, I'm sure, but we ship a few. We can make it anything you want. And what this device does is extraordinary. You can browse the web with it. It is the best browsing experience you've ever had. It's phenomenal to see a whole webpage right in front of you. And you can manipulate with your fingers. It's unbelievably great, way better than a laptop and way better than a smartphone. And you can turn iPad anyway you want, up-down and sideways. It, automatically, just however you want to use it. And again to see the whole webpage is phenomenal like they're holding the Internet in your hands. It's an incredible experience. Phenomenal for mail, when focusing on a message, you can do that. See your inbox. Again, just turn iPad sideways, you can have a different view on your mail. Push the compose window, a keyboard pops up. It's almost life-size. It's a dream to type on. For photos. Your albums are showing stamps of photos. Your album are events, you can unfold them, look at all your photos. Flip through them, got some great slideshows build-in. It's a wonderful way to share your photos with friends and family. Building a calendar, to see your month's activities or your day's activities and everything in between. Building a great address book for your contacts. Have a great map application which works with Google's backing. Show you maps, satellite views, zooming on things. iPad is an awesome way to enjoy your music collection. And of course, we have the iTunes store, built right into the iPad. You can discover music, you can purchase it. Movies, TV shows, podcasts, iTunes university, everything built right into the iPad. YouTube, you can watch YouTube on it. Including YouTube Hign Def now, they've got high-def video. And of course it is awesome to watch TV shows and movies on it.

(Excerpted text of speech by Steve Jobs, CEO of Apple, on the live demonstration of the iPad tablet computer, January 27, 2010)

第 4 单元　同声传译设备
Simultaneous Interpreting Equipment

> **单元学习目标**
> 1. 了解同声传译设备的类型及使用方式。
> 2. 熟悉会展这一口译主题的常用汉英术语和表达方式。
> 3. 独立操作同传设备。

第一部分　知识背景

1. 同声传译会议设备

　　交替传译和同声传译最直观的区别可能是交传译员不需要什么特殊设备，只要一支笔、一个笔记本就可以开始工作了，而同传译员必须要把自己关进特制的"小木箱"里，戴上耳机对着话筒才能进行口译。的确，同声传译是在合适的设备出现以后才真正发展起来的，而这几十年的发展历程也离不开设备的更新换代。口译质量的好坏，译员的水平是关键，但同传设备和工作条件也会成为影响质量的重要因素。

　　国际会议译员协会（AIIC）曾对同声传译员的工作条件作出过详细的规定，如同传厢及设备的标准、会场的大小和位置、同传厢的摆放位置、玻璃窗户的大小和能见度、隔音通风的效果、厢内工作空间及照明等，在有效保障译员的权益、健康的同时也尽可能保证了同传的质量。AIIC 的标准无疑是我国同传行业奋斗的目标，但在目前发展阶段，要求完全达到是不现实的。国内大部分使用同传的会议无法按 AIIC 的标准给译员提供条件，但一般都能按照以下的原则为译员提供合理的工作条件：

　　1) 有独立的同传室/厢，能将译员与会场分隔开来，具有较好的隔音效果。译员进入厢子后，明显感觉会场噪音大大减小，甚至听不到。同时，译员在厢内用正常音量口译时，声音基本传不到厢外。

　　2) 同传室/厢应安置在会场内能直接看到发言人和听众的地方，无障碍物阻挡译员的视线。有些会议室在建造时就设计了同传室，一般位于会场的一边或楼上一层，正面是玻璃墙，译员能清楚地看到会场；而同传室之间也用玻璃隔断，为的是在进行多语种同传接力时，不同组的译员能看到彼此，相互配合。而大多数会议使用的都是可拆卸、方便移动的木制同传厢：正面有宽大的玻璃窗，放在会场的后方或一角。值得一提的是，现在有很多超大规模的会议，几百名听众。由于会场宽大，无论同传厢放置在哪个位置，译员都无法同时看到讲台和听众。不过，这样的会场往往会安装投影仪或大屏幕，同步播放发言人的影像。听众或译员通过大屏幕，反而能更清楚地观察到发言人的表情、手势等。

3）同传室/厢中有合理的工作空间和工作条件。同传室/厢的空间能容纳至少两名译员，译员能自由出入，不会影响同伴。厢中配备有舒适的椅子，译员坐下工作时，空间充足，不会感到局促不适。厢中还应配备宽度适宜的工作台，能摆放同传设备和译员自备的材料、稿纸、笔记本电脑等物品。厢内照明充足或配有台灯，方便译员翻阅讲稿、查看资料。同传室/厢通风良好、温度适宜或配有空调。

4）有专业的同传收发装置。同传室/厢的工作台上放有译员工作系统，配有耳机和话筒。译员通过操作按钮，可选择声音输出和输入频道，自由调节耳机音量，控制麦克风开关等。同传室/厢外，观众通过专用的红外接收装置和耳机选择自己能听懂的语言频道，收听口译内容。同传装置必须保证能稳定地工作，声音的传输必须同步、清晰、无杂音和噪音。同时，会场必须保持至少一个技术人员全程监控设备，以防故障或意外事件。

有经验的译员一般都会提前半小时至一小时到达会场，与技术人员沟通同传室/厢的放置位置，熟悉设备的使用，调试收发装置等。

2. 同声传译教学设备

同传教学应当在专门的模拟国际会议室中进行，特别是经过听辨、跟读训练后，即将进入真正的同传训练，普通的语音室不再适合。进行同传教学的模拟会议室应有几间真正的同传室/厢，足够这个班级一半的学生使用。还应有大的会议桌，可以让学生围坐，聆听指导或点评。最好配备有电脑、投影仪等设备，方便练习时使用。

同传室/厢中需要配备同传译员台，可以是单人台（如图A）或双人台（如图B）。这两种译员台的工作原理和使用方法基本一样。译员台上的按钮一般有：

（图A）

（图B）

1）现场声与译员声通道切换键（Floor 或 Original）

按下声道切换键（Floor 或 Original）可听到现场发言原声，按下接力键（Relay）则切换到其他厢中的译员的输出语言，可进行多语言接力同传。

2）接力语言频道选择键（Relay）

当进行多语言接力同传（Relay）时，可通过拨动按钮或按下按钮1、2、3、4……或者 A、B、C、D……等选择输入语言。

3）输出语言频道选择键

通常有 A、B 或者 1、2 两个频道供译员转换译入语语言。比如：译员在进行中英双向同传，技术人员事先已将 A 频道设为输出中文，B 频道为英文。当译员听英文发言译成中文时，则须选择 A 频道反之则选择 B 频道；否则译文无法正确地传输到听众的接收器中。在实际操作中，工作的译员有可能因为紧张或疏忽而选错了输出频道，在一旁休息的译员则应该帮忙监督，避免出错。

4）暂停静音键（Cough 或 Mute）

在口译过程中，译员可能会觉得嗓子突然很紧，或是想咳嗽一下，清清嗓子；有时会遇到一些问题或特殊情况，需要和同伴短暂交流。按下此按钮后，麦克风暂时关闭，同传厢里的声音传不出去；松开按钮后，麦克风恢复工作。

5）麦克风开关

译员开始工作时要将麦克风打开，休息时要记得关闭，以免影响同伴的工作。现在有一些译员台会自动地控制两位译员各自的麦克风：一个麦克风开启时，另一个自动关闭。

6）收听音量控制键

可让每位译员自由地调节耳机的音量。每个单人台上都设有一个音量按钮，双人台上一般是左右两边各有一个按钮分别调节两个耳机的音量。

在同传厢外，作为听众的老师和同学应每人配备一个同传接收器，以便收听厢内"译员"的翻译。目前，比较通用的接收设备大小如一个眼镜盒，无线，能方便地拿在手中在会场（教室）内自由走动。接收器上连带耳机，打开电源，调至相应的频道，戴上耳机即可收听到相应语言的翻译。

第二部分　操作提示

对于有经验的译员来说，同传设备上的各种功能是他们工作中的好帮手，令他们应对自如。而对于初学者来说，要完成"传译"这件事本身已经很复杂，再配合操作各种仪器和按钮，难免手忙脚乱，常常出错。这时特别需要与同伴密切合作，轮换休息的同学应帮助检查译员台上各个按钮是否都已正确打开或关闭。初学者常会忘了在翻译前打开麦克风，或选错了语言输出频道，这些都需要同伴帮忙及时纠正。在接力同传中，特别是多频道（3个以上）接力时，当值的译员一时会弄不清接力频道，也需要同伴及时的帮忙。两个人在厢子里私下交流或发出噪音时，也要相互提醒按下静音键。总之，与同伴间的协作配合是养成良好的"厢内习惯（booth manner）"的重要因素。

另外，工作译员在厢中翻译的音量也要控制在自然、正常的范围内，长时间的高声喊叫会让自己声嘶力竭，而听众也听得不舒服。一个有效控制自己音量的办法是，不要把耳机收听的音量调得太大，耳机不要带得太紧，在任意一边露出半个耳朵来，监听自己的音量和翻译。同时，还要尽量保持坐姿端正，避免不断地变换姿势而使得声音离麦克风忽近忽远，影响声音输出效果。

第三部分　术语拓展

汉译英

城市，让生活更美好	Better City, Better Life
2007广州（海珠·琶洲）会展经济论坛	Guangzhou (Pazhou of Haizhu District) Exhibition and Convention Forum 2007
颁奖仪式	awarding ceremony
闭幕式	closing ceremony
茶歇	tea break
吹风会	briefing
东方之冠（世博中国馆建筑）	Crown of the East
独立展馆	stand-alone pavillion
高交会（中国国际高新技术成果交易会）	China High-tech Fair
广州国际会展中心	Guangzhou International Conference and Exhibition Center
吉祥物	mascot
剪彩仪式	ribbon-cutting ceremony
礼仪小姐	miss etiquette
联合展馆	joint pavillion
贸促会（中国国际贸易促进委员会）	CCPIT (China Council for the Promotion of International Trade)
特许商品	franchised / licensed product

外国馆	foreign national pavillion
外经贸局	Bureau of Foreign Trade and Economic Cooperation
中博会（中国国际中小企业博览会）	China Exposition for Small-and-Medium-sized Enterprises
中国出口商品交易会	China Export Commodity Fair
中国馆	China Pavillion
《中国会展》杂志	China Conference and Exhibition
主题馆	theme pavillion
总部经济	headquarters economy

英译汉

air freight	空运
amenity	便利设施
badge	证件卡，代表证
Closer Economic Partnership Arrangement (CEPA)	（内地与香港、澳门）关于建立更紧密经贸关系的安排
consignee	收货方 / 代销方
co-organizer	协办方
dismantling the stand	撤展
dress code	着装规则
Economic Cooperation Framework Agreement (ECFA)	海峡两岸经济合作框架协议
epicenter	中心，震中
first-aid centre	急救中心
fizz	泡沫
floor plan	场馆地图，展位图
foyer	门厅
freight forwarder	货代
gala dinner	（有正式发言或表演的）答谢晚宴，欢迎晚宴
Guangdong Beauty & Cosmetic Association	广东省美容美发化妆品行业协会

Guangzhou International Beauty & Cosmetic Import-Export Expo	广州国际美容美发化妆用品进出口博览会
Hong Kong Wine and Dine Festival	香港美酒佳肴巡礼
load-bearing capacity	承重能力
loading dock	装卸区
logistics	物流，后勤
London Stock Exchange	伦敦股票交易市场
mobile toilet	移动厕所
memorandum of understanding (MOU)	谅解备忘录
parking lot	停车场
product catalogue	产品目录
recession	（经济）萧条
setting up the stand	布展
shuttle bus	专线车
stand/booth	展位
supply and purchase system	供采机制
United Business Media Asia (UBM Asia)	亚洲博闻公司
venue	场馆，（会议的）地点
wine auction centre	葡萄酒拍卖中心

第四部分　同传实战

 Listen to the following four speeches and start shadowing. Keep a lag of about a half to one sentence.

Text 1

　　中国 2010 年上海世博会，是中华民族的百年之梦，是我国继奥运会之后举办的又一次国际盛会。在世博兴办以来的 150 多年的历史沧桑中，中华民族不屈不挠，发愤图强，逐步从积贫积弱走向伟大的复兴。以执着的追求和巨大的进步，赢得了国际社会的广泛尊重。如今，曾经是 100 年前文人笔下的世博梦幻，即将在我们手中变成现实。我们深感责任重大，使命光荣。

　　2002 年世博成功申办以来，在党中央国务院的坚强领导下，在中央各部委、各省区市和全国人民的大力支持下，在国际展览局和国际社会的积极参与下，在全体上海市民的共同努力下，各项筹备工作进展顺利，取得了重大的阶段性成果。240 多个国家和国际组织已确认参展，园区场馆及有关基础设施建设顺利推进，各种论坛庆典等重大活动正在精心准备，交通、安保、志愿者服务等运营准备有序推进，宣传推介活动广泛开展。上海世博会的国际知晓率、影响率和吸引力不断提高。广大市民参与世博、服务世博、奉献世博的热情日益高涨。再过100天，举国关注、举世瞩目的中国2010年上海世博会将隆重开幕。世界的目光将聚焦中国、聚焦上海。向世界人民呈现异彩纷呈的世博盛会，兑现向国际社会的庄严承诺，是党中央国务院交给我们的历史重任，是13亿中国人民的热切期盼，是我们的神圣使命和光荣的责任。

最近，胡锦涛总书记在视察上海时，就办好世博提出了"六个确保"的要求。这是全面做好世博筹办工作的总动员令，为我们做好下一步的工作指明了方向。今天，贾主席、岐山副总理等领导同志亲临上海，做临战动员，必将进一步激发我们为国争光的信心和斗志。以志在必得的决心、无坚不摧的豪情、科学严谨的态度、精益求精的作风，再战100天，全面完成各项准备工作，铺就通向世博的成功之路，开启精彩世博的好客之门。我们要用只争朝夕的奋斗精神，铸就办好世博的坚强保障。在最后100天的冲刺阶段，要把世博筹办作为各项工作的重中之重，抓紧完成各项建设工程的收尾工作，抓紧开展试运营的各项准备，特别要把安保工作放在首位。进一步细化实化各项安保工作方案，抓好安保力量的组织培训和落实，及时开展针对性的演练，确保实战期间，指挥高效、运转顺畅和安保万无一失。我们要用科学严谨的工作态度，做好办好世博的运营准备。要进一步细化工作标准、工作流程，确保每一个岗位、每一个细节都落实到位。要深入开展试运营的演练，进一步完善指挥体制，磨合运行机制。要组织力量，设想困难、查找问题，通过逐一解决，问题归零，使可能发生的问题减少到最低限度。要牢固树立为参展者服务，为参观者服务，为市民服务的思想，周到细致、快捷便利地做好各项工作。

我们要用礼仪之邦的当代风采，打造办好世博的良好氛围。深入开展"迎世博、讲文明、树新风"的活动，狠抓礼仪文明、秩序文明、服务文明、环境文明建设。不断提高全社会的文明程度和人民群众的文明素质，大力弘扬志愿服务精神。做好园区和城市志愿者培训和组织工作，使志愿者的微笑成为上海世博会一道靓丽的风景。大力宣传"城市，让生活更美好"的主题，动员社会各界参与世博、服务世博、奉献世博。

（2009年4月29日，上海市市委书记俞正声在"中国2010上海世博会倒计时100天誓师动员大会"上的发言节选，根据录音材料整理）

Text 2

Distinguished Guests, Fellow Investors and Potential Investors in Guangzhou,

I thank the Organizing Committee of this Forum and Conference for inviting me here today to address you. It's always a great pleasure to visit this very important city which is opening up so much of an exciting new era for all our businesses. The infrastructure and people one meets and sees here are very much an indication of the excellent planning and drive that has taken place.

The Economist magazine said in one of its articles last month "It never pays to underestimate the bounciness of Asia's emerging economies." After the region's financial crisis of 1997-98 and again after the dot.com bust in 2001, people considered that the economies would spend a long time not growing. With the recession in most countries during this year it was also said that such export economies would not revive until the European and American economies began to grow. Yet China is still showing good growth rates. The economies of China, Indonesia, South Korea and Singapore grew in the second quarter of 2009 by an average annualized rate of more than 10%.

In China, industrial production rose by 11% in the year (2009) to July. Electricity output which fell sharply last year is growing again and car sales are 70% higher than a year ago! All good news for the exhibition industry as the Chinese government stimulates the economy to ensure it will continue to prosper.

My company, UBM Asia, is one of the pioneer companies in Asia in this B2B business in China. We are today the leading organizer of exhibitions in Asia, and the biggest commercial exhibition organizer in the two fastest growing markets in Asia: China and India, with associated print and online media. Owned by United Business Media Limited which is listed on the London Stock Exchange, we organize over 110 trade shows and publish some 22 publications, of which 32 trade shows are held in major cities in China including Guangzhou, Shanghai, Chengdu, Shenzhen and Beijing.

We have been operating in China for over 15 years now and have experienced the tremendous energy and growth in Guangdong and South China. Our business of "Business to Business Access Provision" through exhibitions, we believe, is the best suited route to enhancing business relationships and encouraging harmonious relations between peoples of different nationalities and industries.

Currently we operate three offices in Guangzhou. The old exhibition grounds served a good basis for industry and gave the introduction to the excellent expansion of these new fairgrounds in Pazhou. The vision needed by those who made this possible have to be truly congratulated. And, of course, it is not yet finished! There are more halls still to be built, more hotels to be finished and offices and retail space to be opened. The access to the exhibition fairgrounds by the metro is a vital part of this development.

As a company, we have achieved many objectives in opening up our exhibitions to South China and Guangdong market through the Pazhou venue. The Haizhu District has made it very easy to have access to the services and foreign investment advice provided by the Guangzhou City government and the Haizhu District government.

South China with Guangzhou as the epicenter of this area and the Pearl River Delta has developed so fast into an international shipping, logistics, trading, exhibition and innovation centre. So through the Exhibition Centres in Pazhou the focus is well made. International standard hotels are now throughout the city, the airport has global links and a good workforce, many with English proficiency.

I have no doubt that by investing in this area that the investment will be strong, and that over time the region will continue to prosper as the GDP increases and the income spend of the inhabitants of this region continues to grow.

I urge you all to come to our next exhibition in Pazhou, the Guangzhou International Beauty & Cosmetic Import–Export Expo (Autumn Show) on September 24-26, which is organized jointly with the Guangdong Beauty & Cosmetic Association, run by our friend, the very well-known Madam Ma Ya.

Thank you again to the Organizing Committee of this Forum and the Conference.

I wish you all good business.

Xie Xie!

(Full text of speech by Michael Duck, Senior Vice President of United Business Media Asia Ltd. at 2009 Forum on Guangzhou Convention and Exhibition Economy <Pazhou & Haizhu> & Investment Promotion Conference on Modern Service Industry, September 11, 2009)

Text 3

各位领导、各位嘉宾、女士们、先生们：

上午好！首先，请允许我代表广州市人民政府对出席"2007广州（海珠·琶洲）会展经济论坛"的各位领导、各位嘉宾、各位朋友表示热烈的欢迎和衷心的感谢！对本次论坛的成功举办表示热烈的祝贺！这次广州市外经贸局、海珠区人民政府、中国会展杂志社联合主办会展经济论坛活动，很有意义也非常及时，这是一个让世界了解广州、了解广州会展业的大好机会，也是广州走出中国、走向世界，实现建成国际会展中心城市目标的良好契机。

广州是一个拥有2000多年历史的城市，是华南地区传统的政治、经济、文化中心。近年来，我市国民经济又好又快发展。2006年地区生产总值达

6068.41亿元，同比增长14.7%；第三产业对经济增长的贡献正不断加大，会展、商贸、物流、金融、旅游等现代服务业蓬勃发展。

中国会展业的历史是从广州1957年举办"第一届中国出口商品交易会"（广交会）开始的，这个"中国第一展"、世界第三大展览已经举办了101届，会展业成为广州外经贸的窗口和引擎。广州是国内仅次于北京、上海的第三大会展城市，会展业硬件设施在国内处于领先水平，现有专业场馆11个，展览面积49万平方米。其中，广州国际会展中心是目前亚洲最大的会展中心。据不完全统计，近年来广州地区举办大型的展览会350多个，各种展示展销会每年1100多场。广州会展业每年直接收入达13亿元，约占广东全省的41%。

会展业的发展将进一步优化广州的投资环境，并有力带动金融、咨询、酒店、旅游等关联产业发展，带来更多的投资机会。广州市紧紧抓住这一发展机遇，首次将会展业发展规划列入广州市服务业发展"十一五"规划，加快发展以会展经济为龙头的现代商贸服务业，提升广州国际会展中心城市地位，并力求通过会展经济活动、会展论坛这些平台加强招商引资，积极发展总部经济，大力吸引和支持跨国公司、国内著名企业和本地企业建立以广州为总部的跨区域经营体系。

今天的会展经济论坛云集了国内外政界、商界、学术界，特别是会展方面的精英人士和权威专家，大家共同就会展经济的发展分享各自的真知灼见和宝贵经验。相信当论坛结束时，每位参加者都会获益良多，对"琶洲"这个名字有更深刻的认识。

我衷心希望今天出席论坛的各位领导、各位企业家、各位嘉宾在论坛上能畅所欲言，为广州会展业的发展多提宝贵意见和建议，继续支持和推进广州的会展经济向更市场化、更国际化、更现代化的方向发展。

最后，预祝论坛圆满成功！

（2007年7月27日，广州市副市长陈明德在"2007广州＜海珠·琶洲＞会展经济论坛"上的发言全文）

Text 4

Jimmy, Mr Lacoste, Your Excellencies, Distinguished Guests, Ladies and Gentlemen,

Good evening. How are we all doing tonight.

It is indeed my great pleasure to join you all here tonight to inaugurate the first Wine and Dine Festival in Hong Kong. This is, indeed, a celebration of the two of our favourite pastimes of any civilisation —wining and dining. We have also, by chance I guess, as a backdrop one of the world's most spectacular cityscapes—all of the ingredients make for a memorable festival.

First and foremost, a warm welcome to you all, and particularly to our special guests from the legendary wine region of Bordeaux. We are delighted that Mr Lacoste, Vice-president of the Bordeaux Chamber of Commerce and Industry, and Deputy City Mayor, Mr Delaux are here this evening. We are grateful to you and your delegation for flying all the way from France to share this unique occasion with us.

Your presence is important to us because this event marks a milestone in our co-operation with Bordeaux under the Memorandum of Understanding on Wine that we signed last year. International co-operation with wine-producing regions is crucial to achieving our goal of becoming a wine trading and distribution hub in Asia. I see that a number of wine-producing nations are represented here this evening as well. Thank you all for your support of our initiatives in developing the wine industry in Hong Kong.

Since eliminating duties on wine in my budget last year, our wine trade has provided some welcome economic fizz during the global financial crisis. The value of wine imports increased by 80% year-on-year in 2008. It further increased by another 42% in the first eight months of 2009, amounting to $2.3 billion.

A number of wine-related businesses have expanded their operations or launched new enterprises here. And they include retail outlets, storage facilities, trading companies and more. We even have a winery now in Hong Kong, which is quite special considering that we don't even produce any grapes.

The industry forecasts that Hong Kong is overtaking London by the year 2009 to become the world's second largest wine auction centre, just behind New York. So far this year, 10 wine auctions have fetched a total of more than $365 million.

Wine and dine activities have also given a boost to our tourism industry during the economic downturn. Indeed, this festival is the main event of our Tourism Board's "Hong Kong Food and Wine Year". Developing Hong Kong as a wine trading and distribution hub in the region has provided an opportunity for us to showcase our city as a premier destination for gourmets and food connoisseurs.

Ladies and gentlemen, thank you for your support of this event, and congratulations to the festival organizers on providing such an inspiring setting to wine and dine good friends.

I wish the festival every success, and I hope you all have a great evening. Thank you very much and, cheers to you all!

(Full text of speech by the Financial Secretary, Mr John Tsang, at the Opening Ceremony of Hong Kong Wine and Dine Festival 2009, on October 30, 2009)

第 5 单元　同声传译基本原则
Principles of Simultaneous Interpreting

> **单元学习目标**
> 1. 掌握同声传译的五大基本工作原则及适用范围。
> 2. 熟悉教育这一口译主题的常用汉英术语和表达方式。
> 3. 能够完成基本的同步听说练习。

第一部分　同传技能

不了解同声传译工作的人往往会对同传持一些偏颇或错误的看法，比如"同传就是把时间占满、不留空隙，只要滔滔不绝讲话就可以了，不用理会意思对不对"。"同传坐在箱子里，只管自己说自己的，根本不关心会场发生的情况"。"同传还需要思考吗？不需要，讲话的人说什么翻译就跟着说什么，字到字的翻译其实简单得很"。那么，实际情况真是这样吗？

同传是一项高强度、高技术性的工作，在听说同步的表象之下，起支撑作用的是译员深厚的双语功底、超强的多任务处理能力、扎实的同传技能、灵活的协调性能以及丰富的知识储备。但仅有这些充分条件还不足以造就好的同传译员，译员还必须深刻理解并切身践行同传工作的基本原则。这些基本原则，有的是译员在具体工作以前就必须把握并能立刻加以践行的，有的需要靠工作中的不断打磨来增进理解、加深领悟。下面对同传工作的基本原则一一简要介绍。

1. 忠实原则

所谓忠实原则，是指译员必须以译入语忠实地传达所听到的源语信息。忠实于源语信息不仅是同声传译工作的基本原则，而且也是评价同声传译质量的基本标准。具体而言，忠实是指译员对信息准确、完整的传译。西方学者通过实证研究指出口译用户对信息准确性、完整性极为重视，在评价口译质量的指标体系中，忠实度也是重要指标之一（蔡小红，2004）。具体到同传的工作过程，要做到忠实于源语信息，要求译员必须在听说同步的工作状态之下对自己的译语产出进行实时自我监测，在信息输入阶段做到完整、正确地听取信息，减少错听、漏听，在信息理解阶段要做到充分理解，不能断章取义、不求甚解，在译语产出阶段要做到表达充分、到位，不能想当然地以自己的想法或理解来置换源语意思，更不能顾前不顾后抓了上句漏下句，尽可能地减少错译、漏译，实现最大限度的准确与完整。

2. 协调原则

所谓协调原则是从同声传译的功能出发而言的。同声传译不是单纯对于语言的翻译，同传译员也不是机械的翻译机器，只负责对语言进行处理。同声传译是非常依赖工作场合的工作，不论是译员还是译员口中传出来的译入语，都要服务于特定的交际场合。有时候同样一句话由于场合的变化可能会呈现出不同的含义，这种情况就需要译员对发言人语调、语气、肢体语言等反映其观点、态度的言外因素进行准确的判断和迅速的把握，并将这些细微之处的变化通过自己的口译来传达给听众，使译语听众有和源语听众相同的机会对发言人及整个口译交际场合有更加全面的把握。同传译员并不像大家所想的只扮演传声筒的角色，在同传过程中，译员为使双方达到充分沟通的效果必须在语言、信息等层面起到一定的协调作用。

3. 释意原则

释意原则，其实也是反映口译区别于笔译的一个重要特点：口译之所以被称为 interpretation 而不是沿用 translation 一词，就是因为口译"在不少情况下，特别是概念不对应、表达形式欠缺的情况下，需要对原文进行解释性翻译"（张维为，1999：40）。塞莱斯科维奇和勒代雷也指出，翻译不是从语言到语言，译员也不是鹦鹉学舌；翻译的过程实际上是对意思的意识过程，"在口语连续的语流中，每7到8秒钟，我们便会忘记语言的形式，产生对意义的'意识'——从这种意识状态出发，译员可以完全脱离源语的语言形式，自发地表达自己的理解"（塞莱斯科维奇、勒代雷著，闫素伟、邵炜译，2007：42）。译员处理的是发言人表达的意思，而不是具体的字、词。对于汉语和英语这一相差较远的语言组合来讲，如果译员不去理解发言人的意思而只是从语言到语言进行直译，或者说意思没有理解透彻就硬译，可能会造成意思的扭曲，最终将会影响交流的效果。

4. 顺译原则

顺译原则，或称顺句驱动，是在承认汉语和英语存在较大差异的前提下，实现双语同传所必须遵循的工作原则。同传的工作模式使得同传译员无法像交传译员或笔译工作者那样听（读）完一段话以后再开始工作；汉语和英语在语序、词序等方面的巨大差异，使同传译员要实现听说同步就必须"按照自己听到原文的顺序，不停地把句子切成个别的意群或概念单位，再把这些单位比较自然地连接起来，翻译出整体的原意"（张维为，1999：41）。遵循顺译原则，可节省译员的等待时间，帮助译员缩小听说时间差，减轻译员的信息处理压力，保障同传工作的顺畅进行及信息产出的最大化。

5. 简约原则

简约原则是同传译员将加工后的源语信息用译语进行表述时所必须遵循的原则。该原则要求译员在不影响源语信息传达的前提下，适当采用简化、归纳、概括、解释等方式来酌情调整无法直接用译语处理的材料或源语中技术性较强的内容（仲伟合，2001）。在同传工作中采取这一原则，原因如下：一是译员必须考虑听众的接受程度；二是同传译员处理的是单位数量大、速度快的信息，高强度的处理任务往往会使译员在个别地方无法迅速反应出译语的最佳表达，与其耗费脑力搜寻完美的表达方式，不如采用简约的表述来舒缓工作压力，避免卡壳。

第二部分　案例讲解

The following passages are from the practice materials for this unit. Sight interpret them into the target language.

Passage 1

的确，我从小学到中学、大学都是念的外国人办的学校，但是它对我来说恰恰是起了个反面教育（1）的作用，因为从西方的先进而看到我们自己国家的落后。(2)

▼ 技能提示

（1）此处不可直译，需灵活处理。"反面教育"的字面意思为"利用反面素材进行的教育"，在汉语中带有负面、否定的意味，有需要引以为戒的意思。译员稍不注意就可能将此处按字面直接处理为 negative teaching materials。但是，这样的直译却与后文的"西方的先进"形成了矛盾：既然外国人创办的学校是 negative 的、不应该学习的，那为什么又说西方是先进的呢？这样的直译从逻辑上解释不通，不仅容易造成误解，而且有违发言人的原意。这里的"反面教育"是指与国内学校相对的、形成对照的一种教育。

（2）此段前半句中英文结构差异不大，可采用顺译原则；后半句需酌情调整，将两句合并为一句，"反面教育"可灵活处理到句末充当状语。

▼ 参考译文

Indeed, the primary school, secondary school and university I attended were all run by foreigners. But this experience enabled me to compare the advancement of Western countries and the backwardness of my own country from the opposite.

Passage 2

So the government, the central government of any country can focus on education, research and development in creating an environment to allow people to be successful and an environment that allows entrepreneurs to succeed. And increasingly we see this sort of entrepreneurial spirit here in China. My company (1) happens to be (2) the largest high-tech venture capital investor (3) in the world. And increasingly we see more and more high tech venture capital investments made here in China. (4)

▼ 技能提示

（1）此处固然可直译为"我公司"、"我所在的公司"，但是译员必须时刻考虑到发言人的身份和背景，并按照译语习惯对部分表述进行调整。此处汉语一般是直说发言人所在公司/机构名称。

（2）happen to be 有碰巧的意味，但考虑到下文的内容不适合直译。

（3）investor 是投资者、投资人的意思，但此处需考虑主语：主语既然为公司，那么译文也应该与之对应，这样更加符合语言习惯。

（4）此段基本可用顺译原则，只是需调整英语中地点状语 in China 在汉语中的位置，并将部分定语从句转化为汉语中的补语成分。

▼ 参考译文

各国政府都可以着眼于教育和研发，以创造良好环境促进成功、培育成长。在中国这种创业精神也越来越多见。英特尔是世界上最大的高科技风险投资公司，我们也看到越来越多的风险投资选择了中国。

Passage 3

我参加共产党，为什么要参加共产党？那个时候参加共产党没有什么名也没有什么利好讲，(1) 谁也不知道中国会这么快地解放。那个时候还是抗日战争的时候，当时我就、我们就看到国民党政府的腐败，(2) 国民党的消极抗日、积极内战。所以当时呢，中国共产党成了我们唯一的希望，所以就凭着这个理想，我参加了革命 (3)。(4)

▼ 技能提示

（1）此处为典型的汉语口头语言，应明确其含义并加以解释。此句可理解为"那时候参加共产党不为名利"。

(2) 发言人自我修正，译员应准确把握主语，避免对已译出的内容进行修正。

(3) 此处译员固然可以直译为 take part in revolution，但稍显直白，欠缺情感；如考虑到发言人的情感和态度，亦可灵活处理为 throw myself into revolution。

(4) 此段为典型的漫谈式中文发言，形式、结构松散，以口语化表述居多，连贯性不强。口译时除需酌情调整顺序以外，还需适当采用衔接手段以避免英语句子过于零散。

▼ 参考译文

Why did I join the Communist Party of China? Being a communist party member at that time could bring you no fame or fortune. No one had expected that China could be liberated so soon. During the Anti-Japanese War, we witnessed the corruption of the KMT Party, who was reluctant in fighting against the Japanese but active in waging a civil war. So the Communist Party became the only hope for us. With such a hope, I threw myself into the revolution.

Passage 4

Finally, I commend Guangwai (1) for its leadership in expanding access to higher education, and I applaud the province of Guangdong and city of Guangzhou for creating the Da Xue Cheng campus in Panyu, which we will go to tomorrow (2). The University City creates a great challenge for us all as educators (3): to learn how to manage not only multi-campus universities, but also multi-university campuses (4).

▼ 技能提示

(1) 此处可适当等待并酌情调整语序，将 for its leadership 和 in expanding access to higher education 两个部分的内容按汉语行文习惯重新安排。

(2) 此处按照顺译原则将 which 引导的非限定性定语从句断成汉语中的小句。

(3) 此句基本顺译，但听到句末的 for us all as educators 时如来不及将 as educators 前置，可采取原词重复的策略。

(4) 此处最好能处理成原文的递进结构，如果顺译时无法做到，也可处理成并列结构，但语气就稍逊于原文。

▼ 参考译文

最后，我赞赏广东外语外贸大学在扩大高等教育方面做出的表率作用，我也赞许广东省和广州市在番禺建立了大学城，明天我们就将去大学城参观。大学城带来了巨大的挑战，给我们这些教育者带来了巨大的挑战，那就是：学会管理拥有多个校园的大学，以及学会管理包含多所大学的校园。

Passage 5

但推算数字显示到了 2007 年,具备大专及以上教育学历的劳动人口将供不应求,短缺逾 10 万人 (1),而学历在高中或以下程度的劳动人口却供过于求,多出达 23 万人 (2)。工作要求的转变明显地不利于低学历人士。解决问题的方法只有一个,就是提升劳动人口的素质。(3)

▼ 技能提示

(1) "具备大专及以上教育学历的劳动人口将供不应求"与"短缺逾 10 万人"这两条信息可简约处理成英文中的单个句子,发挥英文语言精炼、逻辑紧凑的优势。

(2) 此句的处理同上。

(3) 此段在基本顺译的同时,也应注意酌情调整语序和使用合适的衔接手段,以避免英语译文过于松散、缺乏连贯。

▼ 参考译文

But our projections show that by 2007, we will have a shortfall of over 100000 people with education at postsecondary level and above, and at the same time a surplus of 230000 at or below upper secondary level. Clearly, the evolving job requirements are not in favour of persons with lower educational attainment. There is only one way to address this problem – that is to upgrade the quality of our workforce.

第三部分　术语拓展

汉译英

新世纪亚洲各国教育发展策略	Education Development Strategies for Asian Countries in the New Century
博鳌亚洲论坛	Boao Forum for Asia
创意媒体	creative media
慈善家	philanthropist
大学教育资助委员会	the University Grants Committee
副学士资历	associate degree
高级职称	senior professional title
高级文凭 / 专业文凭	the higher diploma or professional diploma
款待学课程	hospitality programme
来料加工	processing with materials supplied by customers

劳动力密集型产业	labor-intensive industry
冷门	a profession, trade or branch of learning that receives little attention
联合国教科文组织	UNESCO
免息贷款	interest-free loan
配对拨款	one-off grant
普及教育	universal education
人才枯竭	exhaustion of human resource
人生观	view on life value
社会活动/实践	social activity/ practice
实习生	intern
授予（学位）	confer
特别训练	special training
提高……的思想品德	enhance the moral awareness of…
通识教育	general education
脱产培训	off-job training
希望工程	Project Hope
香港特区教育统筹局局长	the Secretary for Education and Manpower of Hong Kong SAR
学分	credit
学分制	the credit system
学力	educational level
学历	education/ educational history/ record of formal schooling
学龄儿童	school-ager
学年	school/academic year
学前教育	preschool education
学术活动	academic activity
学习成绩	academic record/ school record
学习年限	period of schooling
学制	educational system
亚洲教育北京论坛	the Education Forum for Asia
在职培训	on-the-job/ in-service training
政治思想教育	political and ideological education
职业教育	vocational education
职业学校	polytechnic

中、小学校长	headmaster (headmistress)/ principal
中国国家留学基金管理委员会	China Scholarship Council
重点大学	key university
重点学科	key disciplinary area / priority field of study
专业	specialty/ major
专业课	specialized course
综合性大学	comprehensive university

英译汉

abroad student	留学生
academy	高等专科院校
accredited	经过认证，接受认证
admission test	入学考试
alumnus	校友
associate professor	副教授
commoner	自费生
compulsory course	必修课
curriculum	课程
diploma mill	文凭工厂 / 野鸡大学
distance education	远程教育
educational background	教育程度
extracurricular activity	课外活动
fee-paying school	付费学校 / 私立学校
freshman	大学一年级学生
government-supported student	公费生
guest professor	客座教授
half-life	半衰期
integrated circuit distance	集成电路距离
junior	大学三年级 / 高中二年级学生
lecturer	讲师
log in	登录
major	主修课
minor	辅修课
normal school	师范院校

online learning	在线学习
optional course	选修课
physical activity	体育活动
post doctorate	博士后
public school	（英国）公学 /（美国、澳大利亚、苏格兰及其他国家的）免费公立学校
recreational activity	娱乐活动
regular school	普通学校
root cause	根本原因
school of continuing and professional studies	继续教育学院
senior	大学四年级 / 高中三年级学生
social practice	社会实践
sophomore	大学二年级 / 高中一年级学生
supervisor	论文导师
teaching assistant	助教
the University City	大学城
transistor	晶体管
undergraduate	本科生
variable	变量
venture capital	风险投资
virtual college	虚拟学院

第四部分　同传实战

Listen to the following four speeches and interpret them into the target language using the skills introduced in this unit.

Text 1

女士们，先生们：

今天我很高兴能够来到这里和大家见面。一进门的时候我感到很惊讶，顺德有一个规模这么大的职业学校。我对旅游业完全是个外行，所以我今天讲的这个题目虽然是我的学习生涯，但是我想先讲一讲我对职业教育的一些看法，因为这个与我年轻时候所受的教育也有很大的关系。

我们在 20 多年以前，有一位香港的爱国的老人，他把毕生的积蓄都捐出来,来支持我们国家的教育事业。这是一笔很大数目的款子,当时拿了这笔款子,我们就考虑该怎么用,用在什么地方,怎么把这笔款子用在国家最需要的地方,用在刀口上。所以经过和有关部门一起研究,反复的研究,我们最后决定把这笔款子用在支持我们国家的职业教育这方面。

为什么我们要做出这样一个决定呢?因为当时我们觉得,国家对我们这个职业教育不是很重视。这个当然,高等教育是我们国家教育方面的重点,每年我们政府要投入大量的资金在高等教育方面。但是,职业教育是一个冷门,普遍地不受到人们的重视。所以国家在这方面的投入也是少得很可怜。那么当时也有许多教育的基金,国内的基金也好、国外来的、境外来的基金也好,这些基金绝大多数都投入到高等教育了。很少,只有个别的来支持我们这个职业教育。你比如说有很多这个,这个,这个大的慈善家,他把这个……建立这个基金,每年要捐很多的钱,上亿的钱来支持我们高等教育,各个大学。但是呢,对职业教育呢,却是一分钱都没有,一分钱都分不到。

那么当然,我们这个高等教育是的确需要来支持,这是个方向,这是对的。但是我们从长远来看,我们觉得职业教育也是非常重要的。所以当时我们就从这一点考虑,决定要把这笔钱用来支持职业教育。

当时因为我们国家的改革开放刚起步,我们引进了大量的来料加工,劳动密集型的这些工业。像这些工业,科技的成分很少,所以一些个工人稍微培训一下就可以上岗了。但是你从长远来看,随着我们经济的发展,这些劳动密集的工业必然慢慢要提高到科技密集的这些工业。到那个时候,就需要大量的技工,不是什么工人都可以上岗的。我们在德国,看到他们对职业教育非常重视,德国的一些工厂里的工人一定要有职业学校毕业的证书才能够上岗。所以这个情况是值得我们参考的,所以我们要从长远来考虑,从这个角度考虑。我们觉得也应该来支持职业教育。

我们对这个……社会上普遍地对职业教育不重视,另外一个原因,是因为当时我们国家的教育制度和人事制度存在一些问题。一个学生中学毕业以后考不上大学,那么好像就定了终身了,往往就一辈子都出不了头。那个时候职业学校的毕业生就不能够再考大学了,所以在政府机关里面也很难当上一个"干部",在其他企业、其他单位工作也很难评上一个高级的职称,所以只能够当一辈子的所谓的"职工"。当时我们还没有在职的进修和自学考试这种制度。所以变成中学毕业以后,大家都要争取要考大学。这样从学生来说,这个负担很重。从进幼稚园就要想着选一个好的幼稚园,从幼稚园到小学就要想着选一个好的小学,小学毕业以后要选一个好的中学,这样最后才能考上大学,结果搞得学生的负担很重。所以这种现象不是一个正常的现象,不是一个好的现象,但是当时的情况就是这样。所以从这个角度来说,我们觉得也应该大量地发展职业教育。

其实从社会上来看，许多的一些个工种不需要有高级职称的，（不需要）这些高等学校毕业的学生来做的。只要经过严格的技术的训练、职业的培训，有一些工作，只要职业学校毕业出来的完全可以胜任。譬如说打字、校对、护理、化验、配药。这些不一定都要大学毕业的什么学士啊、硕士啊、博士生来做的，完全可以由经过正规培训的一些技师来担任。特别是在一些高级技术人才缺乏的农村里面尤其如此。

还有呢，我们觉得当时有很多这个大学毕业生理论和实践是脱节的，他们只会动脑，不会动手。往往是个工科的毕业生，结果家里的水电坏了也不会修；文科毕业的不会打字；工程师，图纸绘制出来以后不知道怎么操作。昨天我还在网上看到了，有些个心理学的博士生不知道怎么做心理咨询。这种现象很普遍，所以，我们觉得非常需要培养一批既能够动脑子又能够自己动手的技术人员。其实呢，我们看我们这个神舟六号上天了，这个火箭当然是要一些个技术人员，一些工程师他来设计，但是它每一个细小的环节都是非常重要的，如果一个螺丝钉它拧得不紧，一个焊头焊得不好、不密，就很可能要出很严重的问题。所以我们的火箭上天，以后要上月球，不是单单靠这些个科学家、技术人员和高级技术员所能够完成的，还是需要大量的经过严密训练的技工一点点、一点点地做成。

（2005年12月16日，前国务院港澳办主任鲁平在"国际旅游与酒店业发展论坛"上的讲话节选，根据录音材料整理）

Text 2

陈先生，方先生，老师们，同学们，朋友们：

大家好！

非常高兴你们给我们机会，很难得的一个机会，参加你们广外纪念四十年的生日，很快乐！今天，我们都是广外人。我们Fullbright的交流项目跟广外有20多年的一个历史。希望我们将来有更大的一个发展。因为我中文说得太差，而且他们翻译得太好，我要用英文。中文有一个成语：天不怕，地不怕，就怕外国人说中国话。所以我现在用英语，那是我的母语。谢谢！

China has expanded its universities dramatically. Between 1998 and 2004, as Professor Fang was saying, the number of first year students has doubled. China now educates almost 20% of all school leavers on further education. When I came to China in 1982, that was less than 5%. China has expanded access to higher education mainly through the growth of its institutions. And the growth of Guangwai is an example of, say, growing from 3000 to 16000 in ten years. How many universities in the world have expanded at that rate and undergone such change? It's remarkable.

This expansion generally across the country has been driven by several factors. The fast economic growth of China has required many more skilled people, especially after the constraints placed on universities in the 1960s and 1970s. The social demand for university education grows in China, especially as the first cohorts of single children per family come of university age. China's traditional cultural value on education has never been stronger. With the globalization of higher education in all countries, Chinese universities are poised to produce PhDs and other graduates in vast numbers, some of whom will go abroad to work in countries with more demand than supply of advanced educated talent.

Some in China may be concerned, as they seem to be in all countries, that not all university graduates can find jobs right away. I suggest this is not a problem of over-supply of graduates, but the need of a more efficient labor market for talented people. By the way, I think Guangwai graduates do not have a problem getting jobs, but graduates of other universities do. It also points to a question of willingness among young people to move to less urban places for their first job after university. Besides, competition for the best jobs in the major cities tends to keep us all on our toes, doesn't it? China cannot have too many educated people. One of China's many remarkable achievements in the past decade is dismantling the *fenpei* – job assignment – system and allowing a new labor market for university graduates and mid career professionals to grow.

When we advocate greater public access to universities, we tend to hear skeptics assume that expanding quantity of higher education necessarily must mean lowering the quality. This is short-sighted. If resources expand to keep pace with the enrollment growth, quality of education can be maintained, and even improved, as access grows. If governments seek to expand universities on the cheap, then universities face real trouble, and quality can suffer over time. By resources, I mean more than buildings and other "hardware" on campuses that you can see right away. Even more important are the adequate resources for the "software" of universities, such as teacher salaries, research funds, student scholarships, exchange opportunities and management systems support. Yes we can achieve greater efficiencies through smarter uses of communication technologies. But the heart of higher education is the interaction between the teacher and student. While this does not have to be done in a face-to-face in classrooms on campuses exclusively, it does have to happen to assure quality while growing access.

Cost is a key factor for access. If higher education becomes too expensive for the public, access declines. Tuition rates have grown in China, as they have all around the world, my country especially. Governments everywhere have argued: let the beneficiaries pay more for their education! Even as universities do seek to diversify their sources of revenue, and I am sure Guangwai has done this, these successes cannot relieve governments at national, provincial and city levels from the responsibility to invest in the next generation. These investments are critical to keeping tuition within reach of many families. China has to be concerned about widening gaps between rich and poor. Access to higher education for poor families with talented children is important for social stability and cultural development. People must believe the university admissions process to be fair and that talent and hard work will be rewarded by access to further education, which is the key to better life chances.

Finally, convenience is a key factor for increasing public access to university. More and more students commute to campus. Dormitories are always in short supply. As cities grow and new campuses rise on the periphery, such as the Da Xue Cheng here in Panyu as an example, efficient and low cost urban transport is critical.

When we speak of access, we do not just mean the traditional student, age 18-22. We also need to create access for non-traditional students, and Sarah Hui was talking about this, who return to further learning even after they continue their work and family lives. They study in evenings and on weekends, balancing job and family commitments with their personal drive for self-improvement. We at universities need to create new chances for young adults to improve themselves and upgrade their work skills. This is central to a learning society. We at universities have to adjust our systems to their needs, and not just simply expect that they can adjust to ours. Our flexibility can create new access for the public to life-long education and training. This includes creating credit unit systems, inter-university transfer policies, online education to complement classrooms, and the like.

Finally, I commend Guangwai for its leadership in expanding access to higher education, and I applaud the province of Guangdong and city of Guangzhou for creating the Da Xue Cheng campus in Panyu, which we will go to tomorrow. The University City creates a great challenge for us all as educators: to learn how to manage not only multi-campus universities, but also multi-university campuses. Such a campus at this scale is unique in the world. We commend all who are involved for this bold initiative and look forward to international academic collaborations wherever that are helpful. We are assured of the continued success of Guang Wai in the next decade and beyond in expanding public access to university education.

Thank you!

(Full text of speech by Glenn Shive, Director of the Hong Kong America Center at the University Presidents Forum on November 5, 2005, as transcribed)

Text 3

周部长，各位嘉宾，各位来宾：

亚洲教育北京论坛举行第二次年会，而我有机会在此向各位嘉宾致词，实在感到万分高兴和荣幸。首先，我谨向举办这次盛会的北京市人民政府、博鳌亚洲论坛、联合国教科文组织和中国国家留学基金管理委员会致贺。

今年会议的主题是"新世纪亚洲各国教育发展策略"。对香港来说，这是一个十分适切的议题，因为我们正在推行多项重大的教育改革，从根本上改变中学和高等教育的学制，以及革新香港新一代的学习经验。今天，我将以香港特区教育统筹局局长的身分，与各位分享推行上述改革的经验，以及我们的愿景。

一如亚太区许多现代化都市，香港正在迅速迈向知识型经济。21世纪为我们带来新的挑战，也催促我们谋求创新的解决方案。但与区内很多现代化城市相比，香港面积小，也没有天然资源，唯一的重要资产就是人才。

过去数十年，香港致力发展成为亚太地区的金融中心，务求在贸易和高增值服务业方面处于领导地位。这些转变对人力供应构成强大压力。去年，香港的总劳动人口是350余万人，但推算数字显示到了2007年，具备大专及以上教育学历的劳动人口将供不应求，短缺逾10万人，而学历在高中或以下程度的劳动人口却供过于求，多出达23万人。工作要求的转变明显地不利于低学历人士。解决问题的方法只有一个，就是提升劳动人口的素质。为此，我们必须致力改善教育服务。

在香港，教育向来是优先的政策项目。本年度的教育开支高达约580亿港元，是我们最庞大的单项开支，占政府总开支23.5%，即本地生产总值的4.4%。以实际金额计算，今年的教育开支比1997年增加了54%。

在教育政策方面，我们提供九年免费普及基础教育，并辅以各类学前高中以及专上教育服务。凡有志求学的学生，几乎都可接受获政府大幅资助的高中教育或职业培训。不过，大学入学试的竞争非常激烈。即使把副学位程度的学额也计算在内，直到上一世纪结束前，香港仍只有三分之一的离校生有机会接受专上教育。

因此，我们在2000年订出一项政策目标，务求在10年内把学额增加一倍，让60%的高中毕业生有机会接受大专教育。这个目标订得很高，但为了维持香港的竞争力，这实在是必要的，教育成本非常高昂。

在香港，由于政府对大学学额成本的资助达80%以上，有关开支尤其庞大。如果我们要以目前的资助模式提供双倍的学额，定会对公共财政构成难以承受的压力。因此，我们从一开始便认为，在增加专上学额方面，自负盈亏的机构应担当重要角色，而政府则应充当支持者和促进者。所以，我们一方面让市场决定课程的数量和种类，另一方面则推出适当的措施，扶助业界发展。有关措施包括：提供50亿元免息贷款；以象征性地价拨地；提供学生资助，以及建立严格的素质保证机制。

政策推出后，新的服务机构纷纷涌现。目前，香港有20所自负盈亏专上院校，提供超过25000个副学位及学位的一年级学额。有机会接受大专教育的年轻人，也由2000年的33%，倍增至今年的66%。换言之，我们已提早五年完成让60%高中毕业生接受大专教育的目标。

学额得以大幅增加的主要原因，是我们引进了副学士资历。香港的教育制度早已设有一些以职业导向为主的副学位课程，例如高级文凭、专业文凭等，而副学士的推出，正好为市民提供多一个选择。

以自负盈亏模式开办副学位课程的教育机构发展蓬勃，情况令人鼓舞。不过，位于知识阶梯顶端的大学，仍然担当独特的角色。

香港政府透过大学教育资助委员会资助8所高等院校，包括两所历史最悠久，擅长学术研究的综合大学，一所较近期成立、并着重科技和商科的大学，两所前身为理工学院的大学，一所推行博雅教育的大学，一所以"全人教育"模式提供高等教育的大学，以及一所教育学院。政府每年动用超过港币100亿元，资助这些院校的运作，并额外拨出校园用地和提供非经常拨款，以支持这些院校的基建发展。为鼓励各院校物色其他资金来源，我们也因应院校自行筹得的私人捐款，不止一次向院校提供高达10亿元港币的配对拨款。

从根本上改革学制，是一项极其艰巨的工作。没有教育家的抱负、政策制定者的决心，以及所有相关者，包括家长、学生、教师、院校、纳税人，以至社会上每个人的充分支持，这项工作决不能完成。我很高兴，经过多年的讨论，社会上终于达成了共识。在未来数年，政府会投入79亿元的非经常拨款，供实行新学制的基本工程及一笔过开支之用，其后每年亦会额外拨款20亿元，应付经常开支。学制改革的道路漫长，但我们知道，我们已朝着正确方向迈进一大步，而推行改革亦是本港教育史上一个新的里程碑。因此，我们会怀着热诚，坚毅不拔地努力前进。

我希望这次会议是对话的开始。我们期望藉着持续的交流和合作，与大家建立更紧密的关系。在此谨祝会议圆满成功，并希望从外地来的朋友此行旅途愉快。谢谢。

（2005年10月15日，香港特别行政区教育统筹局局长李国章在"2005亚洲教育北京论坛"全体大会上的讲话节选）

Text 4

Well, Distinguished Faculty, Students,

It is a pleasure to be on any university campus, but to be on the university site with so many students in such a large university is indeed a pleasure. Today I wanted to briefly talk about the world as a whole and then come down and talk a little bit about China, and then a little bit about university and then a little bit about you as students and what you might expect going forward.

If you look at the world as a whole I think there are two major changes that have taken place in the last ten years and have influenced all of our futures. The first is that practically every country in the world now is part of the world free economic system, part of the world free trade system as others say, easy interchange of goods and services between most countries. And this is a major change from where we were only a few years ago. About half of the world's population has joined the free economic system in the last ten years, China is included, India, Russia, Eastern Europe, some of Latin America. So there has been a major change in the world free economic structure, which means that if you are in any one country, you can deal with any other country, especially in goods and services and ideas which are knowledge based.

The other change that has taken place in the last ten years is associated with technology and the Internet. Today it's very easy to communicate between any two spots on the earth. It is very inexpensive to do so, such as you can transfer knowledge, transfer information and communicate anywhere in the world today for almost nothing. And if you take these two major changes together, what it means is, there's great opportunity in the world as well as great competition. And the competition is what drives us and the opportunity is what drives us. And so every country has to accommodate this change. Every country has to accommodate in its economy this new competition and this new opportunity. So if you look at what countries can do, they can really only do three things for their citizens to make them more competitive going forward. One of the things they can do is the reason you are here at this university. They can provide you good education, and generally standard of living goes directly with education level, so the higher the education level within the country, the greater the opportunity for standard living, the greater the opportunity for economic competitiveness. So providing an education to the whole citizenry is very important.

The second thing that any country can do is in fact to invest in research and development. Research and development creates ideas for the future. And ideas create new products, new services, new companies. So we need to invest in research and development and just as the standard of living of any country is directly related to the education level of the workforce, refine the standard of living and the economic competitiveness of any country is usually related to its investment in research and development. And obviously China has recognized both of these characteristics with a great emphasis on education in the last decade. And the more recent emphasis on increasing and expanding the research and development.

The third thing that any country can do is in fact to create an environment that allows smart people, well-educated people to come together with smart ideas, generated from research and development and create new products, new companies, new services, new economic growth. So the government, the central government of any country can focus on education, research and development in creating an environment to allow people to be successful and an environment that allows entrepreneurs to succeed. And increasingly we see this sort of entrepreneurial spirit here in China. My company happens to be the largest high-tech venture capital investor in the world. And increasingly we see more and more high tech venture capital investments made here in China. It used to be ten years ago those investment were predominantly made in the United States. Now only but 50% of those investments are made in the United States. About 50% are made here in Asia. So those are the three things that any country can do, education, research and development and setting the environment.

By the way, companies are not much different than countries. If you look at our company the three things that we focus on to be successful are hiring the best and brightest in the world, well-educated people, investing a large amount of money in research and development to create the next generation of products, and then providing an environment for our researchers to be successful, to bring their ideas into the market place. So company like Intel or any major successful multinational company today does exactly the same sort of thing that central governments do, trying to promote their competitiveness.

Now you might also then ask what should the individual do? If the world has changed and the world is much smaller today than it used to be, if there's much more competition for jobs, if countries are focusing on education, on research and development and on right environment or atmosphere, what should the individual do? And I have a few just comments for you as individuals going forward. Obviously the reason you are here is to get the best education that you possibly can achieve. And I always recommend to young students that you get the best education you can. That is the best foundation you can have. But once you do that, I think you should recognize that your education has a relatively short half-life. What you learn at the university may be out of date in a few years. So you have to convince yourself that you are going to continuously learn after you leave the university. And you have to continuously learn in your professional life as you go forward. So you never stop learning, you never have the opportunity to stop learning. You must continue the learning as you go forward.

I've a few other pieces of advice for you as well. One of them is even doing your education but perhaps more importantly as you start to work in your professional career, is never being afraid to ask the question why. If you're going to solve problems, if you're going to figure out how to be successful, how to create new things, you always have to ask the question why about five times. Quite often when you're approaching a problem, the first explanation of the problem you will receive from other people is very shallow. It doesn't get to the root cause or the fundamentals of the problem. And you can't be afraid to ask why several times. And I tell all of our employees in Intel to always ask why, why, why. I also like to tell students when they are dealing with their professors to always ask their professors why as well. Don't accept things directly, if you don't understand them, don't be afraid to ask why several times because that's the only way you will totally fully understand the problem. You also obviously need to understand that the problems you will solve as you're going to the outside world, outside of universities are generally very complex problems. They are not simple problems like you're given a homework or assignments in class. For example, if you're in an integrated circuit distance, such as we are in Intel, and you want to solve the problems associated with the next generation of technology, how you go from 65 nm to 45 nm to 30 nm to make these ever smaller transistors. There are usually two or three hundred variables involved in solving that problem. And it's a very complex experimentation to solve that problem. And you have to get used to these very very complex problems as oppose to very simple problems that have a definitive answer. And when you do this obviously you need to collect a large amount of data, and make data-based decisions. So getting used to complex problems and getting used to handling large amounts of data I think is very very critical as you go forward.

I might point out that having read a little bit about your university and the foundation principles for your university, if I understand them correctly. That Sun Yat-sen in 1924 when he founded the university basically said to "study extensively", I think that means to get the best education you possibly can.

(I have to put my glasses on to read the rest of this. Excuse me.)

But "inquire accurately", this means to collect data and ask why several times. To "reflect carefully", make decisions on complex problems, "discriminate clearly" or make clear decisions when you're moving forward, and then to "practice earnestly", practice earnestly might mean that you have to continue to educate yourself as you go forward. So I think the five basic foundations of this university described in 1924, some 80 years ago, line up precisely with what I am trying to tell you today, which is to get the best possible education that you can, to continue to study, continue to learn, to ask why about things that you don't understand, to recognize that you have complex problems to solve, and that you need to spend an immense amount of data to achieve these results.

So let me conclude my prepared remarks with that comment: get the best education you can, never be afraid to ask why, and always deal with data when you are trying to make complex decisions. Thank you and I'll be happy to answer any questions you might have.

(Excerpted text of speech by Craig Barrett, Intel Corporate Chairman at Sun Yat-sen University in Guangzhou on October 30, 2006)

第 6 单元　同声传译常用技巧
Techniques in Simultaneous Interpreting

单元学习目标
1. 了解并初步运用同声传译的八大基本工作技巧。
2. 熟悉经贸这一口译主题的常用汉英术语和表达方式。
3. 能够完成基本的同步听说练习。

第一部分　同传技能

同声传译具有不同寻常的工作模式，前辈译员们经过不断探索与努力实践，终于摸索出了一套有效的用于双语转换、信息加工与重组的同传技巧，使得同声传译由不可能变为可能，并且逐渐为人们所了解甚至熟悉。这些技巧包括：长句切分、词类转换、增补简约、信息重构、归纳总结、信息等待、合理预测和语气强弱。这些常用技巧在实际的同传工作中经常组合使用，方式灵活，需要长期训练才能有效掌握。

1. 长句切分

长句切分是同传中最常用的处理技巧，尤其多用于英汉同传中。长句切分，或者"断句"，是指"在同传时将英语句子，按适当的意群或概念单位，进行切割处理并译成汉语"（张维为，1999：48），英文又称 segmentation、chunking 或 salami technique。琼斯认为，"断句技巧在处理结构复杂的长句、尤其是出现俄罗斯套娃那样的嵌套结构的句子时十分有用（The salami technique is particularly useful when working from languages that have a natural tendency to long, complicated sentences, particularly those that can have Russian-doll-like structures, with one subordinate clause fitting in another one, which in turn fits into a main clause.)"（Jones, 1998: 102）。长句切分不是为了断句而断，它是由英语与汉语在诸多方面的较大差异所决定的：英语是综合型语言，语法严谨，结构严密，使用大量的从属结构；而汉语是分析型的语言，语法和句子结构松散，使用大量的小句、流水句，句子多为并列结构。英语重形合，依赖大量的衔接手段来实现形式上的衔接；汉语重意合，更依赖上下文来表意而基本少用虚词，虽然形式松散，但意义保持连贯。"西洋语的结构好像连环，虽则环与环都联络起来，毕竟有联络的痕迹；中国语的结构好像无缝天衣，只是一块一块的拼凑，凑起来还不让它有痕迹。西洋语法是硬的，没有弹性的；中国语法是软的，富于弹性的。惟其是硬的，所以西洋语法有许多呆板的要求，如每一个 clause 里必须有一个主语，惟其是软的，所以中国语法只以达意为主，……如相关的两件事可以硬凑在一起，不用任何的 connective word。"（王力，1984: 141）

另外，同传译员也面临着信息处理能力（information processing capacity）紧张的巨大压力。按照同传的工作要求，译员不能等待演讲者讲完一整句话以后才开始口译，因为这样不仅会拉大时间差，而且会给自己的短时记忆造成很大负担，甚至有可能因信息过于密集而漏掉部分信息。而使用断句技巧，"可以更快速地减轻记忆力负担，减少短时记忆力的信息处理压力（can save short-term memory capacity requirements by unloading information from memory faster）"（Gile, 1995: 196）。通常情况下，译员在听到半句话以后就开始口译，按照顺句驱动工作的原则，面对源源不断的信息和存在巨大差异的两种语言，如果不适当对源语句子进行切分，再寻求合适时机进行意义的连接，同传工作几乎是无法完成的。

虽然译员在同传时要将句子处理成一段一段的，从形式上来看破坏了句子的完整性，但是就意义而言，这样的处理对源语信息的完整并无减损；把长句化整为零不会增加或者减少信息的数量。

当然，不是所有的英语句子都需要进行切分处理。英语与汉语中存在大量语序基本一致的句子，处理的时候只要顺句驱动，无须改变语序。比如：

- Our delegation wish to thank you for your gracious hospitality and thoughtful arrangement.

  我们代表团要感谢您的热情好客与周到安排。

除了上述英汉双语中概念较等值、表达较对应、语序基本一致的句子以外，英语与汉语中还存在大量在概念、表达和语序方面相差甚远的句子。让我们以一句简单的英文为例来看看同传中长句切分的工作原理：

- ① We/ ② are going to attend the meeting/ ③ at Red Forest Hotel/ ④ from 2 to 4 o'clock/ ⑤ tomorrow afternoon.

在交传的工作模式下，这句话的处理很简单："我们明天下午两点到四点要去红林酒店参加会议。"可即便是这样一句简单的英语句子，在以地道的汉语习惯表述以后，句子成分的顺序也发生了很大的改变：

①我们 / ⑤明天下午 / ④两点到四点 / ③要去红林酒店 / ②参加会议。

在同传中，按照顺据驱动的原理，源语可以被切分为：

"我们要去参加会议，（**地点**）在红林酒店，（**时间**）是明天下午的两点到四点。"

同传工作模式下的这句译文，除了对原文进行切分，还采用了其他的技巧：信息增加与信息等待。按照汉语的话语习惯，时间、地点状语如果放在主句之前说出，则不需额外增加表明时、地的词句；但是按照顺句驱动的原则，我们按照英语的行文习惯先将主谓成分交代清楚，那时间、地点状语就必须增词来加以提示，否则单纯在主句后补充说出会显得别扭，听起来不像地道的汉语。时间状语中，表示日期和时间点的内容在汉语和英语中的语序也有差异，而在汉语中两者的顺序尤为固定，故在表达时应稍加等待，遵从汉语由大（日期）到小（具体时间点）的逻辑。

长句在哪里可断，又如何连起来呢？可依据下列结构：关系词引导的从句、连接词引导的分句、介词短语和分词结构。

1) 关系词引导的从句。关系词包括关系代词和关系副词、连接代词和连接副词，如 who, whom, whose, that, which, what, why, how, when, where 等。这些关系词用来连接主语从句、定语从句、宾语从句、表语从句等，因此断句可以在此进行。例如：

- The WTO is also a powerful force in countering the currents of protectionism and discrimination // which are responsible to a large extent for the economic hardship suffered by less wealthy and less well-endowed economies.

  世贸是对抗保护主义和贸易歧视的重要力量。// 而保护主义和贸易歧视往往导致较贫困、较弱势地区陷入经济困境。

  （对照笔译或交传：世贸是对抗常使较贫困、较弱势地区陷入经济困境的保护主义与贸易歧视的重要力量。）

- Look at the impact on the environment of // what you plan before you do it, not afterwards.

  要了解对环境的影响，在开始之前就要了解计划对环境的影响，而不是过后才去了解。

  （对照笔译或交传：要在计划之前而不是之后去了解其对环境的影响。）

2) 连接词引导的分句。连接词包括并列连词和从属连词 and, or, but, yet, so, however, as well as, either…or, neither…nor, when, while, as, since, until, so…that, unless, lest 等，在听到连接词时便可切断句子。例如：

- This year, the Expo will attract more than 30,000 SMEs // not just from Hong Kong SAR, // but also from Europe, North America, Japan and Korea.

  今年，博览会将吸引三万多家中小企业，// 这些企业不仅来自香港特别行政区，而且来自欧洲、北美、日本和韩国。

  （对照笔译或交传：今年，博览会将吸引三万多家来自香港特别行政区、欧洲、北美、日韩的中小企业。）

- Mr. Donald Tsang has enjoyed strong support // since his election as Chief Executive in June.

  曾荫权先生得到了大力支持，自从六月份当选特首以来便是如此。

（对照笔译或交传：自六月份当选特首之后，曾荫权先生便一直得到极大的支持。）

3）介词短语。介词 with, to, in, at, of, through, on, out 等引导的介词短语处可进行切分。例如：

- We have a five-point plan // for profitable growth here // in China.

  我们有一个五点计划，// 以实现利润增长，// 在中国的利润增长。

（对照笔译或交传：我们有一个在中国实现利润增长的五点计划。）

- We are working with them to ensure // that they meet our rigorous standards // for environment, health and safety as well as for quality.

  我们与他们合作以确保 // 他们符合我们的严格标准，// 关于环境、健康、安全以及质量的严格标准。

（对照笔译或交传：我们与他们合作以确保其符合我们在环境、健康、安全以及质量方面的严格标准。）

4）分词结构。在以现在分词和过去分词引导的状语或定语处可进行切分，将分词结构处理成独立的句子。

- Tourism, a rising industry, has become the major source of economy, // playing a crucial role // in many Asian countries.

  旅游业作为一个新型行业已成为主要的经济来源，// 作用重大，// 对许多亚洲国家而言作用重大。

（比较笔译或交传：旅游业作为一个新型行业已成为主要的经济来源，对许多亚洲国家而言作用重大。）

- Once the resolutions have been adopted, members present may need further information listed in the resolutions.

  一旦决议获得通过，出席成员可能需要更多信息，// 这些信息记载于决议之中。

（比较笔译或交传：一旦决议获得通过，出席成员可能需要更多记载于决议中的信息。）

由上我们不难看出，长句切分作为有效的同传技巧，可以帮助译员在不增加信息处理能力负担的前提下保证信息产出的完整与准确。但是断句也有不可避免的缺点，即会将句子处理得"支离破碎"，在形式上与源语句子有一定差距。因此，译员在采用长句切分技巧时应注意其他技巧（如增补、等待、推迟等）的运用，因为句子切分不是为断而断，在条件允许的情况下，译员也要尽力在形式上对译语信息适当"修补"。

2. 词类转换

词类转换不仅是同传中的常用技巧，也是其他口笔译工作中的常用技巧。笔译中，源语中的某个词不一定被处理为译语中同一词类的词，口译也是如此。英语更倾向于使用名词化表达法，即更多地使用抽象名词或名词短语、介词或介词短语、形容词和分词；而汉语更倾向于使用动词化表达法，大量使用动词和副词，少用抽象名词，不用介词和分词。英语中表示动态时，不像汉语那样连用动词或使用动词短语，而是选择可表示动作含义的抽象名词。英语名词化和汉语动词化的例子，在我们身边随处可见：

- 主席**提议通过**议程，并**提请**大会**注意**他在开幕词中所**说**的话。
- Laser is one of the most sensational *developments* in recent years, because of its *applicability* to many fields of science and its *adaptability* to practical uses.

同传时，根据英汉语的用语特点有选择地进行词类转换，不必拘泥于源语的句子结构和话语偏好，采用更加灵活的方法来处理，使译语产出更地道、更自然。同传中的词类转换基本可分为以下几种。

1）英语名词转换为汉语动词。

- Sadam's *survival* was a *humiliation* to the US-UK coalition aiming at *restoration* of order in Iraq.

  萨达姆还**活**着，这使旨在**恢复**伊拉克秩序的英美联合部队**蒙羞**。

  试比较：萨达姆的**存活**是对旨在实现伊拉克秩序**恢复**的英美联合部队的**羞辱**。源语中的主语和谓语成分均为名词或名词短语，如照搬源语结构和句子成分的词类，译文显得拗口，不符合汉语的话语习惯，而且延长等待时间会增加处理压力。如果采用词类转换，译文明显更通顺、更自然。

- 所有热爱和平的人们都要求全面**禁止**核武器，彻底**销毁**核武器。

  All peace-loving people demand the complete *prohibition* and thorough *destruction* of nuclear weapons.

汉语中连用动词来表示动态，英语适当使用名词，使译文更加简洁流畅。

2）英语形容词转换为汉语动词或副词。

- In order to carry through its policies of economic development, peace is *necessary* for China.

  为了执行经济发展政策，中国**需要**和平。

  将英语中的形容词处理为汉语中的动词，更符合汉语动态的特征。

- 要更好的**理解**这个问题，学习者要**了解**生物多样性这个概念。

  For better *understanding* of this issue, learners need to be *aware* of the concept of biodiversity.

灵活使用转换技巧，更加突出英语名词化的特征。

3) 英语介词转换为汉语动词。

- She escorted the European delegates *round* the sights of Guangzhou.

  她陪同欧洲代表**游览**广州的景点。

将英语介词处理为汉语动词,更符合汉语行文特点。

- 他们用军事力量来**对付**所谓恐怖主义国家。

  They used military force *against* so-called terrorist countries.

汉语中的动态通过连续使用的动词表示,英语则恰恰相反,介词的使用使译语更加严谨、自然。

3. 增补简约

增补与简约是相对存在的两个技巧。如前所述,英语与汉语是两种差异较大的语言,汉语重意合,少用虚词、介词、连接词和关系词,只要把意思表述清楚即可;英语重形合,常用分词、介词、连接词和关系词。面对两种差异巨大的语言,在同声传译时不可能逐字逐句处理,必须视情况酌情增删信息,来保持译语的准确与通顺。增补与简约在同传中的使用十分广泛,桑德拉·黑尔认为,"语言省略与增益往往是必要的,这样可以保证精确度"(1997a:211,转引自 Pochhacker, 2004:132)。司徒罗宾也认为,句法差异会造成处理的瓶颈,而增补技巧可以有效消除这一瓶颈,其本身也是顺句驱动的有效补充策略(Setton, 1999:49-51)。简约,或者省略,是指在不影响信息传达的基础上对源语中无法用译语处理或者技术性过强的内容进行简化,简约的处理必须以不改变源语意义和实质内容为前提,否则就会造成信息遗漏或失误。在英译中时,英文形合虚词的省略现象十分常见,可以更好发挥汉语简洁明快的特色(张维为,1999)。

同传中常见的增补可以分为结构性增补和语义性增补。试举例如下:

1) 结构性增补

- We won't retreat; we never have and never will.

  我们不会退缩;我们过去没有**退缩**过,将来也不会**退缩**。

(试比较:我们不会退缩,过去不会,将来也不会。)

- 我们愿意与美方共同努力,排除一切干扰,排除各种障碍,把一个健康、稳定的中美关系带入下一个世纪。

  We are prepared to work together with the US to remove all kinds of interferences and obstacles *so as to* bring a sound and stable China-US relationship into the next century.

2) 语义性增补

- Recourse to arms is not the best solution to a quarrel between countries.

  武力并不是国家之间争端的最好解决**办法**。

- 今后，我们要加强基础设施建设和农村市场开发。
  In the future we intend to step up the construction of infrastructure and *to open up* the market in rural areas.

同传中的简约则常见于以下的情况：

1) 英译汉时，省略或缩减英语中特有的词或汉语中不需要的词。
- It would be most appreciated if you could pass me a glass of water.
  请给我一杯水。

it 和 there 引导的从句是英语语法中特有的现象，在英汉同传时可以简约处理，发挥汉语简练、自然的风格。

- In the course of the same year, war broke out in that area.
  同年，该地区爆发了战争。

2) 汉译英时，省略或缩减汉语中的冗余或重复表达。
- 从历史悠久的北京和建筑精美的故宫这些缩影中，人们就能够生动地感受到中华文明源远流长、博大精深的深厚底蕴，感受到中华民族自强不息、顽强奋进的壮阔历程。
  From Beijing's time-honored past and the majestic Forbidden City itself, people can learn vividly the long-standing and profound richness of the Chinese civilization and feel the vigor, resilience and pioneering spirit of the Chinese nation.

4. 信息重构

信息重构（reformulation）或信息重组是指按照译语的语言习惯重新组合源语的信息点。这一技巧是相对长句切分而言的：使用切分技巧，译员将源语处理成长短不一的翻译单位；在译成目标语时，为了避免句子过于支离破碎弱化效果，译员常常采取信息重构的手段把切断的句子有机连接起来。因此译员在重构信息时要添加一定的"润滑剂"，使译语片段能够连缀成篇，总体上与源语对等。

同传中，译员可以通过添加衔接成分（如连接词、关系词等）来重构信息，保持译语产出的连贯性。例如：

- 广东是中国大陆最南端的省份，濒临南海，毗邻港澳，历史文化悠久，自然风光秀丽。
  Guangdong, the southernmost province in China's mainland, is adjacent to the South China Sea and close to Hong Kong and Macao, *with* long history, rich culture *as well as* beautiful natural scenery.

源语是汉语中典型的流水句式，一个主语后面跟着一长串谓语。在译成英语时如照搬源语结构不仅会使译语重复、啰嗦，而且逻辑、美感尽失。可考虑添加适当的衔接成分以及将主谓结构灵活处理成同位语短语等手段重构信息，实现译语产出衔接紧密、自然通顺。

- Violation of human rights in that country, originate from anti-terrorist operations, is deeply regrettable.

  该国违反人权的行为，**虽然**是出于反恐的目的，**但**还是让人遗憾。

  源语被切分成三条信息，重构时通过巧妙添加的关联词突显了信息之间的逻辑关系。

5. 归纳概括

同传中的归纳概括指对源语内容进行预测性、总结性、简化性的提炼和总结。

1）预测性归纳常见于对 it 做形式主语引导的主语从句中，如：

- You can tell those factories *it is in their interest to* produce more and waste less.

  你可以告诉那些工厂，对其有利的做法**包括**：多生产、少浪费。

2）总结性归纳是对刚听到的一串信息进行总结，常用词语包括："都"、"这（些）"、"也就是"、"即是"等。例如：

- Mr. Governor, you have already mentioned so many elements on the list of things which should be incorporated in cultivating the innovation that it's difficult to add elements to it.

  省长先生，您已经提到了很多因素了，**这些**因素是培养创新必不可少的，对此我很难再做什么补充。

3）简化性归纳常见于较多的列举项、罗列或技术上较难处理的特殊情况。例如：

- The construction cost of the project is 15,053,7496 yuan.

  该项目建筑成本为一千五百多万元。（压力过大情况下译员可略去听众可能不感兴趣的数字细节，将数字概括化处理。）

- 广东还积极推动包括闽、赣、湘、粤、桂、琼、川、黔、滇9省（区）以及港、澳两个特别行政区在内的"泛珠三角"区域合作，简称"9+2"区域合作。
  Guangdong is also actively promoting the Pan Pearl River Delta regional cooperation, known as the "9+2" Regional Cooperation, which involves nine provinces or autonomous region, Hong Kong SAR and Macao SAR. （在发言人快速列举9个省区简称时，面临极大压力的译员必须迅速做出判断，进行取舍，采用归纳的方式保留信息主干，将列举项进行概括处理。）

6. 信息等待

在上下文不太明晰时,译员要视情况稍作等待,明确上下文以后再开口,这就是同传中的信息等待。英汉两种语言的巨大差异使得英汉同传无法做到完全同步,而译员又不能一味的将句子分割、切断使得译语结构过于松散、充满重复,因此适当使用等待技巧是必要的。

英语结构紧密、逻辑严谨,重视形合,而汉语表达追求达意,重视意合。发言内容相当的情况下,英语句子会长于汉语句子。通常而言,中译英时译员要加快语速,而英译中时译员语速要适当放慢,此时译员要注意不能一味的追求填满时间空隙,而是要根据实际情况来选择是否采取等待策略。另外,由于个人的双语能力以及短时记忆能力均各不相同,译员也必须对合理的等待时长心中有数,避免超出自己能力范围,等待过久,会造成信息的缺失,影响译语产出的完整性、准确性。

英汉同传中,译员在听到由 it 引导的形式主语,由一些介词如 of、in、at、from、to、for 等引导的后置定语等简单结构,there be 存现句型和动词不定式时,即可考虑使用等待技巧。例如:

- The General Assembly decided that capacity-building should remain an essential part of the United Nations system operational activities.
  大会决定能力建设应继续成为(等一拍)联合国业务活动的一个基本部分。
- There are a lot that UK can share with China.
  (等一拍)英国有许多可以和中国分享的地方。
- Dutch philosopher Spinoza was one of the earliest Western thinkers to advocate freedom of ideology and speech.
  荷兰哲学家斯宾诺莎是(等一拍)最早倡导意识形态与言论自由的西方思想家之一。
- We should understand the nature, level and scope of such a commitment.
  我们应当理解(等一拍)这一承诺的性质、层次与范围。

7. 合理预测

预测(anticipation),是贯穿同传过程始终的一个重要技巧。打一个比方:高速公路上有一辆车(B)在追赶另一辆车(A)。如果 B 车始终采取保守的策略,只是埋头在 A 车身后追赶,而不去观察前面的路况或判断其前进的方向,那么两车的车距只会越拉越大,A 车可能将 B 车远远甩在身后。同传也是如此:如果只是被动处理大脑接收到的信息而不留出精力去分析即将到来的信息,那译员的记忆力将会面临极大的压力,甚至可能短路。为了减少压力,译员常常会对接下来的信息进行预测。

预测是译员为减少记忆负担所采取的现实手段。根据吉尔的认知负荷模型（effort model），我们知道，同传可以分解为听辨（L）、产出（P）、短时记忆（M）和协调（C）等子步骤，同传的顺利进行要求加工能力的供给超过加工能力的需求，即 LR<LA、PR<PA、MR<MA、CR<CA。在实际工作中，译员往往要应对语速较快、信息密集、语言组合差异巨大等问题，如果不进行任何预测只是一味的追赶源语发言，那么译员可供使用的加工能力就无法协调分配，译员很快就会疲劳，造成信息错漏，最终影响产出效果。有观察指出，作为最常使用的同传技巧，预测的出现频率高达 85 秒 / 次甚至更高（Van Besien, 1999）。

预测也是英汉语言差异对同传的要求。预测在源语与译语结构差异较大时最为有用，面对结构差异如此大的语言组合，预测技巧的使用不仅可以减少短时记忆负荷，而且可以避免为听完全部信息而出现较长的无声停顿或信息遗漏，从而保持译语的流畅性，同时将更多的精力分配到译语产出上。

译员使用预测技巧的依据是语言信息（linguistic information）与非语言信息（extra-linguistic information），相应的预测也可以分为语言预测（linguistic anticipation）与言外预测（extra-linguistic anticipation）。

语言预测即以词语、短语组合等语言单位为线索进行的预测。

1）词语和固定搭配：各种词性的词语（名词、动词、代词、冠词、介词、连词、形容词、副词，等等）或词组的搭配基本是固定的，因此这些固定搭配可以作为预测的依据。例如：

- The ① *success of Hong Kong's* small-and-medium-sized enterprises ② *in world trade over the past 40 years* has been the ③ *backbone of our economy.*
  香港中小企业过去四十年在世界贸易领域的成功是我们经济发展的支柱。
- There is an urgent ④ *need to improve* public transportation efficiency.
  当务之急是提高公共交通的效率。
- Globalization ⑤ *rests on* a remarkable revolution ⑥ *in information technology.*
  全球化的支柱是伟大的信息技术革命。
- 中国政府一贯主张柬埔寨⑦**问题应该在**联大有关决议和关于柬埔寨问题国际会议宣言的基础上**求得解决**。
  Chinese government has always maintained that the Cambodian problem should be addressed based on the relevant UN resolutions and the declaration of international conference.

分析：①、③处名词 +of/for/in 介词以及④处名词 + 不定式是英语中的常见结构，因此在听到这些名词时可适当预测并加以等待；②、⑥处 in/over 或其他介词引导的状语对时间、地点等范围进行限定，这也是常见的预测线索。⑤处的动宾结构可帮助预测信息走向；⑦处的动词搭配"问题……得以解决"可以帮助预测 address 一词。此外，为了减轻记忆力负担，可将动词转换为名词，将源语主语转换为译语中主语的修饰成分，将整个句子变成开放式结构。

2) 语篇结构：英语中的连词短语可帮助译员判断信息的发展方向，汉语不用或少用连接成分，但是上下文和字里行间隐含的意思可以帮助译员把握逻辑走向。英语与汉语结构差异很大，虽然两种语言的基本句式都是主+谓+（宾）结构，但各有偏向：英语倾向于先出句子主干结构再出状语，而汉语中的目的状语一般置于谓语之前，突出主题；英语中定语如果太长，一般后置，而汉语中的定语不论长短都放在前面，因此，对汉语状语及长定语结构的处理通常少不了预测。例如：

- We will cooperate ⑧ *as long as* we are notified on time.
  只要及时告知，我们就会合作。
- 刚才，我同布什总统⑨**就中美关系及共同关心的国际和地区问题**，深入交换了意见，达成了许多重要共识。
  Just now, President Bush and I have concluded an in-depth exchange of view and reached a broad and important agreement on China-US relations and regional and international issues of mutual interest.

分析：⑧处的连词短语可以帮助预测并把握条件关系；⑨处的"就……问题"短语中的"就"字可帮助预测表示问题、事物的方向，而整个短语作为状语成分又可帮助预测后面谓语成分的内容。

非语言预测即所有语言预测之外的预测行为，通常可以分为场合预测和话题预测。场合预测指译员依据口译场合各类信息，如发言人和/或嘉宾身份、行业背景、职务、大会主题等来进行预测。对于经验丰富的译员而言，这些看似无关紧要的信息对于把握发言人的态度、看法、发言的基调和口吻起着非常关键的作用。话题预测，指根据口译任务类型、文体特征（致词类、介绍类、叙事类文体）等信息进行的预测，话题预测的有效与成功也离不开译员的临场经验和言外知识。

8. 语气强弱

语气的加强或弱化是口头交际独有的交际手段，同传中也很常见。语气强弱技巧的运用分为两种情况，一种是为了传达发言人的语气、意图等言外信息，另一种是用于处理源语中难以处理的结构，在保留源语结构的基础上，通过语气的强调或弱化来实现交际目的。例如：

- We are very grateful to you for your effort to *come all the way from China* to present this document to us.

我们非常感谢您所做的努力，**专程从中国赶来**向我们介绍这份文件。
此处译员采取了语气加强技巧，忠实的传达了发言人的感情色彩。

- 我们国家人均的能源、水资源、土地资源的供应都是严重不足的。特别是在过去，经过多年的经济发展以后，我们面临着越来越紧迫的资源问题和环境问题。

  In terms of per capita energy, water and land supply, we face *severe shortage* in our country. After years of economic development, we are facing increasingly urgent energy issues and environment issues.

加强语气结合信息重组，在完整传达信息的同时也传递了发言的语气色彩。

- It is *a distinct honor* for me to be here today, *especially at Shunde Polytechnic* for two reasons.

  非常荣幸今天能来到这里，**来到顺德职业技术学院**。我来的原因有两个。

加强语气的处理手法可以避免调整译语结构带来的额外记忆负荷，按照源语结构采用强调加增补的方式酌情调整，使译语更加准确、清楚。

- 当今世界**正处在大**变革大调整之中。和平与发展**仍然是**时代主题，求和平、谋发展、促合作**已经成为不可阻挡的时代潮流**。

  The world today *is undergoing tremendous* changes and adjustments. Peace and development remain the main themes of the present era, and pursuit of peace, development and cooperation *has become an irresistible trend of the times.*

顺句驱动时，通过加强语气来传达源语的情感色彩。

第二部分　案例讲解

The following passages are from the practice materials for this unit. Sight interpret them into the target language.

Passage 1

今年是中国改革开放 30 周年。30 年的改革开放（1）使中国经济与世界经济（2）以前所未有的深度和广度（3）紧密地联系在一起。中国已经成为世界第三大、亚洲第一大进口市场，正在日益深入地融入全球化进程。

▼ 技能提示

（1）本句是中文发言中常见的简单结构长句，状语前置，动词的后半部分到句末才出来。为减轻负担，可在原句中主语"30 年的改革开放"之后切分，将其处理为译语句子的时间状语，并将原句中的宾语转换为译语句子的主语，使口译产出更加顺畅、自然。

（2）、（3）处的语序在译语中应按照译语习惯酌情调整，即使用信息重构技巧。

▼ 参考译文

This year marks the 30th anniversary of China's reform and opening-up. After thirty years of reform and opening-up, China's economy has been connected with that of the world in an unprecedented way in terms of both depth and extent. China now is the third largest importer in the world and the largest one in Asia. China has been increasingly and deeply integrated into the process of globalization.

Passage 2

The first reduction (1) for Thailand started in 2003, and was for tariff lines that were parts of the Early Harvest Program which was a result (2) of the Framework Agreement on Comprehensive Economic Cooperation Between ASEAN and China.

▼ 技能提示

（1）如按照原文结构，可译为"泰国首次降税始于2003年"，但略显翻译腔，故可将 reduction 一词转换为动词。

（2）此处又是英文中常见的名词或相当于名词的成分，汉语中也可酌情转换为动词，更符合汉语的表达习惯。在转换时要注意适度等待及信息重构。

▼ 参考译文

泰国于2003年首次开始降税，涉及早收计划之下部分税目商品。而早收计划则源自东盟与中国全面经济合作框架性协议。

Passage 3

立足于"变"、善于捕捉先机（1）、与全球化的发展共进、不断有新作为，是新加坡在短短30年时间里从第三世界一步跨入第一世界的一条重要原因。同时，这（3）也是新加坡至今在世界上仍然能牢牢地保持着名列前茅的国际竞争力的关键所在（2）。

▼ 技能提示

（1）原文开头的两个短语看似无甚关联，如按字面直译，则无法很好的传达效果。可通过增补法进行结构补充或语义补充来明确意思。

（2）汉语中"牢牢"等叠字、"关键所在"等四字格词语十分常见，因此遇到这些内容时可酌情简约，以传意为主。

（3）第一句的处理除增补外还使用了长句切分、信息重构和转换的技巧，为了使上下文衔接更为紧密，此处可以加入总结词 this Singapore-unique feature，避免结果过于松散。

▼ 参考译文

With a change-oriented mindset, Singapore is always good at discerning the earliest unnoticeable sign of the change in the world and quick in grasping the earliest opportunity resulting from it. In this way, Singapore has been successful in making continuous fresh progress, one after another, riding on the waves of globalization. This Singapore-unique feature has played a crucial role in bringing Singapore from the Third World into the First World in one big stride just within a short phase of no more than three decades. This is also the key factor for Singapore to firmly maintain its global cutting-edge competitiveness till today.

Passage 4

Protectionism deepened the economic recession of the 1930s (1). There may be a case for transitional protections to help infant industries grow—but protectionism designed to give established industries time to adjust is rarely effective (2). It is understandable that producers should lobby for it (3), but when help is offered to producers (4) it often comes at the expense of consumers, usually the poorest. It is hardly a sustainable policy.

▼ 技能提示

（1）此处可按照汉语习惯调整信息顺序并转换词语和句子成分。

（2）原句中定语后置，口译时可切分并重构。

（3）按照汉语习惯，调整了源语中 it 从句中成分的顺序。

（4）同（2），在此处切分以后将信息有机粘连起来。除重构信息外，此句还可辅助运用加强语气的技巧。

▼ 参考译文

保护主义加剧了上世纪30年代的经济衰退。也许可以采取一种过渡性质的保护主义帮助幼稚产业成长，但为了给成熟行业足够时间自我调整而施行保护主义，往往不太奏效。生产者四处游说支持保护主义是可以理解的，但生产者获得帮助时，通常由消费者来承担其成本，通常是最贫困的消费者。因此，很难说这是个持续性的政策。

Passage 5

同时，我们也积极鼓励广东的企业利用马来西亚的市场与资源，来马来西亚投资兴业，特别是鼓励优势企业投资马来西亚的制造业、交通、通讯等领域（1），积极（2）参与电力、能源、矿产、工程承包与劳务合作等方面（3）的深度开发与合作。

▽ **技能提示**

(1)、(3) 处列举项信息密集出现，因此译员可酌情将较多的列举项进行简化概括。

(2) "参与开发 / 合作"这一动宾结构中插入了较长的定语，因此可大胆预测，适时调整。

▽ **参考译文**

We will also encourage more Guangdong businesses to utilize Malaysian markets and resources for investment and business here, encourage those with advantages to invest in such areas as manufacturing, communications, telecommunications and others and encourage them to actively participate in in-depth exploration and cooperation in electricity, energy, minerals, project contracting, labor services and other areas.

Passage 6

Now first of all, I'm just going to briefly touch upon the trade relation (1) between our two countries. Thailand and China have a long and cordial trade relations. Trade between the two nations have increased steadily (2) over the recent history, especially after the implementation of ACFTA.

▽ **技能提示**

(1) 在听到 between 时可放慢语速、稍作等待，听到 our two countries 之后迅速产出"两国之间"这一定语成分。

(2) 听到 over 时可预测其为时间状语，因此稍作等待，将时间状语听全以后迅速译出。

▽ **参考译文**

首先，我想给大家简要介绍一下（等一拍）我们两国之间双边贸易的情况。泰中两国拥有悠久、真挚的贸易关系，双边贸易（等一拍）近年来稳步增长，尤其是在实施中国东盟自由贸易区之后。

Passage 7

我坚信，广东作为中国改革开放 (1) 的先行省区，将会在更深入的国际合作进程中，走出一条 (2) 符合广东的新的发展需要和顺应全球化发展大势的科学发展之路。

▽ **技能提示**

(1) 有经验的译员一听到"广东"、"改革开放"等关键词，便可立即从长时记忆中调出相关的信息：先锋、先行者……等与"敢为天下先"相关的内容。此处的预测属于言外预测。

(2) 汉语中的词类搭配使我们在听到"走出一条"这四个字时便可立即

推断出后面的信息应与"道路"有关。因此，译员可以果断的放弃等待策略，大胆先出"道路"一词。此处的预测属于以词语搭配为线索的语言预测。

▼ **参考译文**

I firmly believe that Guangdong, as a pioneer province in China's reform and opening-up, will blaze, in the process of further and deepening international cooperation, a trail of scientific development, which will not only serve the needs of Guangdong's new development agenda but also be in tide with the momentum of globalization.

Passage 8

Over the next couple of days you will be assessing the introduction of Sustainability Impact Assessments (1) into trade policy. The aim of this new system was that it should lead to better policies and a broader and shared understanding of the economic, social and environmental impact (2) of our action – (3) not just on us, but for our children and grandchildren.

▼ **技能提示**

（1）由于语言结构差异导致汉语中习惯前置的限定成分在英语的句末才出现，故可因地制宜，在此处使用加强语气的技巧。

（2）适当等待并加以信息重组。

（3）同（1），可同时加以重复。

▼ **参考译文**

在接下来的几天里，各位将要评价可持续影响评估体系的使用效果，在贸易政策方面。这一新体系的目的是，它应能够带来更好的政策，并使更多的人了解（等一拍）我们的行为对经济、社会和环境的影响，了解这些行为对我们自己和子孙后代的影响。

第三部分　词汇拓展

汉译英

保持双边贸易平衡	balance the two-way trade
保税区	bonded area
财政盈余（赤字）	budget surplus (deficit)
产业结构	industrial structure
产业政策	industrial policy
创汇型企业	foreign exchange-earning enterprise
对外经济贸易	foreign economic relations and trade

工程承包	project contracting
公开招标	call for bid
广东省农垦集团公司	Guangdong Agribusiness Group Corporation
广东省广新外贸集团	Guangdong Foreign Trade Group
国产化	percentage of home-made parts
国民经济	national economy
国民经济的支柱	mainstay of the national economy
国民收入	national income
海洋捕捞	sea fishing
技术、智力、资本密集型	technology, knowledge or capital intensive
减免税收	tax reduction and exemption
经济杠杆	economic levers
经济过热	overheated economy
经济效益	economic performance/returns
经济指标	economic indicators
科研成果产业化	industrialization of research findings
劳务合作	labor services cooperation
片面追求发展速度	seek an unduly high growth rate
沙捞越	Salawak
社会总产值	total product of society
深加工	intensive processing
生产力	productive force
生产资料	capital goods
实际利用外资	foreign investment in actual use
实行全方位开放	practice multi-directional opening
市场疲软	market slump
外贸出口总额	gross foreign export value
中国广东－新加坡经济技术贸易合作交流会	China Guangdong-Singapore Business Conference

英译汉

agricultural protectionism	农业保护主义
aid for trade	促贸援助
bonded warehouse	保税仓库
bulk sale	整批销售，趸售

cash sale	现货
certificate of origin	原产地证明
China-ASEAN Free Trade Area	中国－东盟自由贸易区
comparative advantage	比较优势
condemned goods	没收货物
Council for Trade in Goods	货币贸易理事会
customs clearance	通关
customs liquidation	清关
Doha Development Agenda (DDA)	多哈发展议程
dealer	经销商
Department of Trade Negotiations, the Ministry of Commerce of Thailand	泰国商务部贸易谈判厅
distribution channels	销售渠道
dumping profit margin	倾销差价，倾销幅度
Early Harvest Program (EHP)	早期收获计划
European Free Trade Association	欧洲自由贸易联盟
favorable balance of trade	贸易顺差
fluctuate in line with market conditions	随行就市
free market capitalism	自由市场资本主义
import / export license	进口／出口许可证
inland / home/ domestic trade	国内贸易
International Monetary Fund	国际货币基金组织
marine bills of lading	海运提单
mediation of dispute	商业纠纷调解
middleman	中间商，经纪人
normal track	正常渠道
North American Free Trade Area	北美自由贸易区
partial shipment	分装
Preference Erosion	特惠侵蚀
progressive liberalization	逐步自由化
purchase	购买，进货
Regional Trade Arrangement (RTA)	区域贸易安排
retail	零售
sensitive track	敏感渠道
shipping order	托运单

special preferences	优惠关税
stock	存货，库存
sustainability impact assessment	永续性影响评估
tariff barrier	关税壁垒
tariff line	税目
tariff reduction	关税减让
tax rebate	出口退税
trade commissioner	贸易委员
trade consultation	贸易磋商
trade partner	贸易伙伴
transit trade	转口贸易
unfair competition	不合理竞争
unfavorable balance of trade	贸易逆差
United Nations Conference on Trade and Development	联合国贸易与发展大会
wholesale	批发

第四部分 同传实战

 Listen to the following four speeches and interpret them into the target language using the skills introduced in this unit.

Text 1

尊敬的汪洋书记，尊敬的林瑞生部长，蔡天宝会长，各位嘉宾，女士们、先生们：

上午好！首先（谢谢大家），我对 2008 中国广东－新加坡经济技术贸易合作交流会的成功举办表示最热烈的祝贺！

今年是中国改革开放 30 周年。30 年的改革开放使中国经济与世界经济以前所未有的深度和广度紧密地联系在一起。中国已经成为世界第三大、亚洲第一大进口市场，正在日益深入地融入全球化进程。

30 年来，广东始终走在中国改革开放的前列。广东经济总量已占全国的 1/8，是中国第一经济大省。在对外贸易方面，广东省的贸易额就占了全国贸易总额的将近 1/3。2007 年，广东的 GDP 总额已经达到了 4199 亿美元。以此为基础，广东现在在新的历史起点上，开始了新的征程。我坚信，广东作为中国改革开放的先行省区，将会在更深入的国际合作进程中，走出一条符合广东的新的发展需要和顺应全球化发展大势的科学发展之路。

新加坡是东盟中的发达成员,是本地区发展最快和唯一迈入发达国家行列的国家。立足于"变"、善于捕捉先机、与全球化的发展共进、不断有新作为,是新加坡在短短三十年时间里从第三世界一步跨入第一世界的一条重要原因。同时,这也是新加坡至今在世界上仍然能牢牢地保持着名列前茅的国际竞争力的关键所在。

新加坡也是中国改革开放的热情支持者和积极参与者。无论是在整个中国还是广东省,新加坡的贸易与投资额都是位于前列的。汪洋书记亲自率团来访新加坡并在访问期间出席这场中国广东－新加坡经济技术贸易合作交流会,既为广东更好地借鉴新加坡与时俱进的发展经验,也为新加坡各界朋友更及时地了解广东的最新发展态势从而共同寻求新的合作机遇提供了一个难得的机遇和机会。我相信,两地无限的商机将通过彼此的交流进一步变为合作双赢的现实。在全球化深入发展的今天,互利合作的重要性是无论怎样强调也不为过的。

中新两国关系全面强劲的发展为广东与新加坡深入而富有成效的合作提供了强有力的后盾与保障。自 1990 年两国建交以来,中新合作注重与各自的发展战略相结合,走出了一条务实高效、开拓创新的合作道路,实现了互利双赢,成为一对最具实质内容的双边关系之一。新加坡参加中国地方发展是中新两国政府确定的一大重点合作领域。相信在两国政府的积极支持下,广东与新加坡的深入合作不仅会为中新高效务实的合作增添新的活力与内容,也将会为深化中国与东盟的合作做出积极的贡献。

最后,预祝交流会取得丰硕的成果,也祝贺汪洋和汪洋同志率领的代表团访问成功,谢谢大家!

(2008 年 9 月 16 日,中国驻新加坡大使张小康在"中国广东－新加坡经济技术贸易合作交流会"上的发言全文)

Text 2

I welcome you all to this Conference. In particular, I would like to welcome Minister Christine Lagarde and all the other speakers.

Over the next couple of days you will be assessing the introduction of Sustainability Impact Assessments into trade policy. The aim of this new system was that it should lead to better policies and a broader and shared understanding of the economic, social and environmental impact of our action — not just on us, but for our children and grandchildren.

Have we managed to do this? Have we succeeded in improving the way the European Union shapes its trade policies and objectives? And have we drawn on better analysis to deliver agreements that work for Europe and for our partners around the globe?

I look forward to reading the results of your assessment. Because these questions matter. In my period as Trade Commissioner I have become firmly convinced of the following. Let me share seven observations with you.

First, for the problems of trade policy there are no simple textbook answers. Free market ideologues, even might I add NGO ideologues, need more than a little humility before they lay down the law on these complex questions. I feel this every time I am told by a neo liberal economist that agricultural protectionism is what stands in the way of making poverty history, or by an NGO activist that negotiating better access for industrial goods and services in developing country markets is bound to result in devastating economic and social consequences. The truth is that in virtually every case, it depends on the circumstances.

Second observation, there is no automatic rule that trade liberalisation will lead to greater economic growth, never mind long term sustainability. It can certainly lead to acute short-term adjustment costs as I've seen in my mandate among textile producers and leather shoe manufacturers, not to mention Mauritian sugar growers and Caribbean banana producers. Whether the short-term pain is balanced by a long-term gain depends on many different factors such as the capacity of existing businesses to move up market or a region to integrate and establish new sources of comparative advantage. In ideal circumstances this leads to the creation of sustainable jobs which make use of more sustainable resources — but there is no economic law that guarantees this happy outcome.

On the other hand, third, the history of protectionist policies suggests that these policies are a dead end. Any short-term advantages lead to an erosion of economic strength. Protectionism deepened the economic recession of the 1930s. There may be a case for transitional protections to help infant industries grow — but protectionism designed to give established industries time to adjust is rarely effective. It is understandable that producers should lobby for it, but when help is offered to producers it often comes at the expense of consumers, usually the poorest. It is hardly a sustainable policy.

Here in Europe we have been distracted in recent weeks by a debate about protectionism. Holding shut the doors of international commerce would not be in our interests. It would not be in the interests of our consumers or businesses and it would certainly not deliver new and lasting opportunities for our partners around the world to grow and prosper, from which we would benefit in time.

Fourth, even worse are autarchic strategies for forcing countries on the path of economic progress. These had a disastrous record in the 20th century. I accept of course that it is perfectly legitimate to criticise free market capitalism for the damage it can cause to the environment. One has only to think of the destruction of rain forest in Indonesia or Brazil driven by powerful profit incentives and the unquenchable appetites of consumers in richer parts of the world. I feel that, for all the seriousness of the problems, the market can be made to work for sustainable development through changes in incentives. Europe is, I believe, tentatively showing the way, for example through our emissions trading scheme that has the potential to be a major benefit in tackling global warming.

So, fifth, my observation is under the right conditions of what I call progressive liberalisation, trade can make a huge difference to economic development. That means combining better opportunities to trade through lowering trade barriers with increasing capacities to trade as a result of good governance, assured property rights and a stable legal system, and modern efficient infrastructures.

Sixth observation, we must face up to the consequences of changing production and consumption patterns in the global economy. Of course people affected in Europe need help to adjust to these changes. But if we react positively rather then defensively, we win the chance to shape globalisation, rather than being passively shaped by it. We should also acknowledge that European businesses have significantly contributed to the process of change by relocating production to Asia or elsewhere in many sectors. I sincerely hope that their sense of corporate social responsibility means they carry with them European standards and our strong tradition of social justice. We have influence and leverage here and we should exercise it.

Seventh, we should be committed multilateralists — and not just in pressing for market liberalization. We should be determined about our efforts to strengthen international cooperation and rule-making on trade and environment. This should lead to a more lasting global consensus on core social and environmental standards.

So, those are some basic thoughts. It is more than welcome that this conference comes as the current multilateral trade round, the Doha Development Round, reaches its critical and final stage. Doha can and must make a contribution to development and to making poverty history.

A 1% increase in Africa's share of world trade would deliver more development every year than the continent currently receives all together in aid. Through progressive liberalisation that takes into account the appropriate level of liberalization that different developing countries can bear, effective trade related assistance and aid can be turned from a hand out into a hand up. This is why Doha is still worth fighting for.

From the start of my time as European Trade Commissioner it has been clear that building an agreement in the trade talks means building a consensus — among WTO members of course, but more broadly by reaching out to civil society to show and explain the long-term benefits that such a deal will offer. Civil society and public opinion today play a more crucial role than in any previous multilateral negotiation. And I am happy that this is the case. I believe in transparent rule-making and accountability of trade negotiators to the general public.

So where do Sustainable Impact Assessments fit into this broader picture?

It has been a long road from the Rio World Summit in 1992 which first signalled sustainable development with its three aspects — economic, social, environmental — as a crucial element in sound policy-making. It was on the basis of the debate that started in Rio that back in 1999 my predecessor Pascal Lamy launched the first sustainability impact assessments — or SIAs.

At the time, in trade policy we were pace setters within the European Commission. It was only in summer 2001 that the Commission introduced a more generalised system to assess the economic, social and environmental impacts of its internal policies as part of the Union's overall strategy for sustainable development. Today, these ideas are commonplace. Back in 1999 they were ground-breaking.

By the end of the 1990s it became clear that trade negotiations could no longer be pursued by trade elites behind closed doors on the basis of a simple assumption that trade liberalisation was good for everyone.

In conclusion, let me say, you have an interesting series of debates ahead of you and I am grateful for your participation. I wish you every success, and hope that your work will contribute to helping us improve further the way we shape our policies and negotiating goals.

This is how we can achieve the outcome we seek: a Round which delivers development; a Round that will offer us a positive response to the challenges of globalisation; and a Round that offers new trading opportunities and therefore higher living standards for all. Thank you very much.

(Excerpted text of speech by EU Trade Commissioner Peter Mandelson at the Stocktaking Conference on Trade Sustainability Impact Assessments in Brussels on March 21, 2006)

Text 3

我们高兴地看到,近年来广东与马来西亚经贸合作规模不断扩大,合作领域不断拓宽。马来西亚是广东在东盟国家中进出口贸易最大的国家。2007年双方进出口贸易额达到了144.8亿美元,比上年增长了28%,占中国与马来西亚贸易总额的31.2%。其中,广东进口占到80%,广东与马来西亚贸易的逆差是77亿美元。

与此同时,广东与马来西亚的相互投资也日趋活跃。我刚才在下面看了一下今天马上要上台签署的一些协议额,其中到马来西亚来投资的额度已经超过了1亿美元。我相信下一步,今天的大会开过以后你们还要进行洽谈,洽谈以后我相信还会有一些成果。马来西亚众多的企业也到广东投资并获得了良好的收益,越来越多的广东企业到马来西亚投资兴业。如,华为技术有限公司在马来西亚就设立了地区性的总部,广东省农垦集团公司开展与沙捞越的橡胶资源开发,也取得了积极的成效,今天他们还要在这里签署进一步加大投资的协议。我衷心的希望广东的企业加大对马来西亚的投资力度,更好地造福两国人民。

女士们、先生们,朋友们!

展望新时期广东与马来西亚的合作,商机无限,前景无限。马来西亚是亚洲地区令人瞩目的新兴工业国,近年来经济持续、快速发展,电子业、制造业、建筑业和服务业发展迅速,石油、矿产、棕榈油和橡胶等自然资源丰富,对外贸易和旅游业比较发达,发展潜力巨大。广东是中国乃至世界上的重要的制造业基地,电子、家电、轻工、纺织等一批企业和品牌在国际市场上享有盛誉,金融、物流和会展等现代服务业发展迅速。广东与马来西亚在资源禀赋、产业结构和区位条件等方面各具特色,互补性很强,相信会在更大规模、更高层次上进行合作,也必将促进双方经济共同繁荣、共同发展。

站在新的历史起点,我们真诚地希望在互惠互利的原则下,与马来西亚加强以下几个方面的合作:一是继续扩大双边贸易。马来西亚是广东在东盟的最大贸易伙伴,也是广东在东盟各国最大的进口来源地。目前,广东从马来西亚进口的主要产品是集成电路、二极管、半导体等高技术产品和食用植物油、塑料等,其中集成电路的进口接近一半。广东出口马来西亚的产品主要是纺织服装、家具、鞋类、钢材和陶瓷等产品,其中服装的出口占到20%左右。近两年来,广东与马来西亚的贸易额保持良好的势头,年均增长率超过了23%,如果抓住东盟自由贸易区加快建设的机遇,完全有可能实现到2010年双方贸易额比现在翻一番的目标,达到290亿美元。广东继续扩大进口马来西亚产品,尤其是马来西亚具有比较优势的产品。

二是扩大投资领域的合作。截至去年底,广东吸收马来西亚的直接投资项目累计573宗,实际投资5.35亿美元,投资领域主要集中在电子、旅游等产业。目前广东正在进行产业结构的调整,全力建设包括先进制造业、现代服务业和高技术产业在内的现代产业体系,除此之外,我们还将加大电力、能源、高速公路、城际快速轨道交通等重大基础设施和基础产业的建设。今后,上述领域的5年内投资将超过1500亿美元,涉及200多个重点项目。马来西亚在电子、汽车、机械制造等产业方面积累了比较先进的技术、人才和经验,我们热忱的欢迎马来西亚企业积极参与广东现代产业体系和基础产业、基础设施的建设。同时,我们也积极鼓励广东的企业利用马来西亚的市场与资源,来马来西亚投资兴业,特别是鼓励优势企业投资马来西亚的制造业、交通、通讯等领域,积极参与电力、能源、矿产、工程承包与劳务合作等方面的深度开发与合作。

三是加强旅游领域的合作。我们将积极鼓励广东游客来马来西亚旅游,加大推介马来西亚旅游产品的力度,加强与马来西亚旅游企业的合作。同时欢迎马来西亚的朋友们到广东旅游、观光。

四是加强农业和渔业领域的合作。马来西亚的热带农业和经济作物资源丰富,而广东是棕榈油、天然橡胶、原木等产品的消耗大省。加强双方农业合作大有可为。如本次洽谈会上,广东农垦集团公司将再次投资8000万美元与马来西亚企业合作种植和加工橡胶;广新集团也将签订协议,进口5000万美元的木材。马来西亚海洋渔业资源丰富,而广东拥有比较先进的海洋捕捞和深加工技术,双方可以优势互补,合作开发海洋渔业资源等。

五是建立经贸合作的对话机制,以这次经贸洽谈会的举办为契机,在广东省与马来西亚有关政府部门之间建立省部经贸合作的对话机制,协调双方在投资、经贸合作中的有关事项,全面推进双方经贸关系不断发展。我可以欣喜的告诉大家,在刚才我和慕尤丁部长的会谈中,我们对此已经形成了共识,这个会谈机制将很快会得以建立。

女士们、先生们、朋友们,我和我的代表团来到马来西亚短短两天时间,实际上还不到24个小时。我们既感受到了马来西亚人民与广东人民的友好情谊,也进一步坚定了与马来西亚政府和企业开展经贸合作的决心和信心。昨天,我们刚刚踏上马来西亚国土,巴达维首相阁下就接见了我们代表团的成员,刚才我又与副首相纳吉布阁下、国际贸易与工业部长慕尤丁先生举行了会谈,我们在深化和拓展广东与马来西亚经贸各个领域合作的问题上取得了高度的共识,我们提出的一些想法也得到了他们的积极回应,这为我们双方的合作能够顺利推进并取得成就提供了坚实的保障。

我相信,通过今天的经贸洽谈活动,一定会增进友谊与了解,在双方政府、工商企业界、金融界以及社会各界的共同努力下,广东与马来西亚的经济贸易合作的明天一定会更加美好!

最后，我衷心祝愿"2008 中国广东—马来西亚经贸合作洽谈会"圆满成功，祝愿中马友好合作关系的明天更美好，祝愿中马人民的友谊世代相传！

谢谢大家！

（2008 年 9 月 12 日，广东省委书记汪洋在"2008 中国广东－马来西亚经贸合作洽谈会"上的发言节选）

Text 4

Thank you. Good morning ladies and gentlemen, I'm trade technical officer from the Department of Trade Negotiations, the Ministry of Commerce of Thailand. Today I'm going to introduce you to Thailand's tariff reduction under this ASEAN-China FTA, and update you on our current status.

Now first of all, I'm just going to briefly touch upon the trade relation between our two countries. Thailand and China have a long and cordial trade relations. Trade between the two nations have increased steadily over the recent history, especially after the implementation of ACFTA. From the figure you can see here, from 2005 to 2008, trade value between Thailand and China has increased by more than 78% from 20 billion dollars to 36 billion dollars in 2008. And our latest figure last year, China was Thailand's second largest trade partner and source of import as Thailand become more dependent on Chinese goods as a legitimate option and an alternative of other imports.

And here's a quick introduction to our tariff reductions. In the same case with my Indonesian colleague that has just presented, we are obliged to reduce our tariff under the ASEAN-China FTA modality. Thailand have been implementing the ACFTA for more than 5 years now, and have seen a good growth as the results.

Tariff reductions under ACFTA has been divided into three tracks. The first reduction for Thailand started in 2003, and was for tariff lines that were parts of the Early harvest program which was a result of the Framework Agreement on Comprehensive Economic Cooperation between ASEAN and China. Later reductions were the result of the Trade in Goods or the TIG agreement which came into effect in 2005 and set up for gradual reductions for 5121 tariff lines.

Now, as mentioned in the previous slide, the EHP in which reductions started in January 2004, consisting of unprocessed agricultural goods, was the first group of products set for tariff reductions under the ACFTA. With that said, for China and Thailand, our first reductions came in October 2003, When both parties agreed to accelerate 116 tariff lines consisting of Chapter 07 and 08 which are fresh fruits and vegetables. They were instantly reduced to zero percent in that year.

Now next in line is the Normal Track or NT in which 4770 lines were to be reduced accordingly.

The first step is at least 40% of all tariff lines in NT to be at the rate between zero and 5% by July 2005; next step is to increas that to 60% of all tariff lines to be at the rate between 0-5% by January 2007; and ultimately, all tariff lines in NT are to be eliminated by January 2010 except for those in the NT2 which shall be eliminated by January 2012.

Our sensitive track consists of 351 tariff lines. Those in the sensitive list are to be reduced to no more than 20% by 2012 and to no more than 5% in 2018. For the highly sensitive list, which will be reduced to no more than 50% by the year 2015.

I will move on to our… to Thailand's current status of tariff reductions. Here I show the actual number of tariff lines that were reduced in the ACFTA for Thailand. Last year, more than 90% of our tariff lines were under 10% and up to 59% were between 0 and 5%. Now, in the year 2009 the number of tariff lines between 0 and 5% has almost doubled from 2008. In the next slide, I will elaborate on how many lines have actually come down to zero.

Here you can see that although in the previous slide, I stated that approximately 60% were at the rate of 5% or lower in 2008, the number of tariff line that were actually at zero were only 203 lines which is a comparatively small number. Now in 2009—as you can see in the red column—more than 1700 lines are at zero, an increase of more than 8 folds just this year alone from last year, and Thailand will take another big leap as the number of tariff lines at zero will more than double in this year of 2010. Then finally in 2012, um… Thailand will be virtually tariff free. The reason why not all tariff lines will be at zero in 2012 is due to the rule of reciprocity, which means that we are unlikely to reduce those tariff lines that China puts into the Sensitive Track.

To further elaborate on the significance of tariff reductions in 2009 and 2010, here you see that in 2003, before the ACFTA came into effect, the average tariff rate for tariff lines under the Normal track was 12.93% and the highest tariff rate was a whopping 80%. In 2008, which is last year, the average tariff rate came down to 6.35% and a maximum rate down to 12%. And now in this year 2009, the average rate has come down to 2.79% and maximum rate at only 5%. Furthermore, in 2010, the average rate will be just 0.14% and highest rate to be 5% due to a certain number of products lines that belongs to the NT2, for which will be reduced to zero in 2012, and that brings us to a virtually tariff free Thailand under the ACFTA in 2012.

Now at present, we move on to the Form E: utilization rate of the certificate of origin. Here at present, the utilization of preferential rate, as you may see from this figure — the import from China under the ACFTA and the rate of 4.2% which is currently very small and seems insignificant. For import from China, this means that for Chinese exporters, 4.2% of all the goods that you export to Thailand enjoy preferential tariff rates under the ACFTA, now consider that your total export value of more than 20 billion US dollars in 2008 is not small. There are a lot of potential and opportunities to increase your profit margins. On the other hand, you can see from Thailand figures, as the percentage of total export to China at 10.44%, our percentage of utilization is only a little higher, Thai exporters are still not utilizing the full benefits of the ACFTA. Considering the small reductions in the past, there are reasons to consider skipping the hassles and not utilizing the FTA benefits, but with more than 1700 tariff lines currently at zero this year and will be 4290 lines to do the same for next year, it is time to reconsider and utilize the benefits that you are entitled to under ACFTA.

That's it for my presentation. For more information you can visit the website ThaiFTA. We have the relevant information on the website. Thank you.

(Full text of speech by Mr. Thananchon Rojkittikhun, Technical Officer of the Department of Trade Negotiations, Ministry of Commerce of Thailand, at China-ASEAN FTA Nanning Training Course on March 26, 2009)

第7单元 同声传译视译
Sight Interpreting

> **单元学习目标**
> 1. 掌握同声传译视译工作的难点与策略。
> 2. 熟悉金融这一口译主题的常用汉英术语和表达方式。
> 3. 能够完成基本的同步听译练习。

第一部分 同传技能

所谓视译,是指边阅读发言材料边将发言材料以口头形式翻译成目的语。同传中的视译不仅是同声传译的一种特殊工作形式——发言人宣读稿件的同时,同传译员边对照着手头同样的发言稿或其他相关的文件,边听发言,边做同传,也是从交替传译过渡到同声传译的核心训练方法。

外语学习者对视译并不陌生:我们在阅读外语报刊、书籍时将内容口译出来的做法就是视译。但这种只看文字、不听声音的情况与同传所处的场景有很大的不同。一般视译只需要对照文字材料进行口头翻译,唯一参照就是文字材料,而同传中的视译只能将发言稿或其他材料作为参考,译员不能完全依靠发言稿;一般视译对口译速度无限定,视译语速就是译员理解及产出的速度,而同传中的视译要受到发言人语速的限制,译员必须紧跟发言人,任务难度更高,且相比无稿同传任务类型增多;另外,一般视译没有同传视译现场压力的影响。

由于本书另有章节专门介绍同传视译这一特殊工作形式——带稿同传,故本章将着重介绍一般视译中双语转换的重难点及相应技巧。作为同声传译的核心训练方法,一般视译也必须遵循同传的原则,这样才能进一步接近同传的要求。

1. 视译:原则与单位

如前所述,视译也必须遵循同声传译的原则,即忠实、协调、释意、顺译和简约五大原则。在视译中,忠实和简约原则是就口译产出而言,即视译时要以材料内容为准进行准确、完整的传译,注意减少口头冗余成分,保持话语简洁;释意和顺译原则是就口译过程而言,即视译时不能仅停留在文字信息表层,要以传意为主,而顺译是指不要过多的调整甚至颠倒语序,以免造成错漏；协调原则是就精力分配而言，指译员应合理分配看稿、分析信息和口译产出的精力。

上述原则中，最基本、最重要的是释意原则和顺译原则。视译是一种特殊的口译形式，实际上是以口头的方式进行笔译。视译中，译员很容易完全受到文字信息的吸引，将思路仅仅停留在字、词等微观内容上，这样的做法最容易导致只见树木、不见森林，影响译员对视译材料的整体把握。因此，视译中的译员必须对释意原则更加敏感，避免过度关注字面信息而忽略了对意义的理解。

顺译原则是各种工作形式的同声传译都必须遵循的工作原则，视译也不例外。有的人认为，既然有了文字材料，就可以像做笔译一样大刀阔斧的调整信息顺序了。但在视译中，这是一种危险的做法：一是会延长信息处理所需的时间，减慢视译的速度，二是过于频繁的调整语序很可能会使译员在繁多的文字信息中顾此失彼、迷失方向。如果把经常调整语序的做法延续到带稿同传中，那很可能造成信息的失误、遗漏，反过来也给同传译员造成很大的心理压力，影响同传任务的进行。因此，视译中也要尽量做到顺句驱动，不要对语序进行过大的调整。

视译时有了文字参考资料，这在工作条件上比无稿同传要好了不少：无稿同传条件下，译员完全依赖发言人的信息产出来进行口译，而英汉两种语言在语序、结构、语法等方面的差异使得口译单位有时非常小，这时的译员必须时不时把长句切断，然后再想方设法连起来。从技术上讲这样做是非常必要的，但是就产出内容而言，有时翻译单位太小会使译语支离破碎，影响同传效果。视译则不同，视译时译员可通读文字信息，因此口译单位也可适当放长一些，使得产出更流畅、自然。

2. 视译：难点与策略

英语与汉语存在着许多语序相同的简单句，这种句子的转换遵循顺译原则即可。下面介绍英语中较特殊的语言现象及视译时可采取的做法。

1）英语中以语助词 it 和 there 引导的从句是汉语中没有的语言现象。这种句子的实际主语经常到句中或句末才出现，因此视译时应迅速把握逻辑主语。例如：

- We deem it necessary that theory goes hand in hand with practice.
  理论联系实际很重要。(调整语序、简约)
- There lived an old man at the foot of the mountain.
  一位老人住在山脚。(调整语序)

2）英语中存在大量后置的定、状语短语以及定、状语从句，而汉语则习惯将其前置。这种差异也提醒我们，遇到后置定语和状语短语以及定、状语从句时应酌情调整。例如：

- Access to higher education for poorer families with talented children is important for social stability and cultural development.

  让来自贫穷家庭的有才能的孩子接受高等教育对社会稳定和文化发展至关重要。（调整语序、成分转换）

- Let me lastly thank the people who have contributed to the building of this library.

  最后，我要感谢为图书馆的修建做出贡献的人们。（时间状语、定语从句前置）

- No one was there when I arrived.

  我到的时候，一个人也没有。（状语从句前置）

3) 英语中存在大量被动式，而汉语常用主动式。视译时可根据源语意图和汉语习惯选择保留被动或转为主动。例如：

- He went on to say that protein would probably be prepared chemically in another hundred years to come when the composition of protein became known.

  他接着说，再过一百年，当人们知道了蛋白质的成分之后，就可能化学合成蛋白质。（状语前置、被动转化为主动）

- It is rumored that he will soon be promoted as the general manager.

  小道消息称他很快会被提拔为总经理。（被动，强调施动者）

  小道消息称他很快会升为总经理。（主动，强调事实）

上述几点是视译中常见的调整语序的情况。这里给出的办法并不是唯一的，在操练中如果发现更好的译法也可以采用。出口成章是视译最理想的状态，虽然不能一蹴而就，但是通过练习还是可以不断接近甚至达到这一水平。如前所述，英语和汉语的巨大差异是视译的难点，因此在练习时，重点也应该放在对语言差异的分析和把握上，知道了如何视、视什么，才能译得好。

第二部分 案例讲解

The following passages are from the practice materials for this unit. Sight interpret them into the target language.

Passage 1

正值金秋的时节，今天，"中国－东盟投资合作基金"的推介会在美丽的南宁隆重（1）开幕。请允许我代表中国进出口银行对参加这次会议的海内外的来宾（2）表示衷心的感谢和热烈的欢迎！

▼ **技能提示**

(1) 汉语句子以非人称名词成分作为主语。看完后应可立即决定是保留原有主语（译文一）还是添加人称主语并将原有主语转换为译语的宾语修饰成分（译文二）。

(2) 英语中主语和谓语关系紧密，而汉语中的主语和谓语之间可以插入定语和状语。看到这一典型的汉语句子结构时，应迅速反应，决定不同句子成分在英语句子中的摆放顺序。

▼ **参考译文**

译文一：（添加人称主语，将源语的主语作为宾语的修饰成分）In this golden season of autumn, we gather here for the grand opening of the promotion conference on China-ASEAN Investment Cooperation Fund in the beautiful city of Nanning. Please allow me, on behalf of Export-Import Bank of China, to express to you all my sincere gratitude and warmest welcome!

译文二：（保留非人称主语，按照顺句驱动原则，以源语开头的时间状语做译语的主语）The golden season of autumn witnessed the grand opening of the promotion conference on China-ASEAN Investment Cooperation Fund in the beautiful city of Nanning. Please allow me, on behalf of Export-Import Bank of China, to express to you all my sincere gratitude and warmest welcome!

Passage 2

However, the global economy has only recently emerged from the worst of the crisis, and still has a long way to go (1) until it recovers fully. There are also major tasks ahead of us, including revitalizing the growth potential (2) that was damaged by the crisis, and generating sustainable and balanced growth.

▼ **技能提示**

(1) 如果不看稿只是听发言，在听到 still has a long way to go，然后才听到由 until 引导的时间状语，译员只能采取顺句驱动，将其译为："还有很长的路要走才能完全恢复"。而在视译状态下，则可调整语序，按照汉语习惯将 until 引导的内容提前。

(2) 同理，如果没有稿件辅助，在听到 that 引导的定语从句时，译员可能需要通过重复或强调来处理这一信息，而视译则允许译员按照汉语习惯将定语前置。

▼ **参考译文**

然而，全球经济只是刚刚走出了危机最严重的阶段，在全面复苏到来之前还有很长的路要走。我们也面临着许多重大任务，包括重振受危机严重影响的增长潜力以及促进可持续的平衡发展。

Passage 3

当前,我们的首要任务仍然是应对国际金融危机、推动世界经济健康复苏,(1)同时要坚定不移推进国际金融体系改革,在解决全球发展不平衡进程中(2)实现世界经济全面持续平衡发展。

▼ 技能提示

(1)处可断句,另起一句。

(2)"实现世界经济全面持续发展"是谓语成分,译成英文时注意顺序提前。

▼ 参考译文

At present, coping with the global financial crisis and fostering the healthy recovery of the world economy remains our top priority. Besides, it is necessary to press ahead unswervingly with the reform of the international financial system and to realize comprehensive, sustained and balanced growth of world economy while addressing global imbalanced development.

Passage 4

It occurred in financial market (1) much more generally. Furthermore, they would not have made these investments if they had rationally analyzed the basis for making them (2). (3)

▼ 技能提示

(1)地点状语,可提前。

(2)if引导的条件状语在汉语中常前置,因此视译时可果断调整语序。

(3)全句其他部分可顺译,并加以简约处理。

▼ 参考译文

这在金融市场上更为普遍。另外,投资者如果事先进行了理性分析,那就很可能不会做出这些投资了。

Passage 5

这是中国政府深化中国-东盟双方经贸合作的一项重要举措(1),也表明了我们对东盟市场的信心,对中国和东盟经济发展的信心。(2)

▼ 技能提示

(1)汉语偏好使用动词,源语三个小分句完全体现了这一特点。视译时,如能参照英语名词化的语言特征,则从形式上更能突出"举措"的重要性。

(2)原文采用了并列结构,照搬该结构译成英文则显得结构松散。可将第一分句做状语,将第二、三分句处理为主干成分,使译语结构上更加紧密。

▼ 参考译文

As an important measure made by Chinese government for the further of our cooperation, it is the symbol of our confidence in ASEAN market and in economic growth of our two sides.

第三部分　词汇拓展

汉译英

（基金）发起人	sponsor
保证金	margin
本金	principal
比较基准	benchmark
波动	volatility
不良贷款	non-performing loan
财富分配	wealth distribution
差额，差价	spread
长仓	long position
场外交易	over-the-counter (OTC)
成交量	volume
出口信贷	export credit
初次转换溢价	initial conversion premium
储备货币国家	reserve currency issuing countries
储蓄银行	savings bank
到期收益	yield to maturity
掉期	swap
对冲，套期保值	hedging
对冲基金	hedge fund
对外担保	international guarantee
（中国）对外援助贷款	Chinese government concessional loan
股本回报（率）	return on equity
股权投资	equity investment
股息	dividend
国际结算	international settlement
国库券	treasury bill

坏账	bad debt
货币掉期	currency swap
货币流通量	money in circulation
金融救援机制	financial rescue mechanism
金融信托公司	financial trust
尽职调查	due diligence
进口信贷	import credit
经济繁荣	economic boom
经济复苏	economic recovery
经济衰退	economic recession
经济萧条	economic depression
经济周期	economic cycle
经营利润	operating profit/margin
扩大内需、调整结构、促进增长、改善民生	to expand domestic demand, readjust structures, promote growth and improve people's livelihood
蓝筹股	blue chips
立项	project approval
利率掉期	interest rate swap
零和博弈	zero sum game
流动性	liquidity
路演	roadshow
蒙特雷共识	Monterrey Consensus
普遍接受的金融监管标准	generally accepted financial supervision standard
千年发展目标	Millennium Development Goals
首次公开发行	initial public offering (IPO)
私募股权基金	private equity fund
外国政府金融机构转贷款	onlending loans from foreign government and foreign financial institutions
优化资源配置	optimization of resource allocation
有资质的本地机构投资者	qualified domestic institutional investor (QDII)
有资质的境外机构投资者	qualified foreign institutional investor (QFII)
中国－东盟投资合作基金	China-ASEAN investment cooperation fund
中国进出口银行	Export-Import Bank of China

英译汉

aggregate demand	总需求
animal spirit	动物精神
arbitrage	套利
asset disposition	资产处置
balanced budget	平衡预算
bank holding company	银行持股公司
bank panic	银行恐慌
bank run	银行挤兑
borrow short	借短
capital adequacy requirement	资本充足率要求
capital expenditure	资本支出
certificate of deposit	存款单
commercial paper	商业票据
commission broker	佣金经纪人
convertibility	可兑换性
currency swap arrangement	货币互换安排
current account	经常账户
deposit insurance	存款保险
derivative	衍生产品
discount rate	贴现率
discount window	贴现窗口
Federal Deposit Insurance Corporation	联邦存款保险公司
financial intermediary	金融中介
financial packaging	财务包装
full employment	充分就业
insolvency	破产
instruments of monetary control	货币控制工具
Keynes	凯恩斯
lender of last resort	最后贷款人
leveraged buy-out, LBO	杠杆收购
leveraged loan	杠杆贷款
liabilities	债务
macroeconomics	宏观经济学
monetarist	货币主义者

monetary and fiscal policy	货币政策及财政政策
originator	（贷款）发放机构
Poverty Reduction and Growth Facility	（国际货币基金组织）减贫与增长贷款
price/earning ratio	市盈率
rating agency	评级机构
Scaling-up Renewable Energy Program	（世界银行）可再生能源规模扩大项目
securitization	证券化
shadowing banking system	影子银行系统
solvent	有偿债能力的
stockbroker	股票经纪人
transfer of funds	资金划拨
underlying securities	标的证券
Vulnerability Framework	（世界银行）脆弱评估架构

第四部分　同传实战

 Listen to the following four speeches and interpret them into the target language using the skills introduced in this unit.

Text 1

尊敬的陈武副主席，尊敬的各位来宾，女士们、先生们，同志们、朋友们：上午好！

正值金秋的时节，今天，"中国－东盟投资合作基金"的推介会在美丽的南宁隆重开幕。请允许我代表中国进出口银行对参加这次会议的海内外的来宾表示衷心的感谢和热烈的欢迎！

为进一步深化中国与东盟国家的经贸合作，今年2月，中国国务院决定设立"中国－东盟投资合作基金"，今年4月18日，温家宝总理在博鳌亚洲论坛年会上正式对外宣布。基金由中国进出口银行作为主发起人。在国务院各有关部门的支持和领导下，在社会各界的关心下，经过半年多的时间努力，现在基金的各项设立工作已经取得了实质性的进展，基金很快就会开始运作。

中国与东盟国家的经贸合作由来已久，目前正处于迈上新台阶的关键时期。长期以来，中国政府非常重视与东盟国家的经贸合作，在双方的共同努力下，双边贸易已经取得了显著成果，特别是近几年中国与东盟的经贸合作发展非常迅速，2004年与东盟签署了第一个中国与其他国家的自由贸易协定，2008年尽管受到国际金融危机的严重影响，中国与东盟的双边贸易额仍然达到了2311亿美元，比上年增长13.9%。中国与东盟已互为第三大和第四大贸易伙伴。

2008年以来，全球金融危机对中国和东盟的合作、发展带来了很大的冲击，更加凸显了我们双边贸易合作的重要性。多年来，美欧等发达国家一直是中国和东盟的主要出口市场。但在这次危机中，发达国家经济严重萎缩，购买力大幅度下降。在这样的外部冲击下，中国与东盟国家的经贸合作反而得到了加强，共同度过了这次艰难的时刻，目前正在从危机中得以恢复。从长远看，在世界经济区域化和全球化日益加深的背景下，中国与东盟国家迫切需要进一步加深双边的贸易合作，共同实现可持续的发展。

目前，中国与东盟自贸区的建设已经进入倒计时，明年将进入运行。它将成为世界第三大自由贸易区，将是拥有19亿消费者的大市场。可以说，中国－东盟的经贸合作正在处于一个新的发展的关键时期。

要深化中国－东盟的经贸合作，目前迫切需要加强直接投资，特别是基础设施领域的投资和建设。近年来，中国与东盟国家的贸易往来和人员交流等都呈良好的发展趋势，为进一步加深这些经贸合作，需要加大直接投资的力度，以优化资源的配置，更好地发挥各国的优势。基础设施的投资与建设是经济社会发展的前提条件，交通、电信等基础设施是商品流动、资本流动、人才流动的必要载体。只有基础设施先行，才能加速市场的统一，拓展经贸的发展机会。东南亚作为沟通亚洲、非洲、欧洲以及大洋洲的枢纽，地理条件十分优越。如果能尽快改善交通状况，推进泛亚铁路的建设，打通中国西南到东南亚的国际大通道，将极大地便利物资的交流、产业的转移以及资源和能源的开发，还可带动旅游等产业的发展，有利于形成新的经济增长点。随着中国－东盟自贸区的全面启动，更有必要加快双方基础设施互联互通的建设，以更好地满足中国和东盟人员和贸易的往来需要。

中国政府提出设立"中国－东盟投资合作基金"，用于推进中国－东盟基础设施及网络化建设，其目的就是要通过投资合作基金的引导和扶持，鼓励中国企业"走出去"到东盟进行重大项目的建设，帮助各国经济尽快从经济危机中得以恢复并实现可持续的发展。基金由中国进出口银行主发起，性质为政府指导下市场化运作的私募股权基金。总规模将达到100亿美元，一期的规模为10亿美元。基金一期主要投资于但不仅限于交通设施、公用设施、通讯网络、石油、天然气、矿产资源等。后续资金将从中国－东盟国家经济合作的实际出发，确定适当的投资方向和领域。

作为基金的主发起人，中国进出口银行有信心也有能力在推动中国－东盟经贸合作方面发挥更大的作用。进出口银行是一家执行国家政策、支持国际经济合作的国家银行。成立15年来，始终注重根据宏观形势发展的需要和自身业务范围和职能的调整。目前，进出口银行已经形成包括出口信贷、进口信贷、对外承包工程和境外投资贷款、股权投资业务、中国政府对外援助贷款、外国政府金融机构转贷款，以及对外担保、国际结算等在内的多种业务品种的发展格局。预计到本年底，进出口银行总资产将超过9000亿人民币，支持中国的企业与150多个国家开展经贸合作。多年来，中国进出口银行始终将发展中国家特别是周边发展中国家作为工作的重点，支持了一大批中国企业开拓国际市场，积累了丰富的服务于国际经济合作的经验，锻炼了一支高素质的专业队伍。由中国进出口银行作为"中国－东盟投资合作基金"的主发起人，就是要充分发挥我们的这些优势，把银行信贷业务与基金运作良好的结合起来，把基金管理好、运作好，为中国与东盟的经贸合作注入新的活力。

从国务院批准基金设立到现在，经过8个月的努力，在各界的支持下，我们到目前已经完成了基金的组建工作，基金的筹资工作已经接近尾声，马上就要正式注册，在香港注册设立。

女士们、先生们，朋友们，同志们，

在当前的国际经济形势下，中国－东盟经贸合作的迫切性凸显，面临的机遇前所未有。中国－东盟合作基金的成立，将为双方经贸合作提供了一个崭新的平台。这是中国政府深化中国－东盟双方经贸合作的一项重要举措，也表明了我们对东盟市场的信心，对中国和东盟经济发展的信心。我相信，在我们共同的努力下，基金必将在中国与东盟的经贸合作中发挥重大作用，中国与东盟历史悠久的经贸合作也必将迎来更加富有成果的明天！

最后，我预祝"中国－东盟投资基金"推介会开得圆满成功。谢谢大家！

（2009年10月21日，中国进出口银行董事长李若谷在中国－东盟投资合作基金说明会上的发言，根据录音整理）

Text 2

Honorable Managing Director Strauss-Kahn, Honorable President Zoellick, Mr. Chairman, and Distinguished Participants,

I would like to extend my sincere appreciation to the Turkish government and the citizens of Istanbul for their excellent work in organizing the IMF and World Bank Annual Meeting and the warm hospitality they have shown us. It is my great honor to be here representing (the Republic of) Korea.

Before I begin my official speech, I would like to deliver deepest sympathies of the Korean government to the people of Asian and the Pacific who have suffered so greatly from the destructive earthquakes and severe flooding.

Ladies and gentlemen,

We still remember the sense of dread and despair that hung over last year's Annual Meeting, due to the worst global economic crisis in recent memory. This year, however, we meet with hope, as the global economy begins to show signs of recovery. This is brought by the unprecedented international policy coordination led by the G20, and active support from the IMF and the World Bank.

However, the global economy has only recently emerged from the worst of the crisis, and still has a long way to go until it recovers fully. There are also major tasks ahead of us, including revitalizing the growth potential that was damaged by the crisis, and generating sustainable and balanced growth. At this juncture, I would like to make the following suggestions to overcome the crisis and ensure sustainable growth.

First, exit strategies need to be prepared, but they should be implemented when recovery becomes fully secured.

The premature implementation of exit strategies may impede the emerging recovery and cause the economy to fall into a double-dip recession. Too late an implementation may give rise to market uncertainties and bring about another bubble. In this regard, the strategies should be developed in a concerted manner based on internationally agreed principles, and we should recognize that the scale, timing and sequencing of implementation will vary across countries.

To this end, I call on the IMF to promptly establish the criteria for exit strategies, and come up with specific solutions to provide even-handed, candid and independent surveillance on member countries.

Second, sustainable and balanced economic growth should be pursued by our elaborated and coordinated efforts.

For the global economy to return to a pre-crisis level of trend growth, we have to reject protectionism and develop orderly policy coordination. Countries with a current account deficit should increase government and private savings while keeping the market open. Those with a current account surplus should take further actions to increase domestic demand and openness. To make these successful, it is essential that we expand the global safety net for developing and emerging economies, particularly vulnerable to external shocks. Specifically, currency swap arrangements and regional financial cooperation should continue to be pursued.

Along with these efforts, we need to engage in active promotion of green growth in order to secure a new economic growth engine. Green growth will not only improve living standards but also create new growth opportunities through the green conversion of the current energy and resource-based economy into a more environment-friendly one.

Korea laid out a new national vision of "Low-Carbon Green Growth", and plans to invest around two percent of GDP in the green growth sector annually. At the same time, Korea will increase support for developing countries by participating in the World Bank's Scaling-up Renewable Energy Program (SREP), and will do its part to enhance international cooperation for green growth.

Third, the IMF and the World Bank need to be reformed for effective response to fundamental changes in the international financial system.

It has been more than 60 years since the IMF and the World Bank were established under the Bretton Woods system. In the Asian tradition, 60 years are seen as a period for ending the old and beginning the new.

With the global crisis resulting in significant changes to the world economic order, the IMF and the World Bank need to improve credibility and legitimacy through reforms. In particular, the IMF needs to secure sufficient resources to respond to the economic crisis through a quota increase of at least 100 percent. Also, as agreed at the Pittsburgh G20 Summit, at least five percent of IMF quota shares should be realigned to developing and emerging economies.

The World Bank should also reflect countries' evolving economic weight in its share-holding realignment, which has not been carried out for a decade. In addition, the shareholding of member countries should be periodically reviewed.

Last but not least, I would like to emphasize continued interest and increased support to low-income countries.

Low-income countries are suffering tremendously from the economic crisis, even though they are not directly responsible for the crisis.

In advanced countries, the crisis raises the issues of unemployment and income reduction. In low-income countries, however, it threatens the livelihood of the people.

In this context, I welcome the IMF's recent decision to strengthen support measures for low-income countries and significantly increase the size of loans provided to them. I would like to encourage member countries to actively participate in the efforts by the IMF and the World Bank to increase financial resources for assisting low-income countries.

Korea will also take active part in the IMF's Poverty Reduction and Growth

Facility (PRGF) and the World Bank's Vulnerability Framework.

My fellow Governors and distinguished participants,

There is a saying that "One swallow does not make a summer".

We are beginning to see a glimmer of light in the global economy, which had been in a deep tunnel. To make this light grow brighter, "A Sense of Togetherness" we have built so far must be further enhanced.

I hope the IMF and the World Bank will play a central role in enhancing the global coordination under the spirit of the sense of togetherness.

As the Chair of the G20 in 2010, Korea will earnestly support the IMF and the World Bank in fulfilling their roles.

Thank you for your attention.

(Full text of the keynote speech by Mr. Jeung-Hyun Yoon, Minister of Strategy and Finance of Republic of Korea, at the 64th IMF World Bank Annual Meeting on October 6, 2009 in Istanbul)

Text 3

尊敬的奥巴马总统，各位同事：

很高兴来到匹兹堡参加二十国集团领导人第三次金融峰会。首先，我对奥巴马总统为本次峰会所作的精心准备和周到安排，表示衷心的感谢！

经过华盛顿和伦敦两次金融峰会，国际社会信心增强，金融市场趋于稳定，世界经济出现积极变化。同时，我们也清醒地看到，世界经济形势好转的基础并不牢固，不确定因素仍然很多，实现全面复苏将是缓慢和曲折的过程。当前，我们的首要任务仍然是应对国际金融危机、推动世界经济健康复苏，同时要坚定不移推进国际金融体系改革，在解决全球发展不平衡进程中实现世界经济全面持续平衡发展。

第一，坚定不移刺激经济增长。我们应该充分利用二十国集团这一平台，继续加强宏观经济政策协调，保持政策导向总体一致性、时效性、前瞻性。各国应该保持经济刺激方案力度，无论是发达国家还是发展中国家都应该采取更加扎实有效的举措，在促进消费、扩大内需上多下功夫。主要储备货币发行国要平衡和兼顾货币政策对国内经济和国际经济的影响，切实维护国际金融市场稳定。要坚决反对和抵制各种形式的保护主义，维护公正自由开放的全球贸易和投资体系，继续承诺不对商品、投资、服务设置新的限制措施，在锁定现有成果的基础上推动多哈回合谈判早日取得成功。我们应该大力推动国际新兴产业合作尤其是节能减排、环保、新能源等领域合作，积极培育世界经济新的增长点。我们应该大力加强国际科技合作，充分依靠科技进步增强世界经济增长内在动力。与此同时，我们应该对刺激措施可能产生的负面影响尤其是潜在通胀风险保持警惕。

第二，坚定不移推进国际金融体系改革。二十国集团领导人在前两次金融峰会上达成了推进国际金融体系改革的政治共识，这是我们向全世界作出的庄严承诺。现在，国际经济金融形势有所好转，但我们推进改革的决心不能减弱、目标不能降低。我们应该落实伦敦峰会确定的时间表和路线图，着力提高发展中国家代表性和发言权，不断推动改革取得实质性进展。我们应该完善国际金融机构现行决策程序和机制，推动各方更加广泛有效参与。我们应该推进国际金融监管体系改革，改革应该触及最根本的监管原则和目标，未来金融监管体系要简单易行、便于问责。我们应该加强金融监管合作，扩大金融监管覆盖面，尽快制订普遍接受的金融监管标准，高质量落实各项改革措施。

第三，坚定不移推动世界经济平衡发展。当前，国际社会十分关注全球经济失衡问题。失衡既表现为部分国家储蓄消费失衡、贸易收支失衡，更表现为世界财富分配失衡、资源拥有和消耗失衡、国际货币体系失衡。导致失衡的原因是复杂的、多方面的，既有经济全球化深入发展、国际产业分工转移、国际资本流动的因素，也同现行国际经济体系、主要经济体宏观经济政策、各国消费文化和生活方式密切相关。从根本上看，失衡根源是南北发展严重不平衡。只有广大发展中国家有效实现发展，世界经济复苏步伐才会坚实，世界经济增长才能持久。我们应该完善促进平衡发展的国际机制，支持联合国在解决发展问题方面更好发挥指导和协调作用，推动世界银行增加发展资源、增强减贫和发展职能，敦促国际货币基金组织建立快速有效的金融救援机制，优先向最不发达国家提供融资支持。我们应该加大形式多样的发展投入，二十国集团领导人峰会推动筹集的大量资金应该优先用于解决发展不平衡问题，发达国家应该认真落实蒙特雷共识，切实增加对发展中国家的援助规模，推动联合国千年发展目标的实现。我们应该高度重视技术合作对促进平衡发展的重要意义，降低人为技术转让壁垒，为广大发展中国家缩小发展差距创造条件，尤其要加强绿色技术领域合作，确保发展中国家用得上、用得起绿色技术，避免形成新的"绿色鸿沟"。我们应该着力转变经济发展方式，既要增强紧迫感、积极推进，又要区别情况、从实际出发，允许不同发展阶段的国家在转变经济发展方式过程中选择适合本国国情的路子和节奏，不能挤压发展中国家应有的发展空间。

各位同事！

中国高度重视经济社会全面协调可持续发展。我们坚持把扩大内需特别是消费需求作为应对国际金融危机冲击的基本立足点，积极调整内外需结构和投资消费结构，在经济发展中努力实现速度与结构、质量、效益相统一。

国际金融危机发生以来，中国推出一系列扩大内需、调整结构、促进增长、改善民生的政策措施，并取得初步成效。今年上半年，在外需严重萎缩的情况下，中国国内生产总值同比增长 7.1%。这表明中国通过扩大内需拉动经济增长的政策是有效的，中国经济增长为世界经济复苏作出了贡献。

长期以来，中国积极参加国际发展合作。国际金融危机发生后，中国在自身面临巨大困难和严峻挑战的形势下，仍然积极参加应对国际金融危机的国际合作。中国将继续本着负责任的态度，认真落实各项对外援助承诺和举措，在力所能及的范围内向发展中国家尤其是非洲最不发达国家提供更多帮助。

各位同事！

二十国集团领导人在不到一年的时间内举行了 3 次峰会，取得了积极成效。我相信，在国际社会共同努力下，我们一定能够最终战胜这场国际金融危机，迎来世界经济更加繁荣的明天。

谢谢各位！

（国家主席胡锦涛在匹兹堡 G20 第三次金融峰会上的讲话全文，2009 年 9 月 25 日）

Text 4

I am tremendously honored to be asked to speak at this meeting of the Commission for Growth and Development. I have been asked to speak about my recent book with Bob Shiller, which is *Animal Spirits: How Human Psychology Drives the Economy and Why It Matters for Global Capitalism*. I want to note at the beginning that my talk will be more abstract than the book.

The book has a large number of stories, and we make our points largely in terms of those stories. I am going to concentrate my remarks on how we got into the current economic and financial crisis. I will also concentrate my analysis on the United States, since I believe that the US is at the epicenter of the crisis. Governments the world over are working to solve it. And they are enlisting economists to guide them through it. Economists rely on their vision of macroeconomics. Much of that vision comes from Keynes. Getting it right then calls for a correct vision of how the economy works. The role of Animal Spirits is to provide such a vision.

Current versions of macroeconomics greatly play down the role of psychology in the macroeconomy. But, as we show in our book, there are at least eight fundamental macroeconomic questions whose answers depend largely, although not entirely, on the role of psychology.

So the first task of the book is to explain the role of psychology in the macroeconomy. Keynes called this the role of people's Animal Spirits. The first part of the book describes five different Animal Spirits. They are: confidence, fairness, corruption and bad faith, money illusion and stories. The second part of the book describes how these Animal Spirits play a key role in the answer to these eight macroeconomic questions. These questions are as fundamental as why the economy fluctuates as much as it does; why and how monetary and fiscal policy affects the economy; and why there is involuntary unemployment. Let me review just briefly how these concepts indicate how we have gotten into the current crisis. Then I will review some of the particulars of the crisis in the United States.

The first of these Animal Spirits is confidence. The dictionary tells us that confidence means trust. But trust means that people go beyond the usual rational use of information to make judgments. And that is just what we found in the boom that just ended. People were making all kinds of business investments. Especially they were purchasing, and selling, complex financial instruments, on the basis of their trust. This was not just in the housing and mortgage market.

It occurred in financial markets much more generally. Furthermore, they would not have made these investments if they had rationally analyzed the basis for making them. They made them because they were confident. As it turns out, they were overconfident.

Let me now describe the role of corruption and bad faith. Very few economists foresaw the problems that were developing. The standard view among economists was that private markets would be self-policing. It assumes that people would be knowledgeable buyers and sellers. They would only undertake increased risk if they were duly compensated by higher expected returns. Thus, there was little worry about the absence of regulation in both the securities and real estate markets. But, this self-policing view does not take appropriate account that people were overconfident. And therefore they did not do the self-policing that they were supposed to do. There is a principle of capitalism which means that capitalism will take advantage of overconfidence.

It is true that capitalism will produce what people really want, as long as firms can make a profit. But, more subtly, and more generally, capitalism also produces what people think they want, as long as firms can make a profit. Unregulated capitalism may produce good medicines that cure our ills.

I believe it will. But unregulated capitalism also produces snake oil that does not cure our ills. It may even find it profitable to produce the desire for the snake oil itself. In fact that is one major reason for the Food and Drug Administration in the United States. It protects us against buying snake oil medicine. The book is full of stories, and one of the stories is relevant to this. William Rockefeller, the father of John D. Rockelfeller the first, in the 19th century would tour the US Middle West in his buggy. And when he reached a new town he would go to the Town Square, give a talk and distribute flyers saying that Dr. Rockefeller was in town. He had the miraculous cures. Then he would repair to the best hotel suite in town and sell his wears to those who came for the cure to their ills. Indeed, the contrast William Rockefeller and his son is apt. William was selling snake oil, and represented one side of capitalism, whereas in contrast John D. sold real oil, which really did satisfy people's wants, and represents the productive side of capitalism. The principal of snake oil has special relevance for asset markets. Assets to most people are only pieces of paper. Most investors surmise the value of financial assets from what others, such as accountants and rating agencies, tell about them. These accounting and rating agencies also have their own incentives. And those incentives are not fully aligned with the public's interest. And so when people are overconfident, financial markets tend to produce assets that take advantage of that overconfidence. If unprotected by effective regulation, people will be sold snake oil assets. And an industry will arise to produce them. This is what we have just seen in Wall Street and beyond.

There is a further Animal Spirit which bolsters the previous two. People act and think and live according to stories. That goes for their economic decisions as well as their personal decisions. And there is usually a story about how the economy is behaving as it does. These stories have some grain of truth, but they often are over exuberant, on the one side, or too pessimistic on the other. 10 years ago there was the dot.com story. In the recent past there was the story that financial engineering could make financial assets much more safe than the underlying securities. Modern finance financial packaging had figured out ways to reduce risk. People bought into these stories. They were overconfident. And markets took advantage of those beliefs to sell them what has later proved to be snake oil assets. These three animal spirits then explain how fluctuations in human psychology play a key role, in why the economy fluctuates as much as it does. We think that is the key role in business cycle fluctuations. The confidence comes and the confidence goes. The stories come and the stories go. The snake oil comes, and also goes. We think that the current financial crisis is explained exactly by such fluctuations. That is one major thrust of the book. It tells us the origins of the current financial crisis.

Let's now apply these principles to the current crisis. I am now going to talk about the US, which is what I know most about. I think that it is also especially important here, because I believe that this is a crisis that is centered in the US, but that the same over-exuberance, for the similar reasons, has infected the whole world. So let's turn to the US.

(Excerpted text of speech by George A. Akerlof on Seminar on Financial Crisis and Its Impact on Developing Countries' Growth Strategies and Prospects, April 20, 2009)

第 8 单元　带稿同声传译
Simultaneous Interpreting with Texts

> **单元学习目标**
> 1. 掌握带稿同传工作的操作步骤和练习方法。
> 2. 熟悉文化遗产这一口译主题的常用汉英术语和表达方式。
> 3. 能够完成基本的同步听译练习。

第一部分　同传技能

有的人认为带稿同传的难度低于无稿同传，觉得有了稿子，同传就变成十分容易胜任的工作。有同样想法的某些会议主办方甚至只在会议开始前几分钟才向译员提供稿件，这稿件长达十多页，而且充斥着大量的术语、概念、数据等技术性较强的内容。然而事实并非如此。

严格意义上来说，带稿同传也是视译的一种，与看着稿件做口译不同，带稿同传的译员要边看稿、边听发言、边口译，文字、听觉和视觉这三种信息不停地进入译员的大脑。如果引用吉尔的注意力分配模式，我们可以发现，带稿同传时，译员除了要调动听辨（L）、产出（P）、短时记忆（M）和协调（C）能力，还要抽出精力调动视觉能力。这样一来，等于是给有效的认知能力负荷又增加了一层要求。巴黎高翻学院的塞莱斯科维奇和勒代雷认为这种视译的做法"时间长了会让译员感到难以忍受的焦虑，因而也会使翻译质量迅速下降"（Seleskovitch & Lederer, 2007: 267）。带稿同传使用的稿件都是提前写好，而且大多经过润色修改，具有很强的书面语特征；面对这样的稿件，要译员以既符合源语特点，又遵守译语语法和习惯的要求来处理高度书面化的、以口头表达形式传达的信息，做到准确无误、出口成章，是很困难的。发言人在念稿时只用读出看到的字、词即可，不需要经过自发讲话中连续的心理过程，因此不仅语速比自发讲话更快，而且节奏和语言的表现力也都不同于自发讲话，这与译员理解的节奏和表现力都有较大差距，因此也使得译员对意群的把握更加困难。哪怕是做带稿同传，译员也需要尽早提前获得稿件；如果会议开始前几分钟才拿到稿件且无其他译前准备，翻译的质量将会大打折扣。

一般来说，译员在重要的国际会议之前拿不到任何材料、毫无任何准备的情况是很少见的。在大多数情况下，译员都能提前获得一些准备材料，常见的材料包括：发言人的发言原稿和/或译稿、摘要、提纲、发言时要同步播放的幻灯片文件等。不论拿到何种材料，全面仔细的译前准备都是必要的。

发言人念稿在国际会议中越来越常见，这要求译员必须加强带稿同传练习，更好的适应带稿同传的工作要求。此外，作为从纯视译过渡到无稿同传的必经练习，带稿同传做得好不好也极大地影响着无稿同传能力。

1. 从准备到开始

译员在会议开始之前得到材料的不同决定了带稿同传的准备方法。常见的情况有以下几种。

1）提前获得原稿和译稿

在极其重要的国际性会议上，会议主办方往往会提供重要发言人的发言原稿及其笔译稿，以保证现场口译的效果。在这种情况下，译员可将原稿和译稿对照着通读一遍，进行最终的校对，如果发现错漏或疏忽（如拼写错误、数字不一致、字/句/段缺失甚至缺页等）应及时与主办方核对，以免发言开始后才发现，造成工作被动。另外，拿到原稿与译稿后，如果段落较多，可在两份稿件上做一些相应的段落标记，免得发言人跳过、增加、删除某段落时找不到译文所在。如果原稿和译稿是发言开始之前刚刚送过来的，译员也要抽时间快速浏览稿件，迅速了解发言内容、范围及重点，并至少在开头和结尾处进行标记。口译开始后，译员按照发言人的语速进行"同声传读"即可。同声传读过程中，译员要高度灵活，注意发言人可能对发言稿做出的任何改动并及时处理。

2）提前获得原稿或译稿

在会前同时拿到原稿和译稿的情况毕竟少见，更常见的是只拿到发言稿或只拿到译稿。如果拿到发言稿，译员可以将一些重点、难点的内容（如术语、姓名和职称、机构名称、数字等）事先笔译出来，仔细准备一下稿件的开头和结尾，分析一下发言稿的段落大意、重点和层次，做到心中有数，这样现场就会更有保障。如果会前短短几分钟才拿到发言稿，译员也要迅速通读稿件，以最快速度了解发言内容，时间允许的话可以在稿件上做一些标记（如段落标记¶、重点标记*、难点标记?，等等），尤其是开头和结尾处。开头和结尾处如果处理得好，不仅会获得较好效果，而且可以增强译员的信心。

如果只是拿到了译稿，译员同样需要通读全文，了解段落大意、重点和层次，并选择性地做一些提示性标记，以便在跟读时与发言人的现场发言进行对照。有时发言人可能不会照稿通篇宣读，因此对译稿内容的把握十分必要。同样，如果译稿也是在发言开始之前才送到译员手中，译员还是要尽力抽时间迅速浏览稿件内容，并将重点放在开头和结尾处。

如果译员发现译稿错漏太多，对现场口译工作毫无价值，可以忽略稿件，集中精力做好无稿同传。

3）提前获得大纲/摘要或幻灯片文件

提前拿到大纲/摘要的情况也不少，大纲或摘要可以帮助译员建立合适的翻译语境，并且帮助译员把握信息的走势和范围。面对大纲或摘要，译员可以利用手头的各种资源（参考书、辞典、互联网），以发散式的思维去预测发言人可能会提到的信息，发言人在相同主题的场合发表的言论，相关的重大事件，等等，并且对发言人可能用到的术语进行预测式准备。

提前获得幻灯片是现在国际性会议上较为常见的情况。如果是双语的幻灯片，译员也可对照着通读一遍，把握发言大意和重点内容；如果是单语材料，译员可以参考只拿到原稿或译稿的准备方式进行相应的准备。

不论提前拿到了怎样的稿件，译员在同传时都不能完全依赖手头的稿件，原因有二：一是发言人有可能不会完全照搬发言稿的内容，因此如果出现跳越式发言、增加或删除发言内容的情况，过度依赖稿件会使译员陷入被动；二是过于依赖手头稿件可能会使译员过分关注文字信息而忽略了对由声音信息传递的意义的把握，使得口译产出停留在文字表面。因此，在任何时候，译员都应该以发言人口头传递的发言内容为准进行传译。

2. 带稿同传练习

带稿同传虽然比纯视译更难，但遵循一定的步骤还是可以加以把握的。

首先，可以从"同声传读"开始练习。找一篇有译文的发言稿，一边听录音，一边朗读译文。最开始时可以选择原稿与译稿完全对应的材料，过一段时间以后，可以请同学来扮演发言人的角色，在念稿过程中添加、删减一些内容或者调整部分内容的顺序。口译时，要注意观察听说差的长短，如果发现落得太远，则要注意调整自己的速度。

然后，可以开始尝试脱离译稿、只看原稿进行视译。随着练习的深入，可以不断提高练习难度：语言由简到难，结构由简单到复杂，内容由短到长。如果有同学充当发言人，可请他（她）多一些脱稿发言或多对发言稿内容进行调整。

带稿同传对语言产出的要求与无稿同传相同、甚至更高，因此练习时应注意遵循同传的原则和标准，避免逐字逐句的硬译、死译。两种语言相差越大，瞬间转换的难度也就越大，因此在练习时，也要留心英汉两种语言在结构、语法等各方面的差异，平时多积累，熟能生巧，上场时就能从容应对了。

第二部分　案例讲解

> The following passages are from the practice materials for this unit. Sight interpret them into the target language.

Passage 1

作为一种独特的文化形态，非物质文化遗产为人类构筑起安身立命的精神家园，体现着人类文明的发达程度，显示了人类在思想和实践上达到的智慧高度(1)。今天我们聚集一堂，为保护人类珍贵精神财富、守护共同精神家园进行深入探讨，具有非常重要的意义(2)。

▼ 技能提示

（1）本句可以完全顺译，保留句子结构不变。

（2）本句的处理可以按照笔译的做法，调整语序，使用 it 引导的形式主语从句，也可以按照顺译原则，从"具有非常重要的意义"处拆分另起一句，用总结性词语增强上下文衔接。

▼ 参考译文

译文一：As a unique cultural form, intangible cultural heritage has been a spiritual homeland for human beings. It embodies the high development of human civilization, and represents the intense wisdom of the human mind and practice. Today, we get together to discuss in depth on the protection of the precious spiritual wealth and the safeguard of our shared spiritual homeland. Such discussion is of great significance.

译文二：As a unique cultural form, intangible cultural heritage has been a spiritual homeland for human beings. It embodies the high development of human civilization, and represents the intense wisdom of the human mind and practice. It is of great significance for us to gather here today discussing the protection of the precious spiritual wealth and the safeguard of our shared spiritual homeland.

Passage 2

I was elected as President of the 32nd session of the General Conference (1) just less than two years ago (2).

▼ 技能提示

（1）介词 of 引导的修饰成分放在被修饰名词之后，按照汉语习惯必须全部前置。

（2）顺译时，时间状语仍可以放在句末。

▽ 参考译文

我当选为联合国教科文组织第 32 届大会主席恰逢两年以前。

Passage 3

通过记者图文并茂的现场直击，在民间生活的场域里重现这些非物质文化遗产之美（1），找寻它们不灭的基因，再次唤起人们尤其是年轻人对这些文化遗产的亲切感。

▽ 技能提示

（1）典型的中文无主句，因此需迅速选定译语中的主语。

（2）将小句处理成非限定性定语从句，增强语言的衔接性。

▽ 参考译文

By way of site reproduction with excellent pictures and texts, the report represented the beauty of intangible cultural heritage in folk living environment and tried to find out their eternal genes, which once again reminded people, especially young people, of the fondness of these cultural heritages.

Passage 4

Another major revision to the Law for the Protection of Cultural Properties relating to intangible cultural heritage (1) was made later, in 1975. With this revision, the concept of intangible folk cultural properties was added to the scope of the Law (2).

▽ 技能提示

（1）中心内容 the Law for the Protection of Cultural Properties 前后均有限定成分，处理时需按汉语习惯调整。

（2）可保留被动或转换为主动。

▽ 参考译文

译文一：对《文化财保护法》的另一重大修订是 1975 年做出的，在这次修订中，非物质民间文化遗产被纳入到保护法范围内。

译文二：对《文化财保护法》的另一重大修订是 1975 年做出的，这次修订将非物质民间文化遗产纳入到保护法范围内。

Passage 5

非物质文化遗产交流合作，是落实"中国－东盟全面经济合作框架协议"和《广东省人民政府与东南亚国家联盟秘书处合作备忘录》的一个具体体现（1），必将有利于进一步深化经济、政治各领域的合作（2），实现互利共赢，为各国人民带来更多的福祉（3）。

▼ **技能提示**

(1) 译语中,"具体体现"作为"是"的宾语应前置,同时将汉语中的前置定语后置处理。

(2) 同上,可将"合作"前的定语后置处理。

(3) 汉语没有明示最后两个分句与前面分句之间的关系,因此可以通过添加介词 for 来实现衔接,同时明确逻辑关系。

▼ **参考译文**

The exchange and cooperation of intangible cultural heritage marks the implementation of the China-ASEAN Framework Agreement on Comprehensive Economic Cooperation and Guangdong Provincial People's Government Memorandum of Cooperation with the ASEAN Secretariat. It will further deepen our cooperation in economy, politics and other areas for the mutual benefit and the enhancement of people's well-being in the region.

第三部分　词汇拓展

汉译英

《广东历史文化行》	Historical and Cultural Tour in Guangdong
《岭南记忆——走进广东非物质文化遗产》	Lingnan Memory — Step into the Intangible Cultural Heritage in Guangdong
《文化建设大潮观》	Views on the Cultural Construction Tide
保护为主、抢救第一、合理利用、继承发展	regular preservation, timely rescue, sensible utilization and inheritance and development
传统民间艺术	traditional folk art
非物质文化遗产	intangible cultural heritage
广东凉茶	Guangdong herbal tea
海上丝绸之路	marine silk road
花市	flower market
客家山歌	hakka folk songs
陆丰皮影	Lufeng Shadow Play
木版年画	Woodblock Lunar New Year Print
平面媒体	print media
石湾陶瓷	Shiwan Ceramics
文化身份	cultural identity
文化主权	cultural sovereignty

醒狮	lion dance
阳美翡翠玉雕	Yangmei Emerald and Jade Carving
粤剧	Cantonese Opera
粤绣	Cantonese Embroidery
中国－东盟全面经济合作框架协议	China-ASEAN Framework Agreement on Comprehensive Economic Cooperation
中国文联	China Federation of Literary and Art Circles
中原	Central Plain

英译汉

adult literacy	成人识字率
African Union	非盟
African World Heritage Fund	非洲世界遗产基金
conservation techniques	保存技术
Convention for the Safeguarding of Intangible Cultural Heritage	《保护非物质文化遗产公约》
documentation	立档
enhancement	弘扬
folk techniques	民间技术
identification	确认
Law for the Protection of Cultural Properties	（日本）《文化财保护法》
NEPAD	非洲发展新伙伴计划
oral traditions and expressions	口头传统和表述
performing art	表演艺术
promotion	宣传
Rainbow Nation	彩虹国度
restoration	修复
revitalization	振兴
social practice, ritual and festive event	社会实践、仪式、节庆活动
traditional craftsmanship	传统手工艺
transmission	传承
World Heritage Committee	世界遗产委员会

第四部分　同传实战

Listen to the following four speeches and interpret them into the target language using the skills introduced in this unit.

Text 1

尊敬的国家文化部有关负责人，尊敬的东盟各国代表团成员，尊敬的香港和澳门特别行政区特邀嘉宾，女士们、先生们：

能够出席"广东省与东盟非物质文化遗产保护传承论坛"，我感到非常荣幸。非物质文化遗产是人类文明、智慧的结晶，是社会发展的见证，也是后人传承历史、继往开来的文化渊源。作为一种独特的文化形态，非物质文化遗产为人类构筑起安身立命的精神家园，体现着人类文明的发达程度，显示了人类在思想和实践上达到的智慧高度。今天我们欢聚一堂，为保护人类珍贵精神财富、守护共同精神家园进行深入探讨，是顺应大势、正当其时。借这个机会，我主要谈四个方面的看法，与大家交流探讨。

第一，广东与东盟非物质文化遗产交流合作具有自然天成的基础。首先，基于深厚的历史文化渊源。广东和东盟各国一衣带水，地缘相通、人文相近，历史上就有着频繁密切的文化交流。作为各国人民智慧的结晶，非物质文化遗产既自成一体、特色鲜明，具有高度的独立性和差异性，又相互影响、相互借鉴，包含着一定的同质性和相似性，这是开展交流合作的基本前提。其次，基于高度的文化自觉和担当意识。当前，随着经济全球化的深入发展，非物质文化遗产赖以生存的经济基础、体制环境和社会条件都发生了深刻变化，面临着前所未有的生存危机，许多珍贵的非物质文化遗产濒临消亡，人类的精神家园正遭受侵蚀和破坏。在这样的形势下，探讨加强非物质文化遗产保护的措施、经验，体现了广东与东盟各国文化担当的勇气和信心。最后，基于各具特色的实践积累。广东与东盟各国历来高度重视非物质文化遗产的保护传承工作，并基于不同的实际，探索了各具特色的模式，积累了十分宝贵的经验。因此，通过借鉴经验、共享成果，更好地促进非物质文化遗产保护工作，成为广东与东盟各国的共同愿望。

第二，广东与东盟非物质文化遗产交流合作具有十分重要的意义。我认为，举办这次论坛并加强交流合作，有几个方面的目的和意义：一是统一思想，增进共识。非物质文化遗产不仅是一个国家和民族的独特资源，更是全人类共有的文化财富，是人类文化发展多样性的生动见证。在经济全球化、文化多元化的今天，如何更好地保护传承非物质文化遗产，成为全世界共同关注和必须面对的重要课题。开展广东与东盟非物质遗产保护交流合作，不仅有利于推进广东和东盟各国经济发达、社会和谐、文化繁荣，有利于维护各自独特文化身份、文化主权，而且对推动人类进步、文化延续、国际社会文明对话至关重要。二是促进交流，加深友谊。文化关系是国家关系的重要内容。非物质文化遗产保护的交流合作，必将极大地加深中国与东盟各国人民的相互了解，增进深厚友谊，促进友好往来，丰富对话伙伴国关系的内涵，并最终在文化交流史上留下浓墨重彩的一笔。三是深化合作，达成共赢。非物质文化遗产交流合作，是落实"中国－东盟全面经济合作框架协议"和《广东省人民政府与东南亚国家联盟秘书处合作备忘录》的一个具体体现，必将有利于进一步深化经济、政治各领域的合作，实现互利共赢，为各国人民带来更多的福祉。

第三，广东非物质文化遗产具有开放兼容的鲜明特色。在广东非物质文化交流发展史上，交流合作始终是贯穿其中的永恒主题。一方面，广东是古代海上丝绸之路的发祥地，从汉代开始就与东南亚、欧洲各国发展贸易往来，并不断吸收外来文化的优势和特色，博取众长，为我所用，许多非物质文化遗产具有典型的开放性特征。比如广东音乐大胆采用了外来乐器和曲调，以其音域的宽广和旋律的优美而饮誉世界。另一方面，广东原来是中国古代百越民族聚居的地方，在长期的发展过程中接受了中原四次大规模移民，本土文化和中原文化的交融和变异，使许多非物质文化遗产表现出很强的兼容性。如伴随客家民系的形成而产生的客家山歌，就是中原文化与梅州土著文化融合的产物，也是客家文化最具特色、最为精彩的部分。广东非物质文化遗产保护工作从这两个特点出发，在坚持"保护为主、抢救第一、合理利用、继承发展"方针的前提下，积极探索具有广东特色的保护模式。一是在开展全面普查的基础上，广东省人民政府先后公布了182项省级非物质文化遗产名录项目，其中74项成功列入了国家级非物质文化遗产名录，全省还先后公布了651项市级名录、1121项县级名录，初步建立起国家、省、市、县四级名录体系。二是通过公布命名、授予称号、表彰奖励、资助扶持等方式，对非物质文化遗产项目代表性传承人进行有效扶持保护。三是紧紧依靠各级政府和社会力量，因地制宜建立国有或民间民俗博物馆、专题博物馆和传习所221个，将非物质文化遗产加以集中收藏和展示，同时探索建立广府文化、潮汕文化、客家文化、雷州文化四个省级非物质文化遗产文化生态保护区，实施整体性保护。四是结合每年"文化遗产日"等主题活动，通过举办图片、实物展、传统民间艺术汇演和巡游、专题双传推介等形式，推动非物质文化遗产进入教育体系，提升全社会非物质文化遗产保护意识。五是正确处理保护与利用的关系，探索非物质文化遗产生产性保护的有效措施，使广东凉茶等文化遗产发挥出巨大的经济效益。当然，我们广东的非物质文化遗产的保护工作也存在许多不足，希望借此机会得到各位的指导和帮助。

第四，广东与东盟非物质文化遗产交流合作具有广阔前景。当前，广东与东盟各国关系日益密切，可以说大交流方兴未艾，大合作势不可挡，大发展前景光明。我们要抓住难得机遇，大力开创非物质文化遗产交流合作的新局面，推进各项工作迈上范围更广、层次更高的新台阶。在此，我提出四点建议：一是确立长远的交流合作目标，规划切实可行的推进步骤，同时构建多种平台，建立有效机制，定期商讨合作交流中的重大问题，交流普查、规划、立法等方面的经验，以利于互通信息，发挥优势，实现交流合作的制度化、规范化、长期化。二是合作开展非物质文化遗产理论研究。加强非物质文化遗产保护基础理论和应用理论研究，鼓励召开专题研讨会，扶持专家、科研机构之间合作组织相关课题研究，资助非物质文化遗产研究成果出版。三是加强人才的培训培养。依托高等院校及科研机构，采取委托培训、联合培训、传承人开班授艺等多种形式，重点培养非物质文化遗产保护管理人才和各门类的业务骨干，为保护传承工作提供人才支撑。四是组织展示展演交流。利用"文化遗产日"和民族传统节日，配合国家经济、政治领域的重大交流活动，互派或合作开展非物质文化遗产展览、展演，组织相关文化活动，加强非物质文化遗产的宣传和展示，使其成为广东与东盟各国人民相互了解、升华友谊的重要平台。

各位嘉宾、各位朋友，基于以上认识，我们有理由相信，以这次论坛为契机和平台，大家畅所欲言，集思广益，研究探讨非物质文化遗产保护的理论和实践问题，深入交流各自的创新方法、基本经验和丰富成果，提出推进非物质文化遗产保护的新看法、新视角、新思路，必将收获丰硕成果，达成重要共识，成为各国今后开展非物质文化遗产保护工作的重要指导。我们期待，大家以此论坛为起点，不断拓展文化交流合作的领域，丰富文化交流合作的内涵，使人民创造的优秀文化得以保护、传承、发展，以文化的独特魅力恩泽人民，为促进人类文化发展繁荣、人类社会文明进步做出贡献。

谢谢大家！

(2009年11月7日，广东省文化厅厅长方健宏在"广东省与东盟非物质文化遗产保护传承论坛"上的发言全文)

Text 2

Your Excellencies, Distinguished Delegates, Ladies and Gentlemen, Dear Friends,

Good evening!

It is truly a privilege to address such a distinguished audience. Let me begin my appreciation with warm words of praise and the expression of profound gratitude for the kind hospitality to all the guests and me from our very point of entry at the airport.

Perhaps I should confess that when I was in South Africa, in Cape Town, just last September I had expressed a wish to be back because of the joy that I had at the time. My joy this time around has surpassed that of September and I will not be surprised if I am back again in this great country sooner than you expect! Indeed, it is a pleasure to be here tonight.

The past few days have been intense for all of us. Some have been involved in the African World Heritage Experts' Meeting, while others took part in the deliberations surrounding the African World Heritage Fund. The former was dedicated to the elaboration of the African Position Paper to be presented to both the African Union and the World Heritage Committee while the latter considered innovative, long-term, and sustainable strategic partnership approaches in the context of African World Heritage. In light of this, I shall not monopolise the rostrum for too long. I shall simply spend some time to reflect my term of duty as President of the General Conference of UNESCO.

I was elected as President of the 32nd session of the General Conference just less than two years ago. The LORD has helped me throughout this period to continue the excellent work started on September 29th, 2003 when I was invited to lead the 32nd session of the General Conference. As many of you will recall, we had a historic session as the United States returned to UNESCO after almost two decades of exit, and I had the honour to invite Mrs Laura Bush, the First Lady of the United States, to address the General Conference. Thereafter followed the adoption of some very important conventions including that on the safeguarding of the intangible cultural heritage. Several Resolutions were also adopted to assist our organisation meet the important challenges of the new century. Later this year, in October, I shall be ceding my position, when new elections are held at the beginning of the 33rd session of UNESCO's supreme governing body.

I must admit that these past two years have been extremely exciting and challenging. Most of all, however, these two years have been very fulfilling. I have been privileged to have had the opportunity to travel the globe preaching the laudable and noble goals of UNESCO, representing the organization I cherish and believe in. I have made presentations on such wide-ranging issues as literacy, the abolition of slavery, the relationship between UNESCO and NEPAD, adult literacy, education for all, dialogue among cultures and civilizations; all the way through to the protection of cultural diversity and artistic expression to the subject at hand this week — tangible and intangible cultural heritage. I have also had the opportunity to establish a working group as resolved by the General Conference to examine the relationship between the three organs of the governance of our organisation, the General Conference, the Executive Board and the Secretariat.

Ladies and gentlemen, let me quickly spend some time on the subject that has brought all of us together tonight, namely the protection of the cultural heritage of Africa. Africa has a rich cultural heritage. Indeed, as we have seen, this great heritage is opening other doors. Gatherings such as this, with men and women representing every region, many cultures, languages and religions provide important opportunities to create partnerships, to build synergies and to strengthen relationships. The common interest that brought us together these past few days is the need to do more to reduce the vast disparities between the lives of the rich and the lives of the poor — ultimately making globalization work for the benefit of all through the celebration of our cultural diversity and the promotion of our common cultural heritage. We must take into consideration the social, economic and technological challenges that we face and, especially, those in Africa's developing countries.

Yet, paradoxically, it is through more intense globalization that more and more peoples and communities have begun to recognize the importance of their own cultural heritage — whether tangible or intangible — as a contribution to the world's cultural diversity. Communities in every land have come to realize that their cultural heritage plays a crucial role in their identity and that their engagement in safeguarding activities contributes to a sense of continuity. As a result, while globalization has undeniably contributed to the dissemination of cultures, its effects on cultural diversity can, if we are not careful, also be negative.

How can Africa respond to this challenge? I know that this was on all of our minds these past few days as we all deliberated in order to prepare for the Durban meeting. Let me just say, to paraphrase an old expression, that we have to do our own growing no matter how tall our grand father was. To do so, Africa must cultivate partnerships with those who have traditionally been her friend through support in such initiatives as the abolition of slavery and the dismantlement of apartheid.

Africa ought to ask all these friends throughout the world who have benefited from the contributions of Africans to their own development to show fairness and objectivity and re-invest some of their gains towards the development of our region as a gesture of recognition for the price we paid in their own economic development.

In this vein, it should be considered of extreme importance to have the capital influx necessary for heritage conservation and its promotion. Here governments and the civil society in Africa must be encouraged to seek investments in tourism and capacity-building, thus increasing our own capacity to capitalize on increased world travel. However, tourism must be made responsible, and the people ought to gain an increased awareness of the sensitive nature of the need for conservation when visiting our diverse land.

Ladies and gentlemen, before concluding, please allow me again to convey my thanks to the people and government of South Africa for your warm hospitality, conveyed not only to me, but to the participants of both the African World Heritage Experts' Meeting, and the African World Heritage Fund Workshop. I am sure you will agree with me, without their support, we would not be where we are today in promoting African heritage. UNESCO has always believed in the experts, the brilliant minds that have always worked to provide quality advice and options.

I shall finish by expressing my satisfaction and joy for the excellent meal we were served. It truly has lived up to South Africa's world-famous reputation for excellent cuisine and subliminal wine. Indeed, food here bears witness to a positive effect of globalization: it is an eclectic mixture of ethnic cuisines with indigenous spices and fruits. Our meal exhibited richness and freshness; it boasted elegance in its complex simplicity. The expression "Rainbow Nation" perfectly describes this exceptional meal. Thank you very much for such wonder hospitality and warm welcome in your beautiful country!

(Excerpted text of keynote speech by Professor Michael Omolewa, Ambassador and Permanent Delegate of the Republic of Nigeria to UNESCO at the dinner in honour of the African World Heritage Experts' Meeting and the African World Heritage Fund Workshop on March 17, 2005)

Text 3

女士们、先生们：

大家早上好！

非常高兴能够和大家一起在美丽的佛山庆祝"广东省与东盟非物质文化遗产保护传承交流论坛"的召开，我谨借此机会，代表南方报业传媒集团向此次论坛的召开表示祝贺，并预祝论坛取得圆满成功。

有一句话是这样说的："只有民族的，才是世界的。"非物质文化遗产承担着保持民族文化独特性以及维护世界文化多样性的双重职责。在全球化浪潮冲击的今天，文化认同成为越来越多的国家和地区的内在需求，而强调"活体"传承的非物质文化遗产，凝聚并保存着一个地区、国家和族群的历史记忆。正如中国文联主席孙家正所说的："它不仅是一个民族自己认定的历史凭证，也是这个民族得以延续，并满怀自信走向未来的根基与力量之源。"从这个意义上讲，保护广东的非物质文化遗产，就是留住曾经鲜活的岭南记忆。

今天，越来越多的人们认识到，对于一个地区来讲，珍贵的文化遗产是自身独特的外显文化标志，是不可复制的"文化资本"。当今社会，文化、环境等指标作为"软实力"，成为一个区域经济发展的核心竞争力。所以，代表着一个地区历史文化面貌的文化遗产，不仅不是发展的包袱，相反却是未来发展的资本。尽管它并不能马上成为一棵"摇钱树"，但却是有效促进经济社会协调互动发展的一个"聚宝盆"。从这个意义上讲，保护广东的非物质文化遗产，就是保护广东的可持续发展。

此外，对非物质文化遗产的保护，是对此前"见物不见人"的传统发展观和传统文化价值观的摒弃。非物质文化遗产，突出文化遗产的"非物质"属性，注重知识、情感和技能、技术及其"活体"传承。一言以蔽之，就是要"见物又见人"，"见物更见人"，以人为本。因此，在保护非物质文化遗产时，固然不能忽视这些遗产的物态成果，更要保护创造、传承这些文化遗产的活生生的人。

岭南大地给广东人留下的馈赠是丰厚的，目前广东有 1 个世界级、74 个国家级、182 个省级非物质文化遗产项目。但是随着全球化和社会转型进程的深入，许多地方的非物质文化遗产正在面临消失的严重威胁；一些优秀的非物质文化遗产项目传承人年事已高，后继乏人，有面临失传的危险。

作为此次论坛的唯一平面媒体支持单位，《南方日报》历来重视对保护文化遗产的宣传报道。2004 年《南方日报》的大型系列报道《广东历史文化行》，为全省各地寻找文化坐标，在文化大省建设热潮中起到推波助澜的作用，省内外引起巨大反响。2006 年的大型系列报道《文化建设大潮观》为全省各地文化发展把脉，反响热烈。今年，《南方日报》再次启动大型系列报道《岭南记忆——走进广东非物质文化遗产》，从岭南大地上翻陈出那些深深烙印于百姓生活的文化基因，唤醒属于这片土地的历史记忆，为广东未来的创造力、文化软实力的提升打开了又一扇窗户。为广东非物质文化遗产传承"提灯"，用媒体的力量，照亮他们前行的路，同时唤醒更多民众加入这一征程，是《南方日报》紧迫而又义不容辞的责任。因为除了政府、传承人和学者，保护非物质文化遗产，最终要唤起每个人的文化自觉，《南方日报》甘当做这个"唤起者"和"提灯者"。

《岭南记忆——走进广东非物质文化遗产》选取了广东 30 多个非物质

文化遗产，其中既有产业化程度较高、"钱途"一片光明的阳美翡翠玉雕和石湾陶瓷，也有处境濒危、市场萎缩的木版年画；既有普及度较高、城乡居民喜闻乐见的粤剧、花市、醒狮和客家山歌，也有后继乏人的粤绣和陆丰皮影。通过记者图文并茂的现场直击，在民间生活的场域里重现这些非物质文化遗产之美，找寻它们不灭的基因，再次唤起人们尤其是年轻人对这些文化遗产的亲切感。同时，针对非物质文化遗产信息丰富的特点，采用全媒体报道方式，综合运用文字、图像、视频等多种形式，积极实现平面媒体与网络媒体的互动，实现了传播的立体化。另外，记者带着如何保护与发展的思考，邀请专家，一同寻找存留于南粤大地上非物质文化遗产未来的生存密码，力争成为打通民众与专家、年轻人与历史记忆、岭南文化与未来发展的一个通道。让我们在走远之后重新回望"我从哪里来！"

现在大家手中拿到的《岭南记忆——走进广东非物质文化遗产》一书，就是《南方日报》系列报道的结集。从效果上来看，《岭南记忆》初步实现了报道的意图。我们的采访团每到一个地方，都受到当地政府和"非遗"传承人的热烈欢迎；每篇报道出来以后，都会引起极大的社会反响，报纸在"非遗"申报地非常抢手，可以说是洛阳纸贵；我们选择了天涯等网站作为合作的网络媒体，平均每期报道在天涯上的点击率都超过两万次，高的甚至达10万次以上。

本报《岭南记忆——走进广东非物质文化遗产》的大型系列报道目前已经画上了句号，但是《南方日报》对非物质文化遗产的关注永远没有止境，我们肩负的责任未有穷时。我相信通过此次论坛所提供的深入交流的机会，必将极大地推动对广东和东盟各国非物质文化遗产的保护和传承。

预祝论坛取得圆满成功！谢谢大家！

（2009年11月7日，南方报业传媒集团董事长杨兴锋在"广东省与东盟非物质文化遗产保护传承论坛"上的发言全文）

Text 4

Ladies and Gentlemen,

In this presentation I intend to give a summary of the system for safeguarding intangible cultural heritage in Japan and to briefly outline its relation with the "Convention for the Safeguarding of the Intangible Cultural Heritage," which went into force in April 2006.

First of all, let me confirm what is meant by intangible cultural heritage and the different types of such heritage acknowledged in Japan. There are three categories of intangible cultural properties or matters relating to intangible cultural properties in Japan.

The first category consists of intangible cultural properties, and as specific administrative methods, the government designates those intangible skills that should be protected by the government as important intangible cultural properties or selects them as intangible skills that require measures such as documentation.

The second category consists of intangible folk cultural properties. Since the chief senior specialist for cultural properties of the Agency for Cultural Affairs and the Researchers of the Institute will explain each of these categories in detail, I will only give a brief summary here. With regard to these intangible folk cultural properties, also, administrative methods are taken to designate them as important intangible folk cultural properties or select them as intangible folk cultural properties that require measures such as documentation, and various measures are taken toward the protection of these properties.

Although the third category is not in itself acknowledged by the Law for the Protection of Cultural Properties as cultural property, it consists of conservation techniques for cultural property, or as techniques or skills that are indispensable for the transmission of cultural properties. A certain framework for protection has been established for these techniques through the selection of conservation techniques, i.e. by selecting certain techniques as important techniques for the conservation of cultural properties. In this sense, it may be said that these techniques are acknowledged, from the point of view of administration, as one category of intangible cultural heritage in Japan.

Now let us turn our attention to the actual number of these properties. First of all, in terms of important intangible cultural properties held by individuals, the so-called "individual recognition," the total number is 82, of which 38 are performing arts and 44 are traditional craft techniques. Furthermore, the holders who specifically hold these intangible cultural properties total 111, of which 54 are holders of traditional performing arts and 57 are of traditional craft techniques. These numbers that have been taken from the website of the Agency for Cultural Affairs and may change at any time, for reasons such as the unfortunate death of an individual holder or the addition of newly recognized holders. The greatest characteristics of this system for the protection of intangible cultural properties are that while the system designates techniques and skills as cultural properties, it recognizes individuals or those that exemplify these techniques or skills as holders of these techniques or skills.

In addition to the above, there are also collective recognition and organizational recognition. By this method, groups consisting of a certain number of holders are recognized. In other words, the government, instead of recognizing the one-to-one relationship between an individual and a technique or skill, recognizes a group of people holding a certain technique or skill. In this category the total number of important intangible cultural properties is 25, of which 11 are performing arts and 14 are traditional craft techniques. The number of groups or groups with individuals who hold these techniques or skills total 25, of which 11 are traditional performing arts and 14 are traditional craft techniques.

Earlier I mentioned that in addition to those intangible cultural properties designated as such, there are those that are selected as intangible cultural properties that require measures such as documentation. Currently intangible cultural properties selected as requiring measures such as documentation total 30 for performing arts and 60 for traditional craft techniques. I would also like to note here that roughly 10% of the intangible cultural properties in this group have later been designated as important intangible cultural properties. Thus the list of designated important intangible cultural properties and that of selected intangible cultural properties overlap to a certain extent.

Now let us move on to intangible folk cultural properties. Cultural properties designated as important intangible folk cultural properties consist of three types: manners and customs, folk performing arts, and the newly designated category of folk techniques. There are 146 in folk performing arts, 97 in manners and customs, and three in folk techniques. These numbers do not include the designations that have just recently been made by the government. In the case of folk cultural properties also, as it was the case with intangible cultural properties, there is a system for selecting intangible folk cultural properties that require measures such as documentation. Currently under this category, 346 folk performing arts, 214 manners and customs, and 0 folk techniques have been selected. Of these, roughly 30% have been designated as important intangible folk cultural properties after selection, and there are many such examples especially in the field of folk performing arts.

Finally, with regard to techniques for the conservation of cultural properties, the government has designated a number of techniques as conservation techniques for cultural properties, and the accompanying selection and recognition processes are relatively similar to those of important intangible cultural properties. In other words, the system selects certain techniques and then recognizes the holders or preservation groups of such techniques. In this case also, there is a system for recognizing individuals and a system for recognizing organizations as preservation groups. Currently the number of conservation techniques held by individuals is 46, while the number of individuals holding such techniques is 50. The number of conservation techniques held by preservation groups is 23, while the number of recognized preservation groups is 24.

During this symposium you will be hearing various reports by specialists in each field. However, as there is no presentation specifically dedicated to selected conservation techniques, I will take this opportunity to explain this system in a little more detail. Later in my presentation I will touch on this topic again when I outline the historical background, but it should be noted that this system of selecting conservation techniques did not exist at the time the Law for the Protection of Cultural Properties was first enacted in 1950. In fact, this concept was incorporated into the Law at a much later date. The designated conservation technique is provided for in Article 83-7 of the Law for the Protection of Cultural Properties as follows: "Those traditional techniques or skills which are indispensable for the conservation of cultural properties and must be preserved with positive measures may be selected as "selected conservation techniques." The key concepts here are that the techniques and skills must be indispensable for the conservation of cultural properties and also that the techniques and skills must be traditional. These concepts are the very concepts that are enveloped in the broad sense of intangible cultural heritage as defined in the current Convention. In spite of the fact that Japan has not acknowledged conservation techniques as cultural properties, the above-mentioned definition in the Law is intended to show that conservation techniques for cultural properties are also a part of intangible cultural heritage in Japan. This system is based on the belief that in order to support cultural properties, regardless of whether they are tangible or intangible, techniques, which are intangible, are required in various situations including the safeguarding, maintenance and restoration of cultural properties. In other words, it is extremely important that in order to hand down cultural properties, regardless of whether they are tangible or intangible, intangible skills are indispensable. I think that this fact needs to be communicated to the rest of the world.

I have just outlined the various types of cultural properties as a whole. Intangible cultural properties currently include traditional performing arts and craft techniques; intangible folk cultural properties include manners and customs, folk performing arts and the newly added traditional folk techniques; and conservation techniques for cultural property include traditional techniques necessary for the restoration and transmission of cultural properties. Among these, I believe that the newly added concept of folk techniques, under which the first three designations were made last year, will play a vital role in the world of intangible cultural heritage of Japan from now on. Folk techniques is an important concept that is quite similar to both traditional craft techniques, which are classified under intangible cultural properties, and conservation techniques which are necessary for the protection of cultural properties. I think that unless this concept is skillfully applied and managed, massive confusion may result. The application of folk techniques has only just begun, and I feel that there is a need to fully weigh and consider the direction we are to take with regard to this category.

(Excerpted text of speech by Miyata Shigeyuki from National Research Institute for Cultural Properties at the 30th International Symposium on the Conservation and Restoration of Cultural Property in 2006)

第 9 单元　无稿同声传译
Simultaneous Interpreting Without Texts

> **单元学习目标**
> 1. 掌握无稿同声传译的主要特点。
> 2. 熟悉科技主题的常用汉英术语和表达方式。
> 3. 根据注意力分配原则，熟悉无稿同传的练习方式。

第一部分　同传技能

顾名思义，无稿同传意味着译员在完成同传任务时没有发言人的具体讲稿，获取信息的主要渠道（有时也是唯一渠道）就是听觉，所以译员要将其最主要的脑部精力用于听辨和理解信息之上，一旦这个环节出了差错，就一点补救的机会都没有了，说得再好也没用，毕竟信息准确度大打折扣。

由于缺乏可视的辅助信息，如讲稿、幻灯片、大纲等，译员面临更大的压力，一旦无法通过听辨把握信息，就没有其他渠道来帮助他获取信息，尤其是在数字和专有名词等硬信息（hard information）方面。新译员在各方面能力都不够成熟的情况下，经常会因为听辨负荷过大而无法完成同传任务。但无稿同传也有其有利的一面：译员专注于听辨，不受其他渠道信息的影响，注意力更加集中，符合有效利用注意力、避免干扰的原则；对于新译员来说，无稿同传有时还比有稿同传要简单，因为他们在注意力分配上能力不足，容易受到文字信息的干扰，还不如专注于听辨。

很多同传学员都视无稿同传为一大挑战，觉得手中没稿，心里没底，完全要靠自己的听辨理解来处理繁杂的信息，压力不小，经常是听得断断续续，说得结结巴巴。无稿同传确实难度很大，但却不是无法逾越的鸿沟。通过大量的练习，语言能力的提高，一般性知识和主题知识的积累，以及会前的充分准备，译员还是可以在同传时追求"此时无稿胜有稿"的境界。

1. 无稿同传的类别

无稿同传中，"稿"的范畴可大可小，既可指发言人的详细发言定稿，也可指一切和发言内容相关的信息。一般来说，无稿同传可分为以下几种情况。

1) 绝对无稿：发言人或会议主办方没有给译员任何形式的发言材料，译员只能通过会议主题、议程和官方网页获取发言人及其发言内容的些许信息。同传时，译员几乎完全依赖听力和理解。

2) 相对无稿：译员没有发言人演讲的完整讲稿，但有发言提纲、摘要和幻灯片等信息，从而能够把握演讲的大致方向和内容结构，对演讲信息有相对较为深入的了解（和绝对无稿相比）。在同传时，译员可以适度地边听边看提纲和幻灯片上的信息，以弥补听力理解和短期记忆的不足。

3) 被动无稿：译员自然希望能有发言稿、幻灯片和演讲大纲等信息，从而使准备更有成效，但有时发言人不体谅译员的难处，以种种理由拒绝提供相关材料，使得译员的听辨理解压力剧增。

4) 主动无稿：发言人提供了关于演讲的部分或全部信息，如发言稿和幻灯片，但译员在充分准备之后，主动放弃发言稿，在同传时集中精力于听辨理解上。或者是发言人在会议开始前一刻才把发言稿或相关准备材料提供给译员，译员无暇针对材料做准备，干脆主动放弃这些文字材料。

2. 无稿同传与注意力分配

一方面，译员需要发言稿来缓解听辨和记忆的压力，而另一方面，我们又看到不少译员脱稿同传。这两种看似矛盾的情景说明了什么？带不带稿和译员的水平有关吗？如果都说无稿同传难度更大，为什么还要主动放弃发言稿呢？要搞清楚这些问题，就得回到注意力分配（split of attention）这个关键概念上。

前文已对注意力分配作了一番详尽的解释，此处就不再赘述，只是简单回顾一下基本概念。"注意力分配"是指在同声传译过程中，译员的大脑同时兼顾听辨理解、转换语言代码及译文表达的任务，在听辨理解的同时，迅速组织句子进行连贯流畅的表达。形象地说，就是听一想二说三：译员在传译一节的内容时，还得想着下一节的内容该怎么译，甚至同时还要听着再下一节的内容，"心口不一"。我们都知道要做好一件事，最基本的条件之一就是不能分心，可是在同传过程中，译员不仅要分心，还要每时每刻都一心二用，甚至一心多用，这对人脑的要求极高。

根据吉尔提出的"注意力分配模式"，在同传中，译员应完成"听力分析"、"短期记忆"和"言语表达"三个基本任务，"协调"是指译员必须协调好处理这三项任务的注意力分配，使其顺利进行。

吉尔还指出，同声传译是一个多任务处理过程，要使其顺利进行并完成任务，译员提供给各项任务的总体加工能力必须等于或超过各项任务所需要的总体加工能力，因为同传过程中的多个任务实际上是几乎同时完成的，而且必须在极短的时间内完成，一旦出现了加工能力的饱和（saturation）或不足,同传任务就极有可能失败。不幸的是,每个人的加工能力是有限的,我们不能不切实际地期望译员在同传时能够不断地激发自己的潜能,获得更大的加工精力。既然阈值是固定的,译员要维持或提高表现的关键就在于如何协调精力,如何在多任务处理时确保注意力分配不失衡。

译员在双语能力、"言外知识"和心理素质上的不足都会导致注意力分配失衡,影响同传效果。除此之外,还有一个更为重要的因素——口译任务超负荷,也就是说,译员要处理难度很高的各项任务,其注意力难以集中,从而导致其注意力分配失衡,只能疲于应付。

在无稿同传的环境里,超负荷的口译环节主要集中在听辨理解上。没有发言稿等可视信息的辅助,译员只能通过听辨来接收和处理信息,稍有差池就无法准确地将其传递给目的语听众。一旦发言人用了生僻词、数字、专业术语等信息,译员的听辨负荷就更大了。对于新手来说,无稿同传也会带来更大的心理压力,并加重其听辨负担。所以,要想做好无稿同传,译员就得在减少听辨负荷上下工夫。

3. 如何应对无稿同传

要做好无稿同传,就得减少听辨负荷。吉尔提出,要提高加工精力的有效分配,可以通过如下三种方式:1)提高单项任务的处理能力;2)提高各项任务之间的协调能力;3)提高部分任务处理的自动化能力。放到无稿同传的环境来看,就是提高听辨理解的能力,加强听辨理解和阅读可视材料(幻灯片等)的协调,提高听辨理解的自动化处理能力。具体而言,同传学员应注意以下几方面的训练提高。

1)提高语言能力:双语能力直接关系到译员对源语信息的正确理解和译语表达的质量。语言能力的不足必定会增加译员分配到处理听辨理解和言语表达任务上的注意力,进而影响对其他任务的处理。无稿同传过程中,不熟悉的生词、词组或句子和结构,都可能分散译者的注意力,使其被迫调动更多的注意力来辨识这些信息,进而影响对整体意义的解读、信息记忆和信息转换表达。

2)知识积累:语言不过是表达知识的工具,译员要靠"言外知识"(extra-linguistic knowledge)来理解发言内容。百科知识(encyclopedic knowledge)和专业主题知识(subject knowledge)都很重要,帮助译员和发言人在认知层面上相互靠近,相互理解。无稿同传中,一切语言信息都可能是新知识,稍一迟疑和思索都会把握不及,所以知识结构的扩充也是关键。

3)译前准备:无稿同传并不意味着译员对主题知识和演讲内容一无所知,在得到会议主题和发言人的演讲题目后,译员要主动去收集相关信息,尽早准备。如果发言人提供了讲稿、幻灯片或大纲,也应在会前认真准备,尤其是掌握演讲的大体内容，关键信息和专业术语。到了会场时，尽量不看稿，充分利用长期记忆中积累的知识来帮助理解，减少干扰。充分准备的另一优势在于，即便译员需要书面材料的帮助，也可以迅速找到该信息所处的位置，避免因手忙脚乱寻找信息而导致注意力分散和不够协调的问题发生。

4) 数字和专业术语：译员要加强数字口译的基本功练习，提高数字处理的敏感度和速度；也要通过译前准备和知识积累来提升专业术语上的认知程度。不过同传也是团队合作，译员可以要求轮休的搭档帮自己记录数字，写下或用口形告知专业术语的译文。

5) 同传技巧：同传中最大的一对干扰源就是听和说，一旦处理不协调就很容易导致加工精力的饱和甚至不足。既然译员在无稿同传时要消耗较多的精力于听辨理解之上，那么在言语表达上的精力自然就不会那么充分，所以要灵活处理信息，尽量用简单的词语或句子结构，不要过度使用等待技巧，增加短期记忆压力。使用同传技巧时更要灵活，尽可能让译文简单、易懂、流畅。

6) 极端情况：发言人事先拟好了逻辑严密、结构严谨、内容翔实的讲话稿，如大量复杂的英文句式，或是层出不穷的中英文数字，却不提供给译员，又在会上按照讲话稿快速地"照本宣科"。译员此时切忌慌张，一边要加强听辨，一边要灵活表达，还要在不违背忠实原则的基础上对原文信息加以取舍，果断舍弃次要信息。

无稿同传并非译员的噩梦，反而是帮助译员进一步提高协调能力、处理语言信息的好方法。面对无稿同传中可能出现的问题，译员要找到其根本原因，在场外做好充分准备，才能在场上有优异表现。

第二部分　案例讲解

> The following passages are from the practice materials for this unit. Sight interpret them into the target language.

Passage 1

在广东话中，数目字"九"与今年狗年的"狗"字属谐音，但与足够的"够"字也属谐音（1）。因此，我最好在这里作结。最后，我想引述毛泽东主席一首著名的词："多少事，从来急；天地转，光阴迫。一万年太久，只争朝夕。"（2）

▽ **技能提示**

（1）鉴于英汉两种语言在词汇上的差异，一些具有明显语言烙印的信息很难完全忠实地译出来。如文中此例，译员首先要考虑译文是否达意，然后再看看能否在力所能及的范围作进一步解释，比如加上这几个汉字的粤语读音，让外国听众更好地把握信息。

（2）无稿同传要求译员尽可能地充分准备。主题知识相对来说容易准备一些，但一般性知识的范围太广，往往打译员一个措手不及。一旦发言人引经据典，译员不能慌张，可充分调动知识和语言能力，通过意译还原原文内容。

▽ **参考译文**

In Cantonese, nine rhymes with dog which is the symbol of this new lunar year. It also rhymes with enough. So I'd better stop here. There is nothing political if I end my speech with a quote from one of Chairman Mao Zedong's famous poems, "So many things need to be done, and always urgently. The world rolls on, time passes. Ten thousand years is too long, seize the hour, seize the day."

Passage 2

由创新科技署全权监管的研究及发展中心，很快将落成启用。政府对这两所研究及发展中心承担了 23 亿元的投资。研究及发展中心主要进行与本港资讯通讯科技业相关的研究及发展工作（2），由应用科技研究院管理，并与大学和业界伙伴合作，集中进行通讯科技、电子消费品、集成电路设计和光电子方面的研究工作。（1）

▽ **技能提示**

（1）这段话中出现较多的专有名词和专业术语，给译员不小的挑战，尤其是无稿同传中，因为发言人介绍自己熟悉的内容时总是语速较快，而译员由于知识层面上的不对等，需要更多时间去反应和处理信息。如果没有详细发言材料可准备，译员就得把重点放在相关香港政府机构和电信等行业术语上。

（2）在介绍注意力分配时，我们强调了听力和表达的对立关系，相互干扰，争夺有限的加工能力。为了不让同传任务所需的加工能力超出译员的极限，我们就要减少单任务的工作负荷，有效地调配资源。这里的"研究及发展中心"和"资讯通讯科技"就可以用缩略语——R&D center 和 ICT——来译，省时省力，不影响下文的理解和表达。

▽ **参考译文**

The R&D centers under the overall supervision of the Innovation and Technology Commission will be up and running very soon. Two R&D centers, to which the government is committed to investing $2.3 billion, are particularly relevant to our ICT industry. The ICT R&D center hosted by the Applied Science and Technology Research Institute, or ASTRI, will focus on communications technologies, consumer electronics, IC design and opto-electronics. It will collaborate with universities and industry partners.

Passage 3

It's about the privacy and the economic security of American families. We rely on the Internet to pay our bills, to bank, to shop, to file our taxes. But we've had to learn a whole new vocabulary just to stay ahead of the cyber criminals (1)who would do us harm—spyware and malware and spoofing and phishing and botnets (2). Millions of Americans have been victimized, their privacy violated, their identities stolen, their lives upended, and their wallets emptied (3).

▼ 技能提示

（1）词汇的表达形式是固定的，但意义是灵活的。一个不会释义的译员是很难成功传递信息的，释义可以帮助译员更好地表达，克服产出上的障碍，更好地协调加工能力。例如，"领先于网络犯罪分子"听上去挺别扭，那就不妨换个角度，变成"打败网络犯罪分子"。

（2）同传译员拥有非常迅速的自动处理和反应能力，所以列举信息并不是一个很大的难题，但前提是译员知道译入语中的对应词，否则很容易停在一个词上，不仅这个词译不出，还因为思维的阻断和注意力的过度消耗而无法译出后面的信息。

（3）有些时候译员会卡在一个信息点上，脑子里有东西，但就是表达不顺畅。英文多被动，中文多主动，由于这里描述的情况都是不幸的遭遇，所以用"被"也可以，不过译员也可以把握隐藏的主语——网络犯罪分子，换一个语态。

▼ 参考译文

这关乎美国家庭的隐私和经济安全。我们在网上付账单、办理银行业务、购物、申报个税。不过，要打败那些会伤害我们的网络犯罪分子，我们得先掌握不少新知识，比如间谍软件、恶意软件、网络欺骗、网络钓鱼和僵尸网络。数百万美国人民成为了受害者，隐私被侵犯，身份被盗用，生活被打乱，钱包被掏空。

Passage 4

No single official oversees cybersecurity policy across the federal government, and no single agency has the responsibility or authority to match the scope and scale of the challenge(1). Indeed, when it comes to cybersecurity, federal agencies have overlapping missions and don't coordinate and communicate nearly as well as they should (2)—with each other or with the private sector.

▼ 技能提示

（1）发言人对特定信息的强调可以通过语气的加重或语言结构来实现，译员不仅要锻炼听力，还要通过阅读掌握不同的英文句式，如此例，no single… 有歧义，译员首先要迅速确定合适的含义，再根据上下文的认知语境（cognitive context）作出选择。传译时也要突出重点，如果表达不便，也可以反话正说。

（2）nearly as well as they should 听上去是个很虚的信息，也是中国的英语学习者较少采用的说法。对于译员来说，避虚就实很重要，不要在表达上过多纠缠，灵活套用常见中文表达就行，如"不尽如人意"或"做得不够"。

▼ 参考译文

联邦政府内部没有一个专门管理网络安全政策的官员，也没有一个全权负责如此之大规模挑战的机构。实际上，联邦政府部门在网络安全方面任务重叠，协调和沟通不力，不论是在政府内部还是与私有产业之间。

Passage 5

可以说全球经济都生病了，商业关系也正呈现出前所未有的恶化状态。看一看德国，几乎所有的德国产业都有下降的趋势，在法国已经有 3000 家公司在申请破产，数百万的人都失业了。在日本已经有 200 万人失业，日本的出口下降了 50%。在夏威夷这样的旅游胜地，他们的收入也有很大的下降，游客减少了 40%。在美国、在英国银行情况也不好，在美国有超过 40 家银行破产，失业率高达 7.6%。（1）（2）

▼ 技能提示

（1）汉语中的即兴发言多带有一定的冗余成分，同传时可适当归纳、简化，必要时将过于零散的小句整合，以符合英文表达习惯。

（2）本句中的数字都比较简单，而且不是集中出现，所以译员即便事先不知道发言内容也应该成功地将其一一译出。

▼ 参考译文

Global economy is sick and business relations are deteriorating like never before. In Germany, almost every industry is declining, while in France, 3000 companies are applying for bankruptcy and millions of people are laid off. Two million Japanese have lost their jobs and the country's export has dropped by 50%. Tourist destinations like Hawaii are seeing plummeting revenue as well, alongside a 40% decrease in tourist volume. Banks in America and Britain also have tough times with over 40 banks going bankrupt and a 7.6% unemployment rate in America.

Passage 6

Remembering that I'll be dead soon is the most important tool I've ever encountered to help me make the big choices in life. Because almost everything – all external expectations, all pride, all fear of embarrassment or failure – these things just fall away in the face of death, leaving only what is truly important (1). Remembering that you are going to die is the best way I know to avoid the trap of thinking you have something to lose (2). You are already naked (3). There is no reason not to follow your heart.

▼ 技能提示

（1）发言人不仅通过语言表达信息，还通过节奏、重音、语气等方式传递信息。因此译员需要在表达时把握这些辅助信息，让无法听懂原文的听众获得同样的感受。"语气"是同声传译的一项重要技巧。本句中，讲话人带有比较丰富的感情色彩，译员翻译副词 all、just、only 等词时可以加重语气，从而更好地突出关键信息，表达讲话人的意图。

（2）在无稿状态下，译员听不到完整的意群，而英语往往将修饰或者限定的成分放在句尾，因此译员在翻译的时候经常是话已说出口，听到后半句时才发觉意义有所偏差，处理不好就会前后不一致，有经验的译员要懂得去修补。比如本句中，译员顺句驱动，已经译出"……是我所知最好的方法"，然后听到 to avoid the trap of thinking you have something to lose，发现"最好"的方法并不是绝对的，而是有限定范围的。这时候译员要重新造句已经来不及，所以马上跟着往下说"避免掉入畏惧失去的陷阱里"。这一点信息补充上去，就和前面的信息合起来形成了一个完整的意义。

（3）naked 这个词虽然在上下文中意义是比较清楚的，可是在汉语中一时很难找到一个合适的词来翻译。译员在这种情况下不像笔译那样可以经过长时间的推敲，于是采取"解释"的技巧，把讲话人的意图说清楚即可。

▼ 参考译文

提醒自己快死了，是我在人生中面临重大决定时，所用过最重要的方法。因为几乎每件事——所有的外界期望、所有的名声、所有对困窘或失败的恐惧——在面对死亡时，都消失了，只有最真实重要的东西才会留下。提醒自己快死了，是我所知最好的方法，避免掉入畏惧失去的陷阱里。人生不带来、死不带去，没理由不顺心而为。

第三部分 术语拓展

汉译英

创新科技署	the Innovation and Technology Commission
电讯管理局	Office of the Telecommunications Authority
电讯条例	Telecommunications Ordinance
电讯委员会	Telecommunications Commission
电子促销	e-promotion
工商及科技局	Commerce, Industry and Technology Bureau (CITB)
光电子	opto-electronics
广播事务管理局	Broadcasting Authority
广播条例	Broadcasting Ordinance
规管环境	regulatory environment
国际电信联盟2006年世界电信展	the ITU TELECOM WORLD 2006
汇流	convergence
教育统筹局	Education and Manpower Bureau (EDB)
就职仪式	inauguration ceremony
宽频接达	broadband access
门户	portal
内置接收系统	in-building reception
频谱供应	availability of spectrum
射频识别技术	RFID technology
首席营销官	Chief Marketing Officer (CMO)
数码21资讯科技策略	the Digital 21 Strategy
数码地面电视广播	digital terrestrial television broadcasting
数码声频广播	digital audio broadcasting
腾讯智慧2009高效在线营销峰会	Tencent Mind—2009 Effective Online Marketing Forum
通讯事务管理局	Communications Authority
投资回报率	return on investment (ROI)
无线	TVB
香港电脑学会	Hong Kong Computer Society
（香港）无线科技商会	Wireless Technology Industry Association

谐音	rhyme
亚视	ATV
亚太资讯及通讯科技大奖	Asia-Pacific ICT Award
战略性驱动力	strategic driving force
兆头	omen
资讯通讯技术	information and communications technology (ICT)
自动互动话音装置	interactive voice device

英译汉

Acting Senior Director for Cyberspace	代理网络安全高级长官
Al Qaeda	基地组织
baton	接力棒
biological mother	生母
biopsy	切片
botnet	僵尸网络
brazen	厚颜无耻的
CIA	中央情报局
classified military and intelligence networks	机密军事和情报网络
Conficker	蠕虫病毒
cyber intruder	网络侵入者
Cybersecurity Coordinator	网络安全协调员
diverge	分歧，分化
dogma	教条
endoscope	内窥镜
FBI	联邦调查局
Homeland Security Council	国土安全委员会
industrial spy	工业间谍
intestine	肠子
karma	因缘，因果报应
malware	恶意软件
National Economic Council	国家经济委员会
National Security Council	国家安全委员会

New York Stock Exchange	纽约证券交易所
organized crime	有组织犯罪
pancreas	胰脏
phishing	网络钓鱼
Polaroid	宝丽莱（相机）
Reed College	里德学院
renaissance	复兴
Secret Service	美国特勤局
sedate	（使）镇静，打镇静剂
spoofing	网络欺骗
spyware	间谍软件
Center for Strategic and International Studies Bipartisan Commission on Cybersecurity	网络安全两党委员会战略和国际研究中心
Office of Management and Budget	行政管理和预算局
The Whole Earth Catalog	《全球概览》
thumb drive	拇指驱动器，U 盘
Toy Story	《玩具总动员》
typeface	字体
typograph	活版印刷

第四部分 同传实战

 Listen to the following four speeches and interpret them into the target language using the skills introduced in this unit.

Text 1

各位来宾：

谢谢大家邀请我来这个午餐会。为欢迎工商及科技局新任局长而设的同类午餐会，四年来已是第三次。我向你们保证，政府会贯彻始终，致力在本港推广资讯通讯科技。

身为工商及科技局局长，我的职责是为本港的资讯通讯科技发展展示愿景、制订达成这愿景所需的策略，以及拟订和推行有关措施，务求所得成果，在经济和民生上，都能造福社会。《数码 21 资讯科技策略》已定下一个愿景蓝图，让我引述当中的一段："致力于加强香港的资讯基建设施和服务，令香港在全球网络相连的21世纪成为着着领先的数码城市"。目前我想做的，是更清晰地解构政府达成这个愿景所须担当的角色。我认为政府须积极让业内人士参与——在座各位都是业内翘楚，可助政府制定配合业界需要的政策，制造有利于竞争和保障消费者权益的适当规管环境，以及推动投资和创新，令企业家、就业人士、消费者及整体经济受惠。我们发展资讯通讯科技业的基础非常稳固。现在让我更具体地说说我们未来12个月的工作议程。

首先，为应付汇流所带来的冲击，政府须积极回应，令我们的规管制度更有效，更能鼓励业界善用新机会。下午稍后时间，我们会发表公众咨询文件，提出把广播事务管理局与电讯管理局合并的建议。我的目标是于年底前展开成立单一规管机构所需的立法程序，单一规管机构拟定名为通讯事务管理局。

建议成立的通讯事务管理局将负责施行现有的《广播条例》及《电讯条例》。我们建议把广播事务管理局及电讯管理局现有法定权力和职能，按目前既有情况移交新管理局。为了尽快成立新管理局，我们不打算在此阶段更改该两条条例下的规管及发牌安排。不过，我们打算待通讯事务管理局成立后，立刻展开研究两条条例下若干条文的工作，以期保持连贯性，以及提高规管效率和给消费者更大保障。

公众咨询工作将为期三个月。我深信在座各位，定能把资讯通讯科技业界的真知灼见告诉我们。

第二、本港的资讯通讯科技业界须尽量在国际盛事中曝光，并取得席位，这是非常重要的。

相信你们都知道，香港将于今年年底承办国际电信联盟2006年世界电信展。这是世界电信展自1971年创办以来首次在日内瓦以外的地方举行。在中央政府鼎力支持下，我们于2003年争夺这项盛事的承办权，因为这对本地的资讯通讯科技业界及香港整体均有裨益。世界电信展会令香港及本地的资讯通讯科技业界名闻遐迩，而香港在内地和在世界各地的知名度也会大大提高。香港的地位提升，亚太区电讯和广播枢纽的形象也得以巩固。电信展将吸引900名参展商及6万名访客，并为本地接待服务业带来总值约9亿元的收益，凸显本港亚洲盛事之都的定位。

我们已经有一个很好的开始：目前70%的展览场地已经分配或预留。我们现正着力于市场推广和寻求赞助等事务上。我们会不断努力，期望2006年世界电信展能成为空前成功的电讯界盛事。在这方面，我相信能得到大家的支持。

第三、对本港推出的数码地面电视广播来说，今年是关键性的一年。政府须在年底前决定日后数码地面电视广播的制式。无线及亚视两家现有的地面电视广播机构须于明年推出新数码节目，其新数码网络则须于2008年前覆盖本港75%的地方。这刚好可配合2008年的奥运会。不论是工程基础设施、硬件设计和制造，还是高质量节目制作，均涉及庞大的投入。无线及亚视未来数年会投资数亿元，发展数码地面电视广播。届时不单是传统的资讯科技界，还有数码娱乐等创意工业也会受惠。消费者亦能接收更多元化和更高质素的电视节目服务，包括高清电视，以及有机会使用流动电视和相关的增值服务，如互动多媒体功能项目。相信政府与业界会于多个范畴上合作，例如服务规划、消费者教育、推广数码地面电视广播使用率、大厦内置接收系统、硬件设计和供应等等。

在数码传送方面，由于频谱供应有限和市场预期有需求，我会审慎和正面探讨在本港引入数码声频广播一事。事实上，数码科技带来了声音广播以外的商机。我们看到第三代流动通讯科技可在流动电话中作多媒体及广播用途；在其他地方，崭新的数码科技也可在小巧的掌上流动显示装置上提供多媒体及广播服务。

上述的科技发展制造了新的投资机会，也令消费者受惠，但同时也对规管制度带来了挑战。不过，政府的立场十分明确。我们会在政策方面提供支持，促进科技和商业的发展；但除了保障消费者的权益外，我们不会干预商界如何提供新服务和产品。

如果说过去十年，资讯通讯科技的发展为我们的社会带来翻天覆地的变化，一点也不为过。只消看看互联网、无线及流动通讯科技的发展、宽频技术在家庭的普及程度、网上资讯爆炸、互动娱乐，凡此种种，正改变国家、企业、生活方式、文化和人类行为。在全球化的环境中，我们须认清本身在全球中的定位。我们须反问自己，是否需有新的愿景、新的策略，确保香港继续成为全球领先的数码城市。

我已嘱咐戴启新进行这项工作，并鼓励他大胆尝试，承先"启"后，破旧立"新"。他向我保证，在制定新的《策略》时，会让资讯通讯科技界广泛参与，令政府和业界有共同而深切的认知。新的《策略》将于一年后，即明年首季推出。

各位，我列举了九项我们须于未来十二个月进行的工作。在广东话中，数目字"九"与今年狗年的"狗"字属谐音，但与足够的"够"字也属谐音。因此，我最好在这里作结。最后，我想引述毛泽东主席一首著名的词："多少事，从来急；天地转，光阴迫。一万年太久，只争朝夕。"引述这首词并无政治含意，我只想说，用这首词来形容以科技为本的商业世界，是何等贴切！我深信我们可携手合作，确保业界可达到目标及战胜挑战。我知道我能依赖各位的支持，进行上述九项工作，并为所有人——即社会、业界和消费者——创造全赢局面。

谢谢各位！

（2006年3月3日，香港特别行政区工商及科技局局长王永平在资讯科技团体举办的午餐会上的讲话节选）

Text 2

We meet today at a transformational moment—a moment in history when our interconnected world presents us, at once, with great promise but also great peril.

Now, over the past four months my administration has taken decisive steps to seize the promise and confront these perils. We're working to recover from a global recession while laying a new foundation for lasting prosperity. We're strengthening our armed forces as they fight two wars, at the same time we're renewing American leadership to confront unconventional challenges, from nuclear proliferation to terrorism, from climate change to pandemic disease. And we're bringing to government—and to this White House-unprecedented transparency and accountability and new ways for Americans to participate in their democracy.

But none of this progress would be possible, and none of these 21st century challenges can be fully met, without America's digital infrastructure—the backbone that underpins a prosperous economy and a strong military and an open and efficient government. Without that foundation we can't get the job done.

It's long been said that the revolutions in communications and information technology have given birth to a virtual world. But make no mistake. This world—cyberspace—is a world that we depend on every single day. It's our hardware and software, our desktops and laptops and cell phones and Blackberries that have become woven into every aspect of our lives.

It's the broadband networks beneath us and the wireless signals around us, the local networks in our schools and hospitals and businesses, and the massive grids that power our nation. It's the classified military and intelligence networks that keep us safe, and the World Wide Web that has made us more interconnected than at any time in human history.

So cyberspace is real. And so are the risks that come with it.

It's the great irony of our Information Age—the very technologies that empower us to create and to build also empower those who would disrupt and destroy. And this paradox—seen and unseen—is something that we experience every day.

It's about the privacy and the economic security of American families. We rely on the Internet to pay our bills, to bank, to shop, to file our taxes. But we've had to learn a whole new vocabulary just to stay ahead of the cyber criminals who would do us harm—spyware and malware and spoofing and phishing and botnets. Millions of Americans have been victimized, their privacy violated, their identities stolen, their lives upended, and their wallets emptied. According to one survey, in the past two years alone cyber crime has cost Americans more than $8 billion.

I know how it feels to have privacy violated because it has happened to me and the people around me. It's no secret that my presidential campaign harnessed the Internet and technology to transform our politics. What isn't widely known is that during the general election hackers managed to penetrate our computer systems. To all of you who donated to our campaign, I want you to all rest assured, our fundraising website was untouched. So your confidential personal and financial information was protected.

But between August and October, hackers gained access to emails and a range of campaign files, from policy position papers to travel plans. And we worked closely with the CIA—with the FBI and the Secret Service and hired security consultants to restore the security of our systems. It was a powerful reminder: in this Information Age, one of your greatest strengths—in our case, our ability to communicate to a wide range of supporters through the Internet—could also be one of your greatest vulnerabilities.

This is a matter, as well, of America's economic competitiveness. The small businesswoman in St. Louis, the bond trader in the New York Stock Exchange, the workers at a global shipping company in Memphis, the young entrepreneur in Silicon Valley—they all need the networks to make the next payroll, the next trade, the next delivery, the next great breakthrough. E-commerce alone last year accounted for some $132 billion in retail sales.

But every day we see waves of cyber thieves trolling for sensitive information—the disgruntled employee on the inside, the lone hacker a thousand miles away, organized crime, the industrial spy and, increasingly, foreign intelligence services. In one brazen act last year, thieves used stolen credit card information to steal millions of dollars from 130 ATM machines in 49 cities around the world—and they did it in just 30 minutes. A single employee of an American company was convicted of stealing intellectual property reportedly worth $400 million. It's been estimated that last year alone cyber criminals stole intellectual property from businesses worldwide worth up to $1 trillion.

In short, America's economic prosperity in the 21st century will depend on cybersecurity.

And this is also a matter of public safety and national security. We count on computer networks to deliver our oil and gas, our power and our water. We rely on them for public transportation and air traffic control. Yet we know that cyber intruders have probed our electrical grid and that in other countries cyber attacks have plunged entire cities into darkness.

Our technological advantage is a key to America's military dominance. But our defense and military networks are under constant attack. Al Qaeda and other terrorist groups have spoken of their desire to unleash a cyber attack on our country—attacks that are harder to detect and harder to defend against. Indeed, in today's world, acts of terror could come not only from a few extremists in suicide vests but from a few key strokes on the computer—a weapon of mass disruption.

In one of the most serious cyber incidents to date against our military networks, several thousand computers were infected last year by malicious software—malware. And while no sensitive information was compromised, our troops and defense personnel had to give up those external memory devices—thumb drives—changing the way they used their computers every day.

And last year we had a glimpse of the future face of war. As Russian tanks rolled into Georgia, cyber attacks crippled Georgian government websites. The terrorists that sowed so much death and destruction in Mumbai relied not only on guns and grenades but also on GPS and phones using voice-over-the-Internet.

For all these reasons, it's now clear this cyber threat is one of the most serious economic and national security challenges we face as a nation.

It's also clear that we're not as prepared as we should be, as a government or as a country. In recent years, some progress has been made at the federal level. But just as we failed in the past to invest in our physical infrastructure—our roads, our bridges and rails—we've failed to invest in the security of our digital infrastructure.

No single official oversees cybersecurity policy across the federal government, and no single agency has the responsibility or authority to match the scope and scale of the challenge. Indeed, when it comes to cybersecurity, federal agencies have overlapping missions and don't coordinate and communicate nearly as well as they should—with each other or with the private sector. We saw this in the disorganized response to Conficker, the Internet "worm" that in recent months has infected millions of computers around the world.

This status quo is no longer acceptable—not when there's so much at stake. We can and we must do better.

And that's why shortly after taking office I directed my National Security

Council and Homeland Security Council to conduct a top-to-bottom review of the federal government's efforts to defend our information and communications infrastructure and to recommend the best way to ensure that these networks are able to secure our networks as well as our prosperity.

Our review was open and transparent. I want to acknowledge, Melissa Hathaway, who is here, who is the Acting Senior Director for Cyberspace on our National Security Council, who led the review team, as well as the Center for Strategic and International Studies Bipartisan Commission on Cybersecurity, and all who were part of our 60-day review team. They listened to a wide variety of groups, many of which are represented here today and I want to thank for their input: industry and academia, civil liberties and private—privacy advocates. We listened to every level and branch of government—from local to state to federal, civilian, military, homeland as well as intelligence, Congress and international partners, as well. I consulted with my national security teams, my homeland security teams, and my economic advisors.

Today I'm releasing a report on our review, and can announce that my administration will pursue a new comprehensive approach to securing America's digital infrastructure.

This new approach starts at the top, with this commitment from me: from now on, our digital infrastructure—the networks and computers we depend on every day—will be treated as they should be: as a strategic national asset. Protecting this infrastructure will be a national security priority. We will ensure that these networks are secure, trustworthy and resilient. We will deter, prevent, detect, and defend against attacks and recover quickly from any disruptions or damage.

To give these efforts the high-level focus and attention they deserve—and as part of the new, single National Security Staff announced this week—I'm creating a new office here at the White House that will be led by the Cybersecurity Coordinator. Because of the critical importance of this work, I will personally select this official. I'll depend on this official in all matters relating to cybersecurity, and this official will have my full support and regular access to me as we confront these challenges.

Today, I want to focus on the important responsibilities this office will fulfill: orchestrating and integrating all cybersecurity policies for the government; working closely with the Office of Management and Budget to ensure agency budgets reflect those priorities; and, in the event of major cyber incident or attack, coordinating our response.

(Excerpted text of speech by US President Obama on Securing the Nation's Cyber Infrastructure on May 29, 2009)

Text 3

女士们、先生们，大家下午好，非常欢迎大家再次参加腾讯智慧2009高效在线营销峰会，我在这里见到了很多新朋友和好朋友。

首先问一些互动性的问题，今天是来讲互动的。互动在互联网世界中的确是一大特点，大家通过举手的方式进行互动。第一个问题，在座的各位有多少人认为世界仍处在经济危机当中？又有多少人认为中国仍然处在金融危机当中？第三个问题，有多少人认为这场金融危机会在6个月内结束？

可以说全球经济都生病了，商业关系也正呈现出前所未有的恶化状态。看一看德国，几乎所有的德国产业都有下降的趋势，在法国已经有3000家公司在申请破产，数百万的人都失业了。在日本已经有200万人失业，日本的出口下降了50%。在夏威夷这样的旅游胜地，他们的收入也有很大的下降，游客减少了40%。在美国、在英国银行情况也不好，在美国有超过40家银行破产，失业率高达7.6%。

再看看在现在的市场趋势下，让首席营销官晚上失眠的因素是什么。有5个战略性的驱动力是全球的CMO最为关注的，在这5个战略性驱动力当中有3个都是同数字媒体密切相关的。很多的CMO都需要Web2.0互动性和对企业信息的透明化，因此他们产生了对多种信息进行整合营销的需求。他们希望为最新的Web2.0的技术预留出市场经费，因此需要更高的投资回报率。这都使得全球市场的推广模式越来越多的由传统媒体转到数字媒体。

女士们，先生们，前面的三张图告诉我们世界是处在经济危机中的，危机的程度很多人还没有意识到，但情况是非常糟糕的，而数字媒体又是关键所在，因此腾讯才要讲这样一个主题，就是《经济危机下的数字营销之道》。今天我的演讲主要包括三个内容，首先花一点时间回顾一下在全球，尤其是在中国互联网媒体世界中发生的巨大变化。其次，分析数字营销在经济危机中为什么是最有效的解决方案。再次，讨论如何构建成功的数字营销战略原则。

这个男人在不久前刚刚改写了历史。现在他是全球第一大经济强国的统帅和领导者，其实他也是近年来最出色的首席市场官，为什么这样说呢？他最大的成功是把自己成功地"营销"进了白宫。大名鼎鼎的《广告时代》杂志甚至把奥巴马提名为全球最成功的营销人物。这里我只强调一点，数字营销在他的成功当中的确扮演了关键性的角色。

历史第一次，美国总统的就职仪式和国会演说在网络上实况直播。这样的现象只有当社会大众明确地认知到数字媒体是一种能产生巨大影响力的沟通渠道时才会发生。

从某种意义上说，奥巴马的成功更像是一个成功的营销案例，在总统大选这场营销的攻势当中，他最终赢得市场份额的优势。其实竞选总统就像营销，因为有非常高效的在线沟通策略，所以他才在最后赢得非常好的市场份额。

再看一些数据。根据 ComScore 今年 1 月份的统计数据，全球互联网人口已经达到了 10 亿，其中有 1/3 的互联网用户都在中国和美国。

仅仅一年前中国的互联网用户数量还落后于美国，大家看到今天中国拥有近 3 亿网民，去年刚刚超过美国，成为了世界上最大的互联网宽带市场。令人感到非常惊奇的是美国用了 20 年的时间开展互联网利用，中国只用了一半的时间就成为了世界第一；在美国互联网的普及率高达 80%，中国今天的水平只是比全球平均水平稍微高一点。互联网媒体的专家也意识到在几个月之后中国在线的用户要达到 5 亿人，这么惊人的数据是任何营销者都不会漠视不理的。

就媒体的营销来说，互联网的媒体是唯一在过去 5 年中保持持续增长的种类，而且现在越来越多的中国营销者把广告的预算转向在线的广告，尤其是当品牌寻求非传统的手段来达到目标受众的时候。

女士们、先生们，2008 年对于中国的互联网营销来说是最好的案例。这一年北京的奥运会是首次全方位通过互联网进行传播与展示的奥运会，我们给世界其他地区带去了奥运的热潮。互联网对于中国是具有巨大和深刻影响力的，互联网已成为了中国重要的政治沟通平台。大家或许没有意识到在今年的一些活动中，"两会"期间有超过数以百万计的网民通过腾讯网这样主要门户网站跟领导人进行沟通。

我可以举出许许多多的例子和事实，所有的这些事实都证明了这样一件事情，那就是互联网媒体已经成为影响中国人日常生活极其重要的媒体。原因是非常简单的，就是大家都已经意识到了互联网不再是新的媒体，而是中国的主流媒体。

下面我给大家放一个短片，也是我们这个团队向大家展示的，互联网是如何在短期内成为主流媒体的。这个视频展示了数字视频的巨大影响力，相信大家再也无法忽视数字媒体的巨大影响力了。

(2009 年 6 月 15 日，腾讯公司网络媒体执行副总裁刘胜义在"腾讯智慧 2009 高效在线营销峰会"上的演讲节选)

Text 4

Thank you.

I'm honored to be with you today for your commencement from one of the finest universities in the world. Truth be told, I never graduated from college, and this is the closest I've ever gotten to a college graduation. Today, I want to tell you three stories from my life. That's it. No big deal. Just three stories.

The first story is about connecting the dots.

I dropped out of Reed College after the first six months, but then stayed around as a drop-in for another 18 months or so before I really quit. So why did I drop out?

It started before I was born. My biological mother was a young, unwed graduate student, and she decided to put me up for adoption. She felt very strongly that I should be adopted by college graduates, so everything was all set for me to be adopted at birth by a lawyer and his wife – except that when I popped out they decided at the last minute that they really wanted a girl.

So my parents, who were on a waiting list, got a call in the middle of the night asking, "We've got an unexpected baby boy; do you want him?" They said, "Of course." My biological mother found out later that my mother had never graduated from college and that my father had never graduated from high school. She refused to sign the final adoption papers. She only relented a few months later when my parents promised that I would go to college. This was the start in my life.

And 17 years later I did go to college. But I naively chose a college that was almost as expensive as Stanford, and all of my working-class parents' savings were being spent on my college tuition. After six months, I couldn't see the value in it. I had no idea what I wanted to do with my life and no idea how college was going to help me figure it out. And here I was spending all of the money my parents had saved their entire life.

So I decided to drop out and trust that it would all work out okay. It was pretty scary at the time, but looking back it was one of the best decisions I ever made. The minute I dropped out I could stop taking the required classes that didn't interest me, and begin dropping in on the ones that looked far more interesting.

It wasn't all romantic. I didn't have a dorm room, so I slept on the floor in friends' rooms. I returned coke bottles for the five cent deposits to buy food with, and I would walk the seven miles across town every Sunday night to get one good meal a week at the Hare Krishna temple. I loved it. And much of what I stumbled into by following my curiosity and intuition turned out to be priceless later on. Let me give you one example.

Reed College at that time offered perhaps the best calligraphy instruction in the country. Throughout the campus every poster, every label on every drawer, was beautifully hand calligraphed. Because I had dropped out and didn't have to take the normal classes, I decided to take a calligraphy class to learn how to do this.

I learned about serif and san serif typefaces, about varying the amount of space between different letter combinations, about what makes great typography great. It was beautiful, historical, artistically subtle in a way that science can't capture, and I found it fascinating.

None of this had even a hope of any practical application in my life. But ten years later, when we were designing the first Macintosh computer, it all came back to me. And we designed it all into the Mac. It was the first computer with beautiful typography. If I had never dropped in on that single course in college, the "Mac" would have never had multiple typefaces or proportionally spaced fonts. And since Windows just copied the Mac, it's likely that no personal computer would have them. If I had never dropped out, I would have never dropped in on that calligraphy class, and personal computers might not have the wonderful typography that they do. Of course it was impossible to connect the dots looking forward when I was in college. But it was very, very clear looking backwards 10 years later.

Again, you can't connect the dots looking forward; you can only connect them looking backwards. So you have to trust that the dots will somehow connect in your future. You have to trust in something — your gut, destiny, life, karma, whatever — because believing that the dots will connect down the road will give you the confidence to follow your heart, even when it leads you off the well-worn path, and that will make all the difference.

My second story is about love and loss.

I was lucky — I found what I loved to do early in life. Woz and I started Apple in my parents' garage when I was 20. We worked hard, and in 10 years Apple had grown from just the two of us in a garage into a two billion dollar company with over 4000 employees. We'd just released our finest creation — the Macintosh — a year earlier, and I had just turned 30.

And then I got fired. How can you get fired from a company you started? Well, as Apple grew we hired someone who I thought was very talented to run the company with me, and for the first year or so things went well. But then our visions of the future began to diverge and eventually we had a falling out. When we did, our Board of Directors sided with him. And so at 30, I was out. And very publicly out. What had been the focus of my entire adult life was gone, and it was devastating.

I really didn't know what to do for a few months. I felt that I had let the previous generation of entrepreneurs down—that I had dropped the baton as it was being passed to me. I met with David Packard and Bob Noyce and tried to apologize for screwing up so badly. I was a very public failure, and I even thought about running away from the valley. But something slowly began to dawn on me: I still loved what I did. The turn of events at Apple had not changed that one bit. I had been rejected, but I was still in love. And so I decided to start over.

I didn't see it then, but it turned out that getting fired from Apple was the best thing that could have ever happened to me. The heaviness of being successful was replaced by the lightness of being a beginner again, less sure about everything. It freed me to enter one of the most creative periods of my life.

During the next five years, I started a company named NeXT, another company named Pixar, and fell in love with an amazing woman who would become my wife. Pixar went on to create the world's first computer-animated feature film, *Toy Story*, and is now the most successful animation studio in the world. In a remarkable turn of events, Apple bought NeXT, and I retuned to Apple, and the technology we developed at NeXT is at the heart of Apple's current renaissance. And Laurene and I have a wonderful family together.

I'm pretty sure none of this would have happened if I hadn't been fired from Apple. It was awful tasting medicine, but I guess the patient needed it. Sometimes life's going to hit you in the head with a brick. Don't lose faith. I'm convinced that the only thing that kept me going was that I loved what I did. You've got to find what you love. And that is as true for your work as it is for your lovers. Your work is going to fill a large part of your life, and the only way to be truly satisfied is to do what you believe is great work. And the only way to do great work is to love what you do. If you haven't found it yet, keep looking — and don't settle. As with all matters of the heart, you'll know when you find it. And like any great relationship, it just gets better and better as the years roll on. So keep looking — don't settle.

My third story is about death.

When I was 17, I read a quote that went something like: "If you live each day as if it was your last, someday you'll most certainly be right." It made an impression on me, and since then, for the past 33 years, I've looked in the mirror every morning and asked myself: "If today were the last day of my life, would I want to do what I am about to do today?" And whenever the answer has been "No" for too many days in a row, I know I need to change something.

Remembering that I'll be dead soon is the most important tool I've ever encountered to help me make the big choices in life. Because almost everything — all external expectations, all pride, all fear of embarrassment or failure — these things just fall away in the face of death, leaving only what is truly important. Remembering that you are going to die is the best way I know to avoid the trap of thinking you have something to lose. You are already naked. There is no reason not to follow your heart.

About a year ago I was diagnosed with cancer. I had a scan at 7:30 in the morning, and it clearly showed a tumor on my pancreas. I didn't even know what a pancreas was. The doctors told me this was almost certainly a type of cancer that is incurable, and that I should expect to live no longer than three to six months. My doctor advised me to go home and get my affairs in order, which is doctor's code for "prepare to die." It means to try and tell your kids everything you thought you'd have the next 10 years to tell them in just a few months. It means to make sure everything is buttoned up so that it will be as easy as possible for your family. It means to say your goodbyes.

I lived with that diagnosis all day. Later that evening I had a biopsy, where they stuck an endoscope down my throat, through my stomach into my intestines, put a needle into my pancreas and got a few cells from the tumor. I was sedated, but my wife, who was there, told me that when they viewed the cells under a microscope the doctors started crying because it turned out to be a very rare form of pancreatic cancer that is curable with surgery. I had the surgery and, thankfully, I'm fine now.

This was the closest I've been to facing death, and I hope it's the closest I get for a few more decades. Having lived through it, I can now say this to you with a bit more certainty than when death was a useful but purely intellectual concept: no one wants to die.

Even people who want to go to heaven don't want to die to get there. And yet death is the destination we all share. No one has ever escaped it. And that is as it should be, because Death is very likely the single best invention of Life. It's Life's change agent. It clears out the old to make way for the new. Right now the new is you, but someday not too long from now, you will gradually become the old and be cleared away. Sorry to be so dramatic, but it's quite true.

Your time is limited, so don't waste it living someone else's life. Don't be trapped by dogma — which is living with the results of other people's thinking. Don't let the noise of others' opinions drown out your own inner voice. And most important, have the courage to follow your heart and intuition. They somehow already know what you truly want to become. Everything else is secondary.

When I was young, there was an amazing publication called *The Whole Earth Catalog*, which was one of the "bibles" of my generation. It was created by a fellow named Stewart Brand not far from here in Menlo Park, and he brought it to life with his poetic touch. This was in the late 60s, before personal computers and desktop publishing, so it was all made with typewriters, scissors, and Polaroid cameras. It was sort of like Google in paperback form, 35 years before Google came along. It was idealistic, overflowing with neat tools and great notions.

Stewart and his team put out several issues of *The Whole Earth Catalog*, and then when it had run its course, they put out a final issue. It was the mid-1970s, and I was your age. On the back cover of their final issue was a photograph of an early morning country road, the kind you might find yourself hitchhiking on if you were so adventurous. Beneath it were the words: "Stay Hungry. Stay Foolish." It was their farewell message as they signed off. Stay Hungry. Stay Foolish. And I've always wished that for myself. And now, as you graduate to begin anew, I wish that for you.

Stay Hungry. Stay Foolish.

Thank you all very much.

(Full text of speech by Steve Jobs, CEO of Apple and Pixar at Stanford University Commencement on June 12, 2005, as transcribed)

第 10 单元 同声传译专向技能训练
Skill Training for Simultaneous Interpreting

单元学习目标
1. 了解数字和专有名词、从句及习语处理的特点。
2. 合理利用视译训练,提高专项技能。
3. 熟悉体育主题的常用汉英术语和表达方式。

第一部分 同传技能

在同声传译过程中,译员总是要全神贯注地去理解信息,并用目的语将其传达给译语听众。如此一心多用,自然对译员的要求很高,一些平时看似简单的东西也能带来巨大的理解和记忆压力,要么听不懂没话可说,要么心中有话却不知如何去说。不管译员经验多么丰富,语言能力多么出众,在同传现场,出问题的几率仍然很高,尤其是在细微之处。译员必须苦练基本功,才能以平稳的心态应对可能出现的困难。

不论在同传还是交传中,特定类型的信息、中英句法结构的差异和语法规约的要求都会给译员带来困难,增大译员处理信息的难度。数字和专有名词、英语从句,再加上两种语言里大量的习语,都会给译员带来理解、记忆、处理和表达上的压力。下面我们一起看看这些信息的主要特点和应对方法。

1. 数字

没有一个同传译员敢称自己在数字口译上没有任何问题。在日常生活里,数字不会给人们带来难题,无非就是 0 到 9 十个数字的种种组合,加上个十百千万之类的数位而已。但在同传过程中,数字的真实面目暴露无遗。作为低冗余度的硬信息(hard information with low redundancy),数字所含信息量大,属于独立的信息,与上下文没有语义联系,无法整合,记忆提示也很难设定,所以占据了较多的记忆空间。而数字的表达相对较快,占据了译员较多的注意力,稍有不慎,丢掉其中一个数字,整体忠实性就无从谈起。

这里我们不用很大篇幅来介绍数字究竟该怎么译，而是强调同传中数字口译的重点，从而让学员能够在平时进行针对性练习。

1）数位转换

在百位数之后，中文以"万"为基本数位，而英文用"千"，所以译员会在数位转换上慢一拍，甚至会在较为复杂的数字前栽跟头，究其原因就是数位没搞清楚，转换不成功。译员一方面要通过交传和视译练习加强数字敏感度和处理能力，另一方面又要在同传练习中力求在数字转换上实现自动处理，尽可能避免卡壳，尤其是在关键数位上做到条件反射。

2）计量单位

单位如果弄错了，美元变成英镑，公斤变成吨，即使数字译对了也没有意义（仲伟合，2007：50）。译员比较害怕的是连续几个数字，每个的单位却不尽相同。遇到这种情况，译员需要加强数字处理能力，不要把所有精力都用在数字本身上，还要留有余力去听计量单位，而一般计量单位并不难译，能听到记住就多半能译出，也可以用笔适当记录单位，特别是数字较多，译员本人表述不是特别跟得上时。

3）表达迅速

我们反复提到听与说的相互干扰，数字口译更是如此，若译员还要想这个数字该怎么译，那听的精力就非常有限了。数字表达一定要快，而且要准，尽量使用对自己而言最便捷的表达方式，比如一个位数较多的数字，就可以找一个最大的数位，然后把其余部分放在小数点后，便于表达。

4）把握介词

有时，译员听对了数字，却搞错了关系。简单的 of, by, at, in, to 等几个介词就能把译员原本清晰的思路搅乱。所以说，听数字自然重要，但若听不全面，那也是白用功。

5）模糊处理

遇上语速快、信息量大、数字多的发言，译员肯定会遇到麻烦。如果一连串复杂的数字在你没有任何准备的情况下向你袭来，译员不得不采用模糊处理的策略，把握关键数字，并通过四舍五入来简化表达。但是切记，这种做法违背同传译员的职业标准，我们并不提倡，只能在不得已的情况下偶尔采用。

6）团队合作

一个人的力量总是有限的，况且译员在同传过程中已经消耗了大量的脑力和体力，难免出现注意力不集中或信息丢失的现象。轮休的译员应该在搭档遇到麻烦时伸出援助之手，尤其是在数字方面；一旦听到发言人讲到数字，就要及时帮搭档记录，这样对方就可以把主要精力集中在产出上。记录时，不要只记数字本身，还要加上单位，最好能在搭档要说这个数字之前用手或笔提示他该数字的位置。

2. 专有名词

顾名思义，专有名词指的是特定的人、地方或机构的名称，包括人名、地名、国名、机构名、组织名、公司名，等等。其信息量大，表达语速快，是译员面临的另一个棘手之处。对待专有名词，译员首先要有备而来，既指平时大量积累常用的专有名词，如联合国各机构、中国主要部委和世界各大公司名称，也指译前进行充分的准备，把参会所有代表的姓名、头衔、所在机构等信息一网打尽，倒不用全部熟记在心，至少要心中有数，听到后能立刻反应过来。人名尤其要注意，现在有很多海外友人给自己起了中文名，比如领馆的领事、外交官、跨国企业的中国高管等，译员必须要提前了解，否则的话，水平再高也无法找到准确的译名。此外，译员要有灵活的临场应变能力，尤其是直译能力。一旦不清楚这个专有名词的官方译文，就要学会照字直译，比如"英国国家商务及专业英语协会"，其官方译文是 Business English UK，如果译员事先未能准备，就只能照字译成 The National Association of Business and Professional English in the UK。最后，译员如果实在无法译出新出现的专有名词，就只能采用最后一招——鹦鹉学舌，把原文的发音复述一遍，尤其是在英译中时。当然，这只是一种应急策略，不可滥用，否则听众会觉得译员没做好功课，现场糊弄大家。

3. 从句

从句是英语中常见的形式，包括主语从句、定语从句和状语从句等，稍微复杂点的英语句子里都有关系副词 when, where, why, how 和关系代词 who, which, whom, what, that 的身影。英文句子重心通常位于后面，有了一个固定的主谓搭配后，宾语部分信息可以无限延伸，尤其是通过大量的从句对前文进行修饰。面对这样的嵌入式结构（embedded structure），译员对句子结构的分析至关重要。

此前我们介绍了断句和等待两种技巧，它们是译员为了将表达最优化以及减少记忆和表达压力所采取的灵活方法。断句（或切分），意味着译员要在"一个复杂话语结束前，在短语和从句层面分解和转换独立的话语段"。(Pochhacker, 2004: 133) 等待则要求译员把听到的信息先暂存在脑子里，等到必要信息出现了再重新组织并表达。

从笔译角度来看，从句的主要译法包括前置法和后置法，前者是把较短的定语从句译成带"的"的前置定语，从而把复合句译成简单句；后者是把结构复杂且较长的定语从句后置，译成并列分句。严格来说，这些方法都可以用在同传过程中，帮助译员更好地表达。

但同传不是笔译，没有那么多的时间斟词酌句，只能在极短的时间内力求达意，所以，到底是用前置法（等待）还是后置法（切分），就是译员脑子里一瞬间的决定，没有必要为所有的从句都加上一个刻板的框框。为了能在一刹那间作出最好的选择，译员需要注意如下几点：

1) 熟悉英文句子结构

同传看上去靠的是译员的听、说和反应，实际上依赖于译员各方面的能力。口笔译的结合至关重要，通过笔译，译员能够对英语句子结构有更正确的认识，并且能够在听到一个句子时就主动预判其结构。所以，同传译员不能只把功夫放在嘴皮子上，还要放在笔头上。

2) 合理切分

英文从句结构虽然很复杂，但译员还是可以通过关系副词和关系代词等把握从句和主句的关系，从而准确切分原句。如果说第一点讲的是"理解"，那这一点就属于"表达"了。支离破碎的句子没人喜欢，译员觉得自己听明白了也说清楚了，但如果听众不买账，其工作也是失败的。所以在切分时，译员要注意一个度，不要盲目切，不要切得太细，也千万不能忽视"润滑剂"的作用，通过添加连接词和重复先行词等办法，尽量让表达流畅、符合逻辑。

3) 适当等待

没有绝对的切分，也没有绝对的等待。有经验的译员对等待技巧的把握较好，因为他们有很强的语言功底，丰富的主题知识，出色的信息判断能力，知道如何通过自己的知识来克服记忆的压力。反之，新手往往各方面都很稚嫩，盲目想通过等待来提供完整信息的话，只能徒增短期记忆的压力，很有可能竹篮打水一场空，前面记的信息也全忘了。一般来说，如果译员觉得听到的信息不足以组成一个句子或缺乏足够信息的话，就可以选择适当等待。

4. 习语

习语是一国风俗人情和文化历史背景的反映，其意义植根于各民族特定的历史文化背景中，承载着丰富的民族文化特色。作为一种语言在使用过程中形成的独特而固定的表达方式，习语的范畴非常广泛，包括成语、谚语、歇后语、典故等。发言人可以巧妙地使用习语，给演讲增色，但也会给译员带来更大的挑战。习语口译不仅仅是一个简单的文字解码过程，更是一种语言文化的传递过程。由于地理、历史、宗教信仰、生活习俗等方面的差异，英汉习语承载着不同的民族文化特色和文化信息，它们与文化传统紧密相连，不可分割。同传译员要成功译出习语，先决条件就是对中英两种文化有深入的了解。

可是光有文化意识和知识是不够的，同传译员的首要任务是准确地把发言人所讲的信息传达给译入语听众，既要听得明白，还要说得清楚，表达迅速。没有笔译工作者那么充裕的时间，没有字典提供准确的解释，同传译员要想在最短的时间内高质量完成任务，就必须在场内和场外都做足工夫。

场外工夫自不必说，译员如果能尽可能多的掌握中英习语，自然能更好地完成任务。可是每个人的知识总是有限的，同传难度大，其中一个因素就是译员总是面临新的挑战，如果没稿的话，译员不可能在会前就知道发言人要说的所有内容，再怎么充分的准备也会有盲点，因此场内工夫也很重要。

对于习语采取直译还是意译方法，译员没有时间去考虑，也没有必要去考虑。面对转瞬即逝的信息，译员要做的就是把握其核心的意义，一旦原文的表达形式成为译员理解和产出的羁绊，那么"得意忘形"就是最好的选择。这也符合释意派理论的要求：理解，脱离源语语言外壳，重新表达。

其次，临场中译员必须灵活对待习语，切莫因为一粒芝麻而丢了西瓜。如果死板地试图在习语翻译上尽善尽美，比如将四字成语里每个字的意思解释清楚，或长篇累牍地介绍某典故的背景，那就会无谓浪费大量加工能力，直接影响周边信息的理解和表达。

当然，这份灵活取决于译员的知识沉淀，取决于译员对信息的现场把握，也坚守着"一切忠实于原文"的准则。利用本身的知识，辅以上下文的提示作用，译员要迅速把握习语的核心内容，并将其译出。

第二部分　案例讲解

The following passages are from the practice materials for this unit. Sight interpret them into the target language.

Passage 1

据盖洛普民意调查显示，支持申办活动的北京市民占全体市民总数的94.9%。众所周知，新中国成立前，由于经济凋敝，社会发展落后，国民体质羸弱，中国人曾经被称作"东亚病夫"，给我们留下了刻骨铭心的回忆（1）。

▼ 技能提示

（1）此处有部分习语，虽然难度不大，但也足以引起译员的重视。"东亚病夫"可以直译成 sick man of East Asia，有较强直译能力的译员应该能在无准备的情况下将其译出，但是后面的"刻骨铭心"就需要译员多一个心眼，因为决定一个词的含义的，不仅是其具体的语言形式，还包括语境，尤其是那些可褒可贬的中性词，例如 talkative，往好了说是"健谈"，往坏了说就是"多嘴"。上文主要描述了旧中国落后的现象，因此这里的"刻骨铭心"是痛苦而难忘的，光说 unforgettable 或 be deeply rooted in our mind 还不够，点睛之笔在于加上一个 bitter memory。

参考译文

According to the Gallup survey, the number of Beijing residents who support China's bidding accounts for 94.9% of the total residents in Beijing. It is all known that before new China was founded, the Chinese people were once called "the sick men of East Asia" because of the stagnant economy, the laggard social development and the low physical quality of the Chinese people. Such bitter memory has been deeply rooted in our mind.

Passage 2

Thirteen years ago, my dad and I envisioned helping young people achieve their dreams through education (1). This work remains unchanged and will continue to grow. From the Learning Center students in Southern California, to the Earl Woods Scholars in Washington, D.C.(2), millions of kids have changed their lives, and I am dedicated to making sure that continues.

技能提示

(1) 和从句一样，介词短语做状语在英语里也很常见，而且出现的位置一般在句末，如果前面的信息较长，不宜过多等待，译员就应采用切分技巧将其断开，然后通过连接词、重复先行词或增加补充信息来实现译文衔接。这里的 through education 是表示实现梦想的方式，因此译员就可以加上"实现的方式是……"来衔接上下文。

(2) 译员没有充分准备专有名词，后果会怎么样？译员之所以遇到困难，就是因为发言人提到某些译员的知识体系里匮乏的信息，使得译员措手不及。更为糟糕的是，提到自己耳熟能详的信息时，发言人的语速会加快，让译员的听辨压力剧增，一旦会前没有做好准备，那可能的后果不仅仅是丢掉专有名词传达的信息，还会丢掉更多的后续信息，毕竟新信息的出现很容易打乱译员的节奏；严重的话，整句话都会因为个别的专有名词卡壳而被迫放弃。

参考译文

13年前，我和父亲就设想有朝一日能通过教育（资助）来帮助年轻人实现梦想。这个使命不会改变，规模还会越来越大。从南加州的学生学习中心到华盛顿特区的厄尔伍兹学者协会，千百万的孩子们改变了他们的命运，而我也会致力于帮助更多的孩子们。

Passage 3

举两个例子，一个比如说我们看到在欧洲有四大足球职业比赛，意甲、德甲、西甲、英超（1），这四大足球职业比赛产值、观众的关注度，以及包括体育彩票和竞猜度都是非常庞大的（2）。在美国有四大职业联盟，美国橄榄球、美国棒球、美国篮球和美国冰球（1）。(3)

▼ 技能提示

（1）译员到底需要多少知识？从这里的 8 个专有名词可见一斑。每个国家的职业联赛都有自己固定的名称，如果译员对此一无所知，就只能笼统地译成 professional league。知识从哪里而来？译员可以强记自己觉得重要的信息，也可以通过兴趣的培养来主动汲取新的知识，后者往往更为有效。另外要注意，在美国，橄榄球叫 football，而足球叫 soccer，和欧洲叫法不同。

（2）英文是偏静态的语言，名词占主导地位，而中文是动态语言，动词处于主导地位。可是英文的影响力与日俱增，直接导致大量英式汉语的面世。译员遇到生涩的中文时，首先要听懂意思，然后用自己的话释义，这样翻起来就轻松许多。这句话就可以改为"观众非常关注，大量购买体育彩票并参与竞猜"。

（3）发言人把该说的结构信息丢了，译员要帮他补上。既然是"两个例子"，就不能只有 first 没有 second。当译员发现发言人没交代清楚时，最好在说完这四大美国职业联盟后加一句 and this is the second example，或者用 the other 来导入信息。

▼ 参考译文

I'll give you a couple of examples. The first is the four major professional football leagues in Europe, including Serie A, Bundesliga, La Liga and Premier League. They have received huge profits and great awareness among spectators who take an active part in sports lottery and quiz competitions. The other is the four professional leagues in the U.S., namely NFL, MLB, NBA and NHL.

Passage 4

他说从人类文明进步，从游牧民族到农耕民族，到工业文明，到海洋文明，大海文明（1）这样一个发展，从不同的农耕文明的发展来说，可能是一种形态，比如农耕文明时候的体育，主要是从养生保健出发的，所以我们国家的养生保健是产生于农耕文明，到了工业文明，这个体育形态是对抗人体肢体的发展而创造的体育，到了现代文明，我们说大海文明也好，到了现代文明，我们说鼠标打天下（2），这样的一个时代，休闲它就与人们提高生活质量有关。

▼ 技能提示

（1）面对带稿演讲的发言人，译员需要跟得紧，因为信息比较密集，冗余度低。反之，如果是像这段发言一样的即兴演讲，译员就得把脚步稍微放慢些，跟得太紧，原文里零碎杂乱、没有逻辑或重复的内容也都被译了出来，不但不讨好，反而影响信息的完整和准确。

（2）语言是灵活的，发言人在演讲时可以充分运用自己的知识和语言能力来给演讲增色，不过也会给译员带来更多麻烦。"鼠标打天下"的表层含义是人们很依赖鼠标，深层含义是人们依赖电脑和信息技术。译员应充分发挥认知能力，将鼠标和电脑联系起来，并根据认知情景，传达深层含义，直接用鼠标的英文 mouse，台下听众不一定能立刻反应过来，这就违背了交际原则。

▼ 参考译文

He said that human civilization progressed from nomadic to agricultural, from industrial to marine civilization. In various agricultural civilizations, sports were mainly for maintaining health and that's where China's health maintenance practice was originated. Then in the industrial civilization, sports were developed with an emphasis on bodily competition. In our modern civilization, or marine civilization, when people rely heavily on computers, leisure is about improving the quality of life.

Passage 5

另外长三角作为中国经济增长最快的这样一个区域，休闲体育产业也成为休闲产业一个重要的部分（1）。面对如此各级政府正在大力提升城市生活品质，面对中国人全方位迎接休闲时代到来，我想从区域经济角度来谈一下，可能是非常有必要的（2）。

▼ 技能提示

（1）乍看之下，前后两部分没有直接联系，事实上只差一个词："（它的）休闲体育产业"。我们常说要读懂字里行间的意思，而译员就需要听出这些发言人无意中丢掉的关键信息。

（2）没有必要一见"面对"就用 faced with，虽说字对字非常忠实，但是过于死板，不利于行文，有时用一个 with 就行了，或者干脆把"面对"丢掉，用句子形式译出后面的内容，再根据发言人的信息进行结构上的调整。另外，在"面对……"和"我想"直接加上一个 therefore，突出原文的逻辑关系。

▼ 参考译文

Besides, Yangtze River Delta boasts the fastest economic growth in China and its leisure sports industry is part and parcel of leisure industry. Now with governments at all levels proactively raising the quality of life and Chinese people well-prepared for the era of leisure, therefore I think it's highly necessary to elaborate on that from the perspective of regional economy.

第三部分　术语拓展

汉译英

互不隶属、互不干涉、互相尊重	non-subordination, non-interference and mutual respect
魔高一尺，道高一丈	As vice rises one foot, virtue rises ten.
《奥林匹克标志保护条例》	Regulation on Olympic Symbol Protection
《财富》全球论坛中国体育圆桌会议	China Sports Roundtable Meeting of the Fortune Global Forum
《反对在体育运动中使用兴奋剂哥本哈根宣言》	Copenhagen Declaration on Anti-Doping in Sport
《反兴奋剂条例》	Anti-Dope Regulation
《公共文化体育设施条例》	Regulation on Public Cultural and Sports Facilities
《全民健身计划纲要》	the National Fitness Plan
《中华人民共和国体育法》	Sports Law of PRC
ATP 网球大师赛	ATP Masters Series
大众体育	popular sport
单项体育协会	international federation (IF)
德甲	Bundesliga
反兴奋剂国际公约	International Convention against Doping in Sports
盖洛普民意调查	Gallup survey
经济增加值	economic added value
竞猜	quiz competition
美国棒球（联盟）	Major League Baseball (MLB)
美国冰球（联盟）	National Hockey League (NHL)
美国橄榄球（联盟）	National Football League (NFL)
美国篮球（联盟）	National Basketball Association (NBA)
农耕民族	agricultural people
亲民、便民、利民	being close to people, convenient to people and beneficial to people
全民健身运动	National Fitness Campaign
世界旅游宣言	World Declaration on Tourism
女足世界杯	FIFA Women's World Cup

世界人权宣言	the Universal Declaration on Human Rights
世界休闲大会	World Leisure Congress
世界休闲组织	World Leisure Organization
体育彩票	sports lottery
体育竞赛表演业	sports competition show industry and production
西甲	La Liga
休闲体育产业	leisure sports industry
养生保健	health maintenance
衣食住行	daily necessities
意甲	Serie A
英超	Premier League
游牧民族	nomadic people
中国国家体育总局	the State General Administration of Sports
中华全国体育总会	All-China Sports Federation
自然资源禀赋	natural endowment

英译汉

Accenture	埃森哲
commercial endorsement	商业合同
domestic violence	家庭暴力
Earl Woods Scholars	厄尔伍兹学者会
fair play	公平竞赛
International Olympic Committee (IOC)	国际奥委会
International Paralympic Committee (IPC)	国际残奥委会
Learning Center in Southern California	南加州学习中心
Organizing Committee	组委会
paparazzi	狗仔队
Paralympic Games	残奥会
performance-enhancing drugs	兴奋剂
PGA Tour Commissioner	美巡赛专员
stake out	监视

第四部分　同传实战

 Listen to the following four speeches and interpret them into the target language using the skills introduced in this unit.

Text 1

尊敬的理查德·帕森斯先生，约翰·斯科尔斯先生，特瑞·迈克多诺先生，各位嘉宾，女士们、先生们：

《财富》全球论坛中国体育圆桌会议今天在这里开幕了。首先，我代表中国国家体育总局、中国奥委会、中华全国体育总会，并以我个人的名义，向各位嘉宾以及新闻媒体的朋友们表示热烈的欢迎和真诚的问候！

《财富》全球论坛创建十年来，已经是第三次在中国举办，这是中国经济和社会发展活力的反映。举办以体育为主题内容的圆桌会议，在历届论坛中也是第一次。这为观察中国体育搭建了一个国际化的平台，同时也为通过体育认识中国提供了一个视角，还为中国体育界向世界学习提供了一个机会。

中华人民共和国成立后、特别是改革开放以来，中国积极发展体育事业，大力开展全民健身运动，群众体育活动蓬勃开展，人民体质普遍增强，中国经常参加体育活动的人群已经超过4亿之众；中国运动员在国际赛场上屡创佳绩，竞技体育全面登上了国际舞台，成为世界体坛一支令人瞩目的力量。

在中国，体育的发展始终受到国家的重视。体育事业的发展是国民经济和社会发展规划的组成部分。在经济社会发展的不同阶段，国家都制定了一系列的政策和法律、法规。"国家发展体育事业"的内容载入了《中华人民共和国宪法》；1995年，全国人大常委会通过了新中国成立以来的第一部《中华人民共和国体育法》，国务院颁布了《全民健身计划纲要》。近年来，国务院又先后发布了《奥林匹克标志保护条例》、《公共文化体育设施条例》和《反兴奋剂条例》，为体育发展提供了重要法律保障。

中国体育的迅速发展，得益于国家对体育事业的高度重视，得益于广大人民群众的大力支持，得益于改革开放的不断深入和经济社会的持续发展，得益于人民群众生活水平的迅速提高，也得到了世界各国、各地区朋友们的热情帮助。

2001年，中国获得了2008年第二十九届奥运会的举办权。举办奥运会是中国人民的百年梦想。申办奥运会得到了中国政府和人民群众的大力支持。据盖洛普民意调查显示，支持申办活动的北京市民占全体市民总数的94.9%。众所周知，新中国成立前，由于经济凋敝，社会发展落后，国民体质赢弱，中国人曾经被称作"东亚病夫"，给我们留下了刻骨铭心的回忆。从无缘奥运，到参加奥运，再到举办奥运，不仅仅是中国体育发展的历程，更是中国从封闭走向开放、从贫弱走向富强的见证。

现代奥林匹克运动历经百年，规模日益宏大，影响日益广泛和深远。世界上的绝大多数国家和地区积极投身奥林匹克运动，奥运会成为世界各国团结、交流、竞争、合作的大舞台，其意义已经远远超出了体育的范畴，体现了政治、经济、文化多方面的价值，表现了非同寻常的综合效应和巨大影响。

2008年奥运会在北京举办，为中国体育的全面、协调、可持续发展提供了新的机遇和新的动力。

我们将继续致力于促进体育产业的发展，不断深化体育改革，积极培育体育市场，广泛调动社会力量兴办体育事业的积极性，积极研究制定政策规划，加强行业管理，完善体育公共服务。

面向2008年，中国体育将始终把人民群众的根本利益放在第一位，以举办北京奥运会为契机，以满足人民群众日益增长的体育文化需求为出发点，继续坚持普及与提高相结合，实现群众体育和竞技体育协调发展和相互促进，为建设社会主义物质文明和精神文明服务，为促进经济社会的繁荣、发展、进步服务。当前，中国正致力于努力构建和谐社会，中国体育应当在构建和谐社会的过程中有所作为。

各位嘉宾！

正如社会的发展总是在曲折中前进一样，体育的发展、奥林匹克运动的发展同样受到各种非正常、不健康因素的干扰。兴奋剂就是其中最突出的问题之一，已经成为世界体育的公害。反对在体育运动中使用兴奋剂是中国政府和体育界的一贯立场。2003年，我国作为首批国家签署了《反对在体育运动中使用兴奋剂的哥本哈根宣言》，国务院总理温家宝签署颁布了中国国内的行政立法《反兴奋剂条例》，得到了国际体育界的高度赞赏。目前，我们正在积极配合、推动联合国教科文组织制定反兴奋剂国际公约的努力。中国有一句古话，叫做"魔高一尺，道高一丈"，我们将与世界体育界的同仁一起，与体育发展过程中的各种丑恶现象坚决斗争，共同维护世界体育和奥林匹克运动的公正与纯洁。

体育的发展、奥林匹克运动的发展已经在全球范围内达到了一个空前的高度，同时，体育必将有更加美好的明天。对于中国、对于亚洲、对于世界，体育的发展都面临更广阔的前景，对此我们充满信心。我们愿与在座的各位朋友以及各个国家和地区热爱生活、热爱体育的朋友们携手并进，共同创造体育美好的未来！

最后，祝本届《财富》论坛及中国体育圆桌会议圆满成功！

谢谢各位！

(2005年5月16日，前国家体育总局局长、中国奥委会主席刘鹏在2005《财富》全球论坛中国体育圆桌会议上的讲话节选)

Text 2

Good morning! And thank you for joining me.

Many of you in this room are my friends. Many of you in this room know me. Many of you have cheered for me, or you worked with me, or you supported me, and now, every one of you has good reason to be critical of me.

I want to say to each of you, simply, and directly, I am deeply sorry for my irresponsible and selfish behavior I engaged in.

I know people want to find out how I could be so selfish and so foolish. People want to know how I could have done these things to my wife, Elin, and to my children. And while I have always tried to be a private person, there are some things I want to say.

Elin and I have started the process of discussing the damage caused by my behavior. As Elin pointed out to me, my real apology to her will not come in the form of words. It will come from my behavior over time. We have a lot to discuss. However, what we say to each other will remain between the two of us.

I am also aware of the pain my behavior has caused to those of you in this room. I have let you down. I have let down my fans. For many of you, especially my friends, my behavior has been a personal disappointment. To those of you who work for me, I have let you down, personally and professionally. My behavior has caused considerable worry to my business partners.

To everyone involved in my foundation, including my staff, board of directors, sponsors, and most importantly, the young students we reach, our work is more important than ever. Thirteen years ago, my dad and I envisioned helping young people achieve their dreams through education. This work remains unchanged and will continue to grow. From the Learning Center Students in Southern California, to the Earl Woods Scholars in Washington, D.C., millions of kids have changed their lives, and I am dedicated to making sure that continues.

But, still, I know I have severely disappointed all of you. I have made you question who I am and how I have done the things I did. I am embarrassed that I have put you in this position. For all that I have done, I am so sorry. I have a lot to atone for.

But there is one issue I really want to discuss. Some people have speculated that Elin somehow hurt or attacked me on Thanksgiving night. It angers me that people would fabricate a story like that. She never hit me that night or any other night. There has never been an episode of domestic violence in our marriage. Ever.

Elin has shown enormous grace and poise throughout this ordeal. Elin deserves praise, not blame. The issue involved here was my repeated irresponsible behavior. I was unfaithful. I had affairs. I cheated. What I did is not acceptable. And I am the only person to blame. I stopped living by the core values that I was taught to believe in.

I knew my actions were wrong. But I convinced myself that normal rules didn't apply. I never thought about who I was hurting. Instead, I thought only about myself. I ran straight through the boundaries that a married couple should live by. I thought I could get away with whatever I wanted to. I felt that I had worked hard my entire life and deserved to enjoy all the temptations around me. I felt I was entitled. Thanks to money and fame, I didn't have far — didn't have to go far to find them.

I was wrong. I was foolish. I don't get to play by different rules. The same boundaries that apply to everyone apply to me. I brought this shame on myself. I hurt my wife, my kids, my mother, my wife's family, my friends, my foundation, and kids all around the world who admired me.

I've had a lot of time to think about what I have done. My failures have made me look at myself in a way I never wanted to before. It is now up to me to make amends. And that starts by never repeating the mistakes I have made. It is up to me to start living a life of integrity.

I once heard — and I believe it is true — it's not what you achieve in life that matters, it is what you overcome. Achievements on the golf course are only part of setting an example. Character and decency are what really count. Parents used to point to me as a role model for their kids. I owe all those families a special apology. I want to say to them that I am truly sorry.

It is hard to admit that I need help. But I do. For 45 days, from the end of December to early February, I was in inpatient therapy, receiving guidance for the issues I'm facing. I have a long way to go. But I'll take my first steps in the right direction.

As I proceed, I understand people have questions. I understand the press wants to ask me for the details of the times I was unfaithful. I understand people want to know whether Elin and I will remain together. Please know that as far as I'm concerned, every one of these questions and answers is a matter between Elin and me. These are issues between a husband and a wife.

Some people have made up things that never happened. They said I used performance-enhancing drugs. This is completely and utterly false.

Some have written things about my family. Despite the damage I have done, I still believe it is right to shield my family from the public spotlight. They did not do these things. I did. I have always tried to maintain a private space for my wife and children. They have been kept separate from my sponsors, my commercial endorsements, when my children were born, we only released photographs so that the paparazzi could not chase them.

However, my behavior doesn't make it right for the media to follow my 2½-year-old daughter to school and report the school's location. They staked out my wife and pursued my mom. Whatever my wrongdoings, for the sake of my family, please leave my wife and kids alone.

I recognize I have brought this on myself. And I know above all I am the one who needs to change. I owe it to my family to become a better person. I owe it to those closest to me to become a better man. That is where my focus will be. I have a lot of work to do. And I intend to dedicate myself to doing it.

Part of following this path for me is Buddhism, which my mother taught me at a young age. People probably don't realize it, but I was raised a Buddhist, and I actively practiced my faith from childhood until I drifted away from it in recent years. Buddhism teaches that a craving for things outside ourselves causes an unhappy and pointless search for security. It teaches me to stop following every impulse and to learn restraint. Obviously, I lost track of what I was taught.

As I move forward, I will continue to receive help because I have learned that is how people really do change. Starting tomorrow, I will leave for more treatment and more therapy.

I would like to thank my friends at Accenture and the players in the field this week for understanding why I am making these remarks today. In therapy, I have learned the importance of looking at my spiritual life and keeping in balance with my professional life. I need to regain my balance and be centered so I can save the things that are most important to me: my marriage and my children.

That also means relying on others for help. I have learned to seek support from my peers in therapy, and I hope someday to return that support to others who are seeking help.

I do plan to return to golf one day. I just don't know when that day will be. I don't rule out that it will be this year. When I do return, I need to make my behavior more respectful of the game.

In recent weeks, I have received many thousands of e-mails, letters and phone calls from people expressing good wishes. To everyone who has reached out to me and my family, thank you. Your encouragement means the world to Elin and me. I want to thank the PGA Tour Commissioner Finchem and the players for their patience and understanding while I work on my private life. I look forward to seeing my fellow players on the course.

Finally, there are many people in this room and there are many people at home who believed in me. Today, I want to ask for your help. I ask you to find room in your heart to one day believe in me again. Thank you.

(Full text of Tiger Woods' apology for his affairs on February 19, 2010, as transcribed)

Text 3

非常高兴能够来参加这次会议！我在这里跟各位专家学者谈的话题可能有点不一样，我谈的是休闲体育产业。

这个里面首先想跟大家探讨一个概念问题，就是诸位专家学者更多的是用体育休闲业，我这里面用的是休闲体育，如果想用体育休闲业的话，可能不是所有的体育都带有这样的休闲性质。我们通常是把具有可操作性，具有产业化特征，具有休闲娱乐特征的这样一些体育，称为休闲体育产业。

首先我想提出这样的问题，休闲产业不用说了，主要谈休闲体育产业。休闲体育产业在当今社会当中，发展非常迅速。举两个例子，一个比如说我们看到在欧洲有四大足球职业比赛，意甲、德甲、西甲、英超，这四大足球职业比赛产值，观众的关注度，以及包括体育彩票和竞猜度都是非常庞大的。在美国有四大职业联盟，美国橄榄球，美国棒球，美国篮球和美国冰球。这四大职业联赛也占美国体育娱乐方面的产业也是很大。所以说，休闲体育产业在全世界正在非常快的速度发展。

另外，还给大家说一个事情。可能大家都知道，现在世界休闲组织的前任秘书长吉尼卡塞和现任主席，上午做报告的克里斯多夫·艾丁顿秘书长都是体育出身。所以说，秘书长一是到中国参加会议，是参加体育休闲会议，也可以看到体育产业在世界休闲组织这些官员当中扮演的重要角色。

第二谈一下长江三角洲。长三角被称为全球第六大经济圈，长三角经济就好比飞机已经在跑道上滑行，正在起飞，所以增长的速度非常之快。围绕着国际上休闲体育产业如此快的发展，中国的休闲体育产业到底有哪些资源？我们可以想象2008年在北京进举行奥运会，在长三角也有很多这些赛事，比如说F1，比如说ATP网球大师赛，还有就是女排夺金赛，12号举办的世界女子足球比赛也将在上海开幕，有很多民间和国家大型小型体育赛事，体育活动正在蓬勃发展。所以说，我们必须要来谈点体育市场，这个市场实在是太大了。

我还想谈一下开发休闲体育产业的必要性和可行性。必要性我不多讲了，上午克里斯多夫·艾丁顿已经把关于休闲成为人类社会主流的法律依据，从世界人权宣言到联合国大会，以及世界旅游宣言，都把休闲作为人类追求幸福的一种基本人权。所以这个已经成为我们这个社会当中，法律当中，国家当中非常重要的方面。

另外长三角作为中国经济增长最快的这样一个区域，休闲体育产业也成为休闲产业一个重要的部分。面对如此各级政府正在大力提升城市生活品质，面对中国人全方位迎接休闲时代到来，我想从区域经济角度来谈一下，可能是非常有必要的。2006年在世界休闲大会上，魏小安教授提出一个非常响亮的口号，休闲成为2006年中国休闲元年。我理解休闲经济成为中国经济发展的重要组成部分，一个最大的支柱产业。刚刚王教授说，一旦到休闲时代，可能占国民经济50%以上。二是休闲活动将从精英走向大众，休闲成为普遍的社会现象，休闲成为人们的生活方式。三是休闲与生活品质关系密切，成为提升生活幸福感、满意度的一个重要的元素，第四个是衣食住行、学习环境、工作环境都朝着休闲化的方向发展。

在2006年世界休闲大会期间，我还有幸跟魏小安教授聊了聊，他有一个观点非常值得我的思考。他说从人类文明进步，从游牧民族到农耕民族，到工业文明，到海洋文明，大海文明这样一个发展。从不同的农耕文明的发展来说，可能是一种形态，比如农耕文明时候的体育，主要是从养生保健出发的，所以我们国家的养生保健是产生于农耕文明，到了工业文明，这个体育形态是对抗人体肢体的发展而创造的体育，到了现代文明，我们说大海文明也好，到了现代文明，我们说鼠标打天下，这样的一个时代，休闲它就与人们提高生活质量有关。所以说，我觉得可能不管是成都的休闲文化也好，还是杭州休闲文化也好，我觉得这种休闲的文化形态可能都需要随着文明的进化需要改变。为什么这样说呢？因为成都是土生土长农耕文明发展起来的休闲形态，杭州尽管它有一个吴越文化，包括后来的南宋文化，但是主要形态还是以南宋文化为主，但是现在的文明社会，我觉得休闲的形态是从一种静态要逐渐向动态发展，要从室内逐渐向室外发展，要从家庭休闲逐渐向城市和社区休闲发展。到了现代文明，为什么体育在西方文明国家扮演者如此重要的地位，实际上是适合现在，就是大洋文明，现代文明这种形态出现的一种休闲文化的形态。所以说，我觉得休闲体育产业，在长三角已经出现了拐点，已经作为一个加速器在发展。为了理清这一点，我们有必要对长三角休闲体育的存量资源进行一些考量，比如说第一个，高水平竞赛表演，刚刚我们讲到的美国四大职业联赛，讲到意甲、英超这些市场非常大，我们如何利用2008年北京奥运会，把这块市场做大。

第二，单项体育协会和俱乐部资源，这块是在民间或者大众体育的高端。比如刚刚大家讲的高尔夫球场,在中国高尔夫球场大概有 200 个左右,在美国将近 2 万个左右,所以大家都知道美国高尔夫球场市场是非常大的。现在各种民间的体育赛事,民间的体育协会也越来越多。我的一位朋友今年暑假告诉我,他说今年暑假做了五场大型的民间体育赛事的裁判,这说明民间体育俱乐部和民间体育协会的活动很多,一些高层次人士体育赛事越来越多,大家花钱买娱乐,花钱买幸福,花钱买健康,这个逐渐成为时尚,所以这是一块很大的资源。

第三,城市公共体育场馆资源。随着人民生活水平提高,上海的人均体育用地已经超过 1.5 平方米,浙江已经接近 1 平方米,所以这也是一个很大的趋势。

第四,山水休闲体育资源。山水休闲体育资源实际上是指人们在闲暇时间内,利用山水等自然资源禀赋所进行的以满足人们身心健康愉悦发展为主要目的的体育活动。比如浙江的山水文化,就以它自然资源文化内涵影响着浙江的生活方式、取向、行为特点,也是休闲体育的最大的资源。

(2007 年 9 月 10 日,杭州师范学院体育与健康学院院长凌平在中国休闲产业发展研讨会上的演讲节选)

Text 4

Zun Jing de Hu Jintao ji Fu Ren,

Athletes, Officials, Distinguished Guests, Paralympic Sports fans from all over the world,

Wan Shang Hao, Huan Ying Ni Men

Good evening and welcome!

We are here tonight to celebrate the Opening Ceremony of the Beijing 2008 Paralympic Games.

These Games will have more athletes, more competing nations, and more sporting events than ever before.

As we embrace these milestones in Paralympic history, our hearts go out to the millions of Chinese people who have been affected by successive national disasters in the first half of this year.

Despite these tragedies, China and the Beijing Organizing Committee and its President Liu Qi were able to continue preparations for marvellous Olympic Games and what we are sure will be stupendous Paralympic Games.

I would like to thank you all for this great work and hope that our collaboration over the past seven years has been of a cordial, frank, constructive, temperate and deferential nature.

I would also like to recognize the support of the International Olympic Committee, its President Jacques Rogge and His Excellency Juan Antonio Samaranch who is with us this evening.

Over the next 11 days, the heroines and heroes will undoubtedly be the athletes.

Paralympians, you have invested many years of your lives to be here. Ensure that you perform at your very best, and that you respect fair play. You never know, you may even exceed your wildest dreams.

You are also here to have fun, make new friends, and create memories in the cities of Beijing, Qingdao and Hong Kong. This is not about hope, but about vision and what you represent. We want to experience your confidence and self-determination, ranging from elite performance on the field of play, to voicing your opinions in the IPC Athletes' Council elections.

I want to take a moment with you all to recognize this marvellous stadium. The "Bird's Nest" is a shining example of China's commitment to a modern world.

We all can see its monumental structure of steel, concrete, glass and other hi-tech materials, but this architecturally beautiful stadium truly comes to life when inhabited and animated by people like you, the spectators, performers, and athletes here tonight. When combined with the team and games officials, the media and the sponsors, and China's incomparable volunteers, you all create this unique Paralympic experience.

Starting tomorrow, we will see drama, we will see winning, and we will see disappointment. But above all, when we come together, we will be part of the creation of an almost touchable and definitely breathable distinctive energy source, which is at the heart of the Paralympic Movement, and it is what we call the Paralympic spirit. Once it gets hold, you will never let it go. It will last you a lifetime!

During the 12 days of the Beijing 2008 Paralympic Games, you will realize that the differences that you might have thought existed in the world are in fact, far less apparent.

You will see that we are all people of One World

Xie Xie! (Thank you)

(Excerpted text of speech by IPC President Sir Philip Craven at Beijing Paralympics Opening Ceremony on September 6, 2008, as transcribed)

第 11 单元　同声传译综合训练
Comprehensive Training for Simultaneous Interpreting

> **单元学习目标**
> 1. 掌握国际会议的特点和流程。
> 2. 充分理解同声传译的金科玉律，并运用于同传练习。
> 3. 熟悉环境主题的常用汉英术语和表达方式。

第一部分　同传技能

作为会议口译的主要形式，同声传译的工作场合基本上都是国际会议。所谓"国际会议"，即意味着与会代表来自不同的国家，使用不同的语言，代表不同的文化，体现不同的价值观，并且在会议进程中抒发和分享他们的想法和观点。一个合格的同传译员不仅要在语言和技能上拥有很高的水平，还要熟悉国际会议的基本特点和常见程序；否则的话，上场后难免手忙脚乱、左支右绌，甚至"怯场"（stage fright）。就好比一个本领高强的选手参赛一样，连规则和流程都不知道，怎么能拿下冠军？平时训练得再娴熟也发挥不出来。会议的"场合知识"（situational knowledge）是译员知识结构的必要组成部分，场合知识的缺乏同样会导致翻译不准确、不到位，甚至译不出来的后果（Seleskovitch, 1978）。

1. 国际会议的特点

国际会议最主要的特点是会议参加者的多样性，既指他们来自不同的语言背景，也指他们反映了不同的文化背景。发言人在讲话时使用各自不同的语言，一般来说，会议的工作语言至少两种，如汉语和英语，汉语和法语等。规模大、参与面广的国际会议会有数种工作语言，如 2009 年 11 月在广州举行的 UCLG 大会（世界城市和地方政府联合组织世界理事会会议），就有 7 种工作语言，需要译员进行接力传译；联合国大会更是如此。而且，发言人往往来自不同地域，讲话时往往带有各自地域的地方口音。针对国际会议的这个特点，同传译员必须具备良好的语言基本功，尤其是听力能力，既能应对英美等国发言人的标准英语，也要迅速适应如亚洲、拉丁美洲、非洲和部分欧洲国家的英语"变体"。除此之外，为了避免出现因文化差异而导致的问题，译员也要充分了解参会各国的文化背景。

国际会议的另一特色是千变万化、多种多样的主题。通讯技术和交通的发达，使得国际会议在各个领域遍地开花，今天的会议是关于金融方面的，明天的就可能是知识产权方面的。同一场会议上，由于发言人来自不同的专业领域，知识背景各不相同，发言的侧重点也各有不同。比如金融主题之下，有些发言人会谈宏观政策，有些就关注实际操作。因此，同传译员还必须具备丰富的知识面，像"传声筒"一样准确地传递出方方面面的专业知识。不仅如此，面对林林总总的国际会议主题，同传译员还必须具备快速学习的能力，有一份求知欲和好奇心，毕竟知识面再丰富的人也不可能样样精通。要想成功完成每次会议传译任务，译员必须要能在短时间内迅速了解会议主题的相关内容并熟记有关外语词汇，大脑要像海绵吸水一样快速吸取新的知识并理解相关内容。

2. 国际会议的流程

同传译员应该熟悉国际会议的流程，有备而来。国际会议的一般程序为：

1) 开幕式。这一环节内的发言多为主持人对活动的介绍和礼仪性的致词。其中尤其值得注意的是"来宾介绍"这一部分，里面包含大量与会嘉宾的信息，如姓名、头衔、所属机构等，译得准确与否至关重要，与译前准备相关，译员应注意参考会议的有关资料。

2) 大会主题发言。这是会议的核心部分，发言人往往都是重要人物，如政府主管部门的官员、知名企业代表、学术界带头人等，其发言多为有准备的演讲，就算没有全文原稿，也会有幻灯片演示，译员在会前要根据发言材料对这部分进行重点准备。

3) 问答/讨论/论坛。这部分的发言往往是即兴的，是会议主题发言之外的延伸，而且不同发言之间有互动的关系，译员在翻译时要特别注意这个特点，随时准备处理意料之外的信息。

4) 闭幕式（总结陈词）。这部分的发言既有礼仪性内容也有实质性内容，尤其是"总结陈词"部分，大会主席往往会回顾前面会议进程中各个发言的重要内容，并总结精华所在，译员要对整个会议有全面把握，做到心中有数。

了解会议流程最直接的方法就是会议议程，其中包括每个时间段的具体安排以及发言人信息，译员一般要在会议开始前向主办方索要。

3. 模拟国际会议

"模拟国际会议"是锻炼同传学员在国际会议中的实战能力的有效途径。

这一途径可用于有组织的课堂教学，针对的对象是拥有一定同传技能的学员。对于自学同传的学员，也可以自我组织几个或更多的学员一起进行这种实战训练。

既然是"模拟国际会议"，就要突出"模拟"二字，尽量还原国际会议的特点。学员分角色轮流模拟国际会议的发言，同时进行同声传译。为了使训练达到模拟实战的效果，最好在同传实验室或安装了同传设备的会议室中进行。教师或组织者可事先给学员布置好模拟会议的主题，如："危机之下中国经济发展的前景"、"产品设计与企业营销"、"网络时代的企业发展"等，要求学员自己准备 5-10 分钟的发言两篇（中、英各一篇），并将重点词汇提供给其他学员，最后由学员自己组织会议，轮流发言，轮流进同传厢里做同声传译。

"模拟国际会议"的练习不但能锻炼同传学员的口译技巧，提升同传实战能力，还可以让学员熟悉国际会议的程序，同时也使学员掌握了公众演说这一口译中另一重要的技巧（仲伟合，2001）。

4. 同声传译金科玉律

琼斯在其著作 *Conference Interpreting Explained* 中列举了译员在现场口译中必须遵循的十大"金科玉律"（Golden Rules）。在现场同声传译中，译员如果注意遵循这十条同声传译的"金科玉律"，将会大大增强同声传译的现场效果。它们包括（Jones, R., 2002: 267）：

1) Remember they are communicating. 同传是信息交流的过程，所以同传译员的首要目标是最大程度地实现发言人与听众之间的信息传递。与交替传译不同，同声传译无法在听完一个完整的语段之后再进行口译，而是每听到一个"意义小节"（segment）就要及时把意思传译出去。由于要保持源语与译语在时间上的"近似同步性"（approximate simultaneity），经验不足的译员往往"照字翻译"（word-for-word translation），译语缺乏意义或意义混乱，无法实现信息交流的目的。

2) Make the best possible use of the technical facilities. 同传译员要出色发挥，还得尽最大努力利用好现场的技术设备。首先，同传译员应确认他们能通过同传设备清楚听到发言人的讲话；其次，确认听众使用的同传接收器（耳机）能清楚听到自己的口译声音。这两点在现场会议开始前务必和技术设备操作人员一起确认。否则，发言人讲话传送的频道或者译员口译传送的频道出了问题都很可能延误会议的进行，并给译员自己造成不必要的心理压力。

3) Ensure they can hear both the speaker and themselves. 译员在同传时要时刻监控自己的产出，以便做必要的调整，所以不但要确保听清楚发言人的声音，还要保证能听到自己的声音。译员使用耳机接收源语时，耳机覆盖耳朵不应太紧，应该松紧适度，确保听到两方面的声音。

4) Maximize concentration. 译员在同传过程中一定要集中注意力，一边认真听辨、分析源语信息，一边用目的语进行翻译，绝不能有任何"开小差"的现象，一秒的疏忽都会导致重要信息的遗漏，译员要时刻把自己放在发言人与听众沟通的语境中。

5) Not be distracted by focusing attention on individual problematic words. 同传译员不能因噎废食，由于个别词语有问题而分散注意力，丢了整个句子的含义。口译重在"传意"，在同传过程中，译员要根据发言人讲话中不断涌现的新信息推测发言人的讲话意图及其内在逻辑线索，紧跟总体意义的大方向。这条规则的另一个含义是，同声传译不容译员有太多时间去思考。例如，面对一词多义的情况，译员要迅速根据上下文捕捉最合适的词义；或者说一个词有多种表达方式，译员要根据行文和搭配需要立刻找到最合适的方式，不可能像笔译那样字斟句酌。还有一层含义是，在会议现场，同声传译必须"风雨无阻"地连续进行下去，有错可以纠正，但是不能影响其他内容的传达，更不能为此而分散同传过程中必须高度集中的注意力。

6) Cultivate split attention, with active, analytical listening to the speaker and critical monitoring of their own output. 同传译员应善于"分脑"（split of attention），即一边对发言进行积极的听辨理解，一边对自己的口译输出进行有效的监控。要想边听发言人说话边听自己的声音，一种有效的办法是，控制译员耳机和自己输出内容的音量，保证嘴巴离麦克风的距离不要太远，否则，容易出现两种声音"打架"的现象，而且译员的声音到听众耳机里也像是在"吵架"。

7) Use, where possible, short, simple sentences. 同传时，若过分追求语言表达的美感或采用文绉绉的书面语言，会使译员本就捉襟见肘的加工精力更加稀缺。译语表达的标准是准确顺畅，有经验的译员在现场尽可能使用简短的句子，这样在同传过程中容易把握；把句子分节译出之后，在句间加上一些"润滑剂"，从而保证译语的连贯性和准确性，比如在将句子断为多个意群后，可以加上连词，将单个的句群联系起来，或者加上表示补述的词语，例如，"关于这一点"、"那就是"、"这种情况"等等。

8) Be grammatical. 这点尤其适用于译员用 B 语产出时。译语表达一定要符合语法；尽量让自己的每一句译语都有意义；尽量使自己译出的每个句子都表达完整。切不可因为句子的"切分"（segmentation）而使译语支离破碎。

9) Make sense in every single sentence. 译员所讲的每一个句子都应该是有一定意义的，不要把发言人所讲的"废话"也翻出来。

10) Always finish their sentences. 译员要使用完整的句子。在翻译过程中，

由于发言人的语速过快或译员一时反应过慢等原因,译员会赶不上发言人的速度,在翻译时丢三拉四,甚至没有说完前一句话的内容就直接跳到下一句的内容上来,结果听众听到的都是半句话,得不到完整的信息。

第二部分　案例讲解

The following passages are from the practice materials for this unit. Sight interpret them into the target language.

Passage 1

"一枝独秀",说在百花园里中国这枝花绽放了,但"一枝独秀"不能服众,在百花园里很多花都在开放(1)。"金砖四国"的巴西、印度、俄罗斯,还有"远景五国",还有"新钻十一国(2)……即使中国能一枝独秀,一枝花可能意味着春天的到来,象征着春天的到来,但它是百花园,必须百花齐放,必须大面积地兴起、共同发展(1)。

▼ 技能提示

(1) 译员在处理这部分信息时,主要的问题就是直译还是意译。相比之下,直译的难度更大,因为原文中的"一枝独秀"、"百花园"、"百花齐放"和"春天"等词具有非常明确的形象和引申含义,中国听众能够立刻明白其中的概念,但如果将这么多的"花"搬到英文里,不一定会有等同的效果,而且在选词上的难度更大,甚至还要多加解释。鉴于同传给译员处理分析信息的时间非常短暂,所以建议译员采用意译的形式,将"花园"换成"世界",将"花"译作"国家",将"春天"变成"经济复苏",虽说丢掉了原文的味道,但至少准确传递了信息,也不会因为用词不当而使译语不伦不类。

(2) "金砖四国"的概念早已深入人心,几乎所有译员都能迅速译出来,不过后文出现的"远景五国"和"新钻十一国"知名度相对不大,初次见到,译员恐怕只能照字直译。这说明了知识和准备的重要性。

▼ 参考译文

To say China takes the lead means that we stand out among all nations in terms of development. But it's not convincing since many other countries are developing well at the same time, like Brazil, India and Russia from BRICs, as well as those from VISTA and Next-11…Though the fact that China leads world development may mean the coming of better economic times, all nations have to grow together because we are all members of this world.

Passage 2

The latest science (1) shows us that climate change is a bigger and a more urgent challenge than had been previously understood. The latest report of the Intergovernmental Panel on Climate Change provides an even stronger link between human activities and climate change and clearly demonstrates the need for urgent action to cut greenhouse gas emissions. The economics (2) are also clear: the benefits of strong early action heavily outweigh the costs of inaction and business-as-usual (2).(3)

▼ 技能提示

（1）同传是理解和表达同步进行的艺术，除了要听得懂，还要说明白，这就要译员有扎实的语言基本功，"金科玉律"里提到要遵守语法规则，但也要符合目的语的表述习惯。latest science 很容易理解，但说成"最近的科学"就有点别扭，若能有意识加上"研究"，就能从细微之处见到译员在表达上的功夫。

（2）没有理解就没有发言权，而理解的实现要依赖认知能力和认知语境。economics 和"经济学"看似天生一对，但必须要放到上下文中检验才知道是否需要调整。哪怕译员没有听过 business-as-usual，也可以通过自身的英语词汇知识和上下文将其译成"传统的商业做法"。

（3）英文的嵌入式结构（embedded structure）让译员头疼，一般的做法是化繁为简，不要还原原文的结构，将其切分成短句，中间添加"润滑剂"。切分的关键在于把握原文里的连接词，如介词，关系代词等。

▼ 参考译文

最新的科学研究表明，气候变化给人类带来的挑战比此前所想的更大、更紧迫。联合国政府间气候变化专门委员会在最新报告中点出人类活动和气候变化更加紧密的关联，并明确表明，我们需要采取紧急行动，减少温室气体排放。它带来的经济效益也很明显，尽早采取有力行动的好处远胜于因坐视不理和固守传统商业做法所付出的代价。

Passage 3

2005 年至 2008 年，可再生能源增长 51%。水电装机容量、核电在建规模、太阳能热水器集热面积和光伏发电容量均居世界第一位。2008 年可再生能源利用量达到 2.5 亿吨标准煤。农村有 3050 万户用上沼气，相当于少排放二氧化碳 4900 多万吨。(1)

▼ 技能提示

（1）"金科玉律"里提到：不要因为一个词不明白，就丢掉了周围的重要信息。这不是说译员大可以把不懂的东西丢掉，而是要尽量灵活处理，通过上下文来揣度词义。但是，面对大量的专业术语，光靠猜测是不行的，译员要做好译前准备，丰富主题知识，不断提高自己的语言水平和知识面。

▼ **参考译文**

Between 2005 and 2008, renewable energy increased by 51 percent. China ranked first in the world in terms of installed hydro power capacity, nuclear power capacity under construction, the coverage of solar water heating panels and photovoltaic power capacity. In 2008, the use of renewable energy reached an equivalent of 250 million tons of standard coal. A total of 30.5 million rural households gained access to bio-gas, equivalent to a reduction of 49 million tons of carbon dioxide emissions.

Passage 4

Here at Copenhagen, few (1) organizations can speak with the authority of La Francophonie on the need for a global effort on climate change (2). We speak for both developed and developing economies, for both energy producers and consumers (3). We speak from many perspectives but with a sense of unity, forged by history, and shaped by our common language (4).

▼ **技能提示**

（1）英语里面看似肯定却表达否定含义的词不少，译员遇到这类词时要迅速作出判断，提炼出否定的含义，尤其是在双重否定句中。

（2）此句不长，但结构不简单，尤其是最后的三个介词 on, for, on 给译员带来极大麻烦，如果顺句驱动，就得在中间加上不少连接成分，而且句子会显得支离破碎。建议做法是适当等待，把握完整意思，调整句序，然后产出，这更有利于表达和听众理解。

（3）首先关注 for，在中文译文中重复英语原文省略的 speak，因为英文忌重复，而中文倾向于通过重复来增强语言效果。再看 energy producers and consumers，译员一定要学会利用上下文选择最合适的词义，既然上文说到了法语国家，那这里就该译成"能源生产国和消费国"。

（4）这里可以用顺句驱动，重复 a sense of unity，自然衔接。

▼ **参考译文**

在哥本哈根，要说全球共同应对气候变化的必要性，没几个组织能有法语国家联盟那么有权威。我们替发达国家和发展中国家说话，为能源生产国和消费国说话。我们表达观点的角度不同，但却团结一致，这份团结源于我们的历史，出于我们共同的语言。

Passage 5

The European Union has committed to a 20% reduction in EU greenhouse gas emissions by 2020 on 1990 levels, increasing to 30% when there is an international climate agreement, and committed to 20% of total EU energy consumption to come from renewable energy by 2020. (1)

▼ 技能提示

（1）同传的过程是运用自己的知识弥补听力缺陷的过程，也是运用知识主动预测的过程。在很有把握的情况下，译员可以在发言人还没讲到 by 2020 on 1990 levels 的时候就先把这个信息点说出来，否则就只有等待完整信息再产出。当然，我们并不建议译员总是采用预测手段，毕竟这带有一定的风险，不过，对于经验和主题知识都很丰富的译员来说，主动预测是一个很好的手段。

▼ 参考译文

欧盟承诺，到 2020 年，温室气体排放将在 1990 年的基础上减少 20%，如果世界各国在气候变化上达成一致，减排幅度将增至 30%。同时，欧盟还承诺，到 2020 年，全欧盟能耗的 20% 将来自可再生能源。

第三部分　术语拓展

汉译英

77 国集团	G77 (Group of Seventy-seven)
巴厘路线图	Bali Roadmap
标准煤	standard coal
草原法	Grassland Law
单位国内生产总值能耗比	energy consumption per unit of GDP
低碳经济	low-carbon economy
地热	geothermal energy
风能	wind power
哥本哈根世界气候大会	Copenhagen Climate Change Summit
共同但有区别的责任	common but differentiated responsibilities
光伏发电容量	photovoltaic power capacity
国际转移排放	international transfer emission
核电	nuclear power
环境损害成本	cost of environmental damage
机制保障	institutional guarantee
集热面积	coverage of heating panel

技术转让	technology transfer
减排	emission reduction
焦炭	coke
秸秆	stalk
节能减排	energy conservation and emission reduction
金砖四国	BRICs
京都议定书	the Kyoto Protocol
经济总量	economic aggregate
考核	evaluation
科学发展观	scientific outlook on development
可再生能源	renewable engery
联合国气候变化框架公约	the United Nations Framework Convention on Climate Change
落后产能	backward production facilities
贸易保护主义	trade protectionism
民生	people's livelihood
民意调查	survey/opinion poll
民用建筑节能条例	Regulations on Civil Building Efficiency
木炭	charcoal
排放强度	emission intensity
皮尤中心	Pew Research Center
气候友好技术	climate-friendly technology
清洁生产	clean production
热水器	water heater
人工造林	man-made forestation
森林法	Forest Law
森林碳汇	forest carbon sink
森林蓄积量	forest stock volume
生存排放	survival emission
生物质能	biomass energy
水电	hydro power
太阳能	solar energy
碳排放	carbon emission
退耕还林	return farmland to forest
温饱问题	issue of food and clothing
消费型排放	consumption-attributed emission

小岛屿国家	small-island state
新钻十一国	Next-11
信息披露	information disclosure
循环经济	circular economy
应对气候变化国家方案	National Climate Change Program
远景五国	VISTA
约束性指标	mandatory target
在建规模	capacity under construction
战略研究中心	Strategic Research Center
沼气	bio-gas
中等发达国家	moderately developed country
中国国际问题研究基金会	China Foundation of International Studies
中央经济工作会议	Central Economic Work Conference
装机容量	installation capacity
资源性产品	resource product
最不发达国家	least-developed country

英译汉

British Consulate-General	英国总领事馆
business-as-usual	传统商业模式
carbon dioxide	二氧化碳
carbon footprint	碳足迹
carbon labeling	碳标识
carbon market	碳市场
carbon trading	碳交易
China's Policies and Actions on Addressing Climate Change	中国解决气候变化的政策和行动
city planner	城市规划者
Clean Development Mechanism	清洁发展机制
Clean Energy Dialogue	清洁能源对话
energy efficiency	能效
energy intensity	能源强度
energy-intensive industry	能源密集型产业
extreme weather	极端气候
human migration	人类迁移

Intergovernmental Panel on Climate Change	（联合国）政府间气候变化专门委员会
La Francophonie	法语国家联盟
Marks & Spencer	玛莎百货
National Development and Reform Commission (NDRC)	国家发展和改革委员会（发改委）
post-Kyoto strategy	后京都（议定书）战略
public diplomacy programme	（气候变化）公共外交项目
Quebec	魁北克
renewable energy	可再生能源
sea level	海平面
supply chain	供应链

第四部分　同传实战

Practice in simultaneous interpreting booth by using the following materials. Pay special attention to the Golden Rules introduced in this unit. Organize mock conferences in groups by expanding on the theme of environment.

Text 1

中国日报网：聚焦全球时事，解读中国外交，欢迎收看本期的《外交讲坛》：中国外交2009年终盘点——倾听中国声音。今天我们非常有幸请到了两位嘉宾，一位是中国前驻伊朗大使华黎明，华大使您好。一位是中国国际问题研究基金会战略研究中心执行主任王　生，王大使您好。

今天非常感谢两位能来到演播室，为我们共同点评一下2009年中国的外交亮点与面临的挑战。

中国日报网：说完金融危机，再来说一说气候问题。最近这两天也在召开哥本哈根世界性气候大会。开会之前温总理已经宣布了中国在减排方面的量化目标。两位大使对中国的减排承诺怎么看？

华黎明：中国政府11月26日庄重地宣布，承诺到2020年人均GDP的碳排放比2005年要减少40%到45%。这个消息发表之后，整个世界都非常震惊，觉得中国这样的国家能够做出这样的承诺很不容易。有的西方评论认为很震惊，有的联合国负责气候变化的官员就说这是很令人鼓舞的消息。为什么？因为中国本身是个发展中国家，我们面临的问题是要发展，要解决人民的就业问题，解决城市化问题，解决很多地区的温饱问题。在这种情况下这么高比例的承诺碳排放，一个是中国作为发展中大国对世界气候的变化采取了非常负责任的态度，而且我们是做了牺牲的。根据有些专家的统计，我们做了承诺，从现在开始到 2020 年，我们的 GDP 增长率要影响一个百分点。中国的经济要可持续发展，要真正的按照科学发展观思路进行发展，就必须走"低碳经济"的道路，走低排放的经济道路。昨天刚刚结束的中央经济工作会议也指出了这一点，我们自身有需要，世界的责任也要求中国在碳排放中做出重要的承诺。应该说中国对哥本哈根气候变化会议是做出重要贡献的。

王 生：（关于）我们的承诺，据我的观察，这是经过非常认真、仔细准备承担艰苦责任的一种表现。不管这次会议的成果多大，但大势所趋，"低碳经济"将是未来世界发展的一个方向。低碳经济大家有各种不同的议论，但在我看来它有两个提高，提高生产发展的质量，提高人民生活的质量；它有两个加速，加速生产发展方式的转变，加速经济结构改革的进程；还有两个确保，确保经济可持续发展，确保环境清洁。

华黎明：我们自身的经济发展这些年来，是以高污染、高能耗为代价的，我们已经清楚地认识到这一点。我曾经看到过一个数字，改革开放 30 年中国 48 个湖泊都在重度的污染，我们花了好长时间治理到现在收益甚微。中国出于自身的需要既需要改善环境，对世界降低温室气体效应也要有所贡献。这是问题的一个方面。

问题的另外一个方面，中国毕竟是个发展中国家，世界上造成的温室气体效应和气候变化主要不是中国造成的，而是发达工业国家。他们从 17 世纪英国工业革命之后，400 年来累积造成的这种状况。公平地讲，他们应当对当前的世界气候变化负主要的责任，而且他们是富有国。举个例子，胖的人要减肥，而我们这些发展中国家还没有吃饱肚子，所以不是站在一个立场上讲话。中国不仅要代表自己，而且要代表 77 国集团，所有的发展中国家要发出自己的声音。

中国日报网：正如两位专家所说的，中国在发展经济巨大压力下，在很多全球性问题上展现出了大国的姿态。前几天美国皮尤中心公布了一个最新民调，有四成以上的美国人都认为中国是世界第一经济大国，甚至有人说中国现在是"一枝独秀"，两位大使怎么看这些评价？

华黎明：我也看到了美国的皮尤中心的统计数字，最近英国也做了类似的民调，得出的结论差不多，就是世界上下一个最强的经济大国是中国。其实还有一个统计数字，都不认为中国制造是世界上最好质量的东西，都认为质量是比较低的。这给我们一个警示，西方很多国家都意识到中国的经济总量已经发展很大了，而且很多方面他们指望中国来帮他们解决困难，指望中国来解决当前世界的很多经济问题，希望在中国身上压更多的担子。但另一方面他们又不是很看得起中国，认为中国制造中国的产品质量并不高。我们要清醒地对待，我并不认为中国是一枝独秀，因为中国 GDP 增速是很快，而且今年在这么困难的情况下还能够保 8，确实很不容易。但我们的经济增长质量还不高，中国 GDP 的含金量还不高，中国不是"一枝独秀"。"中国制造"质量的问题也有待于提高，为什么现在中国的产品在世界上屡屡遭到贸易保护主义，原因是出于他们比较狭隘的贸易保护主义思维，另外一方面恐怕也跟我们的产品质量有待提高有很大的关系。

王　生：这次调查我们承认美国舆论的变化，包括他说我们"一枝独秀"，确实在一定程度是从客观上反映出中国发展的速度是惊人的，在解决金融危机这个过程中，中国也是带头起稳定作用的，做了很大的努力。现在有迹象表明，我们跟一些国家会率先复苏。这是值得中国感到自豪和骄傲的，也是催促中国技术奋进的动力。但我们始终要保持清醒地头脑，从科学发展观的角度来看，应该非常清楚中国的定位仍然是一个发展中的社会主义大国，说发展中国家并不是谦虚，而是实实在在的。我们国民生产总值总是说世界第几，但人均收入还不行。原来讲到本世纪中期中国才能达到中等发达国家水平，就算是提前 10 年或者 15 年也还是中等发达国家水平。这个清醒头脑我们要有。

"一枝独秀"，说中国在百花园里中国这枝花绽放了，但"一枝独秀"不能服众，在百花园里很多花都在开放。"金砖四国"的巴西、印度、俄罗斯，还有"远景五国"，还有"宝石十一国（新钻十一国）"，这些答案虽然不是百分之百的准确，但大体上反映了一个趋势，就是发展中大国和相对的大国都在快速地兴起。即使中国能一枝独秀，一枝花可能意味着春天的到来，象征着春天的到来，但它是百花园，必须百花齐放，必须大面积地兴起、共同发展。现在印度、巴西、墨西哥、南非发展都是很快的，当然都有困难，我们也有困难。

现在特别引起我们注意的是，对中国唱颂歌的要具体分析，应该说大部分人是友好的，希望中国强盛起来，而且中国强盛起来之后能够跟他们进行合作，更好地发展。还有一部分人是为了跟中国做生意，还有一部分严肃的学者客观地看待中国，认为中国发展很快。但也确实有一些人是居心叵测的，我不想说他是别有用心，但可能别有企图。60 年来中国没有在围追堵截中被打倒，现在在新时期千万不要被糖衣炮弹、被颂歌迷醉打倒。

（中国日报网《外交讲坛》：中国外交 2009 年终盘点——倾听中国声音）

Text 2

Good morning, everybody.

It's a pleasure for me to be here today at the closing seminar of this project on "Managing Carbon in China's Supply Chains – China Climate Change Training

Initiative". The project is supported by the British Consulate-General through the British Government's public diplomacy programme. Whilst this may be a closing ceremony, I believe it is very much the start of significant new activity by the participating companies, not only to manage their own carbon emissions in their supply chains, but also to gain economic advantage by adopting and implementing low carbon business strategies. I congratulate companies here today for their foresight and active participation in this important project.

I would like to say a few words about why we believe that engagement of the business community is not only crucial to global efforts to address climate change, but it is also inevitable. Fortunately, we also believe it makes sound business sense for companies to take early action on reducing their carbon footprint, and indeed global efforts to address climate change are opening up a vast range of new business opportunities ripe for exploitation. I would also like to outline why we regard this particular project as important to China's national strategy to improve energy efficiency and to reduce greenhouse gas emissions, and I'd also like to outline what further support the British government will be providing to the business community in the coming years.

In the words of my Prime Minister, Gordon Brown, "the climate change crisis is the product of many generations, but overcoming it must be the great project of this generation and the entire community of nations". That's what Prime Minister Gordon Brown said last year. The latest science shows us that climate change is a bigger and a more urgent problem than had been previously understood. The latest report of the Intergovernmental Panel on Climate Change, this United Nations' body, provides an even stronger link between human activities and climate change and clearly demonstrates the need for urgent action for us all to cut greenhouse gas emissions. The economics are also clear: the benefits of strong early action heavily outweigh the costs of inaction and business-as-usual approach.

And let us be clear. The climate change is not just an environmental problem but something that threatens international peace and security, prosperity and development. If we globally follow a business-as-usual approach to energy production and consumption, then by the end of this century we will see mean temperature increases of up to 4 degrees centigrade. This will lead to significant sea levels rises with consequences for ecosystems, for agricultural production, for food and water supplies and for human migration. Here in Guangdong, we can expect more extreme weather, more flooding and greater disruption to supply chains which will affect the business community.

There is a growing international consensus on what needs to be done. The European Union has committed to a 20 per cent reduction in EU greenhouse gas emissions by 2020 on 1990 levels. The EU will increase this commitment to 30 per cent when there is an international climate change agreement. The EU is also committed to 20 per cent of total EU energy consumption to come from renewable energy by 2020.

My own country has even greater ambitions. Last month the British Government announced that Britain would have a long-term target to cut greenhouse gas emissions by at least 80% on 1990 levels by 2050 – this is the most ambitious target set by any country in the world.

And China, as I am sure you are aware, has committed to reduce energy intensity by 20% by 2010 and to increase its use of renewable energy from 5% to 15% of energy production by 2010. Other significant measures were outlined, as you've heard already, in the White Paper on "China's Policies and Actions on Addressing Climate Change" launched by the National Development and Reform Commission in Beijing two weeks ago. We applaud China for the measures it is proposing to undertake.

Whilst there is this emerging international consensus that action must be taken, clearly there is still much work to be done to reach agreement between both developed and developing nations on a post-Kyoto strategy to address climate change. This will be a difficult and complex process to be discussed at the highest levels at a major summit in Copenhagen next year.

But, simply put, agreement has to be reached — and we believe will be reached — if we are to avoid social and economic turmoil and the collapse of food and water supplies, and if our children are to enjoy the quality of life that we here in this room enjoy today. That agreement, in whatever form it takes, and the national strategies that flow from it, will have an impact on everyone, everyone in this room, including government officials, government policy makers, city planners, the general public and, perhaps most significantly, you the business community.

So let us look at the role of the business community, which is very much the theme of the project that we are supporting today. The British government is a firm supporter and advocate for globalisation. Eliminating barriers to the movement of goods, and services, and finance between countries drives global economic growth and we must not allow protectionist arguments in the name of environmentalism to prevent this.

Nowhere is this clearer than here in Guangdong. For 30 years, since the beginning of reform and opening up, Guangdong has led China's economic growth.

Guangdong's success has been down to its willingness to embrace global trade, to open its doors to foreign investment and to adapt quickly to changing overseas market demands. The current crisis in the world's financial markets and the impact that has had on global consumer demand shows how greatly interdependent national economies are today. It also highlights why it is even more important for governments and businesses alike to seek new strategies to stimulate economic revival and growth and to gain market advantage.

Globalisation has also seen the internationalisation and diversification of companies' supply chains, and, as you all know, many of these supply chains pass through Guangdong. You will also know that the international business community has a responsibility to effectively manage its supply chains, wherever they may be, not only to meet local legislation but also to respond to the increasing requirements of consumers and shareholders for production processes that are environmentally responsible and sustainable.

Change, as I'm sure you've all seen, is already happening. Leading international retailers such as Wal-Mart, IKEA, Tesco, Marks & Spencer and many others are seeking to "green" the products on their shelves. New international standards on carbon labelling are being developed. New legal requirements on reporting carbon consumption are being introduced. Over the next ten years we can expect to see a significant increase in demand from buyers, from consumers, from governments and from shareholders for an account of the carbon dioxide and other greenhouse gas emissions arising from production processes. The reason is the growing global awareness of the potentially catastrophic political and economic impacts of unchecked climate change that I have outlined, and the growing consensus about what needs to be done.

My government firmly believes that countries can maintain strong growth while making a transition to a low-carbon economy. Opportunities arise in the development and deployment of low-carbon technologies and services. Opportunities arise in the pursuit and promotion of energy-efficient and energy-saving technologies and in cleaner, more resource-efficient manufacturing processes. And opportunities arise in the evolving carbon markets, CDM projects and carbon trading.

(Excerpted text of speech by Tim Hanson, Consul of Climate Change and Energy, British Consulate General in Guangzhou, at the Closing Ceremony of "Managing Carbon in China's Supply Chains — China Climate Change Training Initiative" on November 12, 2008, as transcribed)

Text 3

拉斯穆森首相阁下，各位同事：

此时此刻，全世界几十亿人都在注视着哥本哈根。我们在此表达的意愿和做出的承诺，应当有利于推动人类应对气候变化的历史进程。站在这个讲坛上，我深感责任重大。

中国高度重视应对气候变化，已经并将继续做出不懈努力。

——中国是最早制定实施《应对气候变化国家方案》的发展中国家。近年来制订了一系列法律法规，把法制作为应对气候变化的重要手段。

——中国是近年来节能减排力度最大的国家。截至今年上半年，中国单位国内生产总值能耗比 2005 年降低 13%，相当于少排放 8 亿吨二氧化碳。

——中国是新能源和可再生能源增长速度最快的国家。2005 年至 2008 年，可再生能源增长 51%。水电装机容量、核电在建规模、太阳能热水器集热面积和光伏发电容量均居世界第一位。2008 年可再生能源利用量达到 2.5 亿吨标准煤。农村有 3050 万户用上沼气，相当于少排放二氧化碳 4900 多万吨。

——中国是世界人工造林面积最大的国家。我们持续大规模地开展退耕还林和植树造林，增加森林碳汇。近五年，森林面积净增 2054 万公顷，森林蓄积量净增 11.23 亿立方米。目前人工造林面积达 5400 万公顷，居世界第一。

中国有 13 亿人口，人均国内生产总值刚刚超过 3000 美元，按照联合国标准，还有 1.5 亿人生活在贫困线以下，发展经济、改善民生的任务十分艰巨。我国正处于工业化、城镇化快速发展的关键阶段，能源结构以煤为主，降低排放存在着特殊的困难。但是，我们始终把应对气候变化作为重要战略任务。1990 至 2005 年，单位国内生产总值二氧化碳排放强度下降了 46%。在此基础上，我们又提出，到 2020 年单位国内生产总值二氧化碳排放比 2005 年下降 40% – 45%，在如此长时间内这样大规模降低二氧化碳排放，需要付出艰苦卓绝的努力。我们的减排目标将作为约束性指标纳入国民经济和社会发展的中长期规划，保证承诺的执行受到法律和舆论的监督。我们将进一步完善国内统计、监测、考核办法，改进减排信息的披露方式，增加透明度，积极开展国际交流、对话与合作。

各位同事，

应对气候变化需要国际社会坚定信心，凝聚共识，积极努力，加强合作。必须始终牢牢把握以下几点：

第一，保持成果的一致性。《联合国气候变化框架公约》及其《京都议定书》是各国经过长期艰苦努力取得的成果，是国际合作应对气候变化的法律基础和行动指南，必须倍加珍惜、巩固发展。本次会议的成果必须坚持而不能模糊公约及其议定书的基本原则，必须遵循而不能偏离"巴厘路线图"

的授权，必须锁定而不能否定业已达成的共识和谈判取得的进展。

第二，坚持规则的公平性。"共同但有区别的责任"原则是国际合作应对气候变化的核心和基石，应当始终坚持。应对气候变化决不能无视历史责任，无视人均排放和各国的发展水平，决不能以延续发展中国家的贫穷和落后为代价，只能在可持续发展的框架下，统筹安排。

第三，注重目标的合理性。应对气候变化既要着眼长远，更要立足当前。确定一个长远的努力方向是必要的，更重要的是要把重点放在完成近期和中期的减排目标上，放在兑现业已做出的承诺上，放在行动上。一打纲领不如一个行动，我们应该通过一个实际的行动，让人们看到希望。

第四，确保机制的有效性。要在公约框架下做出切实有效的制度安排，促使发达国家兑现承诺，向发展中国家持续提供充足的资金支持，加快转让气候友好技术，有效帮助发展中国家、特别是小岛屿国家、最不发达国家、内陆国家、非洲国家加强应对气候变化的能力建设。

最后，我要强调的是，中国政府确定减缓温室气体排放的目标是中国根据国情采取的自主行动，是对中国人民和全人类负责的，不附加任何条件，不与任何国家的减排目标挂钩。我们言必信、行必果，无论本次会议达成什么成果，都将坚定不移地为实现、甚至超过这个目标而努力。

谢谢！

（2009年12月18日，温家宝总理在哥本哈根气候变化会议领导人会议上的讲话全文，根据录音材料整理）

Text 4

Thank you, Monsieur Duhaime, for your kind introduction.

I want to thank Mrs. Dia Touré and her team at l'Institut de l'énergie et de l'environnement de la Francophonie for the excellent work they have done to prepare for today's meeting. I would like to thank all of you for being here.

Here at Copenhagen, few organizations can speak with the authority of La Francophonie on the need for a global effort on climate change. We speak for both developed and developing economies; for both energy producers and consumers. We speak from many perspectives but with a sense of unity, forged by history, and shaped by our common language.

The Francophonie gives voice to those countries that are the most vulnerable to climate change.

The Francophonie also gives voice to those countries that have the capacity to lead, to help, and to provide solutions, countries at the forefront of research, development and deployment, countries that are creating sustainable technologies for a greener economy, countries that can lead and share knowledge, on the basis of their economic strength.

From different perspectives and experiences, we work together on our vision for the future. We pursue the goals that leaders from La Francophonie set forth in October, 2008, at the 12th Summit in Quebec City.

We will include climate change issues in our development policies, and transfer the technology that will help all countries address a problem that knows no borders. We will address the profound issues that are affected by climate change — from the quality of our water to the biodiversity of our ecosystems. We will build upon our strengths as partners in la Francophonie.

For our part, Canada's objectives are clear, transparent, and based on five principles.

First, we will balance environmental protection with economic prosperity.

Second, we will maintain a long-term focus. We will put in place today the policies that will contribute to the goal of reducing global emissions by 50 percent by 2050.

Third, we will work with our international partners to seek commitments from all major economies including all major emitters. At the same time we support the least developed countries who do not have the resources to manage climate change and adaptation. At the Quebec Summit Prime Minister Harper announced that Canada would dedicate $100 million to international climate change adaptation to assist those countries that are especially vulnerable.

Fourth, we will continue to invest in the research, development and deployment of clean technologies, and transfer those technologies to where they are most needed.

And fifth, we will support constructive and ambitious global action.

Canada's message at Copenhagen is simple: Canada will be a positive force in order to get an agreement. Canada will do its share to fight the problem of climate change.

We apply these principles in our domestic and international agendas. But Canada's strength in the global economy comes, in large part, from the integration of our economy within a North American marketplace. Our responses to climate change must be integrated within a North American response.

Canada has committed to a 20 percent reduction in greenhouse gas emissions from 2006 by 2020. This is an ambitious but realistic goal for a country of extreme temperatures, such long distances, energy-intensive industries, and a growing population.

We will continue to work hand and glove with the Obama Administration, aligning our climate change policies.

We work with our American neighbours on the Clean Energy Dialogue launched by Prime Minister Harper and President Obama earlier this year. And we will continue to contribute our economic and technological strength to North American solutions that will be an integral part to global solutions to climate change.

Ladies and gentlemen, colleagues, each country of la Francophonie brings different challenges and different capacities to the global challenge of climate change. Canada brings our potential to integrate efforts on a North American basis. We bring, as well, our capacity for innovation and the development of clean energy. We are a country, after all, that has set our goal at 90 percent of electricity from clean energy sources by 2020.

Canada brings her robust natural environment — the huge expanses of wild regions that serve as the lungs of our mother planet, absorbing carbon dioxide, and breathing out the oxygen.

Canada's wilderness areas provide solutions to climate change. But they also remind us of the vulnerability of fragile ecosystems. They are an inspiration to us, but they are also a stark reminder of what is at stake if we do not reduce emissions.

La Francophonie brings many voices and many perspectives to bear. We have many challenges to address and many solutions to offer.

I look forward to our discussion and I look forward to a constructive and successful collaboration.

(Full text of speech by Jim Prentice, Minister of the Environment in Canada to the Francophonie Luncheon in Copenhagen, Denmark on December 16, 2009)

附录 1　参考译文

第 2 单元

Text 1

　　Lastly, I will talk about the positioning of the promotion of Chinese tourism. For years, we have emphasized the cultural and historical aspects of tourism, like the promotion for the Great Wall and the Forbidden City, but we have not had a slogan, or a tag line that reflects the features of our tourism products.

　　The World Tourism Organization hasn't really had a try on this in China from a macro perspective. But we have had one or two projects. One example is Harbin in Heilongjiang Province. Harbin is not a very attractive city for tourists; at least not a city with top-class tourism resources. Then how do we promote a city like this? After meticulous consideration , we came up with "the Cool Capital of China". C-o-o-l, being cool is very popular among youngsters. Then, why do we call Harbin a cool capital? We have three considerations. The first one is its winter. In winter, Harbin is a city of snow and ice. So it is very cool. The second one is its mild summer. The temperature of Harbin, of the Sun Island, is not very high. The third one is its fad and fashion. Harbin used to be called the Oriental Moscow. So this slogan is the combination of these three features. In fact this is a word trick, too. But once you find a proper one, you should stick to it. It seems that Harbin is still using this slogan.

　　The second example is the overall slogan for Hainan Province. It's not easy to find a proper slogan for Hainan. Hainan is famous for its seaside resort in China, but not in the world. Not many foreigners know that Hainan is a seaside resort. Its fame falls far behind that of Bali in Indonesia or Phuket in Thailand. Then how do we stress Hainan's feature? The slogan we came up with is "Tropical China". Why do we use the word "tropical"? Because when people talk about China, the first thing in their mind is China's history and culture. No one has ever thought that part of China is in the tropical zone. That's why we adopted this slogan to see if it is attractive to tourists.

　　Now Chinese tourism is in a strategic transitional period. During this period, which features a shift from sightseeing to leisure tourism, from quantity to quality, and from mass tourism products to specialized tourism products. Our key priority is sustainable development. Only if we carry out sustainable development, can we maintain the vitality of the tourism industry. So I wish to give you some advice – I hope we do not do so much addition, but do more subtraction, because sometimes the less is more. Thank you!

(Excerpted text of speech by Xu Jing, Regional Representative of Asia and Pacific of the World Tourism Organisation at the International Tourism and Hospitality Industry Development Forum, December 16, 2005)

Text 2

罗思乐先生，尊敬的来宾，女士们、先生们：

早上好！

非常荣幸能与大家齐聚香港迪斯尼扩建工程动土仪式，今天标志着香港迪斯尼和香港旅游业一个重要的里程碑。

香港迪斯尼是我们重要的旅游基础设施。自2005年9月开业以来，已接待了超过1900万游客，为香港经济贡献了100多亿美元。香港迪斯尼每年还创造10000多个就业岗位。

此次扩建工程将增加三个新的主题园区，30多个新的景点和体验设施。一些景点将是香港迪斯尼所特有的。扩建的乐园和新增的景点将继续吸引大批游客，并为大家提供更多的乐趣和惊喜。

去年，香港吸引了来自全球的3000万游客。尽管遭遇了全球金融危机，我们预计今年的游客数量仍将保持这个水平。

我们将继续加强对景点的宣传，以进一步提升香港作为热门旅游目的地的吸引力。

过去的几年中，香港在景点上的投资超过300亿美元。在未来几年中，我们还将投资170亿美元用于旅游基础设施建设。一个世界级的游轮港口已经动工，我们还将进一步提升一些著名景点的吸引力，如尖沙咀、昂坪和鲤鱼门。

香港是一个充满活力的城市。这一年当中，我们举办了很多特色活动，吸引了众多市民及游客。"香港美酒佳肴巡礼"在今年早些时候举行，已被福布斯旅游网评为十大国际美酒美食节之一。中国新年庆典也被"Lonely Planet"公司誉为"世界最具价值的娱乐活动"。

总值1亿美元的"盛世基金"将于今年启动，它将继续吸引国际艺术、文化和体育盛事来到我们的城市。

有了扩建后的香港迪斯尼乐园，我深信香港将继续成为全球各地各年龄段朋友们的首选旅游目的地。

谢谢！祝各位开心！

（香港特别行政区财政司司长曾俊华在"香港迪斯尼乐园扩建动土仪式"上的讲话全文）

Text 3

Distinguished Delegates, Ladies and Gentlemen,

The two day's "China (Guangxi)—ASEAN International Tourism Cooperation Forum", which is co-organised by the Guangxi Tourism Administration, Guangxi Academy of Social Sciences and *China Tourism* magazine, is coming to its conclusion. In the past two days, experts, scholars and tourism officials from ASEAN countries and outside and inside Guangxi Autonomous Region have focused their attention on the theme of "international tourism cooperation between China (Guangxi) and ASEAN" and conducted discussions on relevant issues within the framework of friendship, cooperation and development. They also contributed lots of valuable suggestions and advice. These will greatly promote tourism cooperation between Guangxi and ASEAN. During the two days' forum, delegates have raised many excellent ideas and suggestions after serious and passionate discussion. I would like to summarise the achievements of the forum in the following three aspects.

Firstly, the forum strongly enhanced our friendship. The forum lasted for only two days. However, during the two days' busy schedule, all delegates focused their attention on the commonly concerned topic "tourism cooperation between Guangxi and ASEAN". They listened to speeches and reports, exchanged ideas, and shared experiences. They also made many new friends by crossing the obstacles of culture and language. In the past two days, our friendship has been strengthened. We've also seen that many experts from home and abroad came to join us despite various difficulties. For example, Ms Chan from Thailand participated in our forum though she was not in complete health. Yesterday, she was sent to hospital and is recovering. And we just heard that she came to the forum and presented her paper only four days after receiving surgery in Thailand. It was also on yesterday, during the buffet lunch, she had an in-depth discussion on tourism cooperation with our colleagues from the Tourism Administration and Academy of Social Sciences. So now, let's convey our best wishes to her. We've also noticed that many experts from home and abroad came to the forum by transferring international flights. They also made careful preparation for their speeches. I believe, they come here for friendship and cooperation. And we will appreciate all your efforts forever.

Secondly, we have had better understanding towards each other. In the past two days, many experts and professionals in the tourism industry shared with us information, situation, as well as advanced experience in tourism development in their own countries and regions. Meanwhile, they also promote tourist resources and products of their countries and regions. By informing the current situation of their cooperation with Guangxi, they also expressed the willingness and plans of promoting further cooperation. At the same time, they analyze the problems in the cooperation between the two sides. For example, the security and comfortableness of traveling, language barriers, problems of product positioning for the target market, lack of communication in bilateral tourism promotion, traffic and transporting problems, loose market regulations, inconvenient custom clearance procedures, lack of bilateral cooperation mechanism, and so on. While the experts gave us an objective analysis of the problems in our cooperation, they also expressed strong wishes for further cooperation and spoke highly of the achievements we have made. I think all these have promoted our mutual understanding and pointed out the right direction for us to continue to study and solve all the problems.

Thirdly, the discussion on tourism cooperation is the most important achievement of the forum. In the past two days, we've studied carefully the foundation of our cooperation, suggested measures for strengthening cooperation and foreseen the bright future for that. I believe the forum is an important step of the tourism cooperation between Guangxi and ASEAN. We also believe that Guangxi and ASEAN enjoy rich tourist resources of their own characteristics, and thus are complementary to each other, which form the foundation of long-term cooperation. With the establishment of China-ASEAN Free Trade Area, the cooperation between us will witness a bright future.

(Excerpted text of speech by Xiao Jiangang, Director of Guangxi Tourism Administration on China 〈Guangxi〉—ASEAN International Tourism Cooperation Forum, November 2004)

Text 4

女士们、先生们，朋友们：

"2008广东国际旅游文化节泛珠三角旅游招商会"今天在美丽的广州举办，我很高兴也很荣幸能出席这一盛大的、富有重大意义的活动。我谨代表世界旅游组织对大会表示热烈的祝贺！

20世纪中叶以来，现代旅游在世界范围迅速兴起，成为当代最令人瞩目的发展成就之一，旅游产业规模不断扩大，旅游经济地位显著提升，旅游活动越来越成为各国人民交流文化、增进友谊、扩大交往的重要渠道，对人类生活和社会进步产生了越来越广泛的影响。进入21世纪，全球旅游业的格局发生了重大变化，亚太地区跃居世界第二，欧洲、亚太地区和美洲三足鼎立的局势真正确立。作为东亚乃至亚太地区旅游增长的领军者，中国旅游业近年来的发展取得了尤其令人兴奋的成绩，中国已成为世界瞩目的国际旅游目的地和客源地,也是全球规模最大的国内旅游市场。目前中国每年接待1.5亿的国际旅游者,15亿的国内旅游者,并以每年5%的速度高速增长。按照世界旅游组织预测,2020年中国将超越法国、西班牙和美国等传统旅游目的地国家,成为世界第一旅游目的地国家。

美好的前景迎来了旅游业投资的春天。目前,中国已成为世界普遍看好的旅游投资热点。据初步统计,近年来,中国每年旅游业新增投资超过一千亿元人民币,而投资已成为旅游业发展的支柱之一。

位于中国南部的泛珠三角地区是一片充满希望的热土,商机无限的宝地,它就像一块磁石,不但吸引着近邻的香港、澳门特别行政区的大批游客,而且对亚洲内外的游客也有极强的吸引力。泛珠三角地区旅游以整体形象一起向世界推介,是广东国际旅游文化节的一个突出的特色。这次泛珠三角旅游招商会的举办,构筑了一个加强区域合作、建立广阔的旅游投融资网络、共同拓展国内外旅游市场的平台。泛珠三角的旅游业将会迎来更快更强的增长。

近年来,世界旅游组织与泛珠三角许多省份都进行了良好的合作,例如参与编制了云南、四川、贵州、海南等省的旅游发展总体规划,与世界银行联合参与了贵州等地的旅游扶贫工作。世界旅游组织与广东的合作关系也非常良好,2006年世界旅游组织主持召开的亚太旅游政策部长级会议曾在澳门举行,与会者赴珠海考察,受到了广东方面的热情款待。我们希望进一步发展与广东、香港特别行政区、澳门特别行政区,乃至所有泛珠三角地区的良好合作关系。因为这里是亚洲旅游的心脏,也是亚洲旅游繁荣发展的基石。

今后,在与各省、区业已建立的深情厚谊的基础上,我们将继续关注并大力支持中国旅游业的发展,积极协助和参与泛珠三角地区的国际旅游市场开拓与招商工作,为推动泛珠三角地区乃至全中国旅游业的进一步繁荣竭尽绵薄之力。

祝愿2008广东国际旅游文化节泛珠三角旅游推介大会获得圆满成功!

(2008年12月14日,世界旅游组织亚太部主任徐京在"2008广东国际旅游文化节泛珠三角旅游招商会"上的致词)

第 3 单元

Text 1

So now, many people ask me, "How did you start your business?" Well, five years ago, I was very young and bold. I was confident of my ability to start a business and had many ideas. Fortunately, I got financial support from my mother and gathered a group of good friends to do business. We believed that we could succeed immediately. However, when we started, we found that we still had a long way to go. There were a lot of things that you cannot learn from your teacher in school. I soon found that design was no more than a kind of services. That was to say, your customers paid you to do what they wanted rather than what you wanted to do. Later on, I also understood that in school, when the teacher told you your work was great, it stood for itself and began to promote itself. However, in the market, everything was completely different. You had to know how to sell your work. Another thing is that students in the art school usually ignore mathematics. But once you start a company, you would soon found that it is rather important. You need to calculate your employees' salary and the hourly expenditure of the company. By then, you would find that management is real art, while other things are only services. So, opening a company means beginning to learn to do business. And many designers may not think about this when they decided to start. So if I could come back to four years ago, I would choose to join the blue peer.

Many friends ask me, why did you decide to start your business, or do you think I can open a company? I think you have to ask yourselves several questions: do you open a company for money? Or do you think design companies all look good and you can dress yourselves smart and do whatever you want? Or do you think you can always meet with interesting people in your company? The start of your business is the end of your dream. Or you can also say the end of your dream is the start of reality. This photo was taken by my colleagues who had worked without break for several days. They all lay down on the floor and took the photo. So you can see that we are not different from other business. When you open a design company, apart from your own ability, you will have to face all these problems. And I think these are the things that we haven't been taught in the art school.

I'm a designer myself. I asked myself what I could change with my design and my personal ability. Since I focused on online design, the first thing I can do was to build an online platform to link designers and the market together. We knew many designers who had a lot of artwork, for example, graphic designers, photographers and illustrators. Then how can we help them to reach the market? We can help them through a web-platform. Thus, we built a virtual community, an online design community. We provided them with some free e-commerce tools, and set up a creator network, where there were market places and designers and artists can share their works.

We spent a whole year on developing a network system. Our company, a web-platform, is to help designers and artists to commercialise their products. We also have contacts with some manufacturers in Taiwan. With their support, we make a design into a product.

(Excerpted text of speech by Nancy Chan, designer and entrepreneur from Taiwan, on China–UK Creative Entrepreneur Network Initiative, as transcribed, December 1, 2008)

Text 2

早上好！刘先生，王先生，曾先生，各位来宾，女士们、先生们：

借此机会，我想感谢深圳市政府和香港政府的长期支持。深港创新圈的建立为我们创造了一个理想环境来启动我们的光伏能源事业。因此，我感谢两地政府，感谢我们的合作伙伴和客户，是你们让今天成为可能。此时此刻，世界要决定我们的能源未来。我们所依赖的丰富的自然资源日益稀少，对化石燃料的长期依赖正成为全球焦虑的问题。无论我们是从能源安全的角度，还是从环境的角度来看待这个问题，我们都认识到我们需要节约能源，我们还需要发展可再生能源。正是这个共同关注的问题把我们聚在一起。

杜邦太阳能的研发和生产专业团队将为此提供解决方案。杜邦太阳能是特别的，是中国范围内第一家提供整体太阳能供应系统解决方案的公司。杜邦太阳能拥有先进的技术和生产设施，将为太阳能的未来继续做出贡献。我们的团队富有活力，他们把技术和生产设施结合在一起，创造成功。20年前杜邦在中国建立第一家外商独资企业，即杜邦集团中国有限公司，设在深圳。今天的投产仪式标志着杜邦在中国的又一重要里程碑。在深圳，我们将研究实力与先进的生产设施结合在一起，支持我们在光伏能源市场上的增长。

我要再次感谢深圳和香港政府将我们聚集到了创新圈中。深港创新圈的实力是我们今天共聚在此的真正原因。有了两地政府的支持，有了杜邦研发团队与当地大学的合作，我们对商业的发展和成功充满信心。我希望越来越多的企业能参照我们的范例，抓住珠三角地区独特的优势，发展技术并将之商业化。现如今，有很多其他企业进入到光伏能源市场中，而杜邦在这个行业中拥有25年的经验。我们将会继续推出新的光伏产品和解决方案，提高光伏电池组的效能、性能及寿命。再次感谢光伏能源团队，祝贺你们所取得的成功,再次感谢两地政府,我们的合作伙伴和客户,感谢你们的贡献!

谢谢!

(2009年11月17日,杜邦执行副总裁、首席创新官唐乐年博士在"杜邦太阳能薄膜电池板投产仪式"上的讲话全文)

Text 3

Looking back to the past three decades' development, we find that innovation has become the strongest power for Guangdong's economic development. Guangdong has become the pioneer in implementing China's reform and opening-up policy, an explorer in the process of globalisation and an experiment carrier in system, organisation and technology innovation. Guangdong stands in the front line of China's rejuvenation. It provides a model for developing countries and regions to learn from. The future development of Guangdong must rely on the innovation of development model, so as to maintain its special and important status in the world economy and China's modernisation process as well. Innovation is the hope of Guangdong.

First, the system innovation that supports Guangdong's economic opening-up has made great breakthrough.

During the 30 years' reform and opening-up, Guangdong implemented the great policy with innovation spirit. It took the lead to build up special economic zones, develop the "Three-plus-one" trading-mix (custom manufacturing with materials, designs or samples supplied and compensation trade), acquire advanced foreign technology, facilities and management experience, and open three types of foreign-invested enterprises in China, including Sino-foreign joint ventures, enterprises with Sino-foreign cooperation, and wholly foreign-owned enterprises. It was also the first province in China to reform its foreign trade, trade promotion, pricing and finance systems, and to realise paid land-transfer and ownership reform. It realised the historical transformation from a planned economic system to a socialist market economic system and established the system and environment facilitating its economic opening-up.

Second, Guangdong's economic development model has been innovated. Opening-up economy has become an important driving force for Guangdong's economic development.

The "China model" has already been recognised as a miracle in the world's economic development. Guangdong's development in the past three decades has become a typical example of the "China model", i.e. to have export and foreign investment as the main force for economic development. Through economic opening-up, Guangdong accumulated capital, improved the efficiency in essential productive factor allocation and technology, and enhanced its international competitive edge. By innovating the economic development model, we have adopted an open-economy framework which has become an important driving force for Guangdong's economic growth. It has also helped Guangdong and other provinces to digest a large amount of surplus labour force, promoted the development of domestic-oriented economy, and established Guangdong as the "world factory".

Third, by "learning from doing", Guangdong has continuously improved its ability in technological innovations.

The technological progress realised in the process of Guangdong's economic opening-up is based on the concept of "learning from doing". With the increasing accumulation of its own technological capacity, the province acquires more and more technology transferred from the outside and transforms it into "appropriate technology". In the past 30 years, thanks to the improved technological innovation mechanism and policy environment, the open regional innovation mechanism has taken its initial scale, and technological progress has become important support for Guangdong's economic development. All these have laid a solid foundation for Guangdong to further its economic opening-up, and upgrade its value chain in the world market.

Fourth, Guangdong's capacity of taking mechanism advantages to develop innovation elements, and to concentrate and cultivate the elements has been enhanced remarkably.

The essence of international division of labour and cooperation is the division and cooperation of productive elements among different regions. In the past 30 years, Guangdong has taken the advantages of mechanism to develop innovation elements and concentrate and cultivate productive elements suitable for its economic development. It gathered together low-cost and skilled labour forces, mid-level and senior managers, technicians, and domestic and overseas capital. At the same time, by gradually improving its investment environment, Guangdong has established a sound infrastructure, and laid a solid foundation for concentrating and cultivating mid-to-high-end productive elements through various channels.

Fifth, Guangdong has consistently encouraged industrial and organisational innovations. Its industrial internationalisation has kept progressing.

Since the implementation of the reform and opening-up policy started more than three decades ago, Guangdong has encouraged industrial and organisational innovations, which has accelerated the integration of the division of labour in the international industry, and received international industrial relocation effectively. Today, Guangdong receives more and more knowledge-intensive service outsourcing and subcontracts with high added value from the global market year by year. It also increasingly integrates with Hong Kong, Macao and Taiwan, and participates into the Asian-Pacific economic circle. Its products take more and more share in the international market. A number of industrial clusters with international competitive edge and large enterprises and enterprise groups have taken their initial scale in the province. At the same time, the adjustment of Guangdong's industrial structure has made an important breakthrough. The province witnesses an obvious trend of industrial upgrading and the emergence of the heavy industry in a reasonable amount. Its service industry acquires increasing proportion of foreign investment. The nine pillar industries have taken a stronger and stronger leading role in its economic development. Guangdong's industrial distribution and structure have become more and more reasonable. All these have laid a solid foundation for the province to establish its modern industrial system.

(Excerpted text of speech by Dr. Sui Guangjun, president of Guangdong University of Foreign Studies at the Guangdong Open Forum and the Unveiling Ceremony of Guangdong Academy of International Strategic Research, November 13, 2009)

Text 4

在我们说到那个问题之前，我想先回到1991年，当时苹果发布并上市了第一代PowerBooks，这是第一台现代手提电脑。苹果实际上发明了现代手提电脑，那就是PowerBooks。这是第一款拥有TFT屏幕，即现代液晶屏的手提电脑。这也是第一款手提电脑，把键盘上移设计出手腕放置区，并将定位设备，即轨迹球整合在电脑中。当然，将近20年之后，我们现在已经有了不可思议的手提电脑了。就在几年前，2007年，苹果革新了手机，生产出iPhone。几年之后，我们现在有了美妙的iPhone第三代，世界上最好的手机。现在所有人都使用手提电脑和智能手机。每个人都拥有手提电脑和智能手机。问题就是，最近，是否还有空间容纳第三类产品呢——介于手提电脑和智能手机之间的产品呢？当然，我们也思考这个问题好几年了，要设计真正的新一类产品，门槛儿相当的高。这类产品必须在处理某些关键任务时表现卓越。它们在做一些非常重要的事情时必须做得更好——要优于手提电脑，优于智能手机。什么任务呢？诸如浏览网页，这是个很艰巨的任务，有什么东西在浏览网页时比手提电脑更好用呢？收发电子邮件，欣赏和分享照片，观看视频，欣赏音乐，玩游戏，阅读电子书，如果存在这第三类产品的话，他们必须在处理这些任务时优于手提电脑和智能手机，否则，它们就没有存在的理由。

现在，有人想到了那是台上网本，问题是上网本不擅长做任何事。它们速度慢，显示质量差，运行的是笨拙过时的电脑软件。所以它们比起手提电脑来在任何方面都不优越，只是便宜些。它们就是便宜的手提电脑而已。我们不认为上网本是第三类产品。但我们觉得我们已经有了一些东西。我今天要给你们展示它，这是首次亮相。我们把它称作 iPad。我来给你们展示一下。这是它的外观，我这儿碰巧有一部，就在这儿。这就是它的外观，非常薄。给大家介绍一下，它很薄，你可以改变屏幕背景，在主页屏幕上你可以随心所欲地个性化。大家可以把自己的照片放上去，我们也推出了一些背景，你可以随心所欲地设置。这款机器超乎寻常，你可以用它来浏览网页，那将是前所未有的体验。你会看到整个网页在你的眼前展开，你可以用手指来控制它。这真是难以置信的美妙，比手提电脑好多了，比智能手机好多了。你可以随意翻转 iPad，上下左右翻转，它会自动调整到你想使用的位置。看到整个网页真是棒极了，就像把互联网握在手中，这是难以置信的体验。在处理邮件方面也很棒，你可以查收邮件。把 iPad 转过来，你可以换一个角度来阅读邮件。打开编辑窗口，就会跳出一个键盘来，几乎和现实中的一样大小，这是一个梦幻般的键盘。看照片，你的相册会显示照片的图标。你可以打开相册，看到所有的照片，快速地翻动，还可以幻灯片的方式观看。这是一个与朋友和家人分享照片的美妙方式。建立一个日历，看看你每月的活动、每天的活动或是其他的事情。为你的联系人建立一个地址簿。查看地图，地图功能得到了谷歌的支持。显示地图、卫星图，锁定放大目标。iPad 是欣赏音乐的好工具，当然，我们有 iTune Store，内置到 iPad 里，你可以找寻并购买音乐。电影、电视节目、播客、iTune Universty 等，所有的东西都内置到了 iPad 里。YouTube，你可以在上面看 YouTube，包括 YouTube 高清，那上面有高清视频。当然，用它来看电视节目和电影也很棒。

（2010 年 1 月 27 日，苹果公司 CEO 史蒂夫·乔布斯在"iPad 平板电脑现场演示会"上的发言节选）

第4单元

Text 1

The 2010 Shanghai World Expo is a dream that the Chinese nation has hold for 100 years. It is another international mega event organized by China following the 2008 Summer Olympic Games. In the past 150 years, while the World Expo came into being and gained great development, the Chinese nation fought unswervingly and bravely, and achieved rejuvenation from underdevelopment gradually. China, with its constant efforts and remarkable progress, has gained respect from the international community. Now, the World Expo dream under the pen of great writers 100 years ago is coming true right in front of us. We understand it is a great responsibility and honourable task. Since we succeeded in the World Expo bidding in 2002, with the steady guidance of the State Council and the Central Party Committee, the great support from ministries and departments of the central, provincial and municipal governments and people around the country, the active participation of the Bureau of International Expositions (BIE) and the international community, and the efforts made by all Shanghai citizens, the preparatory work of the Expo progresses smoothly and has achieved important success in different phases. 240 countries and international organisations have confirmed their participation. The construction of complexes and relevant infrastructure is undergoing a smooth process. A series of forums, celebrations and other mega events are being carefully prepared. The work in transportation, security and volunteer services is operated according to schedule. Promotion activities have launched in a large scale. The international recognition, influence and attractiveness of the Shanghai Expo are improving. The passion of our citizens to participate in, serve and contribute to the Expo is increasing. 100 days later, the 2010 China (Shanghai) World Expo is to open. China and Shanghai will become the focus of the world's attention. To provide people from around the world a marvellous Expo and to fulfill our commitment to the international community are the task of historical significance assigned by the central government, the expectation of the 1.3 billion people of China and a holy and honourable duty for us.

Recently, when visiting Shanghai, President Hu Jintao made a "six-ensures" requirement to us. This is the mobilisation for us to complete the preparatory work with a high standard. It also points out a right direction for our work in the next phase. Today, Chairman Jia of CPPCC and Vice Premier Wang paid a visit to Shanghai, and addressed the participants of the mobilisation conference. Their encouragement will surely boost our confidence and passion to win honour and respect for our country. With great confidence, strong passion, rigorous attitude and the spirit of always striking for the best, let us work hard for another 100 days to complete all the preparatory work, lay a solid foundation for a successful World Expo and provide high-quality services for our guests from home and abroad. Making good use of every minute we have, we shall do our best to guarantee a successful Expo. During the next 100 days, we will give the Expo preparatory work top priority, and make good use of every minute we have to complete all the construction projects and be prepared for the trial operation of the Expo garden at the same time. Security is the most important task. We will further detail the security plan, pay special attention to the training of our security staff and conduct security drills for various emergencies, so as to guarantee an effective, smooth and safe Expo. With rigorous attitude, we will try our best to prepare for the Expo. The standards and procedures of all our work will be given further details. We are also going to make sure every single post and detail of work to be taken care of by suitable people. We will hold a large-scale trial operation before the opening of the Expo and improve the command mechanism and operation system. During the trial operation, we shall also encourage all our staff to seek for potential difficulties and problems and find out solutions, in order to minimise problems and mistakes after the opening of the event. All our staff should stick to the principle of serving the exhibitors, visitors and Shanghai citizens, and make sure their work will be completed in a considerate and effective way.

As a country with the tradition of respecting etiquette, we will create a friendly atmosphere for the Expo, by launching special campaigns to encourage polite behaviour, respect to social order, honest and courteous services and environmental protection. We shall promote politeness and good behaviour among all the citizens and encourage them to join in the volunteer services. We will organise and train volunteers to provide services in the Expo garden and around the city, and impress all the guests with volunteers' smile. Last but not least, we will try our best to promote the theme of the Expo "Better City, Better Life", and encourage the whole society to participate in, serve and contribute to the Expo.

(Excerpted text of speech by Yu Zhengsheng, Party Secretary of Shanghai Municipal CPC, at the 2010 Shanghai World Expo 100-Day Countdown Ceremony, January 21, 2010, as transcribed)

Text 2

各位尊敬的来宾,各位来穗投资的客商及未来的投资客户:

感谢本次论坛和招商会的组织单位邀请我到这里向各位致词。在这个令人振奋的新时代,广州为我们的事业腾飞敞开了大门。能到访这样重要的城市,我觉得十分荣幸。在这个城市里看到的基础设施和遇到的人们都充分显示出广州市卓越的规划和发展的动力。

上月的《经济学家》杂志中的一篇文章提到,"人们一直低估了亚洲呈现的经济活力"。1997到1998年的区域经济危机,及其后2001年网络泡沫破灭的危机,人们认为经济的复苏需要一段很长的时间。今年大部分国家出现经济衰退,人们预计直到欧美经济重新增长,出口国的经济才能复苏。然而,中国经济一直保持着良好的增长势头。2009年第二季度,中国、印尼、韩国和新加坡的年平均经济增长率超过10%。

截止2009年7月,中国的工业生产增长了11%。去年急剧下降的发电量已再度回升,汽车的销售与去年同比上升70%,高于前一年。

这些对会展业来说都是好消息,因为中国政府采取了刺激经济、保持繁荣的措施。

我所服务的公司,亚洲博闻,是率先在中国开展B2B电子商务平台的亚洲企业之一。目前,我们是亚洲领先的展会主办单位,同时也是亚洲发展最快的两个市场——中国和印度的最大的商贸展览会主办方,并拥有自己的专业刊物和线上媒体。亚洲博闻隶属英国伦敦上市公司联合企业媒体,每年主办逾110个商贸展会,出版22本专业刊物。其中,我公司在中国的主要城市举办有32个商贸展会,包括广州、上海、成都、深圳和北京。

我们已在中国运营了逾15个年头,经历和见证了广东省和中国南方经济的巨大活力和发展。我们通过展会"搭建商贸平台",深信这是增强商贸联系、促进各国和各行业人士建立和谐关系的最佳途径。

目前,我们在广州市有三个办事处。旧展馆为展览行业提供了很好的基础,也为琶洲新展馆的卓越扩展提供指引。这一切都有赖于规划者的真知灼见。当然,这仅仅是开始而已,有更多展馆将会建成,更多的酒店即将完工,更多商务楼和零售空间会开业。地铁直达展馆的便利也是展览业发展的关键因素。

作为一家企业,我们通过在琶洲展馆举行的展会向华南和广东市场开放,取得了不俗的成绩。在海珠区,我们享受到由广州市政府和海珠区政府提供的良好便捷的服务,以及针对外商投资的建议。

以广州作为珠三角及其中心的华南地区,已快速发展成一个集国际船运、物流、贸易、展览和革新于一身的中心。琶洲会展中心恰恰折射了其焦点所在:国际化标准的酒店现已遍布广州,白云机场成为全球交通枢纽,高素质的劳动力队伍,其中大部分都精通英语。

我确信在此投资,将取得丰厚的回报。随着国内生产总值不断增长,居民消费水平的持续上升,广州将继续走向繁荣。

我诚意邀请阁下莅临于9月24—26日在琶洲展馆举行的第31届广州国际美容美发化妆用品进出口博览会,这是我公司与我们的好朋友马娅会长及她负责的广东省美容美发化妆品行业协会联合主办的展会。

再次感谢主办单位组织这次论坛和招商会。

祝各位生意兴隆!

谢谢!

(2009年9月11日,亚洲博闻展览公司高级副总裁麦高德在"2009广州〈海珠·琶洲〉会展经济论坛暨现代服务业招商会"上的致词)

Text 3

Honourable Leaders, Distinguished Guests, Ladies and Gentlemen,

Good morning. First of all, please allow me on behalf of Guangzhou People's Government to extend our warmest welcome and sincere thanks to the leaders, guests and friends attending the Guangzhou (Pazhou, Haizhu) Exhibition and Convention Economic Forum 2007. I would also like to congratulate on the successful opening of today's event. This forum, co-organised by the Bureau of Foreign Trade and Economic Cooperation of Guangzhou, the People's Government of Haizhu District and *China Conference and Exhibition* magazine, is of great significance and held at the right time. It provides a great opportunity for the world to understand Guangzhou and its exhibition and convention industry. It is also a good chance for Guangzhou to gain recognition from around the country and the world, and realise its target of becoming an international exhibition and convention centre.

Guangzhou, with its 2000 years' history, is the traditional political, economic and cultural centre of southern China. In recent years, Guangzhou's economy develops rapidly and healthily. In 2006, Guangzhou's GDP amounted to 606.81 billion RMB, with a year-on-year increase of 14.7%. The tertiary industry is making greater and greater contribution to the economic growth, while the exhibition and convention industry, the trade, logistics, finance, tourism and other modern service industries develop prosperously. The history of China's exhibition and convention industry started from 1957 when Guangzhou held the first China Export Commodity Fair. This No. 1 Fair in China, and the third largest exhibition in the world, has held 101 sessions so far. The exhibition and convention industry has become the window and engine of Guangzhou's foreign trade. The city, following Beijing and Shanghai, is the third largest exhibition and convention city in China. It has advanced exhibition and convention facilities, including 11 professional complexes with 490 thousand square metres' exhibition area. Among them, the Guangzhou International Conference and Exhibition Centre is the largest exhibition centre around Asia. According to some statistics, in recent years, Guangzhou held 350 large-scale expositions. Every year, it also accommodates 1100 trade fairs and exhibitions averagely. The annual direct income of the industry in Guangzhou reached 1.3 billion RMB, accounting for 41% of that of Guangdong's total.

The development of exhibition and convention industry will further optimise Guangzhou's investment environment, promote the growth of finance, consulting, hotel, tourism and other related industries and bring more investment opportunities. Guangzhou seized this opportunity, and for the first time to include the development plan of the exhibition and convention industry into the 11th Five Year Plan of Guangzhou's Service Industry. Guangzhou will accelerate the development of modern business, trade and service industries with the exhibition and convention industry as the leading force, so as to raise Guangzhou's status as an international exhibition and convention centre. Through exhibitions, conventions and forums, we will attract even more investment and develop headquarters economy. We plan to attract and support multinational corporations, famous Chinese companies and local enterprises to establish a cross-regional business network with Guangzhou as their headquarters.

Today's forum gathers specialists and expertise of political, business, academic, and exhibition and convention circles from home and abroad. They will share and exchange their views and experience of the development of the exhibition and convention industry. I am confident that by the end of the forum, all the participants will learn a lot from each other, and have better understanding of Pazhou.

I sincerely hope all the leaders, entrepreneurs and guests can have a candid discussion, provide valuable suggestions to the development of Guangzhou's exhibition and convention industry, and continue to support Guangzhou to develop a marketised, globalised and modernised exhibition economy.

Last but not least, I wish the forum a complete success.

(Full text of speech by Chen Mingde, vice mayor of Guangzhou at the Guangzhou 〈Pazhou, Haizhu〉 Exhibition and Convention Economic Forum 2007, July 27, 2007)

Text 4

詹姆斯·拉科斯特先生，各位阁下，嘉宾，女士们、先生们：
晚上好！
很荣幸能与大家共聚在此，为第一届香港美酒佳肴巡礼揭幕。这是在为所有文明中最受欢迎的两项休闲活动——美酒与佳肴举行庆典。我们还拥有世界上最壮观的城市景观作背景——所以我们拥有一个难忘的节日所需的所有元素。

首先，对大家的到来表示热烈的欢迎，特别欢迎我们特殊的客人。他们来自传奇的美酒之乡波尔多。我们还欣喜地看到波尔多商会副主席拉科斯特先生，波尔多市副市长戴劳克斯先生也亲临现场。我们感谢您与您的代表团从法国远道而来，与我们欢聚在这个特殊的盛会。

你们的出席对我们非常重要。因为这次盛会标志着我们与波尔多在美酒谅解备忘录下的合作，那是我们去年签署的。与葡萄酒产区的国际合作对我们是至关重要的，因为我们要实现成为亚洲葡萄酒贸易和分销枢纽的目标。我看到了很多葡萄酒生产国代表今晚也来到了现场，感谢大家支持我们发展香港葡萄酒业的计划。

自从去年我在财政预算中取消葡萄酒税以来，我们的葡萄酒贸易已经有了可喜的成果。尽管我们仍处于全球金融危机中，葡萄酒进口总值在2008年同比增长80%，这个数字在2009年的前8个月又增长了42%，达到了23亿美元。

很多与葡萄酒相关的公司已经扩大了经营规模或在此成立了新的企业，包括零售商店、仓储设施、贸易公司，等等。我们甚至还有一个酿酒厂，这是很特别的，因为香港并不出产葡萄。

根据这个行业的预计，香港将在2009年赶超伦敦，成为世界上第二大的葡萄酒拍卖中心，仅次于纽约。截至今年，10场葡萄酒拍卖会已实现超过3.65亿港元的价值。

美酒佳肴活动还刺激了我们处于经济衰退期的旅游业。实际上，此次盛会是我们旅游事业发展局"香港美酒佳肴年"的一项重要活动。发展香港成为区域葡萄酒贸易和分销枢纽为我们提供了一个契机来展示我们的城市，它对于美食家和食品鉴赏家是首选目的地。

女士们、先生们，谢谢你们支持此次盛会，祝贺巡礼活动主办方为美酒佳肴提供了一个振奋人心的庆典，使我们有机会与友人相聚。

预祝巡礼圆满成功！希望各位有一个愉快的夜晚！谢谢！干杯！

（2009年10月30日，香港财政司司长曾俊华在"2009香港美酒佳肴巡礼"开幕式上的讲话）

第 5 单元

Text 1

Ladies and Gentlemen,

I'm very delighted to be here to meet all of you. When I arrived, I was surprised to find such a large-scale vocational school in Shunde. I'm a complete layman of tourism. So my topic today is about my study experience. But first I would like to give my own opinion concerning vocational education, for it is closely related to my educational experience when I was a young man.

Over 20 years ago, an elderly Hong Kong compatriot donated all his savings to support the education in our country. This was a large sum of money. When we received the fund, we considered how to use it, where we should spend it, and how to allocate the fund to the most needed sector in China. After a series of discussions with relevant departments, we finally decided to apply the fund to supporting vocational education of our country.

Why did we make such a decision? Because at that time, we felt our country didn't attach enough importance to vocational education. Of course, higher education is the priority of China's education. Every year our government invests a large sum of money in higher education. However, vocational education receives little attention and our country invests far less funds in vocational education. Funds from home and abroad were mainly directed to higher education; only a very limited sum was used for supporting vocational education. Some philanthropists set up foundations and donated a large sum of money every year to support higher education and to various universities. But there was not even a penny given to vocational education.

Higher education surely should be supported. This is a right orientation of the development of higher education. That is correct. However, in the long term, vocational education is also very important. For this reason we decided to apply this fund to supporting vocational education.

At that time, China's reform and opening-up just started. We introduced a great deal of toll-processing business with materials supplied by customers and a lot of labor-intensive industries. Such industries contained very little technology, so employees with some training could be fit for the post. But in the long term, with our economic development, labor-intensive industries will be gradually replaced by technology-intensive industries. At that time, many technical workers will be needed. Not every worker can live up to the job. We noticed that in Germany great attention is paid to vocational education. Only those workers who have obtained graduation certificates from vocational schools can work in the factories. We should take this into consideration. Therefore we need to think in a long-term perspective, and we felt that we should support vocational education.

Another reason that little attention was paid to vocational education was that there were certain problems with our country's educational system and labor system then. If a middle school student couldn't go to college, it seemed that his or her whole life was determined and he or she wouldn't be successful for the whole life. At that time, graduates for vocational schools couldn't apply for universities, so they could not be promoted as "cadre" in government departments and could not be given senior professional titles in other enterprises and work units. So they could only be a "worker" for the whole life. We didn't have on-the-job training and examination for self-learners at that time. So students must try their best to be admitted into college after finishing high school, which brought heavy burdens to the students. They had to choose a good kindergarten at the very beginning, later a good primary school, and a good high school, so as to go to college. It was such a huge burden to students and it was not a positive phenomenon. But the situation then was just like that. From this perspective, we thought that we should strive to develop vocational education.

In our society, many types of work don't require people with high professional titles or graduating from universities. With strict technical training and professional training, students graduating from vocational schools are qualified for certain work, such as typing, proofreading, nursing, laboratory testing and medicine dispensing by prescription. These types of work don't need college graduates, bachelors, masters or PhDs. Technical workers with regular training can match up to them. It is especially so in the rural areas lacking highly professional human resources.

In addition, at that time, few students could apply theories to practices. They could only use their "brains" and couldn't use their "hands". For example, graduates majoring in engineering didn't know how to fix water and electricity facilities at home. Graduates of arts couldn't type. Engineers didn't know what to do with the finished technical drawing. Yesterday I read on the Internet that some Doctors of psychology don't know how to do psychological consultation. These are very common phenomena in the society. So we think it is necessary to cultivate a group of technical workers both qualified in terms of theory and practice. For example, our *Shenzhou* manned spacecraft has been launched to the outer space. This rocket surely needs technical personnel and engineers to design. However, every single detail of it is of vital importance. If a single screw is not driven tightly or if a single weld is not joined well and seamlessly, serious troubles may arise. So for our rocket to travel in the outer space and even travel to the moon in the future, we need not only scientists, technicians and senior engineers, but also a large number of technical workers with strict training.

(Excerpted text of speech by Lu Ping, former Director of the Hong Kong and Macao Affairs Office of the State Council at the International Tourism and Hospitality Development Forum on December 16, 2005, as transcribed)

Text 2

Mr. Chen, Mr. Fang, Teachers, Students, Friends,

Good afternoon!

I feel extremely delighted for your giving me this opportunity, a very good opportunity, to take part in the 40th anniversary celebration of GDUFS. Today, we gather here as GDUFS people. Our Fullbright exchange program has enjoyed a 20-year history of cooperation with GDUFS. I look forward to our increased and expanded development in the future. Since my Chinese is poor, and the interpreters have done a wonderful job, I will now shift to English. As an old Chinese saying goes, the only thing that should be feared under the sky is a foreigner speaking Chinese. So now, I'll use English, my mother tongue. Thanks.

中国正以迅猛的速度发展其大学，从1996到2004年间，正如方教授所说的，入校新生人数增长了一倍。现在，中国接近20%的高中毕业生都在接受大学教育。1982年我来到中国的时候，仅有不到5%的高中毕业生可以到大学继续深造。中国高等教育普及面越来越广，主要是依靠学校的扩张。广东外语外贸大学的发展就是一个例子。从3000人扩大到16000人，只用了10年时间。世界上有多少所大学经历了这种速度的增长和如此规模的变化？这很不简单。

中国全国范围内的扩招是由很多因素引起的。中国日益腾飞的经济需要更多技术人才，特别是在60到70年代对大学的禁锢解除之后。社会对高等教育的需求增加，特别是当第一批独生子女到了上大学的年龄，这一需求更大。在教育方面，中国传统的文化价值观念没有改变。随着各国高等教育的全球化，中国的大学也准备培养出大量博士生和其他类型毕业生，其中有一些将会到一些人才供不应求的国家去工作。

和所有其他国家一样，中国也有一些人担心不是所有的大学毕业生都能马上找到工作。我想问题不是出在毕业生的供应过剩，而是需要一个更有效的人才市场。顺便说一句，我认为广外毕业生找工作不成问题。同时也反映出这样一个问题，那就是很多刚从大学毕业的年轻学生是否愿意去中、小城市和乡村开始自己的职业生涯。此外，在主要大城市中，好工作的竞争越来越激烈。中国培养的人才并非过多。在过去的10年中，中国取得了许多伟大的成就，其中包括工作分配制度的瓦解，一个面向大学毕业生和处在事业中期的专业人员的新劳动力市场得以扩大。

我们提倡让更多的人接受大学教育，有些持怀疑态度的人认为高等教育扩招就一定意味着教学质量的下降。这是目光短浅的想法。如果资源能跟得上扩招的进度，那么随着更多人接受教育，不仅能够保持教学质量，而且会提高教学质量。但是如果政府对学校的扩张不加大投入和支持，那么大学就会陷入困境，教学质量也会受到影响。我提到的资源不仅指的是大家能够看得见的楼房和校园"硬件"，更重要的是充足的校园"软件"资源，如教师的工资待遇、研究基金、学生的奖学金、交流的机会和管理体系的支持。我们可以通过更有效地利用信息技术来提高效率，但高等教育的重点是教师和学生之间的互动。当然这种互动不局限于校园和教室面对面的互动，然而面对越来越多的学生，一定要确保有这种互动，来保证在扩招的同时质量不下降。

让更多人接受教育，关键是成本问题。如果高等教育对广大群众来说太昂贵，入学率就会下降。学费在中国乃至整个世界，特别是在美国，都在上涨。各国政府声称：让受益人付更多的教育经费。虽然大学都努力使资金来源多样化，我相信广东外语外贸大学也有过这样的努力，但依然不能减轻中央、省、市各级政府对下一代投资的责任。政府的投资对每个家庭是否能够负担得起学费是至关重要的。中国一直以来对贫富差距的扩大十分关注。保证家庭贫困但是成绩优秀的学生接受高等教育对社会的稳定和文化发展都是非常重要的。人们相信，大学入学过程应该是公平的，只要能继续接受高等教育，拥有的才干和付出的汗水就能得到回报，这也是创造美好生活的关键。

最后，方便的设施也是影响更多人接受大学教育的关键因素。越来越多的学生每天乘车去上课，学生宿舍一直都很紧缺。随着城市的扩建，新的大学校园在城市周边地区建立，例如番禺的大学城。所以建立低成本的、有效的城市交通系统是很必要的。

我们说到让更多的学生接受高等教育，不仅指传统意义上年龄在18到22岁的学生，我们需要给非传统意义上的学生，即已经成家立业又重返校园深造的成年学生创造条件，刚才许女士也谈到这个问题。成人学生上夜校和周末班，还要平衡自我进步的要求与对工作家庭的责任之间的关系。大学应该为要求自我进步和提高工作技术水平的成年人创造机会，这对一个学习型的社会是非常重要的。我们大学应该调整自己的体系来满足他们的需求，而不是仅仅要求他们调整以适应我们。我们的灵活性能为公众的终身教育和培训创造更多的资源。这就包括创造学分制体系、大学间转学政策、使用网络教育来补充课堂教学等方式。

最后，我赞赏广东外语外贸大学在扩大高等教育方面所起的表率作用，我也赞许广东省和广州市在番禺建立了大学城，明天我们就将去大学城参观。大学城带来了巨大挑战，给我们这些教育者带来了巨大的挑战，那就是：学会管理拥有多个校园的大学，以及学会管理包含多所大学的校园。这么大规模的校园在世界上是独一无二的。我们感谢参加过这个大胆创新的人们，并盼望进行有益的国际学术合作。我们相信：在未来的10年乃至更长的时间里，广东外语外贸大学在扩大大学教育普及率方面将会不断地获得成功。

谢谢大家！

（2005年11月5日，香港美国中心主任夏龙在"中外大学校长论坛"上的讲话，根据录音材料整理）

Text 3

Minister Zhou, Distinguished Guests, Ladies and Gentlemen,

It is my pleasure and honour to address such a distinguished audience at the Second Annual Conference of the Education Forum for Asia. So, first of all, I would like to congratulate the Beijing Municipal Government, Boao Forum for Asia, UNESCO and the China Scholarship Council for organising this remarkable event.

The theme of this year's conference is "Education Development Strategies for Asian Countries in the New Century". This is a timely subject for Hong Kong, as right now we are undergoing major education reforms that will fundamentally alter the academic structure of secondary and higher education, and revolutionalise the learning experience of our next generations. As the Secretary for Education and Manpower of Hong Kong, I would like to share with you our experience in spearheading these reforms, as well as our vision for the future.

Like many modern cities in the Asia Pacific Region, Hong Kong is moving fast into a knowledge-based economy. The 21st century has brought new challenges to us, and calls for innovative solutions. But unlike many modern cities in the region, Hong Kong is small. We have no natural resources to rely on; our single and most important asset is our people.

Over the past decades, Hong Kong has strived to become the regional financial centre, and to lead in trade and high value-added services. These changes have exerted great pressure on our manpower supply. Total labour force in Hong Kong last year was just over three-and-a-half million, but our projections show that by 2007, we will have a shortfall of over 100,000 people with education at post-secondary level and above, and at the same time a surplus of 230,000 at or below upper-secondary level. Clearly, the evolving job requirements are not in favour of persons with lower educational attainment. There is only one way to address this problem—that is to upgrade the quality of our workforce, and we do this by upgrading our education services.

In Hong Kong, education has always been high up on our political agenda. This year, education spending amounts to some HK$58 billion. It is our single largest expenditure item, representing 23.5% of total government expenditure, or 4.4% of our GDP. In absolute dollar terms, this is a growth of 54% compared with 1997.

In terms of policy, we have put in place a well-established education system providing nine years of free and universal basic education. This is supplemented by a full range of education services at the pre-school, senior-secondary and post-secondary levels. Almost all students who are willing to stay at school can receive senior secondary education or vocational training at highly subsidised rates. Competition at university entrance exam is, however, very keen. Even if you take into account the other education opportunities at the sub-degree level, by the end of the last century, only one-third of our school leavers could receive post-secondary education.

This is why in 2000 we made it a policy objective to double the provision, so that in 10 years' time, 60% of our senior-secondary school leavers should have access to post-secondary education. This is an ambitious target, but is necessary if Hong Kong is to remain competitive.

Education is expensive, especially in Hong Kong where government is subsidising over 80% of the cost of university places. If we were to double the provision using that same funding mode, the burden on public finance would hardly be sustainable. So we recognised from the start that self-financing institutions should be playing an important role in the expansion of the post-secondary sector, with the government being a supporter and facilitator. We have left it to the market to determine the number and types of programmes to be offered, while providing suitable incentives to encourage the development. These include HK$5 billion of interest-free loans; prime sites at nominal premium; student financial assistance; and a rigorous quality assurance mechanism.

As a result, new service providers have emerged. We now have 20 self-financing institutions offering over 25000 intake places at sub-degree and degree levels. The post-secondary education participation rate has also doubled, from 33% in 2000 to 66% this year. In other words, we have achieved our 60% target five years ahead of schedule.

The major driving force behind this is the introduction of Associate Degree into Hong Kong, as an alternative to other more vocationally oriented sub-degree programmes such as the Higher Diploma or Professional Diploma which have always been part of our education system.

The new AD is remarkably well-received. It is now accepted by all our local universities, as well as some 150 tertiary institutions in 10 other regions or countries, for admission to their degree courses or for credit transfer. Outside the academia, 22 professional bodies from the business, engineering, finance, accounting, IT and logistics sectors recognise our AD qualifications for the purpose of granting exemptions from parts of their professional examinations. The AD graduates are also considered for appointment to government posts.

We are delighted to see our self-financing sub-degree sector flourish, but at the top of the knowledge ladder, our universities will always have a special role to play.

In Hong Kong, we have eight institutions that the government funds through the University Grants Committee: the two oldest ones are comprehensive research universities; a younger one focuses on science, technology and business; there are also two polytechnics-turned universities, one liberal arts university, one university which adopts a holistic approach to higher education, and one teacher training institute. Each year the government spends over HK$1 billion subsidising their operation, and this is on top of the prime sites and capital funds for their infrastructural development. To encourage institutions to diversify the funding source, we have also provided one-off grants amounting to HK$1 billion each to match the private donations they receive.

Fundamentally changing the academic structure is a mammoth task. It cannot be achieved without the vision of educationalists, the determination of policy makers, and above all, the full support of all stakeholders—parents, students, teachers, institutions, taxpayers, basically everyone in the community. Hong Kong has taken many years to reach this consensus—and I am glad we did it. In the coming years, the government will have to put in capital funding amounting to HK$7.9 billion for works and one-off expenses, and thereafter an additional HK$2 billion each year to meet the recurrent costs. We have a long way to go, but we will press ahead with enthusiasm, knowing that we are making great strides in the right direction and implementing changes that will become a landmark of our education history.

I hope the conference is just the beginning of a dialogue — we will take it forward through continuous collaboration and sharing. With this in mind, I wish you all a fruitful conference, and for overseas visitors, a most enjoyable stay in our country. Thank you.

(Excerpted text of speech by Arthur K. C. Li, Secretary for Education and Manpower of Hong Kong SAR at the Plenary Session of the 2005 Annual Conference of Education Forum for Asia in Beijing, October 15, 2005)

Text 4

尊敬的老师，同学们：

在任何一个校园里演讲都是很愉快的一件事，在这样一所大的学校，面对如此多的同学，更是如此。今天，我想简单地讲一下整个世界，然后再到中国，然后再讲一点关于大学以及你们学生要如何去努力进步。

放眼世界，我想在过去的10年里主要有两个大的变化，而且影响了我们所有人。首先，世界上每一个国家都加入到自由经济体制下来了，也就是说成为了世界自由贸易体系的一部分，国家之间商品和服务的交流更为方便。这个变化只是发生在数年之前，世界上将近一半的人口在10年前加入到了自由经济体系中来，其中包括中国、印度、东欧、还有拉丁美洲的一些国家。所以世界自由经济结构发生了主要的变化，这意味着如果你在任何一个国家，你可以与其他任何国家做生意，特别是以知识经济为基础的商品和服务，以及创意方面。

过去10年发生的另一个变化是与技术和网络有关。今天，地球上任何两点之间的交流都是很容易的。这一点也不贵，你可以转让知识，转让信息，与世界上任何地方交流，花费很小。如果你将这两个主要变化结合起来，这就意味着当今世界有着很大的机遇，也存在着激烈的竞争。竞争驱使我们前进，机遇也驱使我们前进。所以每个国家都必须适应这个变化。每个国家都要使自己的经济适应这种新的竞争和新的机遇。所以如果你看看国家可以做些什么，国家其实可以做三件事情来让他们的公民在前进过程中更具竞争力。国家可以做的第一件事就是使你们现在能在这里接受大学教育。国家可以提供良好的教育，以及能与你的教育水平相符合的生活标准，所以一个国家教育的程度越高，就越有机会达到标准生活，因此也就更具有经济竞争力。所以，为所有公民提供教育是非常重要的。

国家可以做的第二件事情是投资研发。研发可以创造新理念，理念就可以创造新产品、新服务、新公司。所以我们需要投资研发，就像一个国家的生活标准与劳动力的受教育程度相关，改善一个国家的生活标准和经济竞争力通常都与其研发投资紧密相关。显然中国认识到了这些，所以中国在过去10年很重视教育，近来中国又更重视扩大和增加研发投资。

国家可以做的第三件事是创造一个良好的环境，让人才，受过良好教育的人才可以想出很好的主意，这些主意来自研发，进而创造新产品、新公司、新服务、新的经济增长。各国政府都可以着眼于教育和研发，以创造良好环境促进成功、培育成长。在中国这种创业精神也越来越多见。英特尔是世界上最大的高科技风险投资公司，我们也看到越来越多的风险投资选择了中国。在10年前，这些投资主要是投在美国，但是现在，只有50%是在美

215

国,而 50% 是在亚洲。以上就是我们说的每个国家都可以做的三件事:教育、研发和环境创造。

公司跟国家也没什么不同,如果你看我们公司,我们同样也是注重以上这三件事来取得成功。我们雇请最优秀的人才、受过良好教育的人才,投入大笔资金在研发上,从而创造出最新的产品,然后为我们的研发人员提供良好的环境,把他们的理念带到市场中去。所以像英特尔,或者其他那些大的跨国公司,都做了与政府同样的事情,来努力提高竞争力。

现在你可能会问,那作为个人又能做些什么呢?如果世界发生了变化,变得更小,如果世界的竞争更为激烈,如果国家注重教育、研发和创造良好的环境,个人又该做些什么?下面是我的一些想法。很显然,你们在这里读书的目的就是为了接受良好的教育,我经常建议年轻的学生们,要尽可能地接受最好的教育,这是最好的基础。但是一旦你接受了良好的教育,我想你应该认识到,你的教育还远远不够。你在大学所学到的那些,可能在数年之后就过时了,所以你们要继续不断地学习,在大学毕业后,以及在将来的工作中,都要不断地学习。总之,永远不要停止学习,你也没有机会停止学习,你一生都必须不断地学习。

我还有一些小小的建议。第一,无论是你在学校接受教育,还是在将来的工作中,都不要害怕去问为什么。如果你要解决问题,要知道怎样才能成功,怎样创造新事物,你一定要问为什么,而且不止一次地问。通常当你接近一个问题时,你得到的第一个解释都是很浅显的。这并不接近问题的本质或根源,所以你就要不断地问为什么。在英特尔,我鼓励我的员工要勇于问为什么。我也告诉大学生们要敢于向教授提出这个问题。不要轻易接受事物,如果你不理解它们,要敢于问为什么,因为这是你可以真正理解这个问题的唯一出路。当然你也要明白,你在大学以外的社会上所要解决的问题,通常都是很复杂的问题,这些问题并不像课外作业那么简单。比如说,如果你要解决一个集成电路距离的问题,像我们在英特尔一样,你要解决跟新一代技术有关的问题,你要怎样从 65 纳米到 45 纳米再到 30 纳米或者更小的晶体管。通常要解决一个问题都有两三百个变量,需要很复杂的试验,你必须要习惯这些极其复杂的问题,而不是那些有确定答案的简单问题。如果要做到这一点,你就必须要收集大量的数据,并根据这些数据做出决策。所以习惯复杂的问题以及处理大量的数据是非常关键的一步。

我曾经读过一点你们的校训,如果我的理解是正确的话。孙中山先生在 1924 年创立了你们的学校,基本的校训是"博学",我想它的意思是尽可能地接受好的教育。

(我要戴上眼镜来看其余的内容,抱歉。)

"审问"的意思是收集数据并反复问为什么;"慎思"的意思是在人生中

要就复杂的问题做出决定，即"明辨"或正确决策；"笃行"的意思可能是你要不断地学习。我想这五条基本的校训早在80年前的1924年就与我今天所说的这些遥相呼应。也就是说，不懂就要问，要认识到自己要解决的是复杂的问题，并且需要用大量的数据来达到想要的结果。

所以，我以此来做一个总结，尽可能地接受良好的教育，不要怕问为什么，当你在做出复杂决策的时候，让数据说话。谢谢，我很乐意回答各位的问题。

（2006年10月30日，英特尔公司主席Craig Barrett在中山大学的演讲节选，根据录音材料整理）

第6单元

Text 1

Respected Mr. Wang Yang, Respected Mr. Lim Swee Say, Respected Mr. Chua Thian Poh, Distinguished Guests, Ladies and Gentlemen,

Good morning!

First of all, I would like to extend my warmest congratulations on the successful convening of this conference.

This year marks the 30th anniversary of China's reform and opening-up. Thirty years of reform and opening-up has connected China's economy with that of the world in a way that is unprecedented in terms of depth and extent. China now is the third largest importer in the world and the largest one in Asia. China has been increasingly and deeply integrated into the process of globalization.

Over the past 30 years, Guangdong province has all along stood in the forefront of China's reform and opening-up. Now, Guangdong province is No.1 province in China in terms of economic aggregate, with its GDP accounting for 1/8 of the nation's total, and its foreign trade representing nearly 1/3 of China's total foreign trade . In 2007, the GDP of Guangdong province reached US$419.9 billion. Guangdong province has now embarked on a new journey starting from a new historical height. I firmly believe that Guangdong, as a pioneer province in China's reform and opening-up, will blaze, in the process of further and deepening international cooperation, a trail of scientific development, which will not only serve the needs of Guangdong's new development agenda but also be in tide with the momentum of globalization.

Singapore is a developed member within the ASEAN. As the only developed country in Southeast Asia, it has kept the fastest development over the years. With a change-oriented mindset, Singapore is always good at discerning the earliest unnoticeable sign of the change in the world and quick in grasping the earliest opportunity resulting from it. In this way, Singapore has been successful in making continuous fresh progress, one after another, riding on the waves of globalization. This Singapore-unique feature has played a crucial role in bringing Singapore from the Third World into the First World in one big stride just within a short phase of no more than three decades. This is also the key factor for Singapore to firmly maintain its global cutting-edge competitiveness till today.

Singapore has also been a warm supporter for China's reform and opening-up and actively participated in it. Either with China in general or with Guangdong province in particular, Singapore's trade and investment are both in the front ranking. Party Secretary Wang Yang with his delegation's visit to Singapore and attendance to today's business conference has provided a good chance for Guangdong to draw on Singapore's experience in constantly moving forward with times, and also a good chance for Singaporean friends from all circles to know and understand in person the latest developments in Guangdong, thus jointly seeking fresh opportunities for further cooperation benefiting both. I believe that through mutual exchanges, numerous business opportunities will be turned into reality of win-win cooperation. The importance of mutually beneficial cooperation can never be overstressed.

The comprehensive and vigorous development of bilateral relations between China and Singapore is the strong backing and guarantee for the in-depth and fruitful cooperation between Guangdong and Singapore. Since the establishment of diplomatic relations between our two countries in 1990, China and Singapore have successfully taken a way of highly practical, efficient and creative cooperation by underlining the viable combination of respective development strategies with mutual cooperation, and eventually reaped mutually beneficial fruits. The relationship between China and Singapore has already become one of the most substantive bilateral ties. Singapore's engagement in China's regional development is one of the key areas of cooperation designated by our two governments. It is believed that the in-depth cooperation between Guangdong and Singapore, backed by our both governments, will not only further inject fresh vitality and substance into the effective and practical cooperation between China and Singapore, but also make positive contributions to the deepening cooperation between China and ASEAN.

In conclusion, I wish every success to the conference, to Mr. Wang Yang and your delegation. Thank you all!

(Ambassador Zhang Xiaokang's speech at China Guangdong-Singapore Business Conference on September 16, 2008)

Text 2

非常欢迎各位前来参加会议，尤其是 Chirstine Lagarde 部长先生以及其他各位发言嘉宾，欢迎你们的到来。

接下来的几天里，各位将要评价在贸易政策中引入的永续性影响评估。这一全新系统的目的在于帮助制定更好的政策，并帮助人们更全面、更好地理解我们的行动对经济、社会以及环境等方面的影响；不仅是对我们这一代人，而且是对子孙后代的影响。

我们是否已经做到这一点了呢？我们是否已经成功改进欧盟的贸易政策及目标形成机制了呢？我们是否能做出更好的分析并据此达成协议，以使欧洲及全球伙伴都能受益呢？

我期待看到各位的评估报告，这些问题太重要了。我担任欧盟贸易委员期间，一直有如下坚定的信念，请允许我和各位分享我的一些看法。

首先，对贸易政策方面的问题，我们不可能从教科书中找到简单的答案。自由市场理论家，甚至非政府组织的理论家们，在确立这些复杂问题的规则之前，需要的不仅仅是谦虚一点点。每当有新自由主义经济学家告诉我农业保护主义是消除贫困的障碍，或是有非政府组织的活动家对我说为寻求工业产品和服务进入发展中国家市场的更好渠道进行谈判势必会造成破坏经济和社会的严重后果时，我都会意识到这一点。事实是，在几乎每一个不同的情况中，贸易政策都要依赖具体的环境而定。

我的第二点观察是，贸易自由化必定会带来更大的经济增长这一说法并不会自然发生，更不要说会它带来长期可持续性的增长了。当然，贸易自由化会导致短期调整成本的激增，如同我任内所看到的纺织品生产者、皮鞋生产者，以及毛里求斯甘蔗种植者和加勒比海香蕉种植者所经历的那样。短期阵痛能否以长期所得来弥补取决于很多因素，比如现有商业提升市场的能力，区域整合并建立新的比较优势的能力，等等。在理想的情况下，这会创造很多长期就业机会，这些就业机会使用的是更加可持续的资源——不过没有任何经济规律保证这一切必定会发生。

第三点，保护主义政策的历史告诉我们，保护主义是没有出路的。任何短期的利益都只会使经济实力不断受到削弱。20世纪30年代，保护主义加剧了经济衰退。可能现在也存在着过渡阶段的保护主义以帮助幼稚行业获得发展，但旨在为稳固行业提供调整时间的保护主义往往很少奏效。生产者呼吁实施保护主义可以理解，但当生产者得到帮助时，付出成本的通常是消费者，而且是最贫困的消费者。保护主义很难成为一项可持续的政策。

在欧洲，最近几周一场关于保护主义的争论分散了我们的注意力。关闭国际商贸的大门不符合我们的利益，不符合我们的消费者以及企业的利益，也不会为我们在全球的伙伴带来新的、持续的增长和繁荣的机会，而这些增长与繁荣是使我们可以立刻获益的。

第四，更为严重的是逼迫已处于经济发展道路上那些国家的专制性战略。这些战略在20世纪已经造成了灾难性的后果。当然，批评自由市场资本主义是完全合理的，因为它会对环境造成破坏，对此说法我能够接受。一方面是因为巨额利润而受到破坏的印尼和巴西的热带雨林，一方面是世界上富裕地区人们永远无法满足的胃口，只要想一想这些就够了。我觉得，问题虽然严重，但是如果改变激励方式，市场也可以朝着可持续性的方向发展。

欧洲正在这方面进行尝试，比如我们现在有排放交易计划，这一计划有可能成为遏制全球变暖的主要助力。

第五，在正确的条件下，即在我所说逐步自由化的条件下，贸易对经济发展将会起到十分重要的作用。降低贸易壁垒以获得更好的贸易机会以及提高贸易能力，这两者的出现则是良好的治理、有保障的产权、稳定的法律制度以及现代高效基础设施共同作用的结果。

第六，我们必须面对全球经济中不断变化的生产模式和消费模式所带来的后果。当然，欧洲受其影响的人们需要获得帮助，以调整自己应对这些变化。但是，如果我们做出积极的而不是防御性的反应，我们就会赢得主动塑造全球化趋势的机会，避免陷入被动。我们也要认识到，欧洲企业通过将生产转移到亚洲等地区为变化的过程做出了很大贡献。我也真切希望他们的企业社会责任感意味着他们将欧洲标准和强烈的社会正义传统带到其他地方。我们在这里有影响，因此我们要尽量发挥它的作用。

第七，我们应致力于奉行多边主义，而且不仅仅是为了市场自由化。我们应决心为加强国际合作而努力。这一努力将会使国际社会在核心社会和环境标准上达成更为持久的共识。

以上是我的一些基本想法。本次会议召开恰逢本轮多边贸易谈判——多哈回合谈判——到达关键阶段，即最后阶段，这是再令人高兴不过的了。多哈回合能够，而且必须为发展和消除贫困做出应有的贡献。

非洲在世界贸易份额中的比例增加1%带来的年增长率将超过非洲每年获得的援助总和。逐步自由化考虑到不同发展中国家能够承受的不同自由化程度，所以通过逐步自由化，与贸易相关的有效援助将从过去的"施舍"转变为令人欢迎的做法。而这正是多哈回合值得我们努力争取的原因所在。

从我开始担任欧盟贸易委员以来，很明显，在贸易对话中达成协议等于在世界贸易组织成员中达成一致，但更多的是通过向民间社会团体说明这一做法会带来哪些长远利益。民间社会团体和公众舆论在今天的多边谈判中比以往任何时候的作用都要大，我很高兴看到这一现实。我相信规则制订的透明化，信赖贸易谈判各方对公众负有的责任。

那么，永续性影响评估如何适用呢？

多年前，于1992年召开的里约世界峰会标志着经济、社会、环境三方面可持续发展概念的出现，这一重要概念已成为合理决策的关键因素。正是基于里约峰会的讨论基础之上，我的前任——帕斯卡·拉米先生首先引入了永续性影响评估这一做法。

当时，欧盟执行委员会内部确定贸易政策步调的是我们。直到2001年夏天，欧盟委员会才引入了一个更为宽泛的系统来评估其内部政策作为欧盟可持续性发展总战略的一部分在经济、社会和环境三方面的影响。今天，这样的想法已随处可见，但在 1999 年，这些想法是具有相当开创性的。

到 20 世纪 90 年代末，越来越明显的一点是，不能再由贸易精英们按照自己贸易自由化惠及所有人的简单设想，关起门来进行贸易谈判。

最后，我想说，各位今后几天要参与多场有趣的讨论，多谢各位的参与。祝你们成功，希望各位的工作能帮助我们进一步改进我们制定政策、明确谈判目标的方法。

我们实现追求目标的方式，是一个带来发展的回合，一个帮助我们积极回应以应对全球化挑战的回合，一个提供更多贸易机会、提高全人类生活水平的回合。谢谢大家。

（2006 年 3 月 21 日，欧盟贸易委员彼得·曼德尔森在布鲁塞尔"永续性影响评估盘点会议"上的发言节选）

Text 3

We are very pleased to see that over the recent years the scale of our economic and trade cooperation has been expanding and the fields enlarging. Guangdong has the largest trade volume with Malaysia in all ASEAN countries. In 2007, trade volume between Guangdong and Malaysia reached 14.48 billion USD, increased by 28%, amounting to 31.2% of the total trade volume between China and Malaysia, in which Guangdong's import occupied 80% in our trading volume with a trade deficit of 7.7 billion USD.

Besides, Guangdong and Malaysia also enjoy vigorous mutual investment. Just now I happened to see the total volume in the agreement that we are about to sign, and the investment total in Malaysia already exceeds 100 million USD. I believe that after this conference representatives from both countries will further their talks which will surely bring more benefits to both sides. Many Malaysian enterprises have benefited greatly from their investment in China. While more and more Guangdong enterprises are coming to Malaysia for business and investment, among which are Huawei, who has set up regional headquarters here and Guangdong Agribusiness Group Corporation, who is now developing its rubber business in Sarawak, Malaysia. These enterprises will sign cooperation agreements here at the conference. I sincerely hope that more Guangdong enterprises will come to Malaysia for investment, making your contribution to the benefit of our two peoples.

Ladies and gentlemen, dear friends,

In the future, Guangdong and Malaysia boast great potential for business cooperation. Malaysia, a newly industrialized country in Asia, has a fast growing economy, rapidly developing electronics, manufacturing, construction and service industries, rich natural resources including oil, mineral resources, palm oil and rubber, as well as highly developed foreign trade and tourism. All these indicate the great potential for further development. Guangdong, as an important manufacturing base in China and the world at large, has many well-known enterprises and brands in such industries as electronics, household appliances, light industry and textile, and Guangdong's modern service industry including finance, logistics and exhibition industries are all developing very rapidly. Guangdong and Malaysia are highly complementary in resources, industrial structure and geographical location. Therefore, I believe cooperation between our two sides in larger scale at higher level will undoubtedly promote our common prosperity and development.

At this new starting point, we sincerely hope that under the principle of reciprocity and mutual benefit, our cooperation with Malaysia can be further strengthened in the following areas: firstly, we will continue to expand our bilateral trade. Among the ASEAN countries, Malaysia is the largest trading partner and also the largest import source land of Guangdong. Now, Guangdong mainly imports integrated circuits, diodes, semiconductors and edible vegetable oil, plastics from Malaysia, while the volume of imported integrated circuit takes up nearly half of the total. Goods exported from Guangdong to Malaysia mainly include textile and garments, furniture, shoes, iron and steel and ceramics, in which the export of textile and garments takes up nearly 20% of the total. In the recent two years, trade between our two sides has maintained very good momentum with an annual growth rate of 23%. If we can fully take the opportunity of the acceleration of CAFTA, our goal to double our trade volume by 2010 to 29 billion USD will surely be fulfilled.

Secondly, we will further expand fields for cooperation in investment. By the end of last year, Guangdong has attracted 573 direct investment projects from Malaysia with realized investment of 535 million USD, and the focused areas mainly include electronics and tourism. Currently, Guangdong is undergoing industrial restructuring and going all out to construct a modern industrial system consisting of advanced manufacturing, modern service industry and high-tech industry. Besides, we will also increase our input in key infrastructure areas, such as electricity, energy, highways, inter-city transportation and others. In the following five years, our investment in the above-mentioned key areas will amount to over 150 billion USD, covering more than 200 key projects. As Malaysian enterprises have gained rich experience and expertise in electronics, automobiles, machinery and other industries, we warmly welcome Malaysian enterprises to participate in the construction of the modern industry system, basic industries and infrastructure. Furthermore, we will encourage our enterprises to invest in manufacturing, transportation and telecommunication and we will support our enterprises to participate in in-depth exploration and cooperation in electricity, energy, mineral products, agricultural products, project contracting and labour cooperation.

Third is to enhance our cooperation in tourism. We will encourage more tourists from Guangdong to tour in Malaysia, promote Malaysian tourism in Guangdong and further strengthen our cooperation in this field. We warmly welcome Malaysian friends to Guangdong for traveling.

Fourthly, we will further strengthen our cooperation in agriculture and fishery. Malaysia has rich tropical agricultural resources and cash crops, while Guangdong is a large consumer of palm oil, natural rubber and log, therefore we have great potential of cooperation in this regard. In today's conference, Agribusiness Group Corporation will sign an agreement with a Malaysian enterprise for rubber planting and processing with an investment sum of 80 million USD; Guangxin Foreign Trade Group will sign an agreement with its Malaysian counterpart, importing logs worth of 50 million USD. Malaysia boasts rich marine fishery resources, while Guangdong has advanced marine fishing technology and advanced processing technology, therefore we are highly complementary in exploring marine fishery resources.

Fifthly, an economic and trade dialogue mechanism shall be established. We will take the opportunity of holding this conference to establish a dialogue mechanism between our two governments to coordinate affairs in investment and economic cooperation, thus further promoting our cooperation. I can share with you the good news that in my talk with Mr. Muhyudin just now we have formed our consensus on this part, which means this dialogue mechanism will be established soon.

Ladies and gentlemen, dear friends,

It's only two days since my delegation and I came to Malaysia, but we have already felt the friendly relation between Malaysian people and Guangdong people, and we have strengthened our determination for future cooperation. Yesterday, upon our arrival, His Excellency Mr. Prime Minister kindly met with our delegation, and before the conference I also had a talk with Mr. Najib and Mr. Muhyudin and I'm very pleased to obtain their positive response to our suggestion for furthering our economic and trade cooperation in various areas. Their positive response can serve as the firm base of our future cooperation.

I believe that today's forum will enhance our friendship and understanding, and with the joint efforts from our two governments, business and financial communities and all walks of life, our economic and trade cooperation will surely embrace a brighter future!

Last but not least, I wish the 2008 China Guangdong — Malaysia Business Conference a full success! May the friendship between our two peoples last forever!

Thank you!

(Excerpted text of speech by Guangdong Provincial CPC Committee Party Secretary Wang Yang at 2008 China Guangdong–Malaysia Business Conference, September 12, 2008)

Text 4

谢谢各位。女士们、先生们，早上好，我是来自泰国商务部贸易谈判厅的贸易技术代表。今天，我会给各位介绍根据中国－东盟自贸区安排，泰国的关税减让计划，并给各位介绍一下最新情况。

首先我想简单谈一谈泰中两国的贸易关系。泰中两国贸易联系由来已久，近年来贸易不断发展，尤其是自中国－东盟自贸区启动以来更是发展迅速。从这些数字大家可以看到，自2005年到2008年，泰中双边贸易从200亿增长到了2008年的360亿，增幅超过78%。根据我们去年的最新统计，中国是泰国第二大贸易伙伴和进口来源地，因为泰国越来越依赖中国的产品，中国的产品已成为泰国的首选或是对其他国家进口产品的补充。

接下来给大家介绍泰国的关税减让安排。和来自印尼的同仁介绍的情况一样，我们泰国也是根据中国－东盟自贸协定的模式来进行关税减让。自5年前泰国执行中国－东盟自贸协定以来，泰国的贸易增长十分迅速。

按照中国－东盟自贸协定，泰国的关税减让分成三个渠道进行。2003年泰国开始关税减让，涉及早期收割计划下的部分税目——早期收割计划是中国和东盟国家全面经济合作框架的重要成果。然后，泰国开始按照2005年生效的货物贸易协定进行关税减让，确立了5121个税目的逐步减让安排。

在刚才一张幻灯片里我已经说过，早期收割计划里2004年1月份开始的减让计划里包括未加工农业产品，这是按照中国－东盟自贸协定确立减让关税的首批产品。对泰中贸易来说，关税减让开始于2003年10月，双方同意了按照第7、8章116个税目下商品的减让，主要是新鲜蔬果，其关税当年就减为了零。

下一步要减免的是正常渠道内4770个关税税目下的产品。

到2005年7月以前，正常渠道内至少40%个税目的商品其关税税率要降到0到5%的水平。之后，到2007年1月之前，将正常渠道内60%的税目商品关税税率降到 0 到 5%。最后，正常渠道下全部关税税目将在 2010 年 1 月之前将关税降低为 0，除了正常渠道 2 下的商品以外，这些商品的关税将到 2012 年 1 月以前全部取消。

我们的敏感渠道包括 351 个税目，关税税率到 2012 年之前将降低到 20% 以下，到 2018 年以前降到 5% 以下的水平。高度敏感渠道内的税目将到 2015 年以前降低到 50% 以下。

接下来我给大家介绍一下泰国减税的现状。这里给大家看到的是泰国按照中国－东盟自贸协定已经进行关税减让的税目总数。去年，已经有 90% 的关税税目其税率降到了不到 10% 的水平，59% 的税目其税率在 0 到 5%。今年，税率降到 0 到 5% 水平的税目总数比 2008 年多出了一倍。在下一张幻灯片里我会给大家详细说明多少个税目的税率已经降到零关税的水平。

刚才我说过，2008 年税率不到 5% 的税目约 60%，但税率为零的只有 203 个税目，是个比较小的数字。现在看 2009 年，大家看红色这一栏，1700 多个税目的税率已经降到了零，不到一年的短短时间里增加了 8 倍多。泰国将继续扩大关税减让幅度，到 2010 年争取零关税税目的数字比今年增加一倍。然后，到 2012 年，泰国将实现基本零关税。做不到百分之百零关税是因为我们要遵从互惠原则，也就是说，对那些被中国列为敏感渠道的商品，我们是不能减税的。

为了进一步向各位说明 2009、2010 年关税减让的重要程度，大家可以看到 2003 年的数字，在中国－东盟自贸协定实施以前，正常渠道下税目的平均关税税率为 12.93%，最高税率为 80%。2008 年，也就是去年，平均关税税率降到了 6.35%，最高税率下降到 12%。现在，2009 年，平均关税税率只有 2.79%，最高税率仅达 5%。另外，到 2010 年，平均关税税率将减少到 0.14%，最高税率 5%，因为部分商品属于正常渠道 2 之下，这些正常渠道 2 之下的商品关税到 2012 年会降到零，意味着到 2012 年根据中国－东盟自贸协定泰国将基本实现零关税。

现在我们看一下表格 E，原产地证明的使用率。目前，关于优惠税率的使用情况，大家从这些数据可以看到，在中国－东盟自贸协定下泰国从中国的进口仅为 4.2%，数字很小，看起来很不起眼。这个数字说明中国出口到泰国的全部商品中有 4.2% 根据中国－东盟自贸协定享受优惠关税税率。2008 年中国对泰国出口总额为 200 多亿美元，这个数字可不小。所以中国的出口商有很多机会提高利润。另外，从泰国方面的数字，各位也可以看到，在对中国出口总额里占 10.44%，利用率稍微高一点点，不过泰国出口商也是没有充分使用中国－东盟自贸协定的优惠。可能过去减让的幅度太小，因此大家可能为了避免麻烦没有使用自贸协定的优惠。但是今年已经有 1700 多个税目的关税税率降低为零，明年会继续有 4290 个税目降低到零关税水平，现在大家应该重新考虑享受中国－东盟自贸协定提供的优惠待遇了。

我的介绍就到这里，如果想了解更多的信息，各位可以登录泰国商务部网站 ThaiFTA，我们已经提供了相关信息在网上。谢谢。

（2009年3月26日，泰国商务部贸易谈判厅技术官员 Thananchon Rojkittikhun 在"中国－东盟自贸协定南宁宣讲会"上的发言）

第 7 单元

Text 1

Respected Mr. Chen Wu, Vice Chairman of Guangxi Zhuang Autonomous Region, Distinguished Guests, Ladies and Gentlemen, Dear Friends:

Good morning!

In this golden season of autumn, we gather here for the opening of the Promotion Conference on China-ASEAN Investment Cooperation Fund in the beautiful city of Nanning. Please allow me, on behalf of Export-Import Bank of China, to express to you all my deepest gratitude and warmest welcome.

To further the economic and trade cooperation between China and ASEAN countries, in February this year, the State Council of the Chinese government decided to set up a fund for China-ASEAN investment cooperation. On April 18, Premier Wen Jiabao officially announced this decision at the annual meeting of Bo'ao Asia Forum. Our bank, Export-Import Bank of China, will be the principal sponsor of this fund. Under the support and leadership from relevant departments of the State Council, with the interest from all circles in society, after 6 months' hard work, substantial development has been achieved regarding the establishment of the fund. Soon this fund will begin operation.

The economic and trade cooperation between China and ASEAN countries enjoys a long history and is now at a crucial stage. For a long period of time, the Chinese government has always been attaching great importance to its economic and trade cooperation with ASEAN countries. Under our joint efforts, our bilateral trade has achieved very substantial progress. In recent years, it has experienced very rapid development. In 2004, China signed the free trade agreement with ASEAN countries, the first of its kind that ever signed by the Chinese government with other countries. In 2008, despite the severe impact brought by the global financial crisis, bilateral trade between China and ASEAN reached USD231.1 billion, an increase of 13.9% over the previous year. China is now the third largest trading partner of ASEAN and ASEAN China's fourth largest.

Since the year of 2008, though the global financial crisis has brought huge impact on the cooperation between and development of China and ASEAN, it helped us to realize the importance of our trade cooperation. For many years, American and European developed countries have been the main export market for China and ASEAN countries, but their economy shrank heavily with the sharp decrease in their purchase power due to the current crisis. Despite such severe economic shock, economic and trade cooperation between us has become even stronger. We have both survived the hardest period and are now recovering. From a long-term view, under the background of economic regionalization and globalization, there is more urgent need for China and ASEAN countries to further the bilateral cooperation for sustainable development.

The China-ASEAN free trade area will be fully established and put into operation next year. At that time, it will become the third largest free trade area in the world with a huge market of 1.9 billion consumers. Therefore, we can say that our cooperation is at a crucial point for new development.

The further of our economic and trade cooperation requires more direct investment, especially investment in infrastructure and construction. In recent years, trade and people exchange between our two sides are developing very well. To enhance our cooperation to a higher level, we need to offer more direct investment so that allocation of resources can be optimized and advantages of each country can be given full play. Investment in and construction of infrastructure is the prerequisite for economic and social development, transportation, telecommunication and other infrastructure serve as the necessary carriers for the exchange of commodities, capital and people. Only with the development of infrastructure can we promote the unity of market for more business opportunities. Southeast Asia region enjoys very favorable geographical conditions as the pivot connecting Asia, Africa, Europe and Australia. Therefore, the acceleration of the development of transportation, the construction of Pan-Asia railway and that of the international channel from Southwest China to Southeast Asia will further facilitate the communication of goods, transfer of industries, exploitation of resources and energy, the growth of tourism and other industries as well as the cultivation of new economic growth points. With the launch of the China-ASEAN free trade area, we feel a more urgent need to connect with each other through the development of infrastructure so as to better serve the need for people and goods exchange between our two sides.

The Chinese government proposed the establishment of China-ASEAN Investment Cooperation Fund for the infrastructure and network building with a purpose to encourage Chinese companies to go to ASEAN countries for construction of large-scale projects and help the local countries recover from the crisis for sustainable development with the support and guidance from the fund. Principally sponsored by Export-Import Bank of China, this fund will be a private equity fund with 100% market-oriented operation mode under the guidance of the government. The total scale of fund will be USD10 billion with the scale for the initial phase USD1 billion. The initial phase of the fund will invest, but not limit to, transportation, public facilities, telecommunication network, petroleum, natural gas, mining resources and other areas. The targeted area for the other phases of the fund will be determined based on the real situation of our economic and trade cooperation.

As the principal sponsor of this fund, the Export-Import Bank of China has the confidence as well as the ability to play an even bigger role in boosting China-ASEAN economic and trade cooperation. We are a government policy bank that implements state policies and supports international cooperation. For the past 15 years since its establishment, we have always been paying attention to the need of the macro situation and adjusting our business scope and functions. Currently, our business scope includes: export credit and import credit, loans to overseas construction contracts and loans to overseas investment projects, equity investment, the Chinese government concessional loan, onlending loans from foreign governments and international financial institutions, international guarantee, international settlement and others. It's estimated that by the end of this year our total assets will exceed RMB 900 billion and we will be supporting the economic and trade cooperation between Chinese companies and over 150 countries. For years, we have taken developing countries, especially our neighboring developing countries as key in our work and we have been supporting many Chinese companies in their expansion of international market. Besides, we have trained professionals with high quality and rich service experience for international economic cooperation. As we are chosen as the principal sponsor of China-ASEAN Investment Cooperation Fund, we are expected to give full play to the above-mentioned advantages, integrate credit business with fund operation for the sound management of the fund so that new vitality can be injected into the cooperation between China and ASEAN.

From the approval of the fund by the State Council till now, eight months have passed. With support from all walks of life, we have finished relevant work of the set-up of the fund and almost completed the fund-raising work. The fund will soon be registered in Hong Kong for operation.

Ladies and gentlemen, dear friends,

Facing the current international economic situation, we feel urgent need and unprecedented opportunities in our bilateral cooperation. The set-up of China-ASEAN Investment Cooperation Fund will provide a brand new platform for our cooperation. This is not only an important measure made by the Chinese government for the further of our cooperation, but is also demonstration of our confidence in ASEAN market and in economic growth of our two sides. I do believe that under our joint efforts, this fund can play an ever important role in China-ASEAN economic cooperation and our traditional cooperation will surely be embracing a more fruitful future.

Finally, I'd like to wish the conference every success. Thank you!

(Full text of speech by Mr. Li Ruogu, President of the Export-Import Bank of China, at the Promotion Conference of China-ASEAN Investment Cooperation Fund, October 21, 2009, as transcribed)

Text 2

尊敬的国际货币基金总裁施特劳思·卡恩先生，尊敬的世界银行行长佐利克先生，主席先生，各位尊敬的代表，

我想感谢土耳其政府以及伊斯坦布尔市人民为本次国际货币基金组织和世界银行年会的顺利召开做出的精心组织，同时感谢你们给予我们的热情接待。我很荣幸代表韩国参加此次会议。

在我开始演讲之前，我仅代表韩国政府向亚太地区遭受严重地震和洪水灾害的人民表示深切同情。

女士们、先生们，

我们还记得，由于全球经济危机的严重影响，去年的年会充满了恐惧与绝望的情绪。但是，今年我们怀着希望相聚在此，因为全球经济已经显示出复苏的迹象。这一积极变化的出现，离不开由20国集团主导的前所未有的国际间政策协调，也离不开来自国际货币基金组织以及世界银行的积极支持。

不过，全球经济只是刚刚走出了危机最严重的阶段，在全面复苏到来之前还有很长的路要走。我们也面临着许多重大任务，包括重振受危机严重影响的增长潜力以及促进可持续的平衡发展。值此重大时刻，我想就克服危机、维持可持续发展提以下几点建议：

第一，应建立退出战略，并在经济复苏全面出现时实施该战略。

过早实施退出战略可能阻碍经济复苏并导致经济陷入两位数的衰退，而太晚实施退出战略可能导致市场的不稳定并造成更多的泡沫。因此，我们应该采取一致行动，根据国际间一致认可的原则制定退出战略，并认识到各国实施退出战略的规模、时间和顺序都不尽相同。

为此，我仅呼吁国际货币基金组织尽快建立退出战略的标准并出台具体解决方案以对成员国进行公平、公开和独立的监管。

第二，各国应相互协调，努力寻求可持续和平衡的经济增长。

要使全球经济恢复到危机前的增长趋势，各国必须摒弃保护主义，实现

有序的政策协调。出现经常账户赤字的国家应提高政府和私有部门储蓄率，同时维持市场开放；出现经常账户盈余的国家应采取进一步行动拉动国内需求，提高市场开放程度。要实现上述目标，我们必须为发展中经济体和新兴经济体，尤其是容易受到外部冲击影响的经济体扩大全球安全网络，并且继续货币掉期安排和区域金融合作。

除此以外，我们要积极参与绿色增长模式的推广，培育新的经济增长引擎。绿色增长通过对现有能源的绿色转换将资源依赖型经济转型为环境友好型经济，不仅能提高人民生活水平，而且可以带来新的增长机会。

韩国推出了"低碳绿色增长"国家战略，计划每年将GDP的2%用于投资绿色增长部门。另外，韩国将通过参与世界银行可再生能源规模扩大项目增加对发展中国家的援助，并且积极履行自己的义务，促进绿色增长国际合作。

第三，国际货币基金组织和世界银行应积极进行改革以有效应对国际金融体系的根本性变革。

国际货币基金组织和世界银行建立于60多年前的布雷顿森林体系之下。按照亚洲的传统，60年是一个承前启后、辞旧迎新的时刻。

全球性危机造成了世界经济秩序的深刻变革，对此，国际货币基金组织和世界银行应通过改革积极提升自身的可信度和合理性。国际货币基金组织尤其需要将份额增加至少100%，以确保有足够的资源应对经济危机。另外，在匹兹堡20国集团的峰会上，各国一致同意将新兴市场和发展中国家在国际货币基金组织的份额提高至少5%以上。

世界银行在分配持股比例时也应该重新考虑各国不断变化的经济权重，现有的分配制度已经十年未变了。另外，各成员国的持股比例也应定期审查。

最后，我想强调低收入国家的持续利益以及进一步向其提供援助。

低收入国家受到经济危机的冲击很大，虽然它们不对危机负直接责任。

危机在发达国家造成了失业和收入减少等问题，但在低收入国家却威胁到人们的生计。

在此背景下，我非常高兴地看到，国际货币基金组织决定增强对低收入国家的支持，大幅提高对低收入国家的贷款额度。我想鼓励会员国积极参与国际货币基金组织和世界银行的这一行动，为低收入国家提供更多的财政资源。

韩国也将积极参与国际货币基金组织的减贫与增长贷款项目以及世界银行的脆弱评估架构。

各位来宾，

有句话叫"一燕不成夏"。

我们看到，曾经深深沦陷的全球经济开始发出了一丝光芒，要使这光芒变得更亮，我们必须增进大家努力建立的"共同感"。

我希望国际货币基金组织和世界银行能发挥关键作用，本着共同感的精神，进一步促进国际协作。

作为2010年20国峰会的轮值主席国，韩国将全力支持国际货币基金组织和世界银行履行自己的责任。

谢谢各位。

(2009年10月6日，韩国企划财政部部长尹增铉在"第64届国际货币基金和世界银行年会"上的主题发言节选)

Text 3

President Obama, Dear Colleagues,

It gives me great pleasure to come to Pittsburgh for the third G20 financial summit. Let me first of all express sincere thanks to President Obama for the active effort and thoughtful arrangement he has made for our meeting.

Following the two summits in Washington and London, the international community's confidence has strengthened, financial markets have moved towards stability and the world economy has seen positive changes. We are soberly aware, however, that the foundation of an economic rebound is not yet solid, with many uncertainties remaining. A full economic recovery will take a slow and tortuous process. It remains our primary task at present to counter the international financial crisis and promote a healthy world economic recovery. At the same time, we should stay firmly committed to advancing the reform of the international financial system and achieve comprehensive, sustainable and balanced world economic development while addressing the global development imbalances.

First, we should stand firm in our commitment to stimulating economic growth. We should make full use of the G20 platform to step up macroeconomic policy coordination, maintain the overall consistency of our policies and ensure that they are timely and forward-looking. All countries should keep up the intensity of their economic stimulus plans. Both developed countries and developing countries should take more solid and effective measures and make greater effort to boost consumption and expand domestic demand. Major reserve currency issuing countries should take into account and balance the implications of their monetary policies for both their own economies and the world economy with a view to upholding stability of international financial markets. We should resolutely oppose and reject protectionism in all forms, uphold a fair, free and open global trading and investment system, and impose no new restrictions on goods, investment and services as we have committed. And we should work for the success of the Doha Round negotiations on the basis of locking up the existing achievements. We should energetically promote international cooperation in new industries, especially energy conservation, pollution reduction, environmental protection and new energies, and foster new growth areas in the world economy. We should intensify international scientific and technological cooperation and make full use of the advancement in science and technology to boost the internal dynamism of world economic growth. At the same time, we should stay on alert against any possible adverse impact of the stimulus measures, the potential risk of inflation in particular.

Second, we should stand firm in our commitment to advancing the reform of the international financial system. At the previous two summits, G20 leaders reached the political consensus of reforming the international financial system. This is a solemn commitment we have made to the whole world. The international economic and financial situation is now improving, but we should remain as resolved as ever to advance the reform and our targets of reform must not become any weaker. We should follow through on the timetable and the roadmap agreed upon at the London Summit, increase the representation and voice of developing countries and push for substantive progress in the reform. We should improve the existing decision-making process and mechanism in international financial institutions and encourage more extensive and effective participation of all parties. We should move forward the reform of the international financial supervisory and regulatory regime. The reform should get to the most fundamental principles and objectives of supervision and regulation. The future financial supervisory and regulatory regime should be easy to operate and highly accountable. We should step up cooperation in financial supervision and regulation, expand its coverage, formulate as quickly as possible financial supervision and regulation standards that are widely acceptable, and ensure quality implementation of all reform measures.

Third, we should stand firm in our commitment to promoting balanced growth of the global economy. The issue of global economic imbalances has drawn close attention from the international community. It includes imbalances between savings and consumption, and imports and exports in some countries. But more importantly, it manifests itself in the imbalances in global wealth distribution, resource availability and consumption and the international monetary system. The causes for such imbalances are complex and manifold. Factors at work include deepening economic globalization, international division of labor and industrial relocation, and global capital flow. The existing international economic system, macroeconomic policies of major economies, and the consumption culture and way of life of different countries have also played a direct part. The root cause, however, is the yawning development gap between the North and the South. Only with real development of the vast developing world can there be solid global economic recovery and sustainable world economic growth. We should build up international institutions that promote balanced development. We should support the United Nations in better guiding and coordinating development efforts, encourage the World Bank to increase development resources and enhance its role in poverty reduction and development, and urge the IMF to set up a financial rescue mechanism that will provide prompt and effective assistance and give financing support to the least developed countries on a priority basis. We should scale up input in development in diverse forms. The substantial amount of funds raised through the G20 summits should be used first and foremost to address development imbalances. Developed countries should implement the Monterrey Consensus in real earnest, take concrete steps to increase assistance to developing countries, and promote the attainment of the UN Millennium Development Goals. We should value the important role of technological cooperation in promoting balanced development, reduce man-made barriers to technology transfer, and create an enabling environment for developing countries to narrow the development gap. It is of particular importance to step up cooperation in green technologies, ensure developing countries access to applicable and affordable green technologies, and avoid a new "green divide". We should change our economic growth patterns with a sense of urgency and active measures, and at the same time we should take into account different circumstances and proceed in the light of actual conditions. Countries at different stages of development should be allowed to choose their own approach and pace suited to their national conditions, and the space for development that the developing countries well deserve must not be compromised.

Dear colleagues,

China attaches great importance to comprehensive, balanced and sustainable economic and social development. We have mainly relied on expanding domestic demand, especially consumer demand in mitigating the impact of the international financial crisis. We have taken active steps to adjust the domestic and overseas demand structure and the investment and consumption structure, and strike the right balance among the speed, structure, quality and efficiency of economic growth. In the wake of the international financial crisis, China has adopted a host of policy measures to boost domestic demand, adjust economic structure, promote growth and improve people's well-being. These measures have produced initial results. In the first half of this year, despite the drastic contraction in overseas demand, China's

GDP managed to grow by 7.1% year on year. This shows that our policy to stimulate growth by boosting domestic demand is effective. And China's economic growth has contributed to the global economic recovery.

For years, China has taken an active part in international development cooperation. We have been actively engaged in the international cooperation to tackle the financial crisis ever since it broke out, despite the enormous difficulties and grave challenges confronting us. We will follow through on our assistance pledges and measures in a responsible manner, and offer more help to developing countries, particularly the least developed countries in Africa, within the realm of our capabilities.

Dear colleagues,

The G20 has held three summits in less than a year. These meetings have produced positive results. I am confident that with the concerted efforts of the entire international community, we will prevail over this international financial crisis and usher in a more prosperous future for the world economy.

Thank you.

(Full text of speech by President Hu Jintao at the Third G20 Financial Summit, Pittsburgh, September 25, 2009)

Text 4

很荣幸受邀参加成长委员会会议并发言。会议要我介绍一下我与罗伯特·希勒教授合著的新书《动物精神：人类心理如何驱动经济发展？这对全球资本主义为什么重要？》。开始之前，我想告诉各位，我要讲的内容可能会比书中的更为抽象。

书里有很多很多的故事，我们就通过这些故事来阐述自己的观点。首先，我先介绍一下我们陷入当前这场经济金融危机的原因。我的分析基本会集中在美国，因为我认为美国就是这场危机的震源。全世界的政府都在试图平息这场危机，因此他们向经济学家寻求帮助；而经济学家们依赖于自己对宏观经济趋势的见解，这种见解大部分来自凯恩斯。想要摆脱危机，就必须对世界经济的运作有正确的了解；动物精神恰恰能够使我们做到这一点。

现有宏观经济学的各种版本在很大程度上淡化了人类心理在其中的作用。但是，就像我们在书里写到的，宏观经济学里至少有八大基本问题，其回答基本上——哪怕不是完全地——依赖于心理扮演的角色。

于是，这本书的首要任务就是解释心理在宏观经济中的作用。凯恩斯把这种角色称为人类的动物精神。书的第一部分描述了五种不同的动物精神，分别是：信心、公平、腐败和不良信念、货币幻觉、故事。书的第二部分说明了为什么这几种动物精神能解释宏观经济学的八大基本问题，比如为什么经济是波动的，货币政策和财政政策为什么影响经济、怎样影响经济，为什么会存在非自愿性失业。接下来，我给大家简要介绍一下如何通过这些概念说明我们陷入本次危机的原因，然后我再回顾一下危机在美国的几个特点。

排在动物精神首位的是信心。字典里对信心的解释是信任。信任的意思是，人们超越通常的对信息的理性使用以做出决定。这恰好是我们在刚刚结束的经济繁荣里发现的一种现象。人们做出各种各样的投资决策，尤其是在购买、出售复杂的金融工具时，这一切决策的基础就是信任。这种情况不仅仅存在于住房和抵押市场。

其实，这在金融市场是更为普遍的现象。另外，如果人们对促使他们做出投资决策的基础进行了理性分析，他们可能就不会做出当时的决策了；人们之所以决定进行投资，恰恰是出于信心。但是结果表明他们信心过度了。

现在我再来介绍一下腐败和不良信念的作用。很少有经济学家能提前预见不断发展的态势。他们的标准看法是，私有市场是自我管理的市场，市场里的人是具备相应知识的买家和卖家，只有在回报足够高、能够给他们充分补偿的前提下，他们才会承担不断增加的风险。这样一来，很少人会担心证券市场、房地产市场里缺乏管理会造成怎样的后果。不过，认为市场具备自我监管能力的观点不会考虑人们信心过度这一点，因此市场实际上并没有进行自我监管，尽管这是它应该做到的。资本主义有一个原则，就是要利用人们的信心过度。

的确，资本主义会带给人们想要的一切，只要企业能够盈利；但更为微妙而普遍的情况是，资本主义也带给人们自以为自己需要的一切，只要企业能盈利。不受监管的资本主义也许是我们治病的良药。

我相信它的疗效；但是，不受监管的资本主义也可能是一副假药，根本治不了病。更有甚者，它也许会发现制造更多对假药的需求是一件更加有利可图的事。实际上，这就是为什么美国会有食品和药物管理局的原因：有了它的存在，我们就不会再买到假药了。我们写的书里有很多的故事，其中一个故事就是和这有关的：威廉姆·洛克菲勒，也就是约翰·洛克菲勒的父亲，在19世纪时开着自己的小破车跑遍美国中西部。他每去到一个新的小镇，就会去那里的市镇广场，发表演说，派发传单，告诉人们洛克菲勒医生到镇上来了，洛克菲勒医生有特效药。他会住到镇上最好的旅馆去，把自己穿戴的物品卖给找他治病的当地人。威廉姆·洛克菲勒和他儿子约翰区别太大了：威廉姆叫卖的是假药，代表了资本主义的一个方面，他的儿子约翰·洛克菲勒卖的是真药，满足了人们真实的需求，代表了资本主义有效的一面。威廉姆·洛克菲勒兜售的假药实质上和我们今天的资产市场有着特殊的关联。资产对大多数人来讲不过是几张纸而已；绝大多数投资者是从别人那里了解到自己金融资产的价值的，如会计师、评级机构，等等。这些会计师和评级机构却有着自己的动机，这些动机与公众利益并不完全一致。因此，如果人们信心过度，金融市场就会制造出某种利用人们过度的信心的资产；在缺乏有效监管的情况下，人们买到的资产就有可能是"假药"。于是，某个行业应运而生，保护人们的利益。我们在华尔街等地所看到的情况恰好如此。

另一种动物精神进一步巩固了前面两个：人们的行动、思考和生活依赖于各种故事，不论是经济决策还是个人决定，都是如此。通常，会有一个关于经济为什么会以现在这种形式运行的故事。类似的这种故事多少会有些真实成分，不过往往要么过于乐观，要么过分悲观。十年前，出现了互联网繁荣时期；最近几年，我们听到的是金融工程能够增加金融资产的安全性，比证券更安全；各种现代金融方案已经找出办法降低风险……于是人们相信了这些故事。人们太有信心了。市场于是利用了人们的这种信任，将"假药"资产兜售给了信心过度的人们。以上三种动物精神解释了人类的心理波动如何在经济波动及其原因方面的作用。我们认为这就是经济周期波动的关键所在：信心从无到有，故事从无到有，假药从无到有。我们认为当前的金融危机恰好可以用这种波动来准确地解释，这是我们书里非常重要的一个论点，告诉了我们当前金融危机究竟源自哪里。

我们用这些基本原则来解释一下这场金融危机吧。接下来我要谈的是美国的情况，因为这是我最为了解的。另外，我觉得美国的情况在这里也是非常重要的，因为我相信这场危机的中心就在美国，可是出于同样的原因，同样程度的过度乐观已经影响了全世界。我们现在来看一看美国的情况。

（2009年4月20日，George A. Akerlof 在"金融危机及其对发展中国家发展战略及未来的影响研讨会"上的发言节选）

第 8 单元

Text 1

Distinguished Delegates from ASEAN Countries, Special Guests from Governments of the Hong Kong and Macao SAR, Ladies and Gentlemen:

I am much honored to attend the "Guangdong-ASEAN Conference on the Protection and Promotion of the Intangible Cultural Heritage". Intangible cultural heritage is the crystallization of human civilization and wisdom. It is a witness to the development of society, and it is the cultural base for us to inherit the historical past and to forge ahead into the future. As a unique cultural form, intangible cultural heritage has been a spiritual homeland for human beings. It embodies the high development of human civilization, and represents the intense wisdom of the human mind and practice. Today, we get together to discuss in depth the protection of the precious spiritual wealth and the safeguard of our shared spiritual homeland. Such discussion is of great significance. I would like to take this opportunity to express my thoughts and invite discussions. My speech will focus on four aspects as follows.

One, the exchange and cooperation between Guangdong and other ASEAN members on intangible cultural heritage has an inherent ground.

First of all, it is based on strong historical and cultural backgrounds. Guangdong and the ASEAN countries share proximity in geographical location and humanity. There has been a long history of frequent and intense cultural exchanges. The intangible cultural heritage of each of the countries has its own uniqueness and distinct features, with high degree of individuality and diversity. They influence and learn from each other and share certain extent of homogeneity and similarity, which is the premise for initiating cooperation and exchange. Secondly, it is based on high degree of awareness of culture and sense of responsibility. Along with the economic globalization at the present time, the economic foundation, political environment and social conditions, on which the survival of intangible cultural heritage relies, have changed so greatly that the latter is facing unprecedented crisis and many invaluable intangible cultural heritages are on the verge of extinction; people's spiritual homeland is being damaged and ruined. Under such circumstances, the discussion on the reinforcement of the policies and experiences on the protection of intangible cultural heritage shows the shared courage and confidence of Guangdong and the fellow ASEAN members in assuming cultural responsibilities.

Finally, it is based on the rich resources of practical experience. Guangdong and the ASEAN countries have always attached great importance to the protection of intangible cultural heritage. Each of us have developed our own unique mode of practice according to the different situations and accumulated rich experiences. It is the common goal of Guangdong and the ASEAN countries to advance the work through exchanging experiences and sharing results on the protection of intangible cultural heritage.

Two, the exchange and cooperation on intangible cultural heritage between Guangdong and ASEAN has great significance. In my opinion, there are several layers of purpose and significance in holding this forum and strengthening the cooperation and exchanges. Firstly, seeking the unity of thoughts and enhancing consensus. Intangible cultural heritage is not only the unique resources of a country or nation, but also a shared cultural wealth of mankind, as well as the vivid testimony of the diversity of human cultural development. In the age of globalization and cultural diversity, how to better safeguard the intangible cultural heritage has become an important issue of the world's common concern that we all have to face. To initiate exchange and cooperation on this matter between Guangdong and the ASEAN countries will not only help promote the economic development, social harmony and cultural prosperity, as well as the cultural identity and cultural sovereignty in the region, but will also be important to the inheritance and progression of human culture and to the dialogue among different civilizations. Secondly, promoting exchanges and deepening friendship. Cultural relations are important parts of state relations. The exchange and cooperation in the protection of intangible cultural heritage will greatly enhance mutual understanding between the peoples of China and those of the ASEAN countries, deepen the friendship, promote friendly communications, enrich the relationship between partner countries and, ultimately, leave a significant mark in the history of cultural exchange. Thirdly, deepening cooperation so as to achieve a win-win situation. The exchange and cooperation of intangible cultural heritage marks the implementation of the China-ASEAN Framework Agreement on Comprehensive Economic Cooperation and Guangdong Provincial People's Government Memorandum of Cooperation with the ASEAN Secretariat. It will further deepen our cooperation in economy, politics and other areas for the benefit, win-win and the enhancement of people's well-being in the region.

Three, the intangible cultural heritage of Guangdong possesses a distinctive feature of openness and compatibility. The history of intangible cultural development has always been themed by exchange and cooperation. On the one hand, Guangdong is the starting point of the ancient Marine Silk Road. From the Han Dynasty onward, we began to trade with Southeast Asian and European countries and thus absorbing the interesting and special features of the foreign cultures and integrating them into our own culture. Therefore, the intangible cultural heritage is characterized by its openness. For example, foreign musical instruments and tunes have been boldly adopted in Guangdong music which is famous all over the world for its broad range and beautiful melodies. On the other hand, Guangdong, a place originally inhabited by the Chinese ancient Bai Yue people, has experienced four large-scale migrations from the Central Plains in history. The blending and mutation of the native culture and the culture of Central Plains have rendered much of intangible cultural heritage to demonstrate a distinctive nature of compatibility. For instance, Hakka folk songs, which have become the most characteristic and interesting cultural element, were a result of integration of the culture of the Central Plains and that of Meizhou when the Hakka villages and tribes were formed there. The protection of intangible cultural heritage in Guangdong is set along the principle of "regular preservation, timely rescue, sensible utilization, and inheritance and development" in the research and exploration of protection methods with Guangdong characteristics. First, based on a comprehensive survey, the People's Government of Guangdong Province has announced a list of 182 provincial-level intangible cultural heritage items, of which 74 has been successfully included as state-level intangible cultural heritage. The province has also published a list of 651 municipal, and 1121 county-level directories, all of which have primarily formed a 4-level directory system which includes the national, provincial, municipal and county level. Second, effective protection is carried out on the representative heir of intangible cultural heritage items through the publication of names and titles, the recognition of awards conferred and funding non-government organisations, and so on. Third, closely relying on the strength of the government and non-government organisations, and according to local conditions, 221 state-owned or private folk museums, specialized museums, and education centers will be established which will focus on the intangible cultural heritage collection and display. The establishment of four provincial-level cultural and ecological protection areas for Guangdong Culture, Chaoshan Culture, Hakka Culture, and Leizhou Culture will be explored and overall protection will be implemented. Fourth, combined with "Cultural Heritage Day" and other themed events, exhibitions of pictures, objects, traditional folk art display and parades will be held to promote the combination of intangible cultural heritage with the education system so as to enhance people's awareness of the protection of intangible cultural heritage. Fifth, the relationship between protection and utilization will be correctly handled and effective measures on the protection of intangible cultural heritage will be explored so as to make the most economic benefits of cultural heritages such as Guangdong herbal tea. Of course, there are many deficiencies in our work, and we would appreciate your advice and help.

Four, the Guangdong-ASEAN cooperation and communication on the intangible cultural heritage has a promising future. Currently, the relationship between Guangdong and ASEAN is getting closer and closer. It means that the cooperation is in the ascendant, the cooperation irresistable and the development embracing a bright prospect. So we must catch this opportunity to further promote the cooperation and exchange of intangible cultural heritage at a broader and higher level in every aspect of the work. And I hereby would like to make four suggestions. First, to establish a long-term target for the cooperation in cultural exchange with practical plans and steps. We should build up different platforms, and explore an effective mechanism in order to discuss major issues concerning cooperation and exchange on a regular basis and to share experience in making investigations, plans and laws to protect intangible cultural heritage. In this way, we are able to effectively exchange information and give full play to our strengths so that our exchange and cooperation will be standardized, regular and long-lasting. Second, to conduct theory research in protecting intangible cultural heritage together. We must strengthen the study of the basic theory and applied theory in the protection of intangible cultural heritage and encourage the organization of regular seminars. Moreover, we should support experts and research institutions to study the related topics together and fund the publication of relevant research achievements on intangible cultural heritage. Third, to enhance personnel training. We shall rely on higher education institutions and research institutions and provide different categories of training courses to train personnel for the management and protection of intangible cultural heritage. Fourth, to organize exhibitions. We shall hold exhibitions on Cultural Heritage Day and traditional festivals and at various important economic and political events. We shall also organize relevant cultural activities to strengthen the awareness of protection of intangible cultural heritage. All these will serve as a platform for mutual understanding and enhancement of our friendship between the Chinese people and the peoples of ASEAN countries.

Distinguished guests, ladies and gentlemen, on the basis of the above understanding, we have every reason to believe that if we all take the forum as an opportunity and a platform, speak freely, absorb all useful ideas, explore the theoretical and practical issues on the protection of intangible cultural heritage, and exchange our innovative approaches, experiences and achievements in depth, we will come up with new thoughts, new perspectives and new ideas for promoting the protection of intangible cultural heritage. And we will surely have fruitful results and reach important consensus, which will become the important guidance for the protection of intangible cultural heritage in the future. It is my hope that we take this forum as a starting point and constantly expand areas of cultural exchanges and cooperation, so as to enrich the connotation of cultural exchange. In this way, our outstanding culture will be protected, inherited and developed, and our people can benefit from the charm of our culture. Ultimately, we shall make contribution to the prosperity and progress of human culture and civilization.

Thank you!

(Full text of speech by Fang Jianhong, Director of Department of Culture of Guangdong Province at the Forum of Guangdong-ASEAN Conference on the Protection and Promotion of the Intangible Cultural Heritage, November 7, 2009)

Text 2

各位阁下，尊敬的代表，女士们、先生们、朋友们，

大家晚上好！

面向如此尊贵的客人发言，我倍感荣幸。我和其他的客人自从踏入机场的一刻起就受到了热情周到的款待，首先请允许我对此表示衷心的感谢。

也许我应该坦白告诉各位，去年九月份我在南非开普敦的时候，就表示过自己希望再次回到南非，因为当时我在南非过得十分愉快。而这一次我来南非，感觉更加愉快了，因此我觉得如果自己很快再次来到南非的话我丝毫不会觉得奇怪。能够出席今晚的活动，我十分高兴。

过去的几天对我们来说是十分紧张忙碌的。有的代表参加了非洲世界遗产专家会议，有的代表参与到了非洲世界遗产基金会的活动之中。非洲世界遗产专家会议致力于非洲立场文件的制定，这份立场文件将要提交给非洲联盟以及世界遗产委员会；而非洲世界遗产基金会将会在非洲世界遗产的背景下考虑创新型、长期可持续的战略伙伴关系的建立。有鉴于此，我会花少许时间对我担任联合国教科文组织大会主席职务期间的工作进行简单的回顾。

我当选为联合国教科文组织第 32 届大会主席恰逢两年以前。自从我于 2003 年 9 月 29 日获邀领导第 32 届大会，上帝就一直伴我左右，帮助我开展工作。在座的许多应该还记得，美国在退出联合国教科文组织近 20 年后重

返联合国教科文组织，我当时也有幸邀请美国第一夫人劳拉·布什女士向大会发言。在此以后，联合国教科文组织通过了许多重要公约，包括《非物质文化遗产保护公约》，而且还通过了几个重要的决议以帮助教科文组织应对新世纪的重大挑战。今年10月，我将结束我的任期，届时教科文组织第33届大会将在大会初期进行新领导人的选举。

我必须承认，过去的两年是极为振奋人心的两年，也是相当具有挑战性的两年。过去的两年是意义非凡的两年。过去两年中，我有机会代表我所珍惜和信仰的这个组织，前往各地向人们宣传联合国教科文组织值得称赞的崇高目标。我就广泛主题发表过演说，包括识字率、废除奴隶制度、联合国教科文组织与非洲发展新伙伴计划的关系、成人识字率、普及教育、文明之间的对话、保护文化多样性和艺术表达形式以及本周的重要议题——物质文化遗产与非物质文化遗产。此外，按照联合国教科文组织大会决议，我建立了一个工作小组来检视大会、执行局和秘书处这三大主要机构之间的关系。

女士们、先生们，我接下来想谈一谈今晚让我们聚首于此的重要主题：非洲文化遗产的保护。非洲有着丰富的文化遗产。就我们所见，这一宝贵的文化遗产也开启着其他的门。今晚这样的聚会，使代表不同地区、不同文化、不同语言、不同宗教的宾客有机会建立伙伴关系并增强相互联系。过去几天里，使我们走到一起的共同利益是我们要为消除巨大的贫富差距继续努力，要通过庆祝文化多样性、宣扬我们共同的文化遗产来使全球化为所有人带来福祉。我们必须充分考虑我们面临的社会、经济和技术挑战，尤其是非洲的发展中国家面临的这些挑战。

然而，正是日渐增强的全球化趋势使越来越多的人们和社区开始认识到自己文化遗产的重要性：物质文化遗产和非物质文化遗产都为世界文化多样性做出了重要贡献。各地的社区也已经意识到，他们的文化遗产在自身标识方面扮演着关键角色，而他们保护文化遗产的活动也代表着保护工作的延续性。因此，虽然全球化极大地促进了文化的传播，但是如果我们不注意的话，全球化也会对文化多样性造成负面的影响。

非洲可以如何应对这一挑战呢？我知道我们过去几天在为德班会议做准备的时候一直在思索这个问题。我想到了一句老话，大意是说我们得自己学着长大，不论我们的爷爷多高多伟大。因此，非洲必须与一直以来支持非洲废除奴隶制度和种族隔离制度事业的朋友发展伙伴关系。

对于从非洲获益从而实现自身发展的国家而言，非洲也要请这些国家表现出公正、客观的精神，将其部分获益再投资到非洲以用于本地区发展，以此表示他们对非洲为其经济发展所付出巨大代价的认可。

因此，用于遗产保护和发展的资本流入显得十分重要。非洲各国政府和民间组织应积极寻求旅游和能力建设方面的投资，充分利用旅游业的发展提升自身能力。另外，应该以负责任的态度发展旅游业，使更多的人意识到在发展旅游的同时要保护脆弱的自然环境。

女士们、先生们，在结束我的讲话之前，请再次允许我感谢南非政府和人民给予我本人以及参加非洲世界遗产专家会议和非洲世界遗产基金研讨会各位代表的热情款待。我相信各位也赞成，没有他们的支持，我们今天就不可能聚集在这里推广非洲的文化遗产。联合国教科文组织一直以来对专家都十分信任，我们坚信专家们出色的头脑能不断为我们提供高质量的建议和方案。

最后我想表达我对今晚美味佳肴的喜爱。今晚我们享受到的美食充分体现了非洲在烹饪和美酒方面的美名。的确，今晚的美食也见证了全球化的积极影响：我们享用的食物融合了来自不同民族的菜肴和土生土长的香料与水果。南非享有的"彩虹国度"这一美誉正是对今晚美味食物的完美诠释。再次感谢南非给予我们的盛情款待和热情接待！

（2005年3月17日，前尼日利亚驻联合国大使、教科文组织永久代表M. 奥莫勒瓦教授在"非洲世界遗产专家会议暨非洲世界遗产基金研讨会"晚宴上的主题发言）

Text 3

Ladies and Gentlemen,

Good morning!

I am very glad to be here in this beautiful city of Foshan together with you all to celebrate the opening of the Guangdong-ASEAN Conference on the Protection and Promotion of the Intangible Cultural Heritage. On this occasion, I would like, on behalf of Nanfang Newspaper Media Group, to express my congratulations on the opening of the forum and wish it a great success.

A saying goes like this: "Only national makes international." Intangible cultural heritage bears dual responsibilities of keeping national culture's uniqueness and maintaining world cultural diversity. Today, under the impact of globalization, cultural identity has become the immanent needs of more and more countries and regions, and the intangible cultural heritage, which emphasizes on "living" inheritance, retains the historical memory of a certain country, region and ethnic group. As Sun Jiazheng, the President of China Federation of Literary and Art Circles, has said: "It is not only the self-identified historical evidence of a nationality, but also the foundation and source of strength for the nationality to last and step into future with confidence." In this sense, to protect Guangdong's intangible cultural heritage is to keep the vivid Lingnan historical memories.

Today, more and more people realize that, for a region, the precious cultural heritage is the symbol of its own unique overt culture and its irreplicable "cultural capital." Today in a world when culture, environment and others become the indicators of "soft power" and core competitiveness of a region's economic development, cultural heritage representing a region's historical and cultural appearance is by no means the burden of development, but instead the very base of the future development. It is not the "cash cow" right away, but it would be the "cornucopia" to promote the harmonious and interactive development of economy and society. In this sense, to protect Guangdong's intangible cultural heritage is to protect the sustainable development of the province.

In addition, the protection of intangible cultural heritage is an abandonment of the traditional "rather material than intangible" concept of development and cultural values. Intangible cultural heritage gives prominence to the "intangible" nature of cultural heritage, and attaches importance to knowledge, emotion as well as skill, technology and their "living" inheritance. In a word, it is people-oriented by stressing "both material and intangible" or "intangible over material". Therefore, when we are to protect intangible cultural heritage, we could not ignore its material formats, but more importantly, we should protect the living people who create and transmit the cultural heritage.

The land of Lingnan has left its people abundant cultural heritage. At present, there are one world-class, 74 national-and 182 provincial-level intangible cultural heritage items. However, with the further development of globalization and social transformation, intangible cultural heritage in many places is on the verge of extinction. Some excellent items are endangered because of inheritors' seniority and lack of successors.

As the solely print media organization to support the forum, *Nanfang Daily* has always attached great importance to the promotion and coverage of cultural heritage protection. In 2004, the newspaper's large series report "Historical and Cultural Tour in Guangdong", with the aim to find cultural coordinate for various regions of the province, played an active role in the construction of a great cultural province and triggered strong reaction from both in and out of the province. In 2006, the large series report "Views on the Cultural Construction Tide" commenting on various region's cultural development was also positively echoed. This year, *Nanfang Daily* started again a large series report, "Lingnan Memory—Step into the Intangible Cultural Heritage in Guangdong", which found out and displayed the cultural genes of the land deeply rooted in common people's daily life, evoked the historic memory of the land and opened a new window for Guangdong province to upgrade its future creativity and its soft power in culture.

The urgent and obligatory responsibility of *Nanfang Daily* is to hold the "lantern" for the province in intangible cultural heritage transmission, to illuminate its future road by the use of media power, and to call upon more people to embark on this journey. The protection of intangible cultural heritage needs everybody's cultural consciousness besides the government, inheritance people and scholars. *Nanfang Daily* is willing to serve as the "arouser" and "lantern holder".

The "Lingnan Memory—Step into the Intangible Cultural Heritage in Guangdong" selected 30 intangible cultural heritage items in this province, including Yangmei emerald and jade carving and Shiwan ceramics, whose production has been highly industrialized with a bright profitability prospect, as well as endangered wood-block Chinese New Year pictures with a shrinking market, Cantonese opera, flower market, lion dance and Hakka folk songs with high degree of popularity among both urban and rural residents, as well as Cantonese embroidery and Lufeng shadow play with a lack of successors. By means of site reproduction with excellent pictures and texts, the report represented the beauty of intangible cultural heritage in folk living environment and tried to find out their eternal genes, which once again reminded people, especially young people, of the fondness of these cultural heritage items. Meanwhile, in light of the richness of information of the intangible cultural heritage, with all-media report and comprehensive use of such forms as texts, images, videos and others, the report achieved interaction between the print and the online media, thus creating an all-dimensional effect. Moreover, with the thoughts of how to protect and develop, the reporters invited experts together to search for the future code of survival of the intangible cultural heritage remained in this province, striving to open a channel between common people and experts, between young people and historical memory, and between Lingnan culture and its future development. Let us look back and ask "where did we come from" after a long journey.

Now in your hands, the book *Lingnan Memory—Step into the Intangible Cultural Heritage in Guangdong* is right the result of the large series report of *Nanfang Daily*. From the outcome and effect we can tell that it has basically fulfilled its purpose of reporting. Wherever we went, we received warm welcome from the local government and the "Intangible Cultural Heritage" successors. Every report would cause huge reaction from the society and newspapers were quickly sold out in areas that had applied for "Intangible Cultural Heritage". This can show to you this report was well written in a nutshell. Besides, we selected websites such as www.tianya.com as our online media partners. On average, there were over 20,000 clicks for each issue per day at www.tianya.com, with the record high over 100,000 clicks.

Now the large series report "Lingnan Memory — Step into the Intangible Cultural Heritage in Guangdong" has come to an end, but *Nanfang Daily's* focus on intangible cultural heritage will never stop, and our duty will also continue. I believe that the opportunity for exchanges provided by this forum will provide a strong impetus to the protection and inheritance of intangible cultural heritage in both Guangdong province and ASEAN countries.

I wish the forum a complete success!

(Full text of speech by Yang Xingfeng, Chairman of *Nanfang Daily* Media Group at the Forum of Guangdong-ASEAN Conference on the Protection and Promotion of the Intangible Cultural Heritage, November 7, 2009)

Text 4

女士们、先生们：

在今天的介绍中，我打算简要介绍日本非物质文化遗产的保护制度，并简要说明其与《非物质文化遗产保护公约》的关系。《保护公约》是2006年4月正式生效的。

首先，我想说明非物质文化遗产究竟是什么，在日本有多少种。日本共有三大类别的非物质文化遗产。

第一大类为无形的文化遗产。政府以具体行政手段将应该由政府加以保护的无形的技能指定为非物质文化遗产，或将其列为需要通过立档或其他方式加以保护的无形技能。

第二大类为无形的民间文化遗产。由于文化部负责文化遗产的首席专家以及研究所的研究员稍后将会详细说明这些类别的文化遗产，我就只在这里做简要概述。对于这些无形民间文化遗产的保护，也需要由行政手段将其指定为重要非物质民间文化遗产，或将其列为需要通过立档等方式加以保护的非物质民间文化遗产。

第三大类虽然没有被《文化财保护法》认可为文化遗产，但是这一类别包括文化遗产的保存技术，或在文化遗产传承过程中不可或缺的工艺技术。对此，我们对保存技术进行了筛选，在此基础上建立了一个保护框架，挑选了对保护文化遗产很有价值的重要技术列入其中。因此，可以说这些技术从行政的角度而言已经被视为日本非物质文化遗产的一大类别了。

我们现在来看看这些文化遗产具体有多少。首先，由个别持有者持有的非物质文化遗产或称"个别认定的"，其总数是82项，其中38项为表演艺术，44项为传统手工艺。另外，非物质遗产持有者的总数为111人，其中54人为传统表演艺术持有者，57人为传统手工艺持有者。这些数字来自于文化事务局的网站,随时可能发生变化,比如持有者不幸去世或持有者的新增等等。非物质文化遗产保护制度的最大特点是,该制度指定工艺技术为文化遗产,并且确立代表这些工艺技术的个人为遗产持有者。

除了上面介绍的个别认定,还有集体认定和组织认定的方式,也就是对包含多个个别持有者的群体进行认定。换句话说,政府不是认定持有者和技艺之间的一一对应关系,而是对一个群体加以认定,而该群体即为工艺技术的持有群体。这一类别的重要非物质文化遗产共25项,11项为表演艺术,14项为传统手工艺;这一类别的持有群体共25个,11个为表演艺术持有群体,14个为传统手工艺持有群体。

刚才我说过,除了被指定为重要非物质文化遗产的项目以外,有些非物质文化遗产需要采取立档等保护措施。现在,被列为要采取立档等保护措施的非物质文化遗产包括30项表演艺术、60项传统手工艺。需要在此说明的是,这类非物质文化遗产有大概10%后来也被指定为重要非物质文化遗产。所以说,指定的重要非物质文化遗产与选定的非物质文化遗产有一定程度的重合。

我们现在再来看一下非物质民间文化遗产。被指定为重要非物质民间文化遗产的项目包括三种:风俗习惯类、民间表演艺术类以及不久前被指定的民间技艺类。民间表演艺术类共146项,风俗习惯类共97项,民间技艺类共3项,而政府刚刚指定的非物质文化遗产还没有算在内。非物质民间文化遗产和非物质文化遗产一样,也有一个制度来选定需要采取立档等手段加以保护的文化遗产的项目。目前,已经有346项民间表演艺术、214项风俗习惯、0项民间技术被选定,其中大约30%的项目在选定以后被指定为重要非物质民间文化遗产,这种情况在民间表演艺术类中有很多。

最后,在文化遗产保护技术方面,政府已经指定了一些技术作为文化遗产的保护技术,其相关的选定和认定过程与重要非物质文化遗产的选定和认定过程十分相似。换言之,保护制度选定某些技术并确认其持有者或持有群体。在这一方面,有一个制度来确认个别持有者,另一个制度确认持有群体。目前,由个人持有的保存技术共46项,而个别持有者的人数为50人;由群体持有的保存技术共23项,而持有群体的数量为24个。

在今天的研讨会上,各位会听到来自不同领域专家们的报告。然而,由于今天没有专门介绍选定保存技术的演讲,因此我想借此机会详细谈一谈保存技术选定的制度。我稍后会在简介历史背景的时候回到这个主题上来,但我想值得注意的是,选定保存技术的制度在1950年《文化财保护法》刚刚出台的时候还不存在,是比较晚的时候才被纳入到保护法里的。我们可以看到《文化财保护法》第83条第7款关于指定保存技术的规定:"对于保存文化遗产不可或缺、并且必须加以保护的传统工艺技术可以被选为'选定的保存技术'。"这里的关键概念是,这些工艺技术必须是对保护文化遗产必不可少的，而且必须是传统的。这一概念正好与现行的《保护公约》关于非物质文化遗产的广义定义是一致的。虽然日本还没有将保存技术视为文化遗产，但是《保护法》里的定义已经说明，文化遗产的保存技术也是日本非物质文化遗产的组成部分。这一制度是基于这样一个理念：为了支持有形以及无形的文化遗产，需要将无形的技术用于不同的目的，包括文化遗产的保护、维护和修复等等。也就是说，要明确一个重要的理念，即为了传承有形和无形的文化遗产，工艺技术是不可缺少的。我认为，这一事实也需要传达到世界上的其他国家。

我刚才简单介绍了几种不同类别的文化遗产。非物质文化遗产现在包括传统表演艺术和手工艺，非物质民间文化遗产包括传统习俗、民间表演艺术以及新增加的传统民间技术，而文化遗产保存技术包括对修复和传承文化遗产不可缺少的传统技术。在这些类别中，我认为新增加的民间技术类将在今后对日本的非物质文化遗产保护起到关键作用。去年这一类别下出现了头三个政府指定的文化遗产。民间技术这个重要概念与两种类别的传统手工艺很接近：一个类别是非物质文化遗产，另一个类别是对保护文化遗产十分必要的保存技术。我认为，必须对这个概念进行妥善运用和管理，否则容易造成较大的混乱局面。民间技术的应用才刚刚开始，我觉得有必要充分衡量和考虑这一类别未来的发展方向。

(2006年，东京国立文化财研究所宫田繁幸在"第30届文化遗产保护与修复国际研讨会"上的发言节选)

第9单元

Text 1

Ladies and Gentlemen,

Good afternoon. Thank you for inviting me to this luncheon. This luncheon, which is intended to welcome the new Secretary for Commerce, Industry and Technology, is the third of its kind in four years. I assure you that the government as a whole remains firmly committed to the cause of promoting information and communications technology, or ICT, in Hong Kong.

As Secretary for Commerce, Industry and Technology, my job on ICT development in Hong Kong is to set a vision, devise a strategy to fulfill such a vision and implement the necessary measures to deliver the results which will bring both economic and social benefits to our society. The vision enshrined in the Digital 21 Strategy is, and I quote, "to enhance and promote Hong Kong's information infrastructure and services so as to make Hong Kong a leading digital city in the globally connected world of the 21st century". What I want to do is to define more clearly the role of the government in pursuing this vision. I see the government playing an active part in engaging the stakeholders, and all of you here this afternoon are very important stakeholders, developing industry-friendly policies, creating an appropriate regulatory environment conducive to competition and consumer protection, and promoting investment and innovation for the benefit of entrepreneurs, workers, consumers and the economy at large. We have a strong foundation to develop our ICT industry. Let me tell you more specifically how I see my agenda in the coming 12 months.

First, to meet the impact of convergence, the government needs to respond positively to make our regulatory regime more efficient and to encourage the exploitation of new opportunities by the industry. We will announce later in the afternoon our proposal for the merger of the Broadcasting Authority and the Telecommunications Authority in a public consultation paper. My aim is to introduce the necessary legislation before the end of the year to give effect to the establishment of a unified regulator which we propose to call Communications Authority.

The proposed Communications Authority will administer and enforce the existing Broadcasting Ordinance and Telecommunications Ordinance. We propose to transfer to the new authority the existing statutory powers and functions of the

Broadcasting Authority and Telecommunications Authority on an "as is" basis. To enable it to get on with its job quickly, we do not intend to make any changes to the regulatory and licensing arrangements under these two Ordinances at this stage. However, it is our intention, once the Communications Authority is established, to start examining various provisions in the two Ordinances with a view to maintaining consistency and improving regulatory efficiency and consumer protection.

The public consultation period will be three months and I am confident that I can count on all of you here to provide us with the informed views of the ICT industry.

Second, it is important that our ICT industry secure as much international presence and prominence as possible.

As you know, Hong Kong will host the ITU TELECOM WORLD 2006 at the end of this year. It is the first time this event is held outside Geneva since its inception in 1971. With the sterling support of the Central Government, we fought for the privilege to host the event back in 2003 because we thought it would be beneficial to the local ICT industry and also Hong Kong generally. It is an event that is going to put Hong Kong and Hong Kong IT industry on the map and enhance Hong Kong's visibility in the Mainland and the rest of the world. It will raise the profile of Hong Kong and project Hong Kong's image as the telecommunications and broadcasting hub in the Asia-Pacific region. It is going to attract 900 exhibitors and 60,000 visitors and generate some $900 million worth of income for the local hospitality industry. It will also strengthen Hong Kong's credibility as the event capital of Asia.

We have made a good start: 70% of the exhibition space has now been allocated or reserved. We are intensifying our marketing and fund-raising efforts. We are working hard and we aim to make ITU WORLD TELECOM 2006 the most successful telecommunications event ever held. To this end, I know I can count on your support.

Third, this is a critical year for the rollout of digital terrestrial television broadcasting, DTT for short, in Hong Kong. Before the end of the year, the government will have to decide on the technical standard on which to base future DTT broadcasting. The two incumbents, TVB and ATV, have to start their new digital programmes in 2007 and reach a 75% coverage of Hong Kong with their new digital network by 2008, in time for the 2008 Olympics.

It is a major endeavour in terms of engineering infrastructure, hardware design and manufacture, and high quality production. TVB and ATV will invest hundreds of millions of dollars in the next few years on DTT. It will benefit not just the conventional IT sector, but also the creative industries, such as digital entertainment. The consumers will benefit from more diverse and high quality television programme services, including HDTV, and possibly mobile TV and associated value added services, such as interactive multimedia features. I see the government and the industry working together on various fronts, such as service planning, consumer education, promoting DTT uptake, preparing for in-building reception and hardware design and supply, and so on.

Also on digital transmission, given the availability of spectrum and likely market demands, I would wish to take a critical and positive look at the case for introducing digital audio broadcasting in Hong Kong. In fact, digital technologies offer opportunities that go beyond sound broadcasting. As we have seen the use of 3G technologies for multimedia and broadcasting applications on mobile phones, we are also seeing the adoption of new digital technologies in other places for multimedia and broadcasting services on small handheld mobile display devices.

As these developments give rise to new opportunities in investment and consumer benefits, they also present regulatory challenges. But the government's position is clear. We provide policy support to facilitate technological and business development and we do not interfere with the actual delivery of new services and products other than for consumer protection.

It is almost an understatement to say that developments in ICT in the past decade have transformed our society beyond recognition. Just look at the Internet, the development of wireless and mobile technologies, the penetration of broadband to households, the explosive volume of information that is accessible on line, interactive entertainment, and all that. They are transforming nations, businesses, life styles, cultures and human behaviours. We need to take thorough stock of where we are in relation to the rest of the world in a globalised environment. We need to ask ourselves whether we need a new vision, and a new strategy to ensure that Hong Kong stays as a leading digital city in the world.

I have tasked Howard Dickson to take this forward. I have encouraged him to challenge the fundamentals and be bold. He has assured me that he will engage industry extensively so that the government and our ICT industry will have collective ownership of the Strategy that emerges in the first quarter of 2007, about a year from now.

Ladies and gentlemen, I have counted nine things we need to do in the coming

12 months. In Cantonese, nine rhymes with dog which is the symbol of this new lunar year. It also rhymes with enough. So I better stop here. There is nothing political if I end my speech with a quote from one of Chairman Mao Zedong's famous poems, "So many things need to be done, and always urgently. The world rolls on, time passes. Ten thousand years is too long, seize the hour, seize the day." How apt this is to the technology based business world! I am confident that we can work together to ensure that the ICT industry meets its aspirations and challenges. I know I can count on your support and with this support, I will be able to deal with the nine action items that I have just outlined and create a win-win situation for all of us: society, industry and the consumer.

Thank you!

(Excerpted text of speech by Joseph W. P. Wong, Secretary for Commerce, Industry and Technology of the Hong Kong SAR at a luncheon organised by IT Associations, March 3, 2006)

Text 2

今天，我们在一个变革性的时刻相会。在这个时刻，相互关联的世界既给我们巨大希望，也带来了严重威胁。

过去4个月中，我的行政班子采取果断行动，抓住机遇，应对威胁。我们努力从全球经济衰退中走出来，同时也为持久繁荣打下新的基础。我们加强军备力量，打好两场战争，同时让美国再次成为应对非传统挑战的全球领袖，从核扩散到恐怖主义，从气候变化到流行病。我们给政府和白宫带来前所未有的透明度和责任感，给美国人民带来参与民主的新方式。

可是，如果我们要取得进步，如果我们要克服这些21世纪的挑战，就必须打造美国的数字基础设施，它是繁荣的经济，强大的军队以及开放、高效政府的基石。没有这个基石，我们就会失败。

长期以来，人们都认为信息与通讯技术的革命带来了一个虚拟世界。但千万别搞错，我们每天都依存这个网络世界，它包含硬件和软件、台式电脑、笔记本、手机和黑莓手机，它们都融入了我们的生活。

这个网络还包括脚下的宽带网络，身边的无线网络信号，学校、医院和公司里的本地网，还有为全国提供电力的大型电网。它还包括保卫我们安全的机密军事和情报的网络，以及万维网，让我们以前所未有的方式相互联系。

所以网络空间是真实的，它所带来的风险也是实实在在的。

这是信息时代的一个强烈讽刺：这些技术既帮助我们去创造和建设，也给那些破坏者以力量。无论看得见还是看不见，我们每天都在经历这个矛盾。

这关乎美国家庭的隐私和经济安全。我们在网上付账单、办理银行业务、购物、申报个税。不过，要打败那些会伤害我们的网络犯罪分子，我们得先掌握不少新知识，比如间谍软件、恶意软件、网络欺骗、网络钓鱼和僵尸网络。数百万美国人民成为了受害者，隐私被侵犯，身份被盗用，生活被打乱，钱包被掏空。调查数据表明，仅在过去两年，美国人民就因网络犯罪损失了80多亿美元。

我知道隐私被侵犯是什么感觉，因为它曾发生在我和身边人的身上。大家都知道，我在总统竞选中利用互联网和技术来进行政治变革，不过你们可能不知道的是，黑客在大选过程中侵入了我们的电脑系统。但各位选举捐助者大可放心，我们的筹款网站毫发无损，所以各位机密的个人和财务信息未被盗取。

但是在8月到10月间，黑客获取了我们的电子邮件和一系列选举文件，如政策立场文件和出行计划等。我们和中央情报局、联邦调查局和特勤局紧密合作，聘请了安全顾问，恢复系统安全。这个事件有力地提醒我们，在信息时代，你的最大优势也可以成为最大的弱点，比如我们通过网络与不同的支持者沟通，这就是一把双刃剑。

这也关乎美国经济竞争力。无论是圣路易斯的女性小企业家，纽约证交所的债券经纪，孟菲斯一家全球航运公司的工人，还是硅谷年轻的企业家，他们都需要网络来发下一笔薪水，完成下一手交易，交付下一批货，实现下一个伟大突破。电子商务去年的零售额就高达1320亿美元。

可是，每天我们都见到一波又一波的网络盗贼四处找寻机密信息，比如公司内部不满的员工、千里之外的某个黑客、有组织的犯罪分子、工业间谍、还有越来越多的海外情报机构。去年，网络盗贼无耻地使用偷来的信用卡信息，从全球49个城市130台自动取款机中盗取了数百万美元，只用了半小时。一家美国公司的雇员被控窃取了价值4亿美元的知识产权。人们预计，仅在去年，网络犯罪分子盗取的全球企业的知识产权价值为1万亿美元。

简而言之，美国要在21世纪获得经济繁荣，就得依赖网络安全。

这也关乎公共和国家安全。我们依赖电脑网络来传输油气和水电，运营公共交通和航路管制。但我们知道，网络侵入者潜入了我们的电网，而在其他国家，网络攻击让整个城市陷入黑暗。我们的技术优势对美国的军事主导地位至关重要。但我们的防御和军事网络却经常遭受攻击。基地组织和其他恐怖组织都表明了对美国发动网络攻击的意愿，这些攻击更难侦测，更难防御。的确，当今世界，恐怖主义行为不仅来自采取自杀袭击的极端分子，敲几下电脑键盘也会带来攻击，电脑已成为大规模破坏性武器。

到目前为止，在攻击我国军事网络最严重的案件中，有一起是利用恶意软件感染数千台电脑。尽管没有损失机密信息，但我们的部队和国防人员不得不放弃那些外部记忆装置，也就是U盘，他们放弃了以前每天用电脑的方式。

去年，我们依稀领略了未来战争的面貌。俄罗斯坦克驶进格鲁吉亚，而网络攻击破坏了格鲁吉亚政府的网站。恐怖分子给孟买带来大量的人员伤亡和破坏，靠的不仅是枪炮手雷，还有全球定位系统和网络语音电话。

出于这些原因，我们清楚地意识到，网络威胁已成为美国最严重的经济和国家安全挑战之一。我们也清楚地看到，不论是从政府还是国家的角度，我们都还没有做好应有的准备。近年来，联邦政府做了些改进。不过，正像我们过去在公路、桥梁和铁路等实体基础设施上一直缺乏投资一样，我们也没有在维护数字基础设施的安全上提供足够资金。

联邦政府内部没有一个专门管理网络安全政策的官员，也没有一个全权负责如此之大规模挑战的机构。实际上，联邦政府部门在网络安全方面任务重叠，协调和沟通不力，不论是在政府内部还是与私有产业之间。从我们毫无组织地应对蠕虫病毒就可见一斑，这个网络蠕虫在过去数月中感染了全球数百万台电脑。

我们已无法接受现状，这牵涉到太多利益。我们能够，也必须做得更好。

所以，在上任后不久，我就指派国家安全委员会和国土安全委员会对联邦政府在保卫信息和通讯基础设施方面做的努力进行从上至下的检查，并推荐最好的方法，确保这些网络能够保卫我们的通信网络和繁荣。

我们的检查公开透明。我要感谢今天在场的梅丽莎·哈萨维，她是国家安全委员会的代理网络安全高级长官，领导了检查小组和网络安全两党委员会战略和国际研究中心。我还要感谢这个任期60天的检查小组的所有组员。他们听取了不同团体的意见，很多团体的代表今天也在场，我也想感谢你们提供的信息，包括产业界和学术界，以及推崇公民自由和隐私的人士。我们也听取了政府各级别和各部门的意见，包括地方政府，州政府和联邦政府，民生、部队、国土和情报部门，国会以及国际合作伙伴等。我向国家安全小组，国土安全小组和经济顾问进行了咨询。

今天，我公布了检查报告，也可以向大家宣布，美国政府将采取全面的新方法，确保我国数字基础设施的安全。

这个新方式从政府上级开始执行，得到我的承诺。从今往后，我们的数字基础设施，包括每天所依赖的网络和电脑，将被视为国家的战略资产。保护这个基础设施是国家安全重点。我们将确保这些网络的安全、可靠和可恢复性。我们将阻止、预防和侦查攻击，采取防御措施，并且能够迅速从破坏和损失中恢复。

为了让这些工作得到应有的高层关注和重视，正如本周新委任的独立国家安全官员所宣布的，我将在白宫新设一个办公室，由网络安全协调员负责管理。鉴于该工作的重要性，我会亲自挑选合格人选。在所有网络安全事务上，我将依仗该官员，面对这些挑战，他会得到我的全权支持和帮助。

今天，我要重点谈谈这个办公室的重要责任，包括为政府协调和整合所有的网络安全政策，与行政管理和预算局通力合作，确保机构预算能体现这些工作的重要性，以及在主要网络事件或攻击中协调我们的应对措施。

（2009年5月29日，美国总统奥巴马关于保障国家网络基础设施的讲话节选，根据录音材料整理）

Text 3

Ladies and Gentlemen, good afternoon.

Welcome again to Tencent Mind—2009 Effective Online Marketing Forum. I am seeing many new and good friends here.

Let's kick off with a few questions. Today our theme is interaction, and it is an outstanding feature in cyberworld. Show your response by raising your hands. First, how many of you think the world is still in economic turmoil? Second, how many of you think that China is still in this financial crisis? Third, how many of you think this crisis will end in six months?

Global economy is sick and business relations are deteriorating like never before. In Germany, almost every industry is declining, while in France, 3,000 companies are applying for bankruptcy and millions of people are laid off. Two million Japanese have lost their jobs and the country's export has dropped by 50%. Tourist destinations like Hawaii are seeing plummeting revenue as well, alongside a 40% decrease in tourist volume. Banks in America and Britain also have tough times with over 40 banks going bankrupt and a 7.6% unemployment rate in America.

Let's find the reasons why CMOs can't fall asleep under the current market trend. CMOs worldwide value these five strategic driving forces, and three of them are closely associated with digital media. Many CMOs require the interactivity of Web 2.0 and transparency in corporation information, so there's the need of integrated marketing using various types of information. They want to reserve marketing expenditure for the latest Web 2.0 technology; hence a higher ROI is needed. All of these drive global promotion practice from traditional to digital media.

Ladies and gentlemen, the first three slides tell us that our world is in an economic crisis, the extent of which is yet to be appreciated by many. It's very serious and the key solution is digital media. That's why Tencent proposed this topic: Digital Marketing under Economic Crisis. There are three parts to my presentation. I'll first review the major changes in the Internet media in the whole world, especially in China. Then, I'll tell you why digital marketing is the most effective solution in this crisis. Finally, I'll touch upon the principles to build successful digital marketing strategies.

This man changed our history recently. He is now the commander-in-chief and leader of the largest economic power. Actually, he's also the best CMO in years. Why so? His biggest success is marketing himself into the White House. The renowned *Advertising Age* even nominated him as the most successful marketing person globally. I just want to stress one thing: digital media is crucial to his success.

For the first time in history, the inauguration ceremony and congress speech of the American president is broadcasting live online. It's only possible when the public is keenly aware of digital media as a communication channel with far-reaching influence.

In a sense, Obama's success is a positive marketing campaign. In this campaign of presidential election, he won the dominance of market share. It's indeed a marketing; with effective online communication strategy, he was rewarded with greater market share.

A few more stats. According to ComScore stats in January, the global Internet population has already reached one billion, 1/3 of which are in China and America.

Just a year ago, China was behind America in the number of Internet users. But it surpassed America as the largest Internet broadband market last year, with currently nearly 300 million users. It's amazing that it took America 20 years to popularize Internet but China tops the world with just half the time. Internet coverage is 80% in America, while it in China is only a bit higher than the world average. Experts at Internet media have come to realize that Chinese Internet users will reach 500 million in a few months. No marketing professionals can stay ignorant of that brilliant fact.

In terms of marketing via different media, Internet media is the only category that maintains continuous growth in the past five years. Now, more marketing professionals in China are spending budget on online ads, especially when the brands want to reach target consumers via non-conventional means.

Ladies and gentlemen, the best example for China's Internet marketing is in 2008. Beijing Olympics set the record in broadcasting and promoting the Games online in an all-round manner. We sent the wave of Olympics to other parts of the world, showing the great and profound impact of Internet on China. The Internet is also becoming a major platform for political exchange in China. You may not know that in some events, such as the Two Sessions, millions of Internet users exchanged ideas with state leaders through Tencent and other major portals.

I can cite numerous examples and facts to prove Internet media's important role in our daily life. The reason is simple: just that it dawns on people that Internet is not the new media, but the mainstream media in China.

I'll show you a video clip showing how Internet has become the mainstream media in a short time. It demonstrates the great influence of digital media. And I'm sure no one can afford to ignore it anymore.

(Excerpted text of speech by Shengyi Liu, Executive VP of Tencent Internet Media, on Tencent Mind—2009 Effective Online Marketing Forum, June 15, 2009)

Text 4

谢谢大家。

今天，很荣幸参加世界上最好的学校之一的毕业典礼。说实话，我从来没从大学毕业，所以这是我离大学毕业最近的一刻。今天，我只说三个故事，不谈大道理，三个故事就好。

第一个故事，是关于如何把人生中的点点滴滴串连在一起。

我在里德学院待了6个月就办休学了。到我正式退学前，一共还在学校呆了18个月。那么，我为什么休学？

这得从我出生前讲起。我的亲生母亲当时是个研究生，年轻的未婚妈妈，她决定让别人收养我。她强烈觉得应该让有大学毕业证的人收养我，所以我出生时，她就准备让我被一对律师夫妇收养。但是这对夫妻到了最后一刻反悔了，他们想收养女孩。

所以在等待收养名单上的一对夫妻，我的养父母，在一天半夜里接到一通电话，问他们"有一名意外出生的男孩，你们要认养他吗？"而他们的回答是"当然要"。后来，我的生母发现，我的养母从来没有从大学毕业，养父则连高中都没毕业。她拒绝在认养文件上最后签字。直到几个月后，我的养父母保证将来一定会让我上大学，她的态度才软化。这就是我人生的开始。

17年后，我上大学了。但是当时我无知地选了一所学费几乎跟斯坦福一样高的大学，我那工人阶级的父母将所有积蓄都花在我的学费上。6个月后，我看不出念这个书的价值何在。那时候，我不知道这辈子要干什么，也不知道念大学能对我有什么帮助，只知道我为了念这个书，花光了我父母这辈子的所有积蓄。

所以我决定休学，相信船到桥头自然直。当时这个决定看来相当可怕，可是现在看来，那是我这辈子做过的最好的决定之一。当我休学之后，我再也不用上我没兴趣的必修课，把时间拿去听那些更为感兴趣的课。

这一点也不浪漫。我没有宿舍，所以我睡在朋友房间的地板上；靠着回收空可乐罐的五分钱买吃的；每个星期天晚上得走7英里的路，绕过大半个镇去印度教的哈瑞奎师那神庙吃顿好的，我喜欢那儿的晚餐。就这样追随我的好奇与直觉，大部分我所投入过的事务，后来看来都成了无比珍贵的经历。下面让我给你们举个例子。

当时里德学院有着大概是全国最好的书法教育。校园内的每一张海报上，每个抽屉的标签上，都是美丽的手写字。因为我休学了，可以不照正常选课程序来，所以我跑去上书法课。我学了有衬线与无衬线字体，学到在不同字母组合间变更字间距，学到活字印刷伟大的地方。书写的美好、历史感与艺术感是科学所无法掌握的，我觉得这很迷人。

我从未希望过学这些东西能在我生活中起些什么实际作用，不过10年后，当我在设计第一台Macintosh电脑时，我想起了当时所学的东西，所以把这些东西都设计进了Macintosh里，这是第一台能印刷出漂亮字体的计算机。如果我没沉溺于那样一门课里，Macintosh可能就不会有多重字体跟等比例间距字体了。又因为Windows抄袭了Macintosh的使用方式，因此，如果当年我没有休学，没有去上那门书写课，大概所有的个人计算机都不会有好看的字体。如果我没有休学，我就永远不可能去上书写课，个人电脑也就大概不可能印出现在我们看到的漂亮的字来了。当然，当我还在大学里时，不可能把这些点点滴滴预先串连在一起，但在10年后的今天回顾过去，一切就显得非常清楚。

我再说一次，你无法预先把点点滴滴串连起来；只有在回顾过去时，你才会明白那些点点滴滴是如何串在一起的。所以你得相信，眼前你经历的种种，将来多少会连结在一起。你得信任某个东西，直觉也好，命运也好，生命也好，或者因缘。这种做法从来没让我失望，我的人生因此变得完全不同。

我的第二个故事，是有关爱与失去。

我很幸运——年轻时就发现自己爱做什么事。我20岁时，跟Woz在我爸妈的车库里开始了苹果计算机的事业。我们拼命工作，苹果计算机在10年间从一间车库里的两个小伙子扩展成了一家员工超过4000人、市值20亿美元的公司，在那之前一年推出了我们最棒的作品——Macintosh计算机，那时我才刚迈入30岁。

然后我被解雇了。我怎么会被自己创办的公司给解雇了？嗯，当苹果公司发展起来后，我请了一个我以为在经营公司上很有才干的家伙来，他在头几年也确实干得不错。可是我们对未来的愿景不同，最后只好分道扬镳，董事会站在他那边，就这样在我30岁的时候，公司把我给解雇了。我失去了整个生活的重心，我的人生就这样被摧毁。

有几个月，我不知道要做些什么。我觉得我令企业界的前辈们失望——我把他们交给我的接力棒弄丢了。我见了戴维·帕卡德跟鲍勃·诺伊斯，跟他们说很抱歉我把事情给搞砸了。我成了公众眼中失败的示范，我甚至想要离开硅谷。但是渐渐的，我发现，我还是喜爱那些我做过的事情，在苹果计算机中经历的那些变故丝毫没有改变这一点。虽然我被赶出公司，可是我还是爱做那些事情，所以我决定从头来过。

当时我没发现，但现在看来，被苹果计算机开除，是我所经历过的最好的事情。成功的沉重被从头来过的轻松所取代，每件事情都不那么确定，让我自由进入这辈子最有创意的年代。

接下来5年，我开了一家叫NeXT的公司，又开一家叫皮克斯的公司，也跟后来的太太谈起了恋爱。皮克斯接着制作了世界上第一部电脑动画电影，《玩具总动员》，现在是世界上最成功的动画制作公司。然后，苹果计算机买下了NeXT，我回到了苹果，我们在NeXT发展的技术成了苹果计算机后来复兴的核心部分。我也有了个美妙的家庭。

我很确定，如果当年苹果计算机没开除我，就不会发生这些事情。这帖药很苦，可是病人需要这帖药。有时候，人生会用砖头砸你。不要丧失信心。我确信我爱我所做的事情，这就是这些年来支持我继续走下去的唯一理由。你得找出你的最爱，工作上是如此，人生伴侣也是如此。你的工作将占掉你人生的一大部分，唯一真正获得满足的方法就是做你心中伟大的工作，而唯一做伟大工作的方法是爱你所做的事。如果你还没找到这些事，继续找，别停顿。尽你全心全力，你知道你一定会找到。而且，如同任何伟大的恋情，事情只会随着时间愈来愈好。所以，在你找到之前，继续找，别停顿。

我的第三个故事，是关于死亡。

当我17岁时，我读到一则格言，好像是"如果把每一天都当成生命中的最后一天，你就会轻松自在"。这对我影响深远，在过去33年里，我每天早上都会照镜子，自问："如果今天是此生最后一日，我今天会想做我正要做的事情吗？"每当我连续太多天都得到一个"不是"的答案时，我就知道我必须有所改变了。

提醒自己快死了，是我在人生中面临重大决定时，所用过最重要的方法。因为几乎每件事——所有的外界期望、所有的名声、所有对困窘或失败的恐惧——在面对死亡时，都消失了，只有最真实重要的东西才会留下。提醒自己快死了，是我所知最好的方法，避免掉入畏惧失去的陷阱里。人生不带来、死不带去，没理由不能顺心而为。

一年前，我被诊断出癌症。我在早上七点半作断层扫描，胰脏部位清楚地出现了一个肿瘤，我连胰脏是什么都不知道。医生告诉我，那几乎可以确定是一种不治之症，预计我大概活不到3到6个月了。医生建议我回家，好好把事情料理一下，这是医生对临终病人的标准建议。那代表你得试着在几个月内把你将来10年中想跟小孩讲的话讲完。那代表你得把每件事情搞定，家人才会尽量轻松。那代表你得跟人说再见了。

我整天想着那个诊断结果，那天晚上做了一次切片，从喉咙伸入一个内视镜，穿过胃进到肠子，将探针伸进胰脏，取了一些肿瘤细胞出来。我打了镇静剂，不醒人事，但是我老婆在场。她后来跟我说，当医生们用显微镜看过那些细胞后，他们都哭了，因为那是非常少见的一种胰腺癌，可以用手术治好。所以我接受了手术，康复了。

这是我最接近死亡的时候，我希望那会是未来几十年内最接近的一次。以前我觉得死亡只是个虚幻的概念，但经历此事后，我能更肯定地告诉你们：没有人想死。

即使那些想上天堂的人，也想活着上天堂。但是死亡是我们共同的终点，没有人逃得过。这是注定的，因为死亡很可能就是生命中最棒的发明，是生命交替的媒介，送走老人们，给新生代留出空间。现在你们是新生代，但是不久的将来，你们也会逐渐变老，被送出人生的舞台。抱歉讲得这么戏剧化，但是这是真的。

你们的时间有限，所以不要浪费时间活在别人的生活里。不要被教条所局限——盲从教条就是活在别人思考的结果里。不要让别人的意见淹没了你内在的心声。最重要的，拥有追随自己内心与直觉的勇气，你的内心与直觉多少已经知道你真正想要成为什么样的人。任何其他事物都是次要的。

在我年轻时，有本神奇的杂志叫做《全球概览》，当年这可是我们的经典读物。那是一位住在离此处不远的门洛公园的斯图尔特·布兰德发行的，他把杂志办得很有诗意。那是 1960 年代末期，个人计算机跟小规模出版还没出现，所有内容都是打字机、剪刀跟宝丽莱相机做出来的。杂志内容有点像印在纸上的平面谷歌，在谷歌出现之前 35 年就有了。这本杂志很理想主义，充满新奇工具与伟大的见解。

斯图尔特跟他的团队出版了好几期的《全球概览》，然后很自然的，最后出了停刊号。当时是上世纪 70 年代中期，我正是你们现在这个年龄的时候。在停刊号的封底，有张清晨乡间小路的照片，那种你四处搭便车冒险旅行时会经过的乡间小路。在照片下印了行小字：求知若饥，虚心若愚。那是他们亲笔写下的告别讯息，我总是以此自许。当你们毕业，展开新生活，我也以此祝福你们。

求知若饥，虚心若愚。

非常谢谢大家。

(2005 年 6 月 12 日，苹果电脑公司首席执行官斯蒂夫·乔布斯在美国斯坦福大学毕业典礼上的演讲，根据录音材料整理)

第 10 单元

Text 1

Honorable Mr. Richard Parsons, Mr. John Scholes, Mr. Terry McDonell, distinguished Guests, Ladies and Gentlemen,

China Sports Roundtable Meeting of the Fortune Global Forum raises the curtain here today. First of all, on behalf of the State General Administration of Sports, the Chinese Olympic Committee and All-China Sports Federation as well as myself, I would like to extend my warm welcome and sincere wishes to all the guests and friends from press and media.

It has been the third time for Fortune Global Forum to be held in China since it was founded over ten years ago. It reflects the economic and social development in China. It is also the first time to have a roundtable meeting with the theme of sports compared with the previous forums. It helps building up a globalized platform for observing China's sports, providing a visual angle to understand China through sports and at the same time offering China's sports circle an opportunity to learn from the world.

Since the founding of the PRC, especially the policy of reform and opening-up, China has been actively developing its sports undertakings and national fitness campaign. Mass sports activities have been greatly promoted and the physical quality of the Chinese people has been strengthened. There have been already 400 million people who often take part in sports activities in China. Chinese athletes continuingly achieve remarkable results in international competitions. China's competing sports have gone up onto international stage in an all-round way and is becoming a compelling strength.

In China, the state attaches great importance to the development of sports undertakings. The development of sports undertakings is a component of national economy and social development plans. At different stages of economic and social development, China has formulated a series of relevant policies, laws and regulations. The content of "developing sports undertakings" has been written into the Constitution of PRC. In 1995, the Standing Committee of National People's Congress approved the first Sports Law of PRC since the founding of New China. Later, the State Council promulgated the National Fitness Plan. During these years, the State Council has successively promulgated Regulation on Olympic Symbol Protection, Regulation on Public Cultural and Sports Facilities and Anti-Dope

Regulation. These have formed crucial legal guarantee for the development of sports.

The fast-speed development of China's sports is attributed to the great attention of the state on sports undertakings and the mass support of the general public. It is also due to the further growth of reform and opening up, sustained economic and social development and the friendly support and help of friends from every country and every region in the world.

In 2001, China successfully won the bid for holding the 2008 29th Olympic Games. Holding Olympic Games is the dream of Chinese people for over a hundred years. Bidding for Olympics has won the firm support of the Chinese government and its people. According to Gallup survey, the number of Beijing residents who support China's bidding accounts for 94.9% of the total residents in Beijing. It is all known that before New China was founded, the Chinese people were once called "the sick men of East Asia" because of the stagnant economy, the laggard social development and the low physical quality of the Chinese people. Such bitter memory has been deeply rooted in our mind. From being kept away from Olympics to participating in Olympics and from participating in Olympics to holding Olympics is not only the process of China's sports development, it also witnesses China's transformation from an isolated society to an open one and from poverty to wealth and prosperity.

After over a hundred years' development, modern Olympic Games enjoy larger scales and more extensive and further influence. Most of the countries and regions in the world have played active roles in participating in Olympics. Olympic Games have become a broad stage for solidarity, exchanges, competition and cooperation between different countries worldwide. The significance of Olympics is far more than that of the field of sports. What's more, it embodies the values of politics, economy and culture etc. It shows the extraordinary comprehensive impact and huge influence.

Beijing's holding of the 2008 Olympic Games provides new opportunities and impetus for the comprehensive, coordinated and sustainable development of China's sports.

We will commit ourselves in promoting the development of sports industry and deepening sports reform. We will actively cultivate the sports market and comprehensively stimulate the enthusiasm for sports undertakings sponsored by non-governmental organizations. At the same time, we will take the initiative to study and formulate policies and plans, enhance industrial management and optimize public service for sports.

Facing the year 2008, China's sports undertakings will give the top priority to the people's interest. We will take the opportunity of holding Olympic Games in Beijing to meet the increasing demands for sports of the public. We will continue to combine popularization with improvement, realize the coordinated development and mutual complementation of mass sports and competing sports, serve the development of socialist ethical and material progress and serve the prosperity, development and progress of the economy and the society. Today, China is striving to build up a harmonious society, on which China's sports should have a huge impact.

Distinguished guests!

Like social development is always twisting forward, the development of sports and Olympics is also influenced by some non-conventional and unhealthy factors. Doping is one of the most prominent problems and has become the evil of world sports. Anti-doping is, as always, the standpoint of the Chinese government and the circle of sports. In 2003, China, among the first group of countries in the world, signed the Copenhagen Declaration on Anti-Doping in Sport. Premier Wen Jiabao of the State Council signed and promulgated the domestic "Anti-Doping Regulations", which has won the high praise of international sports circles. Till now, we are striving to cooperate and promote the Anti-Doping International Convention formulated by UNESCO. There is an old saying in China, "As vice rises one foot, virtue rises ten." We will join hands with colleagues in the international sports circles to fight against any evil phenomenon during the process of sports development and to safeguard the fairness and chastity of world sports and Olympic Games.

Globally speaking, the development of sports and Olympics has entered into an unprecedented high stage. In the meantime, sports will surely have a bright future. We are fully confident that for China, Asia and the world, there is a promising prospect for the development of sports. We are willing to join hands with friends here and those who are fond of life and sports in every country and region to create a better future for sports!

Finally, I hope the Fortune Forum and China Sports Roundtable Meeting a complete success.

Thank you very much!

(Excerpted text of speech by Liu Peng, former Director-General of the State Sports Administration and President of the Chinese Olympic Committee at the China Sports Roundtable Meeting of the 2005 Fortune Global Forum, May 16, 2005)

Text 2

早上好，感谢大家的到来。

在座很多人都是我的朋友，很多人都认识我，曾为我喝彩，和我共事，或支持过我。而现在，你们每个人都有充足的理由来批评我。

我想对你们每个人都直接明了地说声对不起，我对我的不负责任、自私自利的行为表示深深的歉意。

我知道大家都想知道我为何如此自私和愚蠢，想知道我如何能够做出伤害自己的妻子艾琳及孩子的事情。虽然我一直是个注重隐私的人，但现在我有些事情需要澄清。

我和艾琳已经开始商讨如何弥补由我的行为所造成的损失。她向我指出，我如果真的想悔过自新，那就需要用日后的行动来证明，而不能光在嘴上承诺。我们俩谈了很多，不过内容不便于公开。

我也清楚我的行为给在座各位带来了极大的痛苦。我让你们失望了。我让支持我的球迷失望了。从个人角度来说，我的行为让你们其中的很多人感到失望，特别是我的朋友。对那些和我共事的人来说，我在个人和工作层面都让你们失望了。我的行为也给生意合伙人极大的担忧。

对于每个与我的基金会有关的人而言，包括员工、董事会、赞助商以及最重要的，那些基金会所接触的年轻学生们，我们的工作更加重要。13年前，我和父亲就设想有朝一日能通过教育（资助）来帮助年轻人实现梦想。这个使命不会改变，规模还会越来越大。从南加州的学生学习中心到华盛顿的厄尔伍兹学者会，千百万的孩子们改变了他们的命运，而我也会致力于帮助更多的孩子们。

尽管如此，我知道我还是让各位感到非常失望。我让你们质疑我的为人，猜想我怎么会做出那样的事情。我为此感到很狼狈。对我的所作所为，我说声抱歉。我有太多的过失需要弥补。

不过，还有一件事我很想拿出来说说。有人曾臆断，说艾琳曾在感恩节那晚伤害或攻击过我。人们竟然能编出这样的谎言，让我非常生气。那天晚上她没有打过我，从来也没有过。我们的婚姻从未出现过家庭暴力，从来没有。

从始至终，艾琳在这次痛苦的事件中都展现了她的风度和稳重。她应该得到赞赏，而非责备。这件事的责任都在我，是我接二连三地做出不负责任的事情来。我不够忠诚，我有很多婚外情，我越过轨。我的所作所为是不能让人接受的。这全都怪我。我违背了从小就灌输给我的核心价值观。

我之前就知道自己做错了，但我自以为我可以跳出生活中的条条框框，从不考虑我的所作所为会伤及到谁，只考虑我自己。我肆意地冲破了已婚夫妇应该恪守的界限。我曾认为我可以得到我想要的一切。我曾觉得我这一辈子都在努力工作，也该去享受一下身边的诱惑。我曾觉得我有权利那样去做。拥有金钱和名声，我无须费力就能得到那些。

我错了，我太愚蠢了。生活的规则不会给我网开一面。限制别人的界限同样也适用于我，是我自取其辱。我伤害了妻子、孩子、母亲、妻子的家人、我的朋友、基金会，还有全世界仰慕我的孩子们。

我花了很长时间去思过，我的过错让我重新审视自我。我现在应该改正自我了。从不再重蹈覆辙做起，我要开始诚实正直的生活。

我听过这样一个说法，我也相信事实确是如此，就是说，一个人一生中取得何等成就并不重要，重要的是他克服了何种困难。想要树立榜样，我在高尔夫球场上取得的成就只不过是一小部分而已，品格和正派作风才是真正重要的。有些孩子的家长拿我当作孩子的榜样。对他们，我感到尤其的抱歉。我想告诉他们，真的对不起。

虽然很难启齿，但是我还是承认我需要帮助。从去年12月底到今年2月初，45天里我一直在接受住院治疗，通过医生指导来解决这些问题。我还有很长一段路要走，但是我的这一步算是走对了。

渐渐地，我懂得了人们总是心有疑问。我明白为何新闻界想问我出轨的细节，我也知道人们都想看我和艾琳是否仍在一起。不过在我看来，这些问题和答案所涉及的内容都是我和艾琳之间的私事，一个丈夫和他妻子之间的私事。

有些人编造了莫须有的谎言，他们说我曾用过兴奋剂。这真是天大的谎话。

有些人写了关于我家庭的文章。虽然我的所作所为伤害了大家，但是我仍然认为我的家人不应成为舆论的焦点。事情都是我做的，和他们无关。我一直都为妻子和孩子留一点私人空间。他们不接触我的赞助商，不被牵扯进我的商业合同。我的孩子出生时，我们只公开出一些照片，以免狗仔队穷追不舍。

然而，我的过错不意味着媒体能去跟踪我两岁半的女儿到学校，并公开学校的位置。他们还监视我妻子，跟踪我母亲。不管我做错了什么，为了我的家庭，请不要再骚扰我的妻子和孩子。

我知道自己自食其果，我也知道我必须先做出改变。为了我的家人和与我关系莫逆的朋友，我需要做出改进。这是我关注的重点，而且要做的事情很多，我决定要全力以赴。

信佛是我在改变自我上要迈的一步。我的母亲在我小的时候就教我信佛。很多人可能都不知道，但我打小都是佛教徒。孩提时，我就是个虔诚的信徒，不过到了近几年，我渐渐地背离了自己的信仰。佛教讲求无欲则无求，对外界事物的欲望只会让人痛苦而无谓地寻求安全。信佛让我学会了避免冲动，克制欲望。显然，我全然忘记了我所学的东西。

在我改进的过程中，我将不断地接受帮助，因为我清楚，人要想真正改变自我就必须得到他人的帮助。从明天开始，我将会接受新一轮的治疗。

我想感谢在埃森哲工作的朋友们，以及这周在球场上遇到的几位球员，感谢他们理解我为何说今天这番话。接受治疗时，我懂得了关注精神生活以及平衡家庭和工作的关系是多么重要。我需要重新找到这个平衡，不再偏离方向，这样才能留住对于我来说最重要的东西：我的婚姻和我的孩子。

那也意味着要寻求他人的帮助。我学会了从病友身上寻求帮助，我也希望有一天能够帮助那些也需要帮助的人。

我确实打算重返球场，只是不知道确切时间，不排除今年的可能性。当我重返赛场，我得保证我的一言一行都配得上这比赛。

最近几周，我收到了成千上万的电邮、来信及电话，大家都祝福我。感谢所有关心我和家人的人们。你们的鼓励对我和艾琳来说非常重要。我要感谢美巡赛专员蒂姆·芬臣和参赛的球员们，感谢你们的耐心和谅解，等待我处理完私事。愿我们能在球场上再相见！

最后，现场和在家中观看直播的人中，有很多曾信任过我。今天，我向你们寻求帮助，希望有朝一日，你们仍将信任我，谢谢！

（2010年2月19日，伍兹就婚外情发表正式道歉，根据录音材料整理）

Text 3

Thanks for joining me in this conference. I am taking a different perspective from those experts and scholars by talking about leisure sport industry.

Let's get to a concept first. Many experts and scholars mentioned the sport leisure industry, whereas I put it as leisure sport industry. If we adopt the first title, then not all sport categories are of a leisurely nature. So we usually group those sport activities with operability, potential of industrialization and a touch of leisure and entertainment under the type of leisure sport industry.

First of all, I'll put away the general leisure industry, but focus on leisure sport industry. It's been growing really fast in the contemporary society. I'll give you a couple of examples. The first is the four major professional football leagues in Europe, including Serie A, Bundesliga, La Liga and Premier League. They have received huge profits and great awareness among spectators who take an active part in sports lottery and quiz competitions. The other is the four professional leagues in the US, namely NFL, MLB, NBA and NHL, which also account for a big portion in the sports and entertainment sectors in the States. So, this industry is developing fast worldwide.

I'll share with you another story. You may be aware that Mr. Derek Casey, the former secretary general and current president of World Leisure Organization, and Mr. Christopher Edginton, the secretary general who addressed the audience this morning, both have a sports background. So, the presence of Mr. Edginton in this sports leisure conference indicates the importance of sport industry in these senior officials of World Leisure Organization.

Second, the Yangtze River Delta, or YRD. YRD is the 6th largest economic community in the world. Its economy, like a taxiing plane on the runway, is on the rise, in a fast way indeed. With this speedy growth in the world leisure sport industry, what resources does China possess? Well, we all know the Beijing Olympics in 2008, and many events in YRD, such as F1, ATP Masters Tournament, Women's Volleyball Championship, and the impending FIFA Women's World Cup on 12th this month in Shanghai, a whole bunch of sports events of all scales at the local and national level. Sports events are booming, therefore a discussion of the sport market is a must for it's too big to be ignored.

Then I'd like to talk about the necessity and feasibility of developing leisure sport industry. I won't elaborate on necessity since this morning Christopher Edginton already mentioned the legal evidence that leisure is now a mainstream practice in our society, and the fact that it is a fundamental human right in pursuing happiness stated in the Universal Declaration on Human Rights, UN Assembly and World Declaration on Tourism. It has been a key aspect to the global community, legal systems and individual countries.

Besides, the YRD boasts the fastest economic growth in China and its leisure sport industry is part and parcel of leisure industry. Now with governments at all levels proactively raising the quality of life and Chinese people well-prepared for the era of leisure, therefore I think it's highly necessary to elaborate on that from the perspective of regional economy. In the World Leisure Congress 2006, Professor Wei Xiao'an proposed a high-sounding slogan, that is, 2006 marked the birth of leisure industry in China. To me, leisure economy is a main component and the largest pillar industry of Chinese economy. Just now Professor Wang mentioned that leisure industry could account for over half of national economy in the leisure era. Secondly, leisure activities are no longer the privilege of the elites, but a right of all and a common social practice, a lifestyle. Thirdly, leisure, closely related to quality of life, is key to improving the happiness and satisfaction of life. Fourthly, the leisure element can be found in our daily necessities, learning and working environment.

During the World Leisure Congress 2006, I had the privilege of talking with Professor Wei Xiao'an, who proposed a thought-provoking point. He said that human civilization progressed from nomadic to agricultural, from industrial to marine civilization. In various agricultural civilizations, sports were mainly for maintaining health and that's where China's health maintenance practice was originated. Then in the industrial civilization, sports were developed with an emphasis on bodily competition. In our modern civilization, or marine civilization, when people rely heavily on computers, leisure is about improving the quality of life. Therefore, be it the leisure culture in Chengdu or Hangzhou, I think it is adapting to the evolution of civilization. Why so? For leisure culture in Chengdu is built from the original agricultural civilization, while Hangzhou's is primarily affected by the culture in the Southern Song Dynasty, though there is the well-known culture of Wu and Yue Kingdoms. However, leisure in the contemporary civilization is shifting from being static to dynamic, from indoor to outdoor, and from family-based leisure to city- and community-based leisure. The reason that sport is so important in Western civilization is that it takes the form of leisure culture in the marine, or modern, civilization. So I think leisure sport industry in YRD is now at a turning point to accelerate growth. To better understand the situation, we have to think about the existing resources of leisure sports in YRD, such as high-standard competitions. Just now I mentioned the huge market of the four leagues in America, and Serie A and Premier League. We'll learn how to capitalize on Beijing Olympics 2008 to expand this market.

The second category is resources from international federations and clubs, which are at the higher end of local or popular sports. Some speakers just mentioned golf courses. We have around 200 in China, while there are nearly 20000 in the States. Everyone is clear about the huge golf market there. Also we are seeing more local sports events and associations. A friend of mine told me that he worked as referee for five large-scale local sport events this summer vacation. It clearly exemplifies the growing number of activities from local and private sport clubs and associations, and of events for high-profile participants. People spend on entertainment, on happiness and on health. This is in vogue and indeed a huge market potential.

The third type is resources of public stadiums and gymnasiums in cities. With a higher living standard, the per capita land for sport purposes in Shanghai has already exceeded 1.5 square meters, while in Zhejiang Province, almost 1 square meters. So this is a significant trend as well.

The fourth type is resources of natural landscapes, which implies that people are engaged in sport activities with the purpose of having well-being in life by using natural endowments like hills and rivers in their spare time. For instance, the culture of landscape and natural resources in Zhejiang is influencing the lifestyle, orientation and behavior of people there. It's also the largest resource of leisure sports.

(Excerpted text of speech by Ling Ping, Dean of the School of Sports and Health, Hangzhou Normal University, at the Symposium of Chinese Leisure Industries, September 10, 2007)

Text 4

尊敬的胡锦涛主席及夫人，各位运动员，各位官员，尊敬的各位来宾，来自世界各地的残奥运动支持者们：

晚上好，欢迎你们！

今晚，我们在此相聚，共同庆祝北京2008年残奥会隆重开幕。

本届残奥会的规模空前，无论是运动员人数、参赛国家和地区数量还是体育项目数量，都超过往届残奥会。

这是残奥运动史上的一座里程碑。我们为此感到欢欣鼓舞，我们的心也与今年上半年接连遭受自然灾害的数百万中国人民在一起。

灾难没能阻挠中国，没能阻挠北京奥组委和刘淇主席继续筹办奥运会。北京奥运会精彩绝伦，相信北京残奥会也一定会圆满成功。

我想对你们致以谢意，感谢你们的出色工作。七年以来，我们的合作一直是友善、坦诚、稳健、互敬和富有建设性的。

我还要感谢国际奥委会给予我们的支持，感谢雅克·罗格主席，感谢终身名誉主席胡安·安东尼奥·萨马兰奇先生，今晚他也与我们在一起。

毋庸置疑，今晚以及此后的十一天当中，运动员们将是真正的英雄。

残奥运动员们，你们为了来到这里，历经了无数个春秋的苦练。你们一定要淋漓尽致地发挥，一定要尊重公平竞赛的精神。谁都无法预知，你们将如何超越最大胆的梦想。

你们来到这里，也是为了愉悦身心，结交朋友，将北京、青岛和香港留存为永恒的记忆。这不是关于希望，而是关于远见卓识和你们所代表的一切。无论你们在运动场上展现风采，还是在国际残奥委会运动员委员会选举中坦陈意见，我们都想从中领略你们的自信与独立。

此刻，我想与大家一同欣赏这座美轮美奂的体育场。"鸟巢"是一个活生生的例证，象征着中国对于建设现代化世界的承诺。

我们都可以看到，这座由钢筋、混凝土、玻璃和其他高科技材料建造而成的建筑气势恢宏。然而在今夜，当你们大家，观众们、演员们和运动员们置身于这座极富建筑美感的体育场时，它才真正被赋予了生命。而当随队官员、赛事官员、媒体、赞助商以及中国无与伦比的志愿者们也来到这里时，你们将共同创造独一无二的残奥经历。

从明日起，我们将看到一幕幕的好戏，我们将看到胜利，我们将看到失望。然而，最为重要的是，当我们相聚在一起，我们将融入那独特的力量之源,它似乎触手可及,又的确可被呼吸,它存在于残奥运动的核心,我们称之为残奥精神。它一旦占据你的心灵,你将难以割舍。它将伴随你的一生!

在北京2008年残奥会的十二天当中,你将会发现,那些你本以为存在于世上的差别其实远非那么明显。

你们将会看到我们共处同一个世界。

谢谢!

(2008年9月6日,残奥委会主席克雷文在北京残奥会开幕式的致词,根据录音材料整理)

第 11 单元

Text 1

Chinadaily.com.cn: Global issues and Chinese diplomacy. Welcome to this session of Diplomatic Forum, The Voice of China—Reviewing Chinese Diplomacy in 2009. We are honored to have invited two guests, Mr. Hua Liming, former ambassador of China to Iran, and Mr. Wang Yusheng, executive director of the Strategic Research Center of China Foundation of International Studies.

Thanks for coming and commenting on the highlights and challenges in China's diplomatic relation in 2009.

Having covered the topic of financial crisis, let's move on to climate change. Currently we are having the Copenhagen Climate Change Summit. Prior to its convening, Premier Wen declared China's quantified objective in emission reduction. What do you think of China's commitment to emission reduction?

Hua Liming: On 26th, Nov., the Chinese government declared solemnly that it's committed to reducing carbon emission per unit of GDP by 40% to 45% in 2020 on the level of 2005. It shocked the whole world, which thought that for a country like China, it's indeed a daunting promise. Well, some Western critics were shocked, while officials of climate change in the UN thought that really encouraging. Why so? It's because China is a developing country whose major tasks are development, employment, urbanization and providing daily necessities. Making a commitment of such a high ratio indicates China's accountable position in coping with global climate change as a major developing country, and its sacrifice as well. Estimated by some experts, China's commitment will drop its GDP growth by one percentage point from now to 2020. However, if Chinese economy is to pursue sustainable development with a truly scientific outlook, we'll have to adopt the low-carbon economic pattern with low emission. The Central Economic Work Conference, just concluded yesterday, pointed out that it was the national demand and global responsibility for China to deliver important commitment in carbon emission. Therefore it's fair to say that China contributed a lot to the Copenhagen Convention on Climate Change.

Wang Yusheng: As regards our commitment, according to my observation, it is a demonstration of our deliberate willingness to shoulder arduous responsibility. Regardless of the outcome of this convention, low carbon economy is the future trend. People hold different opinions towards this approach, but to me, it improves the quality of production and people's living standard, accelerates the transformation of production pattern and reform of economic structure, and guarantees economic sustainability and clean environment.

Hua Liming: China's economic growth is completed at the cost of heavy pollution and high energy consumption in these years, which we've clearly realized. I once came across some statistics, saying that 48 lakes in China have been heavily polluted in the three decades of reform and opening-up. We spent much time on treatment, with little result. China needs to improve the environment out of its own demand, and has to contribute to mitigating greenhouse gas effect globally. This is one side of the issue.

The other side of the story is the fact that China is, after all, a developing country, and it's not China that created the greenhouse gas effect and climate change in the world, but developed, industrialized countries, which have incrementally led to this situation in the over 400 years since the industrial revolution in the UK in the 17th century. Fairly put, they should be held accountable for the current climate change. These are rich countries. For example, over-weight people want to lose weight while people in developing countries are still hungry, so we are not on an even footing. China needs to get its voice heard for itself, for G-77 and for all developing countries.

Chinadaily.com.cn: As was mentioned by both experts, China, under the huge pressure of economic growth, presents itself as a global power on many international issues. Recently the Pew Research Center of the US released the result of a latest survey, saying that over 40% of Americans considered China as the largest economy in the world, and some even claimed that China now "takes the lead". What's your comment on that?

Hua Liming: I also read the statistics from Pew Research Center. Recently a similar survey was done in the UK with the same results, claiming that China is the next greatest economy. Actually, there comes another conclusion that products made in China are not the best in quality; they are inferior. It warns us that, on the one hand, many Western countries are aware of China's huge aggregate economic strength and are counting on China to overcome difficulties and solve many economic problems in the world by giving China greater responsibilities. While, on the other hand, they don't think highly of China as its products are of inferior quality. We have to be sober-minded. I don't think China takes the lead. Despite the overwhelming GDP growth and the hard-earned feat of maintaining an 8% growth rate against all the hardship this year, our GDP growth is of unbalanced nature. China is in no way taking the lead. We'll have to improve the quality of products made in China. The reason that Chinese products are battling with frequent trade protectionism is the narrow-minded trade protectionist mindset of Western countries, and also their less than satisfactory quality.

Wang Yusheng: We recognize the change in the public opinion of America, saying that China is taking the lead, which to some extent reflects the truth of China's speedy growth. China also took the lead in making efforts to stabilizing the situation when overcoming the financial crisis. Now there are signs indicating that China, alongside some countries, will recover first. It's really something we can take pride in and an impetus for our technological progress. But we still have to be clear that, in terms of the scientific outlook of development, China is by far a developing socialist country, indeed. We are among the leading ranks in GDP, but not in per capita GDP. We originally planned to be a moderately developed country in the middle part of this century. Yet, even though we reach that target 10 or 15 years ahead of time, we are still not a developed country. We have to be clear about that.

To say China takes the lead means that we stand out among all nations in terms of development. But it's not convincing since many other countries are developing well at the same time, like Brazil, India and Russia from BRICs, as well as those from VISTA and Next-11. These are not fully accurate answers, but they reflect a trend in general, that is, some developing powers and developed ones are emerging quickly. Though the fact that China leads world development may mean the coming of better economic times, all nations have to grow together because we are all members of this world. Countries like India, Brazil, Mexico and South Africa are growing fast. Sure they have problems; so do we.

What's worth special notice is an analysis of all those who applaud China. The majority is friendly, expecting a stronger China that can better cooperate and develop with them. Some are for doing business with China. Some are serious and decent scholars who objectively recognize China's fast growth. But, there remain some others who are ill-purposed, or at least they may have some hidden intentions. China withstood all the containment in the past six decades and it should not be overtaken by those ill-intended lauds.

(The Voice of China—Reviewing Chinese Diplomacy in 2009, from the Diplomatic Forum at www.chinadaily.com.cn)

Text 2

大家早上好。今天很高兴能参加"中国供应链的碳管理——中国气候变化培训项目"的总结研讨会。该项目通过英国政府的公共外交项目得到了英国总领事馆的支持。虽然这是个总结会，但我觉得它启动了一个重要的新活动，使得参与公司不仅能在供应链里管理碳排放，还能通过采取和实施低碳商业战略获得经济优势。在此，我想向各公司表示祝贺，感谢你们在这个重要项目里的远见卓识和积极参与。

我想谈谈，为什么我们认为企业界的参与对全球解决气候变化工作如此重要，而且也是大势所趋。幸运的是，我们也相信，企业尽早采取行动，减少碳足迹，也符合企业的商业利益，而且解决气候变化的全球努力为我们带来了亟待利用的无限商机。我还想说一下，为什么这个项目对于中国节能减排的国家战略至关重要，以及英国政府会在未来数年给企业界提供什么样的帮助。

英国首相戈登·布朗说过，"气候变化危机是多代人行为的产物，但克服该危机是当代人和世界各国的巨大任务。"这是他去年说的。最新的科学研究表明，气候变化给人类带来的挑战比此前所想的更大、更紧迫。联合国政府间气候变化专门委员会在最新报告中指出了人类活动和气候变化更加紧密的关联，并明确表明，我们需要采取紧急行动，减少温室气体排放。它带来的经济效益也很明显，尽早采取有力行动的好处远胜于因坐视不理和固守传统商业做法所付出的代价。

我们一定要明白，气候变化不仅是环境问题，更是威胁国际和平与安全、繁荣与发展的问题。如果我们在全球还以传统商业模式进行能源生产和消耗，那么到本世纪末，平均气温将增高4摄氏度，导致海平面的大幅上升，从而影响生态系统、农业生产、食物和水供应、以及人类迁移。在广东，我们会遭遇更极端的天气、更多洪灾、对供应链更严重的破坏，这都会影响企业界的发展。

世界各国就应对行动日益达成共识。欧盟承诺，到2020年，温室气体排放将在1990年的基础上减少20%。如果世界各国在气候变化上达成一致，减排幅度将增至30%。同时，欧盟还承诺，到2020年，全欧盟能耗的20%将来自可再生能源。

英国提出了更宏伟的目标。上个月，英国政府宣布其长期目标，到2050年，温室气体排放将在1990年的基础上至少减少80%，这是世界上最雄心勃勃的国家目标了。

我想大家也都知道，中国承诺，到2010年，能源强度将减少20%，能源生产中可再生能源的比例从5%增至15%。大家刚才也听到了，两周前，发改委在北京公布了"中国解决气候变化的政策和行动"白皮书，其中列出了其他的重要措施。我们很欢迎中国提出的相关举措。

虽然全球各国日益达成共识，认为必须采取行动，但如果要在后京都议定书战略上达成一致，使得发达国家和发展中国家共同解决气候变化问题，

依然任重而道远。在明年哥本哈根峰会上，各国最高领导人将就此开展艰难而复杂的磋商，

不过，简而言之，我们必须达成一致，我们也相信能够达成一致，如果我们要避免社会和经济混乱，避免食物和水供应的崩溃，如果我们的孩子也能享受在座各位今天所享受的生活。不论形式如何，不论它能产生如何的国家战略，这个共识会影响在座每一个人，包括政府官员、决策者、城市规划者、普罗大众，还有最重要的，各位企业界代表。

我们一起看看企业界的作用，这也是我们今天支持的项目的主题。英国政府坚定支持并积极推动全球化。消除各国间商品、服务和资金流动的障碍能够推动全球经济发展，我们不能容忍有些人借环境保护之名行贸易保护之实。

最好的例子非广东莫属。自改革开放30年以来，广东引领了中国的经济腾飞。广东之所以成功，源于它主动开展国际贸易，吸引海外投资，迅速适应不断变化的海外市场需求。当今的世界金融危机以及它对全球消费者需求的影响告诉我们，各国经济非常紧密地相互依存。它也说明，政府和企业要找到新战略，促进经济复苏和增长，赢得市场优势，其重要性不言而喻。

伴随全球化的是公司供应链的国际化和多样化。各位知道，很多供应链都经过广东，你们也知道，世界各国企业都有责任去有效地管理供应链。不论是在哪个国家，不仅满足当地法规要求，还要响应消费者和股东对生产流程的更严格要求，希望其环保、可持续发展。

我相信大家已经看到了变化。全球领先的零售商，如沃尔玛、宜家、乐购、玛莎百货等，正在把货架上的产品变成绿色产品。我们正在制定碳标识的新国际标准，引入碳消耗报告的新法律要求。未来十年，更多的买家、消费者、政府和股东会要求公司说明生产过程中产生的二氧化碳和其他温室气体的数量。这么做是因为世界各国日益明白，如果气候变化不加控制，必将带来我刚才所说的灾难性的政治和经济影响，还因为我们已经就未来的行动达成更多的一致。

英国政府坚信，各国在保持强劲发展势头的同时也可以向低碳经济转型。机遇来自于开发和采用低碳技术和服务，来自于寻求和推广高效及节能技术，来自于更加清洁、更节约资源的制造流程，来自于不断发展的碳市场、清洁发展机制和碳交易。

（2008年11月12日，英国驻广州总领事馆气候变化和能源领事韩天恩在"中国供应链的碳管理——中国气候变化培训项目"总结研讨会上的讲话节选，根据录音材料整理）

Text 3

Prime Minister Rasmussen, Dear Colleagues,

At this very moment, billions of people across the world are following closely what is happening here in Copenhagen. The will that we express and the commitments that we make here should help push forward mankind's historical process of combating climate change. Standing at this podium, I am deeply aware of the heavy responsibility.

China has taken climate change very seriously. We have exerted, and will continue to exert unremitting effort.

China was the first developing country to adopt and implement a National Climate Change Program. We have formulated a series of laws and regulations as an important means for us to address climate change.

China has made the most intensive efforts in energy conservation and emission reduction in recent years. By the end of the first half of this year, China's energy consumption per unit of GDP had dropped by 13 percent from the 2005 level, equivalent to reducing 800 million tons of carbon dioxide.

China is the fastest growing country in new and renewable energy. Between 2005 and 2008, renewable energy increased by 51 percent. China ranked first in the world in terms of installed hydro power capacity, nuclear power capacity under construction, the coverage of solar water heating panels and photovoltaic power capacity. In 2008, the use of renewable energy reached an equivalent of 250 million tons of standard coal. A total of 30.5 million rural households gained access to bio-gas, equivalent to a reduction of 49 million tons of carbon dioxide emissions.

China has the largest area of man-made forests in the world. We have continued with the large-scale endeavor to return farmland to forest and expand forestation, and made vigorous effort to increase forest carbon sink. In the past 5 years, China's forest coverage registered a net increase of 20.54 million hectares and forest stock volume rose by 1.123 billion cubic meters. The total area of man-made forests in China has reached 45million hectares, the largest in the world.

China has a 1.3 billion population and its per capita GDP has only exceeded 3,000 US dollars. According to the UN standards, we still have 150 million people living below the poverty line and we therefore face the arduous task of developing the economy and improving people's livelihood. China is now at an important stage of accelerated industrialization and urbanization, and, given the predominant role of coal in our energy mix, we are confronted with special difficulty in emission reduction. However, we have always regarded addressing climate change as an important strategic task. Between 1990 and 2005, China's carbon dioxide emissions per unit of GDP were reduced by 46 percent. Building on that, we have set the new target of cutting carbon dioxide emissions per unit of GDP by 40-45 percent by 2020 from the 2005 level. To reduce carbon dioxide emissions on such a large scale and over such an extended period of time will require tremendous efforts on our part. Our target will be incorporated into China's mid-and-long term plan for national economic and social development as a mandatory one to ensure that its implementation is subject to the supervision by the law and public opinions. We will further enhance the domestic-statistical, monitoring and evaluation methods, improve the way for releasing emission reduction information, increase transparency and actively engage in international exchange, dialogue and cooperation.

Dear colleagues,

To meet the climate challenge, the international community must strengthen confidence, build consensus, make vigorous effort and enhance cooperation. And we must always adhere to the following three principles:

First, maintaining the consistency of outcomes. The United Nations Framework Convention on Climate Change and the Kyoto Protocol are the outcomes of long and hard work by all countries. They serve as the legal basis and guide for international cooperation on climate change. And as such, they must be highly valued and further strengthened and developed. The outcome of this conference must stick to rather than obscure the basic principles enshrined in the Convention and the Protocol. It must follow rather than deviate from the mandate of the "Bali Roadmap". It should lock up rather than deny the consensus and progress already achieved in the negotiations.

Second, upholding the fairness of rules. The principle of "common but differentiated responsibilities" represents the core and bedrock of international cooperation on climate change and it must never be compromised. It is totally unjustified to ask developing countries to cope with climate change in disregard of historical responsibilities, per capita emissions and different levels of development. And it should by no means compromise the efforts of developing countries to get rid of poverty and backwardness, but be organized in a coordinated way under the framework of sustainable development.

And third, paying attention to the practicality of the targets. In tackling climate change, we need to take a long-term perspective, but more importantly, we should focus on the present. It is necessary to set a direction for our long-term efforts, but it is even more important to focus on achieving near-term and mid-term reduction targets, honoring the commitments already made and taking real action. One action is more useful than a dozen programs. We should give people hope by taking credible actions.

Fourth, ensuring the effectiveness of institutions and mechanisms. We should make concrete and effective institutional arrangements under the Convention and urge developed countries to honor their commitments, provide sustained and sufficient financial support to developing countries, speed up the transfer of climate-friendly technologies and effectively help developing countries, especially small island states, least developed countries, landlocked countries and African countries, strengthen their capacity in combating climate change.

I wish to conclude by underlining that it is with a sense of responsibility to the Chinese people and the whole mankind that the Chinese government has set the target for mitigating greenhouse gas emissions. This is a voluntary action China has taken in the light of its national circumstances. We have not attached any condition to the target, nor have we linked it to the target of any other country. We will honor our word with real action. Whatever outcome this conference may produce, we will be fully committed to achieving and even exceeding the target.

Thank you.

(Full text of speech by Chinese Premier Wen Jiabao at the Leaders' Meeting of the Copenhagen Climate Change Summit, December 18, 2009, as transcribed)

Text 4

谢谢杜汉姆先生对我的介绍。

我想感谢蒂亚·图雷女士和她在法语国家能源环境学会的团队,感谢她们为此次会议所做的出色准备。我还要感谢各位的光临。

在哥本哈根,要说全球共同应对气候变化的必要性,没几个组织能有法语国家联盟那么有权威。我们替发达国家和发展中国家说话,为能源生产国和消费国说话。我们表达观点的角度不同,但却团结一致,这份团结源于我们的历史,出于我们共同的语言。

法语国家联盟替那些最受气候变化影响的国家说话。

法语国家联盟也替那些有能力去领导、帮助和提供解决方法的国家说话,替那些走在研发和应用前沿的国家说话,替那些打造可持续发展技术以建立更环保经济的国家说话,替那些能够在经济实力之上领导和分享知识的国家说话。

拥有不同的视角和经验,我们一同为实现愿景而努力。2008年10月,法语国家联盟的领导人在魁北克市举行的第十二届峰会上制订了发展目标,我们将追求目标的实现。

我们将气候变化问题纳入发展政策中，通过技术转让帮助各国解决这个跨国界的问题。我们将解决受气候变化影响的那些重要问题，包括水质和生态系统的生物多样性。所有法语国家联盟的合作伙伴都将充分利用自己的力量。

　　就我们而言，加拿大拥有明确透明的目标，秉承五大原则。

　　首先，我们将均衡发展环境保护和经济繁荣。

　　其次，我们有长远目标。通过制定今天的政策，我们能实现2050年全球减排50%的目标。

　　第三，我们将携手国际性伙伴，要求各主要经济体——包括主要的排放国——做出承诺。同时，我们也支持那些没有资源来管理气候变化和适应工作的最不发达国家。在魁北克举行的峰会上，哈珀首相宣布，加拿大将斥资1亿美元，帮助那些格外受气候变化影响的国家适应需求。

　　第四，我们将继续在清洁技术上的研发和应用，并将该技术转让给最需要的国家。

　　最后，我们将支持有建设性和有抱负的全球行动。

　　加拿大在哥本哈根大会上传达了简单的讯息：她将积极促进达成协议。加拿大将尽其所能，应对气候变化问题。

　　我们在国内和国际事务上运用这些原则。但是，很大程度上来说，加拿大在全球经济中的力量来自我们与整个北美市场的经济一体化。我们对气候变化的反应也必须要和北美各国的反应一致。

　　加拿大承诺，到2020年，温室气体排放将在2006年的基础上降低20%。这个目标既雄心勃勃，也非常实际，因为加拿大有着极端的气候条件，广阔的领土，能源密集型产业和不断增长的人口。

　　我们将继续与奥巴马总统领导的美国政府合作，协调我们的气候变化政策。

　　我们与邻邦美国在今年早些时候开展了由哈珀首相和奥巴马总统负责的清洁能源对话。我们还将继续利用经济和技术优势，制定北美地区的解决方案，使之成为全球气候变化解决方案的重要部分。

　　女士们、先生们，各位同事，法语国家联盟的各成员国为气候变化的全球挑战带来了不同的问题，也提供了不同的能力，加拿大也帮助北美各国协调合作。我们也有提供创新和发展清洁能源的能力。在此之上，我们的目标是到2020年使用清洁能源发电比率达到90%。

　　加拿大有着非凡的自然环境，大面积的野生地带成为地球的天然肺部，吸入二氧化碳，呼出氧气。

　　加拿大的野生地带提供解决气候变化的方法，但也提醒我们生态系统的脆弱。它们激励我们，也残酷地告诉我们，如果不减少排放，我们会面临何等风险。

法语国家联盟代表了不同的声音，提供了诸多的视角。我们面临众多挑战，也有各类解决方法。

非常期待和各位的讨论，期待我们开展有建设性的成功合作。

（2009年12月16日，加拿大环境部长吉姆·普伦迪斯在哥本哈根法语国家联盟午宴上的发言全文）

附录 2　参考文献

Gile, D. Conference Interpreting as a Cognitive Management Problem. *The Interpreting Studies Reader*, London and New York: Routledge, 2002.

Gile, D. *Basic Concepts and Models for Interpreter and Translator Training*. Amsterdam/Philadelphia: John Benjamins, 1995.

Jones, R. *Conference Interpreting Explained* (2nd edition). Manchester: St. Jerome Publishing, 2002.

Jones, R. *Conference Interpreting Explained*. Manchester: St. Jerome Publishing, 1998.

Pochhacker, F. *Introducing Interpreting Studies*. London and New York: Routledge, 2004.

Seleskovitch, D. *Interpreting for International Conferences*. Washington: Pen and Booth, 1978.

Setton, Robin. *Simultaneous Interpretation: A Cognitive-Pragmatic Analysis*. Amsterdam/Philadelphia: John Benjamins, 1999.

Van Besien, Fred. Anticipation in Simultaneous Interpretation. *Meta*, vol. 44, no. 2, 1999, pp.250-259.

蔡小红．口译质量评估研究的历史回顾．《中国翻译》第 3 期，2004.

塞莱斯科维奇、勒代雷著．闫素伟、邵炜译．《口译训练指南》．北京：中国对外翻译出版公司，2007.

王斌华．《口译：理论・技巧・实践》．武汉：武汉大学出版社，2006.

王力．《中国语法理论》．济南：山东教育出版社，1984.

张维为．《英汉同声传译》．北京：中国对外翻译出版公司，1999.

仲伟合．英汉同声传译技巧与训练．《中国翻译》第 5 期，2001.

仲伟合．《英语口译教程》．北京：高等教育出版社，2006.

仲伟合等．《基础口译教程》．北京：高等教育出版社，2007.

仲伟合．《英语同声传译教程》．北京：高等教育出版社，2008.